ON TO
VICTORY

EDITED BY BETTINA FRIEDL

ON TO VICTORY

PROPAGANDA PLAYS OF THE WOMAN SUFFRAGE MOVEMENT

Northeastern University Press
Boston

Northeastern University Press

Copyright 1987 Bettina Friedl

Library of Congress Cataloging-in-Publication Data

On to victory.

  Bibliography: p.
  1. Suffragettes—Drama. 2. Women—Suffrage—Drama.
3. American drama—19th century. 4. American drama—
20th century. 5. American drama—Women authors.
I. Friedl, Bettina.
PS627.S7405 1987   812'.008'0352042   87-12194
ISBN 1-55553-018-4 (alk. paper)

Designed by Melinda Grosser
This book was composed in Electra and Windsor Condensed by Crane Typesetting Service, Inc., Barnstable, Massachusetts. It was printed and bound by Halliday Lithograph, Hanover, Massachusetts. The paper is 55# Sebago Cream, an acid-free sheet.

Manufactured in the United States of America

91 90 89 88 87   5 4 3 2 1

DEDICATION

For Herwig

TABLE OF CONTENTS

PREFACE

My discovery of the existence of suffrage propaganda plays, of which this edition presents a selection, is anecdotal. It happened to coincide with my discovery of the significance of the resources in the Schlesinger Library at Radcliffe College for my research during the summer of 1979. As I was scanning the shelves for materials, picking up volumes at random, a slender brochure accidentally was pulled out with another book and fell to the ground. It was a privately printed play called *Election Day: A Suffrage Play*. I had never heard of a "suffrage play" and I did not know its author, Emily Sargent Lewis. But I became curious, especially after I found some more early feminist plays at the Schlesinger Library and a few at Harvard's Widener Library during that summer. This was the beginning of my collection.

Three years later, in 1982–83, I had gathered enough material to teach my first class on selected English and American suffrage plays. During that semester, Norman Pettit (Boston University) was doing research in Stuttgart; when I learned from him that his grandmother was Emily Sargent Lewis, who had been an active suffragist in Philadelphia and had written plays for the movement, I hastened to invite him to give a lecture on *Election Day* and its author in my class. The success of the seminar convinced me that these plays might deserve an edition to bring them to the attention of other teachers of American studies or American drama, or, indeed, of the general reader interested in the history of American feminism. My plans met with the encouragment and support of editor Nancy W. Waring, and I am delighted that a selection of suffrage plays will now re-appear in print after more than seven decades.

My special thanks go to the students at the University of Stuttgart, who participated in the two seminars on suffrage plays I taught in 1982–83 and 1986–87. They were enthusiastic and perceptive in their own readings of the plays, helping me to evaluate the genre; but, they were also critical enough to point out occasional weaknesses in the propagandistic argument or defects in dramatic structure.

I am very grateful to the American Council of Learned Societies whose fellowship provided financial support in 1984. At the Bunting Institute of Radcliffe College in 1983–84, the sustaining scholarly and personal interest of the other women also meant that some of the energy they gave me could go into the planning of this collection, although I was working on a different project then and still am. Sharing their experiences, memories, and insights, the members of the "Mother and Daughter Group" during that year did more for me than can be said in words.

Staff at Widener Library, Harvard University; the Boston Public Library; the John Hay Library, Brown University; the New York Public Library, especially at the Annex and at the Performing Arts Research Center, were very helpful. I gratefully acknowledge the assistance of Jill Erickson at the Boston Athenæum, and Jessica Randolph and Catherine Craven at the Massachusetts Historical Society. At the Schlesinger Library, Patricia King, Barbara Haber, and Karen Morgan deserve special thanks for their friendly assistance and knowledgeable suggestions during many summers in Cambridge, and Marie-Hélène Gold, for her help with my last minute requests for illustrations.

I count myself fortunate in having found enthusiasm and editorial support at Northeastern University Press, first in Nancy W. Waring, formerly of the Press, and then in Deborah J. Kops, editorial director, who did not feel daunted by the transatlantic complications of this edition.

I am very grateful to Mrs. Millicent Lewis Pettit for taking time to tell me what she remembered about Emily Sargent Lewis's life, and for allowing me to reproduce her mother's photograph. I owe profound thanks to friends in Germany and America: to Christine N. Brinckmann, Judith Fryer, Renate Hof, and Claudia Yukman, who listened patiently and made valuable suggestions; to Ruth Nestvold-Mack for taking time off from her own work to help with the preparation of the manuscript; to Daniel Aaron for many years of generous and stimulating criticism; to Elizabeth Bergeson, Rachel Snow, and Mary White for creating the perfect feminist ambience during my time in Cambridge in 1984; and to Norman Pettit for his hospitality as well as his prolonged interest in this project.

Most of all, I wish to thank Kathryn and Robert Preyer, whose friendship and intellectual support has come to mean so much to me, and Herwig Friedl, to whom I dedicate this book.

* * *

I am grateful to the following libraries for permission to reprint plays from their collections: the Harvard College Library, to reprint Mrs. O. H. P. Belmont and Elsa Maxwell, *Melinda and Her Sisters*; [Ariana R. W. Curtis and Daniel Sargent Curtis], *The Spirit of Seventy-Six*; William B. Fowle, *Woman's Rights*; Eleanor Freeman, *When the Women Vote*; Charlotte Perkins Gilman, *Something to Vote For*; Hester N. Johnson, *On to Victory*; George Rugg, *The New Woman*; Ella Cheever Thayer, *Lords of Creation*; and excerpts from Alice Duer Miller, *Women Are People!*; The Schlesinger Library, Radcliffe College, to reprint Marie Jenney Howe, *An Anti-Suffrage Monologue*; Emily Sargent Lewis, *Election Day*; Catharine Waugh McCulloch, *Bridget's Sisters*; George Middleton, *Back of the Ballot*; and Mary Winsor, *A Suffrage Rummage Sale*; the John Hay Library at Brown University, to reprint Kate Mills Fargo, *A Voting Demonstration*; Florence Kiper, *Cinderelline*; Mary Shaw, *The Woman of It*, and *The Parrot Cage*; Alice C. Thompson, *A Suffragette Baby*; and the Boston Public Library, to reprint Alice E. Ives, *A Very New Woman*.

GENERAL

INTRODUCTION

"When we have achieved reforms enough to bring our institutions as far into harmony with the feelings of women as they now are with the feelings of men, there will no longer be a Woman Question.
No conflict, no question."

—George Bernard Shaw

The Boston suffragist and former Lowell mill operative Harriet Hanson Robinson noted with deep satisfaction in 1881 that the American novel had begun to reflect the achievements of the woman's rights movement. Fictional accounts of women were reaching far beyond the literary stereotypes or romantic idealization of the pre–Civil War decades. The drama, however, she found sadly remiss because it spoke "too feebly on the right side of the woman question. No modern successful dramatist has made this 'humour' of the times the subject of his play. An effort was made in 1879, by the executive committee of the New England Woman Suffrage Association, to secure a woman suffrage play; but it was not successful, and there is yet to be written a counteractive to that popular burlesque, 'The Spirit of '76.' " It is to be regretted, she observed, "that the stage still continues to ridicule the woman's rights movement and its leaders."[1]

The Spirit of Seventy-Six: or, The Coming Woman, a Prophetic Drama had been published anonymously in 1868, but was probably performed for the first time in 1866, a decade before the projected time of action. Although the book version of this play, together with two "other little pieces," came out in a thoroughly professional looking edition with Boston's Little, Brown and Company, the authors still found it necessary to point out that their "play was not written for the stage, nor with any view to publication, but simply for amateur

1

performance; and therefore all scenery, stage-properties, &c., were purposely dispensed with, and the action limited by the resources of a drawing-room." This prefatory note clearly indicates that their play, like most popular farces and burlesques written for private performance in the nineteenth century, was never intended to compete with professional drama. William B. Fowle had published his play *Woman's Rights* in 1856 as part of a collection of similar one-act plays called *Parlor Dramas, or, Dramatic Scenes, for Home Amusement.* The title identifies these plays as belonging to the specific dramatic genre of the parlor farce, and implies that their author does not regard himself as a "playwright" in the professional sense.

Private theatricals were probably the most important form of educated home amusement in the nineteenth century. Documentation of actual performances is sadly lacking, apart from the wealth of instruction manuals for avid bourgeois amateur actors and stage managers. Nevertheless, the importance of parlor theatricals for the study of the American theater has been emphasized by eminent drama scholars like Richard Moody, who even included one of William Dean Howells's parlor farces in his anthology of *Dramas from the American Theatre, 1762–1909.* "Although Howells's parlor farces appear as a minor chapter in our theatre history," he writes, "neither they nor Howells deserve to be neglected as they have been. Amateur home theatricals constituted a widespread middle-class family amusement through the last twenty-five years of the past century, and the little plays of Howells were certainly the best of the type designed for this purpose."[2] Literary scholarship until recently excluded the genre as too slight for serious consideration because the quality of many of these unassuming plays did not measure up even to the works of other eighteenth- and nineteenth-century American playwrights like Royall Tyler, William Dunlap, and Anna Cora Mowatt, let alone to works of the European stage of the same period. Moody's selection offers the combination of a big name and a much neglected genre as a useful compromise for the purpose of introducing an amateur play, although Howells's parlor farces in fact constitute neither the best nor the earliest examples for the American amateur theatrical.

It is all the more important, therefore, to note that cultural historians have recently begun to study the significance of parlor theatricals for the middle classes in nineteenth-century America as a cultural rather than a strictly literary phenomenon. Karen Halttunen devotes a full chapter of her excellent book, *Confidence Men and Painted Women,* to parlor theatricals and their cultural meaning. She establishes the decade after 1850 as the beginning of an "explosive popularity of theatrical parlor games"[3], a fact that is supported by the publication of William B. Fowle's *Parlor Dramas* as early as 1856. Magazines like *Godey's Lady's Book* became trendsetters for popular parlor entertainment by publishing suitable acting charades and acting proverbs; guides and manuals "reassured their readers that parlor theatricals were a perfectly respectable form of entertainment."[4] Halttunen interprets these theatricals as evidence of the new bourgeois self-confidence that exhibits itself in performances in and about the inner sanctum of the American home—the parlor. To turn the parlor into a stage for the ritualized performance of charades, tableaux vivants, and amateur theatricals, Halttunen writes, meant that members of the middle classes "were casting aside some of their sentimental aversions to theatrical conduct."[5] At the same time, the rage for parlor theatricals "testified to a growing acceptance by the American middle classes of the underlying theatricality of all their claims to genteel social status."[6]

The popularization of amateur acting as an exciting new form of amusement for well-to-do Americans soon led from the strictly private parlor theatrical to newly founded drama clubs that staged performances at member's houses, often taking turns so that each member with a parlor large enough to accommodate a temporary stage would receive other members and additional guests for an evening's entertainment. The audience was provided with handwritten playbills—later these gave way to printed playbills, particularly once a drama club became more ambitious—and participants were offered refreshments after the performance. Apart from the infrequent collections of nineteenth-century playbills in rare book libraries and historical societies, personal scrapbooks are now the only source of information about private theatricals. These private records of social gatherings and amusements meticulously list casts for tableaux vivants and farces, note the addresses at which the performances were to take place, and sometimes even comment on the quality of acting in brief penciled remarks.[7]

Town halls, ballrooms of resort hotels, and even small professional theaters were rented whenever large audiences might be expected, or when dramatic clubs gave benefit performances for philanthropic purposes and charged admission. Occasionally there were efforts to give the simple theatrical amusements a didactic underpinning, probably in the attempt to make them seem not only innocent but also useful, educational, and therefore more respectable. Some drama societies favored performances of burlesques in French or Latin; at the time of the Centennial, some specialized in presenting acting charades or pageants with scenes from American history. The activities immediately connected with acting—dressing up, making up, declamation, and the actual attempt to represent a different character—which had formerly been regarded as somewhat frivolous, especially in their professional and public forms, were made acceptable by giving them a private, edifying, or charitable function.

Membership in the dramatic clubs and the audiences invited to private theatricals were carefully restricted, pointing to a basic similarity between the parlor farce and the genteel social performance itself, as Halttunen suggests.[8] Playbills of some of the theatrical groups, therefore, read like the social register of the respective town or city, confirming the existing social barriers as well as the new acceptability of amateur acting, even among the strictest and most reputable families. The printed handbill for the performance of *The Ladies' Battle* and *The Chimney Corner* (no authors mentioned) at the Cambridge Lyceum Hall in March 1868 listed Mr. Fuller, Mr. Cabot, Mr. Shaw, Miss Howe, and Miss Parkman. In January 1878, Mrs. S. B. Schlesinger and Mr. Francis S. Sturgis acted in *Fire in the Convent*, followed by *York* with Mr. S. M. Quincy and Mr. Charles Curtis, a relative of Ariana Wormeley Curtis; both adaptations from "the French of Octave Feuillet" were performed in aid of a "Temporary Home for Working Women." Mrs. Edward D. Boit and two of her daughters—who had already become famous as participants of a different visual parlor presentation in John Singer Sargent's large portrait "Daughters of Edward D. Boit" (1882)—acted in *A Charade* and *The Rendezvous* on New Year's Eve in 1886; and the Boston Amateur Dramatic Club cast Mrs. J. Lodge in the role of a domestic servant as "Martha (Karl's housekeeper)" in a comedy played at Horticultural Hall in Boston.[9]

By the end of the nineteenth century, private theatricals were once again regarded as dangerous, though for different reasons than forty years earlier. Too many women had supposedly succumbed to the dreadful temptation of regarding themselves as would-be actresses, seeking applause and, some critics claimed, even notoriety. They were confusing a strictly private entertainment with professional ambitions, wrote Fannie A. Mathews in the *North American Review*, and were beginning to lose their hold on reality.[10] Her article "Women and Amateur Acting" (1894) describes the craze for parlor theatricals as one would a drug; the addiction to "an applause that is too often totally insincere as well as totally unmerited," she warns, leaves women "glorying in a non-descript phase of self-adornment, which for lack of the courage to christen it *demi-mondaine*, we impertinently designate as 'actress-like'." Mathews declares that amateur acting had long since ceased to be an innocent amusement and had instead "become a literal profession."

While the author of this article soberly attempts to prevent stage-struck young women from taking their fascination for acting, and perhaps even the professional stage, too seriously, the gradual professionalization of amateur theatricals continued to attract actresses like Mary Shaw, who had actually begun her career in amateur performances before she joined the company of Madame Modjeska. As middle-class Americans had formed a habit of engaging in theatricals, they had apparently ceased to regard the theater itself as entirely frivolous or suspicious. The growing respectability of the theater, on the other hand, eventually opened the parlor socially to the American actress. During the 1890s, however, the parlor and the theater began to merge in a completely unforeseen way that moved beyond the vague bond of a mutual fascination for the stage. Similar political interests in the Woman Question worked to unite middle-class women and actresses, and it became evident that these hitherto segregated, if not antagonistic, social groups could actually cooperate by using the stage as a forum for their common goal. The performance of women's pageants, tableaux, and suffrage propaganda plays helped to integrate the previously separate spheres of the theater and the American home.

The specific genre of the suffrage play grew out of a long tradition of writings on woman's rights. From its beginnings, the Woman Question appears to have stimulated the dialogic imagination, to take Mikhail Bakhtin's term literally. This is evident in Charles Brockden Brown's *Alcuin: A Dialogue* (1798 and 1815), or Margaret Fuller's dialogic insertion in her essay "The Great Lawsuit—Man *versus* Men; Woman *versus* Women" (1843), although these examples formally still belong to the essay tradition, not that of the drama. As literary diaglogues, however, they already indicate that the Woman Question would always be more than a mere topic for politics, restricted to a homogeneous group of combatants interested in the subject at hand. The fact that the issue involved one-half of the population and reached deep into private structures like marriage, family, and household arrangements prevented its limitation to the strictly public and theoretical level. Since the antagonists in this controversy were confronting each other daily, their argument began to turn into a continuing discussion as a matter of fact. In short, the debate about woman's rights had taken the shape of a dramatic dialogue in actual life, before it ever reached the stage. But, unlike the genteel performance in the parlors of the middle classes where social restrictions ensured a tone of polite conversation and a general observance of forms, the Woman Question was "performed" in bedrooms and kitchens rather than drawing rooms, eventually turning American homes of all classes into a stage where the topic was enacted with a considerable amount of passion.

The earliest plays, written immediately before and after the Civil War, were true parlor farces written for those bourgeois audiences who had already heard of the Woman Question and were in turn troubled, amused, or perhaps genuinely interested by its implications. The early plays are modeled on the drawing room comedy and the popular burlesque; they playfully enact the absurdities envisioned as the possible results of a temporary or permanent reversal of gender roles. The anti-suffrage plays of the nineteenth century are insufficiently documented, with the possible exception of *The Spirit of Seventy-Six* (1868), which gained considerable popularity outside of the parlor. It is even more difficult, however, to locate information about audiences and modes of performance of pro-feminist plays of the same period. Some of them appear to have been closet dramas, written for reading purposes only. Eleanor Freeman's *When the Women Vote* (1885) seems to have belonged to this category. Other plays, like Alice E. Ives's *A Very New Woman* (1896), were brief enough to be published in widely read feminist journals with the intent to motivate suffrage associations and perhaps even women's clubs to perform them for propaganda purposes. *The Woman's Journal* published a significant number of short plays over the years, and in 1896 *The Woman's Column* reprinted a play from the *Chicago Post* that may well be considered not only the shortest suffrage play but also a typical example of the way in which the debate on the Woman Question tended to turn into dialogic scenes:

As to Voting

"You see, Maria," he said, as he looked up from his newspaper, "it is useless to give women free suffrage because they won't vote anyway. Reports from Massachusetts show—"

"Did you vote at the last election, John?"

"I—why, you see, the fact is—"

"Did you vote?"

"Maria, I can't understand why you—"

"Did you vote?"

"You know very well, Maria, that I was too busy to spare the time to."

"Then what right have you to criticise the women of Massachusetts or any other State?"

"But they don't realize their duties and obligations to the—"

"Do you?"

"Maria, I must decline to discuss this subject with you any longer. A woman cannot argue without descending to personalities, and I cannot permit that."[11]

In the nineteenth century there seems to have been a widespread reluctance even among organized feminists, however, to regard the political play as a serious mode of enlightenment. Speeches and patriotic pageants were far more common as forms of public address during the early campaign for the cause of woman's rights. The "problem plays" of European dramatists like Brieux, Ibsen, and Shaw were commonly regarded as immoral, and the more conservative suffragists were extremely concerned not to have their movement linked with the obvious notoriety of these plays. In my research for this part of the collection, therefore, it was necessary to rely on fragments of information and on a single, fairly well-documented case of an anti-suffrage play.

After 1900 and in western states, where the possibility of gaining full suffrage was far greater than in the East, suffrage plays were often performed as part of the campaign. A document from the Washington Campaign in 1910 mentions that a "suffrage play, A Mock Legislative Session, written by Mrs. S. L. W. Clark of Seattle, was given in the State House and repeated in other cities."[12] This play, *Entertainment to Make Votes for Women* by Sophie Louise Wepf Clark, was also performed during the campaign in California and Oregon, along with Selina Solomons's *The Girl from Colorado; or, The Conversion of Aunty Suffridge* (1911). The achievement of the vote in western states began to make it necessary to teach women how to register and vote; didactic plays like Kate Mills Fargo's A *Voting Demonstration; or, An Election in Primerville* (1912), therefore, became useful as local instruction material.

The early twentieth century eventually saw a radical change in the attitude of suffragism toward performance and drama even in the East. The two main reasons for this change may be, first, suffragists' realization that they, like their sisters in the West, needed to rally popular support for the ballot by all possible means; second, actresses in the eastern metropolitan centers tended to become active suffragists. Important work on this connection between suffragists and actresses has been done in recent years. The pioneering collection of essays edited by Helen Krich Chinoy and Linda Walsh Jenkins, *Women in American Theatre*, as well as Claudia D. Johnson's recent study, *American Actress*, helps to explain the radical shift in the social position of actresses in American culture from the nineteenth to the twentieth century.[13] Albert Auster's *Actresses and Suffragists* is indispensable for research on the important role of feminist actresses at the turn of the century.[14]

The alliance between the suffrage movement and the theater in America, as in England, was formed early in the century.[15] By 1909, the theater magazine *Billboard* stated in an article, "Women of the Stage All Desire to Vote": "It may only be a passing fad, but woman's suffrage is just now the subject of general discussion of people of the stage. Some of them have really become worked up about it, to such an extent that at teas and after theatrical performances, it is the sole topic of conversation."[16] Political awareness among popular actresses like Mary Shaw and Lillian Russell certainly led to an increase of feminist activism in the American theater. Mary Shaw had become a suffragist before 1900. She was an early member of the Professional Woman's League and participated in the club's tenth anniversary "Woman's Exhibition" at Madison Square Garden in October 1902. She acted in plays by Ibsen and Shaw, and, by linking performances of the works of these two progressive playwrights to her personal convictions, became notorious by touring the country with Shaw's *Mrs. Warren's Profession*. In 1909 she played the lead in the first New York performance of her friend Elizabeth Robins's suffrage play, *Votes for Women*, and later wrote and produced suffrage plays of her own, *The Woman of It; or, Our Friends the Anti-Suffragists* and *The Parrot Cage*. In 1913, she and co-actress Lillian Russell founded the all-female Gamut Club and in the same year tried to set up a National Woman's Theater. The actress and suffragist Fola La Follette, daughter of Senator Robert La Follette and wife of the playwright George Middleton, gave speeches and led the actresses' division in more than one suffrage parade in New York City. Her husband joined the Men's League for Woman Suffrage and at her request supported the woman's movement by writing *Back of the Ballot* in 1915.

Simultaneously with the rising activism among actresses, students of pres-

tigious women's colleges, who had become increasingly interested in the suffrage mvoement after 1900, began to write and perform plays and pageants in
support of the cause. A few brave and solitary women, like Maud Wood Park
at Radcliffe and Inez Milholland at Vassar, had openly joined suffrage organizations shortly after the turn of the century—usually against the explicit
recommendation of their college presidents—and recognized the opportunity
for publicity in dramatic performance. By 1910, however, support from students
had grown significantly, according to a curt article in the New York Times,
which was an anti-suffrage paper at the time:

Suffrage Play at Barnard

Unless appearances are deceptive, woman's suffrage has been gaining
adherents in Barnard College. The college is not pledged to the cause by
any means, but some 150 women students advocate it openly and many
others say they are interested.

For several weeks posters advertising a suffrage entertainment in
Brinckerhoff Theatre yesterday had been posted about the college. This
entertainment consisted of a one-act play entitled, "How They Won the
Vote." There were ten characters in it. There were no pretty girls selling
tickets at the door, as there usually are at Barnard plays, because the
performance was free. But the commercial spirit was manifested in suffrage
literature, which was sold at the door to help pay expenses. [17]

Once college women, actresses, and society women of New York City
began to join forces, however, the articles in the New York Times became
markedly longer and somewhat less condescending. The paper could hardly
afford to snub Mrs. Vanderbilt, Mrs. Gould, or other equally prominent social
leaders, whose dinner dances and European trips they would still have to report.
When Mrs. Clarence Mackay persuaded other New York society women to
participate for the first time in a public series of tableaux in aid of the Equal
Suffrage League, the Times devoted three consecutive issues to details of the
event at Maxine Elliott's Theatre in January 1911. The article, "Smart Set
Leaders, in Historical Poses, Will Represent Woman's Advancement," is an
excellent example of newspaper writing for the society page that tries to avoid
mentioning the political issue: "A dress rehearsal of the tableaux was held
yesterday in the theatre, and the programme presented a review, indicative of
the progress of women. A large and fashionable patronage is promised for the
performance. Each tableaux [sic] will represent a famous painting or statue.
Scenic artists and costumes have been working for weeks on the backgrounds
and settings, and famous tapestries, chairs and other accessories as well as a
dazzling array of jewels have been loaned by the society women for the review."[18] After correctly, though briefly, having stated the purpose of the benefit

performance, the review of the performance itself two days later wanders off into a proper society report about the illustrious participants of the various tableaux and meticulously describes their elegant costumes.[19]

In New York City, suffrage plays were either performed at commercial theaters like the Broadway Theatre and the Republic Theatre, which were also rented for political meetings by the Woman Suffrage Party and other organizations, or at fashionable hotels such as the Waldorf or the Astor that had facilities for theatricals. In Philadelphia, the Broad Street Theatre became a favorite location for performances arranged by the Pennsylvania Equal Suffrage Organization. On February 16, 1911, for instance, Mrs. Otis Skinner and Beatrice Forbes-Robertson organized a matinée performance of three English suffrage plays at the Broad Street Theatre, "Given under the Auspices and for the Benefit of" the Pennsylvania Limited Suffrage League, the Equal Franchise Society of Pennsylvania, and the College Equal Suffrage League. Performances like these were usually done for fund-raising purposes, and suffragists explicitly informed their audiences in the program that a "collection for the benefit of the Suffrage Cause will be taken before the last play."[20] Successful plays and tableaux often traveled on the invitation of local suffrage groups. The series of tableaux *A Dream of Brave Women* by Emily Sargent Lewis, a leading Philadelphia suffragist, was performed at the Broad Street Theatre on February 27, 1912, with Mrs. Otis Skinner as the reader of the poems.[21] At the invitation of the Woman's Political Union, the same production was then given at the Republic Theatre in New York on April 12, 1912, together with an English suffrage play. The *New York Times* called it a "Stage Riot for Suffrage" but conceded that it turned out as a "big benefit matinée" advertising the forthcoming suffrage parade on May 4, which was to have more than ten thousand participants.[22]

Marie Jenney Howe, a former Unitarian minister and friend of both Mary Shaw and Fola La Follette, had founded her own theatrical company in Manhattan's Twenty-fifth Assembly District of the Woman Suffrage Party, which successfully toured in and around New York. Early in 1912, a second theater company began to compete with Howe's Twenty-fifth District Players, as the *New York Times* reported:

> The Woman Suffrage Party has gone into theatricals for good. It has
> organized a regular stock company, under the direction of Mrs. Helen
> Griffith, to play in New York and nearby towns. One of the Assembly
> districts organized by the Party, the Twenty-fifth, has for some time had a
> theatrical company, which has been doing good business. It was known as
> "The Twenty-five Players of the Twenty-fifth." This company has given
> suffrage and other plays all over the city with much success and has raised
> considerable money for suffrage work. The new company will work on the
> same lines and will also go on the road.[23]

While suffrage organizations began to realize the benefits of large-scale theatrical performances, feminist actresses, on the other hand, persuaded directors of commercial theaters to permit suffragists to address theater audiences during intermissions of regular evening performances. The satirical report in an undated suffrage pamphlet, however, testifies to the obvious lack of interest in propaganda sandwiched between the acts:

The Drama

MISGUIDED theatrical managers are allowing suffragists to make speeches in the intermission during plays. The theater is no place to get real ideas, and it is to be hoped that women in the audiences will show their disapproval by following haughtily in the footsteps of the male sex who scud out between the acts. [24]

Theatrical propaganda for the vote had become less self-conscious and produced wittier plays as the campaign drew on. Authors were beginning to use stereotypical anti-suffrage arguments for their own ironic purposes, from Marie Jenney Howe's *Anti-Suffrage Monologue* to Mary Shaw's *Our Friends the Anti-Suffragists*. Their comedies demonstrated that the arguments of the "Antis" were so ridiculous and puerile that one needed simply to pronounce them publicly in order to achieve the desired comic effect. Suffragists set out to prove that they had the greater sense of humor. As George Middleton explains in his memoirs, a feminist like Marie Jenney Howe could even organize an evening of anti-suffrage mock speeches as a form of popular entertainment. She brought together twenty-five eminent speakers at the Metropolitan Temple in New York City on March 11, 1912, and at her suggestion each "speaker took a trite objection to suffrage and had five minutes to mop it up. Thirty seconds before the end of the allotted time Marie rang a bell: On the sentence her gavel would drop."[25] Charlotte Perkins Gilman was invited to speak on the topic "Woman Suffrage Would Unsex Women"; Howe's husband, Frederic C. Howe took up the argument that "Women Don't Understand Politics." Inez Milholland, for example, replied to the demand of anti-suffragists that "Woman's Place Is In the Home": "If woman's place is in the home, how does it happen that there are about eight million women in the United States who are out of the home—working in gainful occupations?"[26] This version of improvised speech-making with a sense of dramatic rhetoric became such a success that Howe repeated it twice in similar form at the Cooper Union early in 1914. Arguments of the "Antis" had gradually begun to work for, and no longer against, enfranchisement. By 1915 Alice Duer Miller could ridicule some of the most popular anti-suffrage arguments of the past four decades in a mock write-up on women's fashion:

Fashion Notes: Past and Present

1880—ANTI-SUFFRAGE arguments are being worn long, calm and flowing this year, with the dominant note that of woman's intellectual inferiority.

1890—Violence is very evident in this season's modes, and our more conservative thinkers are saying that woman suffrage threatens the home, the Church and the Republic.

1900—A complete change of style has taken place. Everything is being worn à l'aristocrate, with the repeated assertion that too many people are voting already.

1915—The best line of goods shown by the leading anti-suffrage houses this spring is the statement that woman suffrage is the same thing as free love. The effect is extremely piquant and surprising. [27]

Numerous "Votes for Women" balls, "Suffrage Carnival" balls, and vaudevilles between 1913 and 1916 already seemed to anticipate and celebrate the approaching end of a long campaign. Yet, after the outbreak of World War I in Europe, large suffrage organizations like the National American Woman Suffrage Association felt the obligation to turn to war relief work instead of suffrage theatricals; the National Woman's Party, on the other hand, favored picketing, not performance. One of the last flamboyant productions in New York City, therefore, was *Melinda and Her Sisters*, the suffrage operetta by Mrs. O. H. P. Belmont and Elsa Maxwell, which was performed by a mixed cast of professional actresses and New York débutantes in the grand ballroom of the Waldorf Astoria on February 18, 1916, as one of the great social events of that season. In spite of the enthusiasm and success with which suffragists agitated on the stage before the United States entered the war, it took another four years to ratify the Nineteenth Amendment.

Suffrage plays, especially those written and performed in the early twentieth century, are plays with a propagandistic purpose. The plays reflect the topics of the controversy at that time, proving that the arguments of suffragists were far more varied than a mere battle cry for the vote, as historians have occasionally claimed. The issues range from the Pure Milk debate to legal questions of alimony and child support, from attacks against "social evil" to the well-known argument against "taxation without representation." Although it is true that the ballot was generally regarded as the remedy for these problems, the plays prove that the campaign for "Votes for Women" addressed a greater diversity of issues than is commonly assumed. The open discussion of many problems, however, that could not possibly be resolved by the enfranchisement of women alone also disappeared along with the interest in suffrage plays after the ratification of the amendment. The main provocation was now missing. George Bernard Shaw, in his essay on the problem play and the drama of propaganda, explains that since "a drama with a social question for the motive cannot outlive the solution of that question . . . when a play depends entirely on a social question—when the struggle in it is between man and a purely legal institution—nothing can prolong its life beyond that of the institution."[28] American literature, in fact, has a long and much neglected tradition of polemic plays about social and political controversies or grievances at specific periods in history, beginning with a surprising number of eighteenth-century propaganda plays of the Revolution, some of which were made accessible by Norman Philbrick in his excellent collection, *Trumpets Sounding*[29], to nineteenth-century temperance plays, or more recently, pro-union, anti-segregation, and anti-war plays. All of these plays lost, or will necessarily lose, their impact with proper social or political "improvements," according to Shaw, but they will certainly retain their value as cultural documents.

Literature that has its origin in the immediacy of political struggle or a specific political event is purposefully designed to respond to or aid that event. It is pragmatic in a basic sense of the term, and can be read and understood properly only in connection with the actual historic situation. In fact, it presupposes an intimate knowledge of the event in question, or a specific development, and keeps referring to it. Unlike any other part of literary culture, it cannot be cut off from this origin or source without serious impediments, and any interpretation that disregards this mutual dependence of historic context and literary work will distort its meaning. Propaganda literature is of necessity polemic, didactic, referential, and usually dated, because its true purpose dies with the cause. During the decades of the equal rights debate and the suffrage movement, propaganda plays accompanied the actual political issues in a way that makes them valuable as documentations and illustrations. Suffrage and anti-suffrage plays developed into a genre of their own, giving the historical discussions of the time an immediacy that other events relying entirely on written sources will not possess for us. The plays, even if they are amateurish at times, re-create for us some of the passion, energy, and moral fervor of the actual controversy in a situation that became decisive for American women.

THE PLAYS

William Bentley Fowle (1795–1865). Woman's Rights (1856). In *Parlor Dramas; or, Dramatic Scenes, for Home Amusement*. Boston: Chase and Nichols, 1856, pp. 7–17.

Published eight years after the first Woman's Rights Convention at Seneca Falls, New York, in July 1848, the play by Fowle probably constitutes the first acknowledgment of the woman's rights debate in dramatic form. As befits both the genre and the topic, the scene of *Woman's Rights* is "The Parlor" of the main antagonists, Mr. and Mrs. Manly. Voicing her growing dissatisfaction with the traditional legal and economic dependence of wives, Mrs. Manly wishes to revoke the marriage vow and warns her sister Myrtilla not to give up her freedom as a single woman for a state of bondage. She openly deplores the inequality between the sexes, insists that by divine purpose men and women were created equal, and, like Shakespeare's Rosalind, finally exclaims in exasperation, "O, would I were a man!" Myrtilla's position seems as yet untinged by negative experiences; she therefore plays the role of Portia in this unresolved conflict and suggests the Manlys exchange their respective roles as breadwinner and housekeeper.

The outcome of the experiment is predictable: Mr. Manly, the business man, proves to be a disastrous housekeeper, unable to organize the most commonplace details of housework, while Mrs. Manly spends a harrowing day at the store, only to find out that she has no talent for business. Although Manly had tacitly assumed that his part of the bargain would be the easier one and would give him the opportunity to take a day off, his inability to manage the servants antagonizes the uppity Irish cook and the incompetent Irish maid, who make no attempt to hide their derision of the "henpecked husband" and are subsequently fired by Mr. Manly. Before the day is over, husband and wife gladly revoke their playful experiment at role reversal, and Myrtilla fulfills her role as the wise judge and declares that the "hen was never made to swim" (p. 51).

The message of the play, as voiced by Myrtilla, is an affirmation of the "natural order" which assigns separate spheres to men and women. Yet in spite of the conservative pattern of the plot, the couple's final reconciliation promotes a few surprising concessions. Being temporarily forced into a position of economic dependence, Mr. Manly has to realize that it can be a very demeaning experience to have to beg one's spouse for money to cover basic household expenses; and Mrs. Manly, from the brief experience in her husband's store, suddenly comprehends that being in business and having access to the cash register cannot necessarily be equated with economic independence. As it turns out, Mrs. Manly is more dissatisfied with the fact that she has no budget than with marriage as an institution, or the legal state of women. With some mutual understanding and an allowance for wives, that is, with a little diplomacy the woman's rights debate could easily be settled. Thus the play simply establishes the *status quo ante* as the "natural state," and it does so in the tone of traditional farces; only fools, says Fowle, meddle with the convention of separate spheres for men and women.

The generic name of the Manlys clearly designates them not as dramatic characters but as types. They are mouthpieces for the then-current opinions on the roles of men and women in marriage, if not in life. It is quite surprising, though, to note that the main arguments of the early feminists had been popularized so quickly. During the first part of the play, Fowle alludes to a number of points that had been discussed before and after Seneca Falls. Lucy Stone's refusal to include the verb "to obey" in her marriage vow when she married Henry Blackwell in 1855 could easily have been the model for Mrs. Manly's high-spirited revocation of the marriage vow at the opening of the play. Similarly, her comparison of women and slaves as equally unfree was one that was often used in speeches and pamphlets by early feminists who were, after all, supporters of Abolitionism. Mrs. Manly's arguments at the beginning of the play reflect the level of discussion about woman's rights before the beginning of the Civil War. Like the early feminists, she deplores the whole concept of the supposed inferiority of women and insists on adequate control over property and earnings. Suffrage for women, however, has not yet become the topic of a play.

True to the pattern of parlor theatricals, *Woman's Rights* operates with stereotypes that were easily recognizable in spite of improvised stages and amateurish acting. Yet Bridget Killmallybone, the cook, and Kitty, the maid, are distortions of stock characters, vicious caricatures of domestic servants that were quite typical for nineteenth-century burlesques. As exhibited in these farces, middle-class insensitivity for what were regarded as "the lower orders" almost invariably influenced the portrayal of the recently immigrated Irish as incompetent, foul-mouthed, dishonest, and potentially insurgent. The economic

dependence of the two servants is taken lightly in Fowle's play: it is regarded
an impertinence when they ask Mr. Manly for the ten weeks' wages due them,
and Kitty's solidarity with Bridget is seen as an insubordination that comes
close to an act of criminal bonding. When she finally steals a pencil-case and
a pair of gold glasses, this merely confirms widespread prejudices about servants
of a different race or creed.[30]

*   *   *

Ariana Randolph Wormeley Curtis (1833–1922) and Daniel Sargent Curtis
(1825–1908). *The Spirit of Seventy-Six; or, The Coming Woman, A Prophetic
Drama, Followed by A Change of Base, and Doctor Mondschein*. Boston: Little,
Brown and Company, 1868, pp. 7–73.

Amateur plays rarely reached the professional stage. Usually they were
one-act plays, and as such were both too short and dramatically too simplistic
to justify a costly theater production. Their dialogue was explicitly geared to
the needs of amateur actors, as was the required quality of acting, and most
plays did not even offer enough parts to satisfy the professional interests of a
larger stage. *The Spirit of Seventy-Six* is a notable exception. Its success as a
parlor farce was outstanding and lasted more than three decades; in 1889 the
published play had already reached its twenty-third edition. Although it was
originally written for private performance, it was then successfully transferred
to the professional stage. The press announcement for its first commercial
performance on April 20, 1868, claims: "At Selwyn's tonight the entertainment
will have peculiar local attractions. The 'Spirit of '76' has been found so
sparkling and bright in private theatricals, that it can hardly fail of making a
hit with its numerous and humorous hits on the regular stage. Something more
than curiosity will be gratified by its representation. It has intrinsic merits of
dialogue, situation and characterization to insure its success."[31] Its surprising
dramatic quality caused the play to run almost three weeks at Selwyn's Theatre
and it was received "at each representation with great enthusiasm, laughter
and applause, by large and fashionable audiences," as the last advertisement
proudly announced. Like so many popular nineteenth-century farces, however,
it was still short enough to run on a double bill with another burlesque to fill
an evening of theatrical amusement, and there was musical entertainment
during the intermission.

The Spirit of Seventy-Six had been written for the well-educated and
genteelly urban audience of the Boston area that was clearly much amused by
the idea of a world turned upside down through the zealousness of radical
woman reformers. Bostonians, of course, were all too familiar with the various
reform movements of their fellow citizens, and before the Civil War had had
little reason to laugh about any of them. With the end of the war, however,
when many of the former Abolitionists had begun to turn to different causes,
the possibility emerged to satirize certain "excesses" of the Woman's Rights
Movement. The main thrust of the seemingly absurd exaggeration of *The Spirit*

of Seventy-Six is therefore directed against the alleged attempt of radical reformers to reverse the traditional gender roles. Like the plays and speeches of
many of the educated antifeminists to come, the play does not necessarily
ridicule higher education or positions of responsibility for women. Rather, it
satirizes universal role reversal as a ludicrous possibility, and its sarcasm attacks
those "deluded females" who attempt to cover their own undersirability or
incompetence with the authority of the new movement.

The play opens at the Newton Corner Railway Station. Tom Carberry has
just returned to Boston after a ten years' absence in China, and he is stunned
to find that the world, as he had known it, has been turned upside down
through the enfranchisement of women. He has to confront Mrs. Badger, a
New Woman in Bloomer costume, smoking a cigar in what once was "the
gentlemen's waiting-room" of a public railroad station. To his amazement,
women now hold all the important offices in and around Boston and have
relegated men to the home. Men, in fact, are being found sadly deficient in
consistency and the ability of logical argumentation; the only occupation for
these useless creatures seems to be child care and the mending of stockings,
while their wives attend important political meetings or spend their evenings
at the club. Tom Carberry finally seeks refuge from this awesome new regime
in a marriage with his old friend's somewhat backward daughter, Victorine
Wigfall, who refuses, however, to propose to him as she should. To his utter
dismay, two of the fiercely strong-minded new women claim him for their
husband—breach of promise seems to be the only old law that survives in the
new era—and threaten him with a duel, until Victorine's mother, the Judge,
reluctantly intervenes in her daughter's behalf.

The play is, of course, not only more daring than Fowle's *Woman's Rights*,
but also more consistent in its utopian design. Men and women have not
simply exchanged their spheres for a brief and ill-fated experiment. Rather,
the consolidated votes of women at the first national election after their enfranchisement have brought them dominance in all areas because they hold
the majority. Men and women therefore experience a complete reversal of all
roles and positions—not only of their respective professions and occupations,
but also of those supposedly generic attitudes and characteristics that were once
identified as feminine or masculine when men were still socially, politically,
and economically superior. According to the complex argument of the play,
the new revolution seems to prove that, since they attained political power,
women also automatically acquired previously male characteristics which had
been thought necessary prerogatives for precisely that power, not its result.
Male loss of social dominance, on the other hand, has quickly produced in
them those feminine traits that had formerly been regarded as inherent in
women: "Men have such frivolous minds,—they don't care for anything but
dress and company" (p. 62), complains one of the women. Men are now the
weaker sex in every sense of the word, and as a necessary consequence, they

have to suffer and be still; they now have to listen patiently to the boring self-aggrandizements of women, the tedious expressions of female superiority, and the vain exhibition of their wives' importance.

The authors' intention was clearly anti-feminist, and there is little sympathy for radical woman's rights leaders, as the animal names of Wolverine Griffin and Mrs. Badger show. In fact, Mrs. Badger was played by a male actor at Selwyn's Theatre to emphasize the grotesqueness of the character; the hand-written cast for a private performance, in which "Mrs. Daniel Curtis" herself played Judge Wigfall, lists two male actors, Jeremiah Abbott as Wolverine Griffin and Hal Lee as Mrs. Badger. The play clearly ridicules the new movement as already having gone too far, but it also permits a number of interesting ambiguities in presenting Tom Carberry as an unenlightened male chauvinist who eventually expresses the strong (un-American) desire to return to China, as "the only country fit to live in,—they drown the superfluous females young!" (p. 69). And although both Griffin and Badger feel jilted in the end, they firmly refuse to drown themselves in the Chestnut Hill Reservoir for a man.

The topos of the world turned upside down is not used simply to draw a caricature of an imminent and fearfully masculine generation of emancipated women; it also cleverly reveals the existing injustices and incongruities of American social standards. The application of reverse clichés must have been considered wonderfully absurd; but since satirists have always used laughter to reveal incongruities of human thinking and behavior, these lines also backfire. As in Swift's *Gulliver's Travels*, crass exaggeration is here used to produce the dual effect of causing laughter *about* and *with* existing conditions and their reversal. The play satirizes discrimination of men by the new women leaders, but it thereby points simultaneously to existing discrimination—for instance, when Judge Wigfall solemnly declares that she herself does not favor the "popular doctrine of the complete Mental and Moral Inferiority of Man" (p. 66), although the more conservative women of the new era will only tolerate men in their proper sphere. Hence, social and cultural standards are here comically reversed in a way that occasionally seems almost revisionist to us. The new leaders have discovered, for example, that Shakespeare was a woman, which for us is reminiscent of Virginia Woolf's essay "A Room of One's Own." In addition, an impressive list of Great Women has taken the place of a list of Great Men to celebrate the cultural achievements of womankind, reminding the modern reader of Judy Chicago's "Dinner Party." What makes the play interesting, therefore, are the curiously dialectical consequences of such a reversal of prejudices and cultural clichés.

The Spirit of Seventy-Six is a utopian centennial play. It anticipates conditions in Massachusetts at the forthcoming centenary celebrations of the Revolution, foreseeing yet another, though rather ludicrous revolution: "A hundred years ago it was thought a fine thing for a few American men to throw off the British Tyrant's yoke,—but that was a trifling achievement, compared to the new Revolution, in which twenty millions of ladies have thrown off *all* restraint, and now plant their victorious feet on the neck of the Male Oppressor!" (p. 63). And when Tom Carberry begins to feel the negative consequences of his present inferior state, he sees this as an outrageous injustice and exclaims in rebellion against the oppressor: "And *I've* a right—an inalienable right—to life, liberty, and the pursuit to happiness! Are Men's Rights trampled underfoot? Is there no Antislavery sentiment left in Boston? No Society for the Abolition of Women? What are all the philanthropists about, now-a-days, I should like to know?" (p. 70). The ambiguity of his evocation of the Declaration of Independence would certainly have reminded a Massachusetts audience of Abigail Adams's plea to "Remember the Ladies," and Carberry's furious demand that Abolitionists should now concentrate on the emancipation of Man involuntarily reveals the arbitrary injustice against one half of the population by the other. By using the literary model of the centennial play, the Curtises end their prophetic drama with a judicial epilogue reminiscent of Margaret Fuller's "The Great Lawsuit," which addresses the women in the audience as the jury that has to decide "either for or against the defendant,—MAN," and then offers refreshments in the next room, true to the manner of the traditional parlor theatrical.

   The Spirit of Seventy-Six, together with the other two plays in the volume, was published anonymously. Although bibliographical sources usually list both Ariana R. Wormeley Curtis and her husband, Daniel Sargent Curtis, as joint authors of the collection, the manuscript note by a contemporary in an early edition not only lists Ariana Curtis as a member of the cast, but also credits her with sole authorship of the title play—"by Mrs. Daniel Curtis."[32] She was the youngest daughter of the American-born Rear Admiral Ralph Randolph Wormeley of the English Royal Navy, and both her sisters, Elizabeth Wormeley Latimer and Katherine Prescott Wormeley, were well-known American authors and translators, according to the biographical dictionary *A Woman of the Century* (1893).[33] Together with her sisters, Ariana Curtis wrote the recollections of their father, printed in 1879. Considering the topic as well as the ambiguity of argument and tone in *The Spirit of Seventy-Six*, it seems likely that Ariana Curtis composed this particular play without her husband as co-author. Yet it is hardly surprising that neither she nor her husband wished to be officially known as the authors of plays that were regarded as mere recreation.

*   *   *

Ella Cheever Thayer. *Lords of Creation: Woman Suffrage Drama in Three Acts.* Boston: Geo. M. Baker & Company, 1883.

   With the heated debate over the Fourteenth and Fifteenth Amendments, the woman's rights movement had changed gears. While the American Equal Rights Association supported the Fourteenth Amendment under all circumstances and after its ratification in 1868 introduced a text for the Fifteenth Amendment that once again left out discrimination on the grounds of sex,

Elizabeth Cady Stanton, Susan B. Anthony, and their supporters became avid woman suffrage advocates. Two years after Harriet H. Robinson's complaint that there was as yet no proper woman suffrage drama, *Lords of Creation* was published as the first self-pronounced "Woman Suffrage Drama."[33]

The plot of Ella Cheever Thayer's play in three acts is effectively modeled on that of the standard drawing-room comedy: Mr. Grovenor, "the Head of his Family," is almost brought to ruin by his spendthrift son and his thoughtless wife, but his smart and competent daughter Kate takes over her father's business while he is ill, and saves him from bankruptcy. Dr. Endicott, "a true Man," supports Kate and wins her hand after some romantic complications, while her sister, Alice, opts for the rich but stupid Doughlass to support her in style. The main plot is accompanied by the typical comedy subplot of the servant couple that tries to imitate the leading characters.

The various arguments for and against equal rights for women, rather than the plot structure, are what make the play so interesting. Thayer, in fact, uses the standard comedic characters to present the main anti-suffrage arguments that had become popular at the time of the first debate on woman suffrage in the Senate, namely, that the vote for women would destroy the home, that women were sufficiently represented by men, and, most important of all, "that women *should* not vote or hold office because they *could* not."[35] Kate's father complains about his wife and younger daughter, Alice, for regarding him mainly as the provider of costly clothes, but he also opposes Kate's plans for getting an adequate education and her attempt to help him with his business. Mrs. Grovenor and Alice are stereotypes of those passively dependent women whose parasitical existence Harriet Beecher Stowe had criticized as "the pink and white tyranny" in her novel of that title,[36] but Mr. Grovenor is convinced that working women constitute the greater social danger. Entangling himself in the kind of contradiction that will later become the hallmark of all suffrage propaganda plays, he suggests that women should work for their living in order to learn the value of money; yet as soon as Kate points out that women's wages are only half that of men's, her father replies, if "a woman did her work as well as a man she would get the same wages; but she does not. She isn't thinking of her work. When she is young she is thinking of getting married, when she is old she is mad because she can't" (p. 88). Many of the lines in the play, in fact, sound quite authentic if one compares them with the diatribes of the anti-suffragists. It would not be farfetched to claim that, in spite of its propagandistic intentions, Thayer's play has more of the ring of realistic dialogue than most other American plays before the arrival of James A. Herne and William Vaughn Moody.

The comedy ends on a conciliatory note. Once his defenses are down, Kate's father is grateful for her help and business expertise, and eventually concedes that the independent and strong-minded woman may even be an improvement on the utterly dependent one. Reason and common sense are re-established when even the spoiled younger daughter begins to realize her mistake in having encouraged a wealthy but stupid suitor; when Jim, the coachman, is willing to grant equal rights to Jennie, the maid; and when— most important of all—Kate is reconciled to Dr. Endicott, the perfect spouse for the new woman. The final toast sounds like a belated constitutional guarantee of happiness for everyone: "Equal rights to all." This enlightened projection of an ideal future for the Grovenor family ultimately depends on the certainty that civic justice will eventually follow equal rights.

Lords of Creation is not, strictly speaking, a suffrage propaganda play. It pleads for woman suffrage, to be sure, but it uses many of the more general arguments of the mid-nineteenth-century woman's rights debate that were occasionally given up in the woman suffrage movement proper after the turn of the century, once the activities of the woman's movement began to concentrate on the campaign for the vote. Like most of the plays written during the last decades of the nineteenth century, Lords of Creation argues against the double standard, ridicules the metaphor of the sturdy oak and the clinging vine as the ideal image for a good marriage, and exposes the male privilege of sowing wild oats as a disastrous license for irresponsible young men. The author openly deplores taxation without representation as tyranny and describes marriages for economic reasons as socially sanctioned prostitution—in short, the play contains the full spectrum of arguments of the moral and social reform movement as well as the woman's rights movement, and it interprets woman suffrage as an important element, but not the only step toward a change of women's position in society.

In spite of the obvious didacticism of the dialogue, Lords of Creation avoids the danger of becoming a mere tract by giving the arguments plausibility through plot. The melodramatic conflict may seem contrived to us nowadays—Kate mistakes her brother's girlfriend for Dr. Endicott's and refuses to marry him until the third act—and the equally melodramatic subplot between Kate's irresponsible brother and the trusting young girl, whom he betrayed, may jar our more sophisticated dramatic perceptions. To theater audiences of the late nineteenth century, however, who were used to the improbabilities of popular melodrama and the undisguised didacticism of temperance plays and other propaganda drama, Lords of Creation may well have appeared almost as stage realism.

*　*　*

Eleanor Freeman. When the Women Vote: A Colloquy. Cincinnati: Standard Publishing Company, 1885.

Dialogue has been used as a learned form of reasoning about ideas and philosophical propositions since the days of Plato. As an interplay of ideas, dialogue can be more effective than a mere presentation of the idea in a lecture or tract; and as a literary convention, it is often livelier than the usual essay. Charles Brockden Brown, the first American author to have used the form of dialogue for a discussion on woman's rights, presents the fictitious debate between Alcuin, the shy but old-fashioned schoolmaster and scholar, and Mrs. Carter, the independent and almost radical woman of the world, in *Alcuin: A Dialogue*. Eleanor Freeman's "Colloquy" may have been modeled to a certain extent on Brown's "Dialogue"; at any rate, it presents a similarly spirited exchange of opinions in a bourgeois household, but extends it to include the voices of two women and two men. Like *Alcuin*, Freeman's *When the Women Vote* expands the form of a strictly dialectic and didactic dispute to a controversy that contains rudimentary elements of the drama without actually attempting to become a play.

The temporal setting of the debate is the future, immediately after women have won the vote. While Mrs. Van Arden, the suffragist, tours the country giving a series of lectures for the "Cause," her husband and child are left under the care of Bridget, the stereotypical Irish maid, who cannot cope with the new-fangled kitchen equipment and futuristic machines. Although the opening lines of Freeman's *When the Women Vote* sound precisely like a continuation of the anti-feminist arguments of *Woman's Rights* and *The Spirit of Seventy-Six*, it soon develops four major conflicting opinions that clearly support the argument for the emancipation of women. Apart from the voice of Mrs. Van Arden, the "ardent" suffragist, there is Mrs. Rivers, her sister-in-law and a moral reformer, who may not be in favor of Universal Suffrage, but who will certainly support even militant women in their "efforts to elevate humanity, whether in the form of man or woman" (p. 119). Although Van Arden deplores his wife's frequent absences from home even more than her opinions on the advancement of women, he still prefers to be married to a strong-minded woman, because he is not "an admirer of the milk and water type" (p. 120). Mr. Jones, the neighbor, on the other hand, may have a wife who stays at home, but he "has grown to hate the whole sex, because he married a woman for her beauty, her wealth, and her *supposed* submission to the male sex. He is reaping just what he sowed" (p. 120), as Mrs. Rivers informs her temporarily malcontent brother.

These four conflicting opinions of one militant and one moderate supporter of each of the two sides are merely pitted against each other without any pretense of dramatic plot or character development. The propagandistic purpose of the "Colloquy," therefore, corresponds to its structure, and the seeming artlessness of Freeman's dramatic dialogue should be seen as the attempt to revive the literary dialogue as an adequate form for an ongoing debate. In fact, the rather inconsequential remarks about Bridget's relationship with Dennis, the drunken Irish coachman, and the somewhat confusing introduction of the effeminate dandy Oscar Vere de Vere rather serve to obscure the strictly dialogic structure. Both incidents are mere vehicles for two specific arguments—that drunkards and illiterates should certainly not be allowed to vote, and that pretentious fops, whose affectations make them repulsively hermaphroditic creatures, are harder to bear than militant suffragists—and as arguments they might easily and more effectively have been integrated into any of the other speakers' parts.

The obvious and disturbing class arrogance articulated by the two emancipated women in Freeman's "Colloquy" is a phenomenon that, unfortunately, tainted many remarks by leading woman's rights activists during the first decades after the Civil War. Especially before the ratification of the Fifteenth Amendment in 1870, Elizabeth Cady Stanton and, to a somewhat lesser degree, Susan B. Anthony openly began to oppose Black suffrage at the expense of white middle-class women. As Ellen DuBois explains in her edition of speeches and letters by Stanton and Anthony: "On the one hand, they argued that white women, educated and virtuous, were more deserving of the vote than the ex-slaves. On the other hand, they attempted to build feminism on the basis of white women's racism. At times, Stanton even fueled white women's sexual fears of Black men to rouse them against Black suffrage and for their own enfranchisement."[37] Apart from the early racism that gradually subsided during the next decades, the general feeling that white middle-class women were more deserving of the vote than many uneducated or socially unacceptable men again became more pronounced after the beginning of the new immigration in 1880, when illiterate foreigners from poor European countries were able to vote, while the vote was still withheld from women of old American stock. This argument was initially used by feminists during the last decades of the nineteenth century, but eventually became a counter-argument of anti-suffragists who maintained that women should not defile themselves with politics since too many people were voting as it was.

✻   ✻   ✻

George Rugg. *The New Woman: A Farcical Sketch with One Act, One Scene and One Purpose.* Boston: Walter H. Baker & Company, 1896.

Alice E. Ives. *A Very New Woman.* In *The Woman's Column* 9, no. 11 (March 14, 1896).

In a number of articles published in leading journals and magazines, the term "New Woman" was introduced during the late 1880s and early 1890s. Oddly enough, the epithet at first had a negative, or at least critical, implication, characterizing a woman as brash, self-centered, or even irresponsible. Eventually the meaning was transformed from "strong-minded" or "unwomanly" into a positive denomination for the emancipated, educated, or progressive woman of the day. After 1900 especially, the expression became so popular that it was worn like a badge by many women who simply thought of themselves as fashionable. The fact that there are at least twenty or thirty plays of this title proves not only the popularity of the term itself but also the ambivalent usage that allowed both feminists and anti-feminists to claim the "New Woman" as an ideal or as a warning to others, respectively. The two plays by George Rugg and Alice Emma Ives, both published in the same year, represent both positions.

The farce by Rugg is one of the many anti-suffrage plays especially, but not exclusively, written by male authors around the turn of the century. These burlesques usually depict the emancipatory endeavors of women as outrageously funny, the stuff for "sidesplitting" domestic comedy and anti-feminist farce. The intention of Rugg's play is to show henpecked husbands a ridiculously simple trick to relegate women to their proper station. The sad present state of man, his blatant suppression by the dangerous New Woman, according to Rugg and other playwrights, is the result of men's foolish lenience. Although they have forfeited their superiority, men could easily disempower the New Woman by threatening her with the archenemy of all women: the mouse. A brave mouseslayer will immediately be reinstalled in his previous position of natural authority and male dignity.

The single purpose of Rugg's farce, as stated in the subtitle, may even then have been too simplistic to make it effective as counter-propaganda; its crude slapstick quality now merely succeeds in making the play and its argument unintentionally funny. Rugg uses the term "New Woman" to revive the stereotype of the mannish emancipated woman still modeled on mid-nineteenth-century caricatures in popular magazines. As in most of the other anti-suffrage plays written around the turn of the century, suffragists are seen as screeching females with ridiculous assumptions of equality who have to be brought to their senses by firm males before they actually endanger the social order. Yet, unlike even the most amateurish of the feminist plays, these later anti-feminist farces usually lack the careful argumentation of an effective propaganda play. Rugg actually patches together lines and ideas from earlier plays, using the concept of a world temporarily turned upside down from Fowle's play, the boxing females and scrubbing males from *The Spirit of Seventy-Six*, and the name Vere de Vere from Freeman's *When the Women Vote*, but without any of his predecessors' originality or wit. Within the context of this collection, however, his farce exemplifies the increasing sterility of anti-feminist arguments. At the same time it is representative of the numerous stereotypical anti-feminist parlor farces written particularly between 1890 and 1910. Their surprising number attests that the conservative movement had gained momentum during those years until the new generation of American suffragists became active.

Alice Ives's *A Very New Woman*, on the other hand, proudly presents two generations of New Women. Mrs. Curtis Twillington, an "advanced woman," is appalled when her only son, Arthur, presents her a "womanly woman" as his future wife. Arthur is afraid that his mother's revolutionary ideas might shock the "dear, housewifely little thing," whereas Mrs. Twillington's polite and insincere questions soon prove that Edith, her future daughter-in-law, is in fact the secretary of a Woman Suffrage League and a law student about to take her exams. She is tremendously relieved that her conservative son has been deceived by Edith's docile appearance and gleefully suggests an alliance of New Women. Completely overwhelmed by the bond of interests between the two independent women, Arthur proposes partnership in his law firm to his future wife. This revolutionary incident in the play was probably inspired by Catharine Waugh McCulloch's position as a partner in her husband's Chicago law firm, which was renamed McCulloch & McCulloch after their marriage in 1890.[38] The author originally came from Detroit, before she settled in New York as a journalist and playwright. In Detroit she had been a member of the Illinois Equal Suffrage Association, in which Catharine Waugh McCulloch was legislative superintendent.[39] Ives was certainly familiar with the partnership of the McCullochs and may well have used them as the model for the marriage of a truly advanced couple.

The little sketch by Ives describes Edith as the ideal type of the New Woman, who is sweet and feminine yet independent, modest and shy yet intellectually curious and determined to succeed in her profession. She does not belong to the first generation of militant woman's rights advocates, but to an inoffensive second generation of New Women who, according to Ives, have found a compromise between femininity and emancipation. Edith appears to be the "womanly New Woman," and the author's presentation reads like a direct response to George Rugg, refuting his vision of the grotesque and bossy New Woman. A Very New Woman is directed against the common prejudice of the "Antis" that the New Woman's unnatural demands would prove to be the ruin of the institution of home and family, and provides the counter-image of the intelligent emancipated woman who plans to combine professional and private spheres—with the help of her husband. After Thayer's Lords of Creation, this is the first, if brief, dramatic treatment of the new kind of marriage that would need to rely on the willingness of husbands to support their wives' emancipatory efforts. Marriage as an emancipated relationship between equal partners was a notion popularized by suffragists and social reformers alike, and other American playwrights struggling for stage realism would eventually treat the question of the "new marriage" in topical plays like Alice Groff's Freedom (1904), Rachel Crother's He and She (1911), and George Middleton's Nowadays (1914).[40]

* * *

Charlotte Perkins Gilman (1860–1935). Something to Vote for. In The Forerunner: A Monthly Magazine 2, no. 6 (June 1911): 143–153.

Many suffrage organizations had begun to feel the opposition of women's clubs to the question of the vote. Although most women's clubs continued to work for an impressive variety of social causes, they often avoided strictly political issues. Occasionally, the question of universal suffrage was introduced like any other interesting and edifying lecture topic of the day, but in many cases women's clubs actually excluded references to the suffrage debate in order to avoid a fundamental split on political grounds. The more radical suffragists, on the other hand, often regarded all women's clubs as sources of conservativism and anti-suffrage sentiments, an opinion that is hardly justified as a generalization. According to recent studies by social historians, club women preferred to see their activities as an expression of domestic feminism.[41] In an afternoon lesson, the members of the Woman's Club in Gilman's optimistic play learn that public health issues may have strong political implications and that, even in matters of housekeeping, women need the vote in order to control their own interests.

Charlotte Perkins Gilman, well-known sociologist, socialist, suffragist, lecturer, and prolific writer, had early shown her interest in household reform and eventually wrote *What Diantha Did,* a novel on the possibilities of communal kitchens, serialized in her journal, *The Forerunner,* in 1909. The question of "social evil" became the topic of another novel, *The Crux,* serialized in 1910, in which the responsibility of doctors is emphasized by a tough and unsentimental woman doctor from Colorado who is clearly the model for Dr. Strong in *Something to Vote for.* The play deals with the topic of Pure Milk, an interest that should concern every mother and could turn club women into more than mere domestic feminists. As Gilman stated on a different occasion: "Politics governs even the purity of the milk supply. It is not 'outside the home,' but inside the baby."[42] The joint efforts of the determined woman doctor and the honest new milk inspector reveal the corrupt methods of the milk trust that sells good milk to the rich and influential and impure milk to the poor. The anti-feminist club members, however, are actually more convinced by the heartrending story of the death of a poor Irish woman's only child, which moves them to a new solidarity with all mothers. Gilman's play demonstrates that the human interest angle often works more effectively in propaganda literature than purely scientific arguments. The club women all decide to become good suffragists, and the integrity of the milk inspector is rewarded when he wins the charming and rich president of the Woman's Club.

* * *

Catharine Waugh McCulloch (1862–1945). *Bridget's Sisters; or, The Legal Status of Illinois Women in 1868.* Chicago: Illinois Equal Suffrage Association, 1911.

Standard histories of the woman suffrage movement of the nineteenth century usually make a rough distinction into two early phases: from the 1840s to the Civil War and from the post-war decade to the 1890s. These phases were devoted, respectively, to the struggle for the abolition of slavery, social reforms, and promotion of equal rights. According to this generalized division, a third phase of the movement, after 1900, made the vote for women its sole issue. It is therefore usually considered as being more exclusively and radically political compared to the reform tendencies of the movement before the turn of the century. Occasionally these three phases are regarded by some historians almost as separate movements, the last being a radical narrowing down of the former era, which not only brought a rigid concentration on the political issues at hand, but also a refusal to consider the value of the wider legal and psychological implications of equal rights and social reforms.[43] The suffrage plays written during the second decade of the twentieth century, however, contradict this assumption and suggest a far greater variety of topics than historians generally seem to include in this phase of the movement. Charlotte Perkins Gilman's play articulates a Progressive's interest in the pure food reform and her socialist vision of female solidarity beyond class barriers; Catharine Waugh McCulloch's play demonstrates a professional interest in legal matters, such as the remnants of a patriarchal English Common Law, as well as a pronounced historical interest in past achievements of the women's movement. In fact, *Bridget's Sisters* is the first of a number of historical plays about the early women's movement, later followed by Josephine Preston Peabody's play about Mary Wollstonecraft, *Portrait of Mrs. W.* (1922); Maud Wood Park's *Lucy Stone* (1938), a dramatization of Alice Stone Blackwell's biography of her mother, which Park had written for the Federal Theatre Project; and finally Olivia Howard Dunbar's *Enter Women* (1939), a play about the World Anti-Slavery Convention of 1840 in London, which had excluded women abolitionists from the floor. Even Gertrude Stein's opera libretto, *The Woman of Us All* (1946), about Susan B. Anthony and Anna Howard Shaw might be included here as a dramatic treatment of the history of the women's movement.

Catharine Waugh McCulloch was certainly well qualified to give a dramatic rendering of cases in legal history that had become relevant for women. Her legal training in Chicago, her professional experience as a partner in her husband's law firm, and her continuing involvement in the suffrage movement gave her a rare expertise to write about women and the law. Her novelistic tract, *Mr. Lex* (1899), on the legal status of married women and widows became widely known. When she wrote *Bridget's Sisters* in 1911, she had already been Justice of the Peace of Evanston, Illinois, for two years.[44] McCulloch used the actual case of Myra Bradwell who, together with other women, founded the Illinois Equal Suffrage Association and also achieved the establishment of an Illinois law that secured a wife's wages to her own use as early as 1869. Although *Bridget's Sisters* pretends to be strictly a historical play, emphasizing its own documentary value as a treatment of legal history, it is at the same time a suffrage play about the contemporary situation of 1911, challenging women to show solidarity with their sisters. For example, when the Justice of the Peace explicitly states that women will need the ballot to press for legal changes in their favor and mentions the Fifteenth Amendment as a forthcoming event that will serve to protect the rights of black men, the text in fact points to the continuing validity of these demands for women.

The general didacticism of the play resembles that of fables, especially in its usage of "telling names," names that signify character traits.[45] But while Mr. Vulture, the saloonkeeper, is just a familiar stock character from the temperance play of the nineteenth century, Bridget's various woman employers are mouthpieces for the different opinions on woman's rights that continued into the twentieth century. Bridget's case teaches Mrs. Bradley and the other women that indirect influence in legal and political questions is hardly enough when the male members of a family are unwilling to support their wives' demands. The most important message of the play, however, beyond the fact that Bridget will actually have to use her wages to pay for her husband's drinking debts, is the demonstration that women have to organize, exchange information, and learn to cooperate in order to effect change. The suspicion and even derision of the Irish in many of the nineteenth-century plays has almost uniformly given way to compassion and loyalty in these later plays by Charlotte Perkins Gilman, Catharine Waugh McCulloch, Emily Sargent Lewis, and others. The pathetic portrait of the hardworking and enduring Irish washerwoman, who has to raise her children alone because her husband drinks and may beat her or take her money as well, reads like a retrospective exoneration of the Irish characters from earlier stereotyped presentations, and—in the case of McCulloch—pays tribute to her own Irish ancestry.

* * *

Kate Mills Fargo. A *Voting Demonstration; or, An Election in Primerville*. [Redlands, Calif.]: privately printed, 1912.

After the enfranchisement of women in California in October 1911, propaganda plays were no longer needed for the suffrage debate on the state level. Women like Kate Mills Fargo, however, realized the tremendous need for didactic material to instruct the new and inexperienced women voters. In addition to statewide information for new voters published in the newspapers, special classes were held for women voters. As the author's prefatory note indicates, A *Voting Demonstration* is an instruction manual in the form of drama; it reads like a script for a classroom demonstration in which the guiding voice of the teacher explains the relevant steps in the casting of the ballot and points to a number of common mistakes made by novice voters. Kate Mills Fargo printed her play in January 1912, carefully selecting those cases in which uninformed or uneducated women might easily be embarrassed by the official character of the voting procedure or simply feel insecure about the various steps of casting a ballot. To make it valuable for adult education, the play had to include virtually all technical details as well as the relevant legal requirements for voting in California, and the teacher recapitulates these points after the dramatic presentation.

The claim at the end of the play that the "thought of voting will be a positive burden to the majority of women until they have learned how" may seem rather exaggerated to present readers. It should be a reminder, however, of the extent to which recently enfranchised women were regarded as pioneers and proud representatives of emancipation by the women of those states who still had a long way to go. The act of voting was seen as requiring courage, and the effect of voting as changing women's self-esteem; both aspects were found quite remarkable at the time. Four years after women had won the vote in California, the unpracticed, shy, and puzzled women voters of Kate Mills Fargo's play were already regarded as models of freedom on the East Coast. In 1915, Inez Haynes Gillmore wrote in an article for the Special Suffrage Number of *Harper's Weekly*: "It seemed to me at first that the California women were the most brilliant women I had ever known. I learned gradually that they were not superior to other women—except that they had become real citizens. That little link—the ballot—had made the connection between their ideas and ideals. . . . The thrill came however in that combination, so new to me, so calmly accepted by them, of progressive politics, equal suffrage and labor. Go West, young woman!"[46]

*   *   *

Alice C. Thompson. *A Suffragette Baby: A Comedy in One Act*. Philadelphia: Penn Publishing Company, 1912.

As one western state after the other was granting women the vote and the movement in the remaining states gained supporters at all levels of society, suffragists were beginning to think about the consequences of women's emancipation beyond the immediate political results. Alice Callender Thompson, one of the numerous women playwrights who were still producing farces and burlesques for amateur or semi-professional performances, deals in this play with the modern dilemma of professional women who are no longer economically dependent on male support but cannot reconcile their new independence with the old desire to have children. Although the four young suffragists in *A Suffragette Baby* visibly participate in the campaign by wearing sashes and waving banners, the real concern of the play is the question of individual rights and the possibilities of self-fulfillment for women. As was often the case in the conventionally structured suffrage propaganda plays, there is an astounding awareness of the current debate and the perceptible shift in interests and arguments. Ellen DuBois describes the change of tenor in referring to Elizabeth Cady Stanton's last speeches written in the 1890s as feminism's important new "concern with the 'personal' elements of women's experience."[47] Thompson's play, about a community of working women, demonstrates that even the less innovative burlesques eventually began to deal with such elements.

The young suffragists of the play find the ideal comedy solution for their maternal instincts by their joint adoption of a baby, whom they rescue from the orphanage by handing her over to the loving care of the Irish landlady. Their enthusiastic plan to bring up the suffragette baby "in the true faith" sounds splendid, but should not be considered as more than the witty ending of a proper farce. The play had no serious intention to encourage single women to make up for the lack of family and home by sharing babies. There is nothing arbitrary, however, about the play's title because babies were a topic treated with a great deal of pompousness by the "Antis." The lightness of tone at the end of the play may well have been a reaction to their rather absurd arguments, with which the "Antis" either continued to blame suffragists for neglecting their babies while going to meetings or had begun to criticize them for bringing their babies along to these meetings. By 1911, babies seemed to have become a regular media feature at tableaux and suffrage meetings alike, as the New York Times reports, calling them "suffrage babies" and making them in turn a feature of the paper's suffrage articles.[48]

* * *

Emily Sargent Lewis (1866–1931). *Election Day: A Suffrage Play*. Philadelphia: privately printed, 1912.

Emily Sargent Lewis came from an old New England family and grew up in New York before she married and moved to Philadelphia. She belonged to the new generation of "genteel suffragists" who began to join the cause in growing numbers after the turn of the century. The feminism of these more progressive society women, of course, antagonized conservative upper-class women who had been strict and careful guardians of their own social privileges, usually exerted through membership restrictions in the traditional women's clubs of their home towns. The confrontation between privileged suffragists and "Antis" resulted in a new and amusing comedy of manners that was to dominate the last years of the campaign.

In 1911, the Pennsylvania Limited Suffrage League, of which Emily Sargent Lewis was an active member and a patroness, had produced three English plays under the direction of Mrs. Otis Skinner and Beatrice Forbes-Robertson. According to the "Program of Suffrage Plays" of February 16, 1911, the Special Matinée at the Philadelphia Broad Street Theatre included Bessie Hatton's *Before the Dawn*, Gertrude Jennings's *A Woman's Influence*, and *How the Vote Was Won* by Cicely Hamilton and Christopher St. John, probably the most popular suffrage play both in England and America.[49] In 1912 Maud Durbin Skinner also directed *Election Day* and Lewis's pageant *Dream of Brave Women* at the Broad Street Theatre. Compared to the earlier parlor theatricals and modest amateur performances, these productions might almost be considered professional.

Lewis's witty play reflects the entire spectrum of the ideological rather than political problems relevant to the controversy within the same social class. Mrs. Gardner is not really opposed to woman suffrage for any convincing reason, but because she is snobbish, thoughtless, and self-centered. She stands for the numerous "Antis" of the affluent upper middle classes, who felt no immediate personal need for equal rights and lacked imagination to consider the possibilities or the necessity of equality for other women. Although the author attacks the general superficiality and lack of political interest of women of her own class, she is especially angered by the Lady Bountiful attitude of those society women whose vague social consciences are easily satisfied by gestures of condescending charity. Dorothy and Mrs. Carter, as the feminists of the play, have all the enlightened, logical, and genuinely humane arguments on their side. But, although they may convince the audiences, the truly upper-class "Anti" will be converted only by the realization that it is actually becoming more fashionable to be "pro" than "anti."

*   *   *

Mary Winsor. A *Suffrage Rummage Sale*. Haverford P.O., Penn.: privately printed, 1913.

Mary Winsor became president of the Pennsylvania Limited Suffrage League soon after it was founded in 1909. Although the league was still opposed to universal suffrage in 1911, a number of controversial and even radical speakers had been invited to Philadelphia during those first years, ranging from Emmeline Pankhurst and Charlotte Perkins Gilman to Alice Paul, who was to found the National Woman's Party. Mary Winsor's short history of the league also mentions that "Mrs. Thos. N. Hepburn, now president of the Connecticut Woman Suffrage Association, gave us a beautiful, earnest and refined address on 'Social Purity,' speaking with great feeling on the moral dangers to which the working girl is exposed."[50] Katharine Houghton Hepburn (the mother of actress Katharine Hepburn) was a knowledgeable and frank lecturer on the white slave trade and birth control; she scandalized audiences by appearing in public during her pregnancies and by taking her small children along to meetings and rallys as "suffrage babies." Her speech "Woman Suffrage and The Social Evil" had been distributed by the National Woman Suffrage Association, and her husband, who shared her feminist interests, used his influence as a Hartford physician to distribute and eventually produce *Damaged Goods*, the English version of Eugène Brieux's *Les Avariés* (1901).[51] The play dealt with the problem of venereal disease in marriages, a topic that interested Progressives from Upton Sinclair, in his novels *Sylvia* and *Sylvia's Marriage*, to Charlotte Perkins Gilman, in *The Crux*.

Under Mary Winsor's presidency, the league had produced suffrage plays and pageants by members like Emily Sargent Lewis and in 1913 staged A *Suffrage Rummage Sale*. Winsor's intention was to organize an auction for the benefit of the cause and to have the actual play interrupt the auction. "The Auctioneer's Speech" existed only in the form of a typescript, which had to be returned to the author after the performance. The play reprinted here is the dramatic interlude of the auction, "The Auction Interrupted," in which Mrs. Grundy, the Mad Hatter, and Mrs. Partington personify the silly aspects of anti-feminism with which they confront the supposedly pro-feminist audience. In Winsor's humorous literary allegory, the Mad Hatter is the last male crazy enough to support Mrs. Grundy's dictum for proper womanly behavior, and Mrs. Partington, who has turned into a strong, bellicose scrubwoman, tries in vain to stop the progress of the woman's movement with her broom.

Unfortunately for the "Antis," their arguments are not particularly consistent; Mrs. Grundy interrupts the auctioneer with endless talk, proposing to speak for silent womanhood; Mrs. Partington claims to be only a weak woman who cannot fight and then knocks down the Mad Hatter with her broom; and the Mad Hatter manages to confuse matters as usual, but he nevertheless encourages Mrs. Partington to keep on sweeping against the tide.

*   *   *

Marie Jenney Howe. An Anti-Suffrage Monologue. New York: National American Woman Suffrage Association, 1913.

The tendency of suffragists to ridicule the "Antis" by simply repeating their arguments had become one of the most popular forms of dramatic amusement. There were mock debates, mock speeches like Howe's Anti-Suffrage Monologue, and mock plays, like Mary Shaw's The Woman of It; or, Our Friends, the Anti-Suffragists, pretending to be against the movement, just as there had once been anti-suffrage plays with titles like The New Woman or The Suffragettes, which had ridiculed women's emancipation. The suffragists had eventually begun to profit from wide public support and could now afford to denounce many of the traditional arguments by simply turning them against their opponents. What had helped the cause tremendously was the changing attitude among younger women in the cities. Many young working-class women were organized in the pro-suffrage Women's Trade Union League, young college women supported the College Equal Suffrage Leagues, and, once women like Inez Milholland headed suffrage parades on a white horse and made headlines, the smart set of young, upper-class urban women no longer feared being ostracized by society for their suffrage activities. The mixed crowds that participated in pageants and parades in New York City and Washington, D.C., where "Mrs O. H. P. Belmont walked but a few steps ahead of Rebecca Goldstein, who runs a sewing machine in a shirtwaist shop,"[52] showed that suffragism began to create a new solidarity between women that, at least temporarily, cut across class boundaries.

Marie Jenney Howe, who had organized her own theater group of professional and amateur actresses and actors in the Twenty-fifth District of the New York Woman's Suffrage Party, modeled her Anti-Suffrage Monologue on the emotional public address of an "Anti." The main arguments are arranged in couplets, in which two popular statements mutually exclude each other and therefore help to support the anti-suffragist's womanly appeal to disregard facts and statistics. Some of the statements ironically play on common prejudices by veiling them in a semblance of logic, like the suggestion that women should stay at home to answer the telephone because there is no longer any other relevant reason why woman's place should still be in the house. Other arguments, however, disclose the full sarcasm of Howe's attack, as for instance, when the anti-suffragist proposes to protect working women and children from the vote to prevent a change in their conditions.

*   *   *

Florence Kiper [Frank]. *Cinderelline; or The Little Red Slipper.* Chicago: Dramatic Publishing Company, 1913.

In a review article in *Forum*, Florence Kiper, journalist, drama critic, and occasional poet, noted that, from the viewpoint of the feminist, contemporary American playwrights with the exception of Rachel Crothers failed miserably in presenting social plays relevant to the new role of women in society:

> In a drama whose themes are almost entirely those of contemporary social life, few among our playwrights are attempting to interpret to us the meaning of the growing divorce "evil," of the suffrage agitation, of women in the professions, of young girls in industry, of the sudden awakening of the sheltered woman to a knowledge of prostitution and venereal diseases. Almost none among our clever writers for the stage are bringing to these vital themes a conscious philosophy or an informed understanding. Yet the woman movement is undoubtedly, if perhaps the class-consciousness in the labor struggle be excepted, the one most important tendency of the century. It is important because it deals not with a limited and selected class of society, but with the very fundamentals of society. [53]

Kiper, of course, was not alone in her scathing critique of American theater, but her outspoken feminism makes her view particularly valuable in the context of this collection. Not only were there far too few attempts at realistic presentation in drama, she continues, but the American stage also lacked even good "thesis plays" by native authors, which, though not of great quality, would at least have "the educational value of their propaganda."[53] The pressing topics of the day, in the opinion of the feminist critic, were neglected in favor of "provincialism, prudishness and sentimentality."

Cinderelline was praised as a delightful poetic play at the time, "very well suited to presentation by college students, as the one male part (a young poet) can easily be taken by a girl."[54] Kiper had no intention to compete with professional dramatists with her suffrage play; *Cinderelline* should be considered as her dramatic attempt to be heard as a feminist and a supporter of the movement. In the play about the modern Cinderella, the two wicked sisters are personifications of the "domestic drudge" and the spoiled "sex parasite," in Margaret Ladd Franklin's terms, who compete for the rich, young heir, while Cinderelline is the suffragist who fights for women's freedom against their wishes. She is not necessarily looking for a husband and only agrees to try the modern prince's magic red slipper after she has tested his views and is reassured that he supports her ideas, likes children, and is "pure in thought and pure in deed." In the new version of the fairy tale, Cinderelline accepts the poet-prince, not vice versa, because he can prove that he will be the perfect companion for the New Woman.

*   *   *

Mary Shaw (1854–1929). *The Woman of It; or, Our Friends the Anti-Suffragists: A Satirical Comedy in One Act*. Chicago: Dramatic Publishing Company, 1914; *The Parrot Cage: A Play in One Act*. Chicago: Dramatic Publishing Company, 1914.

Mary Shaw had been active in the women's movement since the early 1890s. In 1892 she became a charter member of the Professional Women's League, and she played the part of Rosalind in the league's all-female performance of *As You Like It* in 1893–94.[56] She acted in the major "woman's plays" of the day, in Ibsen's *Ghosts* and *Hedda Gabler*. It was her decision to open the highly controversial *Ghosts* on Broadway in 1903, and she even toured the country with the production, which drew mixed responses. In 1905 she defied public and critical opinion by playing Mrs. Warren in Arnold Daly's first American production of Shaw's play *Mrs. Warren's Profession*, which had already caused a scandal in London. According to Albert Auster, "the furor caused by *Ghosts* was mild in comparison with the controversy that surrounded Mary Shaw when she played in George Bernard Shaw's *Mrs. Warren's Profession*."[57] The New York police commissioner closed the play on opening night and arrested all those connected with the performance. In 1907 and 1908, after the play had become more acceptable, at least in New York City, she took it on tour, as she had toured with *Ghosts*, in a conscious feminist effort to confront American audiences with the topics of modern political and psychological drama. Wherever she appeared on her tours, writes Auster, she made a point of speaking before the local women's clubs and encouraged women not to listen to male critics, but rather to decide for themselves how they felt about these plays.

The New York opening of Elizabeth Robins's *Votes for Women* at Wallack's Theatre, March 15, 1909, was not nearly as controversial, but it became the first large-scale, professional theatrical event for woman suffrage. The reaction of unsuspecting male members of the audience was almost paranoid because "suffragettes were everywhere." Suffragist Mary Shaw played the leading part, and there

> were Suffragettes and Suffragists of every shade and degree from the
> curbstone militants to the parlor auxiliaries. They filled every seat and all
> available standing room. There were club women in blocks and advanced
> thinkers in boxfuls. Everywhere yellow flowers, ribbons, and buttons
> flaunted themselves. From an upper box gleamed the banner of the
> American Suffragettes. In the lobby young women did sentry-go with
> placards swung about their necks, from which it appeared that in four of
> these United States women have votes—why not in all, pray?[58]

One of the men complained that he had come "to see a play. All I've seen has been a woman's rights meeting."[59] Shaw had organized the performance "for the glory of women and for the benefit of the building fund of the Actor's Society."[60] Vote for Women was criticized for being boring beyond expression, a problem play, mere theatrical propaganda, just a tract. According to the unanimously unsympathetic reviews, it was Mary Shaw's superb acting that saved the play; in fact she "was so much better than the play that one felt sorry for her."[61] In spite of her stunning personal success, the play closed after only six nights.

Shaw's own suffrage play, The Woman of It; or, Our Friends the Anti-Suffragists, was performed at an Equal Suffrage meeting at the Hotel Astor in January 1912. Marie Jenney Howe and her Twenty-fifth District Players, who presented the play at this meeting, also performed The Parrot Cage in 1913, and on March 7, 1915, Mary Shaw produced this second play at the Gamut Club, of which she served as president for many years. This rather bitter suffrage allegory shows a number of women as caged birds who cannot remember life in freedom. As female parrots, they obediently and pathetically repeat the meaningless phrases their male owner tells them. When the only rebellious bird, the Free-Souled Parrot, finally breaks her chain and calls out to the others to follow her, they are too afraid of a life in freedom to try their clipped wings. Although they lack the courage to try for the Unknown, they have had a brief glimpse of other possibilities and are suddenly conscious of their own imprisonment. Solemnly and sadly they continue to repeat that "Polly's place is in the cage." Shaw's play recalls Kate Chopin's brief and early story "Emancipation: A Life Fable." Both authors try to convince women that the dangers of independence might be outweighed by the exultation of freedom, but Shaw's dramatic fable ends on a more wistful note because it stays behind with those who remain caged and hopeless.

*　*　*

Hester N. Johnson. On to Victory: A Comedy in Two Acts. Boston: Walter H. Baker & Company, 1915.

At the turn of the century, most American plays were not published until they either had been successfully performed or showed promise of becoming sufficiently popular because of their topic, unless, of course, they were written by playwrights like Sir Arthur Wing Pinero, Dion Boucicault, or David Belasco. Most suffrage propaganda plays therefore remained unpublished. If they were of particular local interest, the author or the local suffrage organization occasionally printed them privately, hoping to gain greater publicity and more frequent performance. Samuel French in New York and London and Walter H. Baker in Boston were the two publishing companies with the widest distribution for playscripts, especially inexpensive scripts of farces and burlesques suited to amateur theater groups. Since women's clubs rarely endorsed suffrage during the early decades of the movement, but demanded plays specifically related to women, French and Baker sold large quantities of anti-feminist formula plays. Even if plays were moderately feminist, the typical advertisement for a farce like Lillian Clisby Bridgham's *A Suffragette Town Meeting* (1912) would read as follows: "Presents a town meeting as it will be conducted by and by when the ladies have taken full charge of the public business. A shrewd and good-natured satire of present feminine peculiarities applied to this problem written for laughing purposes only. Just the thing for women's clubs."

Samuel French's eventual publication of George Middleton's *Back of the Ballot* and Walter H. Baker's announcement of Hester N. Johnson's *On to Victory* as a "very bright and pretty little 'suffrage' piece, strongly recommended," were clear indications that public opinion had begun to change. By this time, feminist plays were portraying suffragists as pretty, unmarried young women, who were no longer in danger of risking their chances on the marriage market as soon as they confessed their political opinions. On the contrary, in these plays their determination to fight for the cause wins them the sympathy and respect of attractive men. Hester Johnson's play presents a suffrage romance in which the young heroine needs a strong man to carry her heavy banner with the "On to Victory" inscription in the forthcoming suffrage parade, and then marches on toward the happy ending.

✻   ✻   ✻

George Middleton (1880–1967). *Back of the Ballot: A Woman Suffrage Farce in One Act.* New York/London: Samuel French, 1915.

George Middleton was an early-twentieth-century playwright who is almost forgotten today, although feminist scholars have every reason to save him from oblivion. Like Rachel Crothers and a few others, he had begun to write plays about the New Woman around 1910. In 1911 he married the actress and suffragist Fola La Follette, who kept her own name after their marriage. Middleton marched in suffrage parades, participated in suffrage debates, gave speeches, and rallyed for the cause. Like Frederic Clemson Howe, he fully supported his wife's activities and accompanied her on lecture tours. Through her, he met numerous other feminists of the stage and also some of the most prominent woman's rights advocates of the time, such as Jane Addams, Lillian D. Wald, and Charlotte Perkins Gilman. In his memoirs, he recalled his own participation in the suffrage movement with evident fondness: "The mite of interpretation I contributed was nothing to what I got out of the suffrage cause. My instinctive sympathies were now reinforced by facts and feelings which stemmed from the group of wonderful women with whom it was my privilege to be closely associated."[62]

In 1915 Middleton finally complied with the wishes of his wife and her friend Marie Jenney Howe by writing his "one straight suffrage propaganda play."[63] His own interest in *Back of the Ballot* was only mild. He never saw it acted, he wrote, but was "told it went well enough. I was more interested in writing about the particular personal problems feminism created. Of course I was called a propagandist, as is any author who dips into such passing contro-versies."[64] He reported far more proudly that the Woman's Party performed *Tradition*, one of his more serious one-act plays, at the Berkeley Lyceum in New York on January 23, 1913. Later that year he expanded the topic of *Tradition*—the confrontation of a professional young woman with her father, who cannot comprehend that she will not give up her hard-won independence to come back home—into a three-act play, *Nowadays*. He based his heroine upon Fola, he wrote, and although the play was never produced on the profes-sional stage, it was highly praised by prominent feminists and leading papers of suffrage organizations, such as Gilman's *Forerunner* and the *Woman Voter*.

Middleton's difficulties in getting his controversial works performed con-vinced him of the importance of publication. In his article "The Publication of Plays" for *Harper's Weekly*, he wrote that only publication might keep a play alive, even if it was not performed adequately or never produced at all; he also claimed that published plays had already "raised the standards of amateur performances—and it is in these organizations, so frequently sneered at, that the taste of the future is being moulded."[65] Years before Susan Glaspell and Eugene O'Neill began to popularize one-act plays through the Provincetown Players, Middleton had used the one-act play as an appropriate form for the treatment of serious topics. His one-act plays about the psychological aspects of the double standard, the inadequacy of sex education for young women, the problems of modern marriage and divorce made him a leading represen-tative of what was then called the "drama of sincerity."[66]

Although *Back of the Ballot* was a mere dramatic pastime to him written for the amateur stage, the thoroughly professional quality of his suffrage farce is obvious. The composition is that of a classic drawing-room comedy, in which the absurdity of the plot is expertly balanced by verbal wit. It skillfully combines the didacticism of pro-suffrage arguments with the fast-paced dialogue of an effective comedy. Jennie Martin, the pretty, young suffragist, unexpectedly finds an ally in her battle for the ballot. The puzzled, and eventually exhausted, burglar points his gun at all those who dare oppose votes for women. The title alludes to Lincoln's anti-slavery argument that the ballot is stronger than the bullet. Taking Mr. Martin's slogan, "Back of the ballot lies the bullet," at face value, Middleton uses it as both a title and a structural element. The converted burglar becomes Jennie's representative for Direct Action and vows: "Lady, if he don't vote for yer, I'll kill 'im."

✻   ✻   ✻

Mrs. O. H. P. Belmont (1853–1933) and Elsa Maxwell (1883–1963). *Melinda and Her Sisters*. New York: Robert J. Shores, Publishers, 1916.

Socially prominent women who became interested in suffrage after 1900 were regarded with suspicion by those suffragists who remembered the early years of the women's movement with fondness. Their fear that the movement might change in character once members of New York high society joined the suffrage organizations was somewhat justified because these new woman's rights advocates brought along not only their money but also their names, social and political influence, and often a certain notoriety. Mrs. Oliver Hazard Perry Belmont, formerly Mrs. William Kissam Vanderbilt, had been the indefatigable duchess of the Gilded Age, as Dixon Wecter described her in *The Saga of American Society*.[67] The story of her marriage to the grandson of Commodore Vanderbilt, her successful invasion of the New York aristocracy in the 1880s, her daughter Consuelo's marriage to the Duke of Marlborough, and finally her divorce from Vanderbilt and marriage to O. H. P. Belmont made her seem like a socially ambitious character straight out of an Edith Wharton novel on the conflict between Old New York and the rich invaders. When Alva Smith Belmont turned to the cause of women after her second husband's death in 1908, feminists therefore doubted her sincerity. Especially those women who constituted the rank and file of the movement were skeptical and even embittered, because once Mrs. Belmont endorsed suffragism the leading papers began to follow the movement far more closely and favorably than before.

Alva Smith Belmont, however, did not treat the women's movement as a passing fad. She turned out to be an experienced organizer and fund-raiser; she published articles in the *North American Review*, the *Forum*, and other major journals,[68] went to England with Inez Milholland to study the possibilities of militant suffrage activism, and in 1914 brought Christabel Pankhurst to the United States for a lecture tour. She also invested large sums of her Vanderbilt and Belmont funds in support of the cause. She financed the New York headquarters of the National American Woman Suffrage Association and the Political Equality League, helped support Max Eastman's socialist magazine, *Masses*, and even bought a house on Capitol Hill as the headquarters for the National Woman's Party in Washington, D.C. The New York production of what was called her "propagandist operetta" served fund-raising purposes and at the same time became the social event of the 1916 season. Mrs. Belmont had collaborated with Elsa Maxwell, an experienced songwriter and composer of musical comedies, in writing *Melinda and Her Sisters*. They persuaded the well-known comedienne Marie Dressler to take the part of Melinda's mother. Four weeks before the actual performance, the rehearsals were already receiving tremendous publicity because New York débutantes were acting side by side with professional actresses: "Yes, indeed! The 'cause' that has been argued from the platform, talked from automobiles, declaimed from the stage and swallowed with afternoon tea is now to be warbled by opera stars, concert singers and society buds—the suffrage opera is with us!"[69]

The production on February 18, 1916, at the Waldorf Astoria, was very favorably reviewed, although most critics confined their comments to Mary Dressler's jewels, the daring costumes of the débutantes, the spectacular gowns of the society women in the audience, and the supper Mrs. O. H. P. Belmont gave after the performance for illustrious members of the cast and the audience. Very little was said about the operetta itself, and one reviewer dared criticize the mixed cast of professionals and amateurs:

> While it was undoubtedly a great triumph for Mrs. Belmont—and I suppose Mrs. Belmont argues that she can do anything she likes—there is, nevertheless, some question as to just how far it is advisable to mix people up. Amateur performances are all right so long as they are confined to amateurs and kept, as it were, a close corporation; but when it comes to mixing up young débutantes with seasoned professionals, painting their faces and dressing them up in diaphanous and abbreviated costumes, to kick about for the amusement of a mixed public, it seems to me there should be a limit somewhere. . . . No matter what the cause may be or how great the vanity of its propagandist, we should remember that the protection of our young girls is of paramount importance and that to exploit them behind the footlights farded and tinseled has a vulgarizing effect that robs them of much of their admirable sweetness and naïveté. The manners of the stage are not the manners of the drawing-room, no matter how much the drawing-room manners are essayed on the stage. . . .[70]

The familiar late-nineteenth-century concern about blurring the boundaries between the parlor and the stage was obviously still an issue.

Together with the expensive program and Mrs. Belmont's libretto, "bound in suffrage yellow and blue," sold at the performance, the suffrage operetta brought in more than $8,000 for the cause. As a propaganda comedy, *Melinda and Her Sisters* is quite effective because it cleverly combines the well-known arguments for suffrage with the pretentious society chatter of Mrs. Grundy and Mrs. Malaprop, as well as Mrs. John Pepper's pseudo-refined views about the purely decorative function of women in high society. Melinda, the youngest of the eight marriageable Pepper daughters, successfully rebels against the combined silliness of fashion arbiters, social climbers, and conservative politicians, convincing even her ambitious mother that women should not be satisfied with being ornaments for society or their husbands.

❋ ❋ ❋

Alice Duer Miller (1874–1942). *Unauthorized Interviews*. In *Women Are People!* New York: George H. Doran Company, 1917, pp. 87–98.

Alice Duer Miller came from a distinguished New York family and entered Barnard College in 1895, where she majored in mathematics and astronomy, a revolutionary decision for a nineteenth-century débutante.[71] She began writing to pay for her tuition and continued to write after her marriage. She worked for the National American Woman Suffrage Association and became a popular novelist, playwright, and journalist, whose witty feminist sketches and poems appeared under the title "Are Women People?" as a weekly column in the Sunday edition of the *New York Tribune* between 1914 and 1917. In her two collections, *Are Women People?* (1915) and *Women Are People!* (1917), she exhibits a wonderful sense of the bizarre in some of her parodies of anti-suffrage arguments.

Her three "Unauthorised Interviews" in verse were not written for performance, but they use the form of dialogic argumentation for women's equality common over a century ago. Representing the Queens and Goddesses of history, Cleopatra and Pallas interrupt a woman suffrage debate in Congress taking place between men, and they intimidate the speaker by forcing him to tell the truth whenever he intends to talk about women in the future. The second sketch confirms in an almost realistic fashion the experiences of any suffragist who ever tried in vain to argue with a politician, confirming the suspicion that male logic in connection with woman's rights is too irrational to be understood. In the final interview, the Suffragists accuse the Statue of Liberty of maltreating the women of the nation, but the statue explains that men put her up as "a milestone, not an inspiration," and that she waits for the women to fulfill her promise.

NOTES

1. Harriet H. Robinson, *Massachusetts in the Woman Suffrage Movement: A General, Political, Legal and Legislative History from 1774 to 1881*, second ed. (Boston: Roberts Brothers, 1883), pp. 170–71. Harriet Robinson wrote a melodrama on a woman's struggle for professional equality, whose rather heavy-handed use of dialect and unbalanced plot structure prevented its success. See *Captain Mary Miller*. Boston: Walter H. Baker & Company, 1887.

2. Richard Moody, ed., *Dramas from the American Theatre, 1762–1909* (Boston: Houghton Mifflin Company, 1969), p. 616.

3. Karen Halttunen, *Confidence Men and Painted Women: A Study of Middle-class Culture in America, 1830–1870* (New Haven: Yale University Press, 1982), p. 174.

4. Halttunen, p. 175.

5. Halttunen, p. 179.

6. Halttunen, p. 186.

7. The Boston Athenaeum and the Massachusetts Historical Society, for instance, hold a significant number of those rare early scrapbooks that became my source of information.

8. Halttunen, p. 184.

9. These and other programs are to be found in the collection of the Boston Athenaeum. The wealth of playbills in the library of the Massachusetts Historical Society, of course, is equally impressive and perhaps more easily accessible because Katherine M. Doherty, a former member of the library staff, published an extensive

checklist of the society's holdings, including an index of names, titles, and actors. *See* Katherine M. Doherty, "Playbills of the Massachusetts Historical Society of Amateur Theatricals, 1775–1921," *Proceedings of the Massachusetts Historical Society* 91 (1979): 101–211.

10.   Fannie Aymar Mathews, "Women and Amateur Acting," *North American Review* 159 (December 1894): 759–760.

11.   *The Woman's Column* 9, no. 11 (March 14, 1896).

12.   "Document 69 (VI:675–682): Washington Campaign, 1910," in *The Concise History of Woman Suffrage: Selections from the Classic Works of Stanton, Anthony, Gage, and Harper*, eds. Mari Jo Buhle and Paul Buhle (Urbana, Ill.: University of Illinois Press, 1978), pp. 388–389.

13.   Helen Krich Chinoy and Linda Walsh Jenkins, eds., *Women in American Theatre* (New York: Crown Publishers, 1981); and Claudia D. Johnson, *American Actress: Perspective on the Nineteenth Century* (Chicago: Nelson Hall, 1984).

14.   Albert Auster, *Actresses and Suffragists: Women in the American Theatre, 1890–1920* (New York: Praeger, 1984).

15.   Julie Holledge, *Innocent Flowers: Women in the Edwardian Theater* (London: Virago Press, 1981).

16.   Auster, *Actresses and Suffragists*, p. 85.

17.   *New York Times*, December 16, 1910.

18.   *New York Times*, January 16, 1911.

19.   *New York Times*, January 18, 1911.

20.   "Votes for Women—Program of Suffrage Plays," Schlesinger Library, Radcliffe College.

21.   Emily Sargent Lewis, *A Dream of Brave Women* (Philadelphia: privately printed, 1912), p. 22.

22.   *New York Times*, April 13, 1912.

23.   *New York Times*, April 10, 1912.

24.   Undated suffrage pamphlet, the Schlesinger Library, Radcliffe College.

25.   George Middleton, *These Things Are Mine: The Autobiography of a Journeyman Playwright* (New York: Macmillan Company, 1947), p. 125.

26.   Inez Milholland, "Woman's Place Is in the Home," in *Twenty-five Answers to Antis*, ed. Marie Jenney Howe (New York: National American Woman Suffrage Association, 1912), p. 19.

27.   Alice Duer Miller, *Are Women People? A Book of Rhymes for Suffrage Times* (New York: George H. Doran Company, 1915), p. 45.

28.   George Bernard Shaw, "Should Social Problems Be Freely Dealt with in the Drama?" *The Humanitarian* 6 (May 1895).

29.   Norman Philbrick, *Trumpets Sounding: Propaganda Plays of the American Revolution* (New York: Blom, 1972).

30.   This class arrogance, of course, is more than equaled by the blatant racism of the dozens of "Ethiopian" plays predating the minstrel shows.

31.   *Boston Daily Evening Transcript*, April 20, 1868.

32.   The copy belongs to the Harvard College Library and is listed in the Union Catalogue under NC0843719.

33.   Francis A. Willard and Mary Ashton Livermore, *A Woman of the Century: Fourteen Hundred-Seventy Biographical Sketches Accompanied by Portraits of Leading American Women in All Walks of Life* (Chicago/New York: Charles Wells Moulton, 1893), pp. 451 and 802–803.

34.   Further information about Ella Cheever Thayer is scant. According to *The*

Boston Directory of 1879, the author had briefly worked as a telegraph operator at the Hotel Brunswick in Boston, and in the same year she published a novel called *Wired Love: A Romance in Dots and Dashes* (New York: G. W. Carleton, 1879), obviously using her professional experience.

35. Eleanor Flexner, *Century of Struggle: The Woman's Rights Movement in the United States* (1959; repr. New York: Atheneum, 1974), p. 149.

36. Harriet Beecher Stowe, *Pink and White Tyranny* (Boston: Roberts Brothers, 1871).

37. Ellen Carol DuBois, ed., *Elizabeth Cady Stanton/Susan B. Anthony: Correspondence, Writings, Speeches* (New York: Schocken Books, 1981), p. 92.

38. *See* the articles in *A Woman of the Century*, p. 485, and by Paul S. Boyer in *Notable American Women 1607–1950: A Biographical Dictionary*, ed. Edward T. James et al. (Cambridge: Belknap Press of Harvard University, 1971), 2:459–460.

39. *See* the article on Alice Emma Ives in *A Woman of the Century*, pp. 412–413.

40. Useful articles dealing with the New Woman in American plays at the turn of the century are Lois Gottlieb, "The Perils of Freedom: The New Woman in Three American Plays of the 1900's," *Canadian Review of American Studies* 6 (Spring 1975): 84–98; Deborah S. Kolb, "The Rise and Fall of the New Woman in American Drama," *Educational Theater Journal* 27 (1975): 149–160; Yvonne B. Shafer, "The Liberated Woman in American Plays of the Past," *Players* 49 (1974): 95–100; John Tibbetts, "The 'New Woman' on Stage: Women's Issues in American Drama, 1890–1915" *Helicon Nine* 7 (1982): 6–19.

41. The expression is Karen J. Blair's, in her book *The Clubwoman as Feminist: True Womanhood Redefined, 1868–1914* (New York/ London: Holmes & Meier Publishers, 1980).

42. See the pamphlet "Eminent Opinions on Woman Suffrage," New York: National American Woman Suffrage Association, [191?], p. 40.

43. This unbalanced view was criticized most recently by Judith Papachristou, in the *Newsletter of the Organization of American Historians*, August 1986.

44. For further biographical information on Catharine Waugh McCulloch, *see* the article by Paul S. Boyer in *Notable American Women*, 2:459–460. Unfortunately, Boyer misnames the play *Bridget's Daughters*, which is not nearly as suggestive to feminists as "Bridget's Sisters."

45. This is a direct translation of the German literary term *sprechende Namen*. Unfortunately, there seems to be no precise term for names that carry either allegorical or symbolical meaning in English.

46. Inez Haynes Gillmore, "The Result in California," *Harper's Weekly* 60 (May 8, 1915): 441.

47. DuBois, *Elizabeth Cady Stanton/ Susan B. Anthony*, p. 246.

48. *New York Times*, January 18 and January 28, 1911.

49. Dale Spender and Carole Hayman included the two plays by Jennings and Hamilton/St. John in their recent edition of seven English suffrage plays. *See* Dale Spender and Carole Hayman, eds., *How the Vote Was Won and Other Suffragette Plays* (London: Methuen, 1985; Methuen Theatrefile). In 1981 Julie Holledge had already reprinted three English suffrage plays in *Innocent Flowers*, pp. 167–201.

50. *See* "Program of Suffrage Plays," February 16, 1911, in the Schlesinger Library, Radcliffe College.

51. Katharine Houghton Hepburn, *Woman Suffrage and The Social Evil* (New York: National Woman Suffrage Publishing Company, 191?). For information about

Dr. Thomas N. Hepburn's activities to introduce Brieux to American audiences, *see* Auster, *Actresses and Suffragists*, p. 5.

52.   Flexner, *Century of Struggle*, p. 259.

53.   Florence Kiper, "Some American Plays: From the Feminist Viewpoint," *Forum* 51 (1914): 921.

54.   Kiper, p. 922.

55.   Margaret Ladd Franklin, *The Case for Woman Suffrage: A Bibliography* (New York: National College Equal Suffrage League, 1913), p. 182.

56.   For more details about Mary Shaw's biography, *see* the article by Pat M. Ryan in *Notable American Women*, 3:277–278. *See also* the excellent chapter in Auster's *Actresses and Suffragists*, "Mary Shaw: The Actress as Clubwoman and Suffragist," pp. 67–90. The article by Robert A. Schanke on Shaw is stimulating, but unfortunately contains many inaccuracies; *see* Schanke, "Mary Shaw: A Fighting Champion," *Women in American Theatre*, pp. 98–107.

57.   Auster, *Actresses and Suffragists*, p. 79.

58.   Unidentified newspaper clipping, March 16, 1909, Harvard Theatre Collection, Harvard College Library.

59.   Unidentified newspaper clipping, March 16, 1909, Harvard Theatre Collection, Harvard College Library.

60.   Unidentified newspaper clipping, March 16, 1909, Harvard Theatre Collection, Harvard College Library.

61.   Unidentified newspaper clipping, March 16, 1909, Harvard Theatre Collection, Harvard College Library.

62.   Middleton, *These Things Were Mine*, p. 126.

63.   Middleton, p. 131.

64.   Ibid.

65.   George Middleton, "The Publication of Plays," *Harper's Weekly* (January 24, 1914): 26.

66.   The term is Sheldon Cheney's, in his article "The American Playwright and the Drama of Sincerity," *Forum* 51 (April 1914): 498–512.

67.   Dixon Wecter, *The Saga of American Society: A Record of Social Aspiration, 1607–1937* (1937; repr. New York: Charles Scribner's Sons, 1970), pp. 336–341. *See also* the article by Christopher Lasch in *Notable American Women*, 1:126–128.

68.   Mrs. Oliver H. P. Belmont, "Woman's Right to Govern Herself," *North American Review* 190 (November 1909): 664–674; idem, "Woman Suffrage As It Looks To-Day," *Forum* 43 (March 1910): 264–268.

69.   *Musical America*, January 22, 1916.

70.   *Town Topics*, February 24, 1916.

71.   For information about Alice Duer Miller, *see* the article by Sue G. Walcutt in *Notable American Women*, 2:538–540.

EDITORIAL NOTE

This edition arranges the plays in chronological order according to the first publication or private printing, even where performances prior to the publication date attest to earlier manuscript or typescript versions. Historic spellings and phraseology have been retained throughout; however, obvious misprints have been silently emended. Authors' names appear as on the original title pages of the published plays. In the case of anonymous publication and uncertain publication date, the names of authors and supposed time of publication are given in brackets. The names of the characters have been uniformly given in full, even where they were abbreviated in the plays, to facilitate easier reading.

WOMAN'S RIGHTS

WILLIAM B. FOWLE

In *Parlor Dramas, or, Dramatic Scenes,*
for Home Amusement.
Boston: Chase and Nichols, 1856, pp. 7–17.

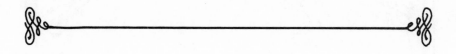

CHARACTERS

Mr. Manly, a merchant.
Mrs. Manly, his wife.
Myrtilla, her sister.
Bridget, the cook.
Kitty, the chambermaid.

SCENE I.

The Parlor

Mrs. Manly *and* **Myrtilla.**

Mrs. Manly. I am resolved, Myrtilla! This last outrage has determined me, and I henceforth revoke the promise, that in my folly I once made, to serve, to honor, and obey. Out on me for a traitor to my sex!

Myrtilla. The traitors far exceed the loyal; and I, you know, am soon to increase the number.

Mrs. Manly. You surely will not make any such promise?

Myrtilla. I am no wiser than the rest of womankind.

Mrs. Manly. Profit by my experience, and renounce the yoke before it is imposed.

Myrtilla. My word is given, and this very moment, as you know, my future is expected. Shall I renounce him?

Mrs. Manly. Better so than wear his chain. I tell you, sister, matrimony is a balance, and the weight is ever in one scale.

Myrtilla. What matters it which scale is highest?

Mrs. Manly. Every thing. The moment you ascend, you lose your foothold, and must swing as the greater weight commands.

Myrtilla. Sister, I pray you to enumerate a few of the ills I may expect; nay, tell me some of those that you endure. The world supposes you a favored wife, and named but to be envied.

Mrs. Manly. I am married; and this word expresses all a noble mind abhors. Since the world began, woman has been a slave.

Myrtilla. If this be true, usage would seem to indicate that He who made us intended we should serve.

Mrs. Manly. He made us equal; and an eternity of usurpation cannot alter the decree.

Myrtilla. I think it would *annul* it most effectually. But to the point. You just now complained of outrage. May I ask in what the wrong consisted?

Mrs. Manly. I wanted money, and my *lord* told me I could not have it.

Myrtilla. Well, spoke he not the truth?

Mrs. Manly. The truth, Myrtilla! You will drive me mad! 'Tis bad enough to be compelled to ask my lord; 'tis infamous to be refused.

Myrtilla. I do not see it thus. If I should ask another, be he lord or serf, for what he has not, his refusal is a necessity that would not move my wrath, however it might disappoint me.

Mrs. Manly. I could shake you, Myrtle, for your tameness! If that sex usurps the purse and holds it, 'tis but just that we should have all we demand, and at the instant, too.

Myrtilla. We, then, should be the tyrants. I expect to marry a husband, not a purse; and, if I manage him aright, I have no fear but all I need will be supplied.

Mrs. Manly. O, yes! I think I see you now informing him of what he ought to have seen,—that you are not dressed befitting your condition, and he must not be offended if you say, that you have worn out all the wardrobe you brought with you from your father's, and are sorry, extremely sorry, to be obliged to say that you must look to him for a new outfit! O, 'tis glorious to kneel thus in the dust!

Myrtilla. If I dress as well as he does, and have a reasonable share of what he may possess——

Mrs. Manly. You never will know the fact. He is the judge, and you must take the pittance he allows; inferior in this to the drudge who knows her wages, and with independent face can claim her pay.

Myrtilla. You go upon the ground that every husband is a tyrant and unjust. I am inclined to think the husbands I have seen have given too freely, and the ruin of too many has been hastened by the lavish bounty of the lord who could not say his lady nay.

Mrs. Manly. There comes my precious keeper! I will propose a plan at once to set me free.

Enter **Mr. Manly.**

Mr. Manly. Good evening, wife! and you, Myrtilla! How do you bear the approach of the dread hour that will suffuse the eye with tears of joy or sorrow?—which, 'tis hard to say.

Mrs. Manly. I have been warning her of her danger; but, like a bird beneath the serpent's charm, she waits her willing doom.

Mr. Manly. It is not well to alarm her, when the course before her is so bright and free.

Mrs. Manly. Free! Call you it freedom to hold nothing, have nothing, and what you humbly ask to be refused? O, would I were a man!

Mr. Manly. That might involve the necessity of my becoming a woman.

Mrs. Manly. Why so?

Mr. Manly. I did not know you wished for a divorce,—the natural consequence, if one alone should change.

Myrtilla. Better stay as you are, and let the wife and husband change their duties. My sister to the business may attend, and her liege lord may govern here at home.

Mr. Manly. Done! I will surrender on the moment, and only regret the change can't be complete.

Mrs. Manly. Agreed! You hear, Myrtilla, he agrees to let me have full swing abroad, while he remains at home, to sew, or cook, or entertain the callers with an account of his experience in the kitchen, or perhaps with a hash of sentiment, which, on such occasions, always flows from the heart, you know.

Myrtilla. I hear, and I will judge between you; for on your experiment may hang my destiny. I pray you to begin this morning; for my hour of grace is nearly spent, and I would not plunge in the dark.

Mr. Manly. Come on! Here is the trunk, the bank-book, cash-book, notes, and all. Take them, and give me all the ensigns of your office,—the keys, the cook-book, and the broom. O, what a king—a queen—I am already!

Mrs. Manly. You soon will feel the chain that I have worn so long. While I am dressing for the store, you may prepare a note, informing all the clerks that I am master there.

Mr. Manly. I will do so; but, lest you should repent too soon, I'll hint that I am ill; and you can then retreat, if you desire, and feel no shame or mortification.

Mrs. Manly. Word it as you please. I have no fear of a relapse, and will contrive to make perpetual your sudden illness.

Mr. Manly. Be it so. Let us lose no time.

(**Mrs. Manly** and **Myrtilla** go out.)

Mr. Manly. (Writing and talking.) Well, I shall have a day of rest at last. Since the banks refused to discount, I have had no peace. To-day my payments are heavier than usual, and I have not slept a wink. If wife does not get cured of any wish to change, she must be more than my equal. (Folding his billet as she returns.) There, wife! That document will make you head of the concern. Now, manage carefully.

Mrs. Manly. Never fear. Women are too cautious, and never speculate.

Mr. Manly. And always fail, I believe.

Mrs. Manly. I'll have some pocket-money, at any rate; and you shall never ask me twice for what you want. I will be a model husband.

Mr. Manly. More likely you will make me turn my coat twice. Business will make you economical.

Mrs. Manly. It shall not make me mean. I feel more concern on your account. You never did a thing in the house.

Mr. Manly. No matter; there is no mystery in keeping house. I'd teach it to an ape in half a day.

Mrs. Manly. I dare say the ape would soon know as much as his teacher. But I am wasting time. Good morning. You will not see me again till dinner; and then I shall expect a banquet.

Mr. Manly. You shall have one worthy of the occasion. Good bye. Success to you!

Mrs. Manly. I shall no doubt obtain it. *(She goes out.)*

Enter the Cook.

Mr. Manly. Well, Bridget, what would you?

Bridget. Plase, sir, madam says I must look to yourself for the dinner.

Mr. Manly. What is there in the house?

Bridget. Nothing in the wide world but the praties and ungyuns.

Mr. Manly. What else do we need, Bridget?

Bridget. Mate, sir, or fish, or both, as it may plase.

Mr. Manly. I'll have a chowder, Bridget. Mrs. Manly would never let me have my favorite dish; and, now I am mistress, the inauguration dinner shall be chowder. Can you make a chowder, Bridget?

Bridget. Aw, yis, sir. Do you think the likes of me can't make that same?

Mr. Manly. How do you begin? What fish do you prefer?

Bridget. Fish, is it? Sure, there's nothing aqual to the sahlt fish taken fresh from the wather, already sazoned, as it always is.

Mr. Manly. What?

Bridget. The sahlt fish for me! It has no innards, you know, and needs no claning.

Mr. Manly. Bridget, you don't know what a chowder is!

Bridget. It's the first time a genthilman ever towld Bridget Killmallybone that she didn't know her business! It is not I will put up with the insult from a miserable, hen-pecked, meddlesome, impartinent——

Mr. Manly. That will do, Bridget! You may pack up and be gone.

Bridget. Be gone is it, indade? It's not I will stay in your dirty presence another blessed minute! You may make your own chowther, and ate it, too, for all Bridget Killmallybone! *(Putting her hands on her hips, insultingly.)* I'll thank you for my wages!

Mr. Manly. Wages! What is due?

Bridget. Ten weeks, come Saturday.

Mr. Manly. *(Aside.)* Twenty dollars! I have not ten in my pocket, and wife has carried off the trunk. Bridget, you must wait till Mrs. Manly comes home, or call to-morrow.

Bridget. I want me money now!

Mr. Manly. Call Miss Myrtilla.

Bridget. Do your own cahling! I am no longer your sarvant.

Mr. Manly. This is too bad! *(He goes out to call **Myrtilla**.)*

Bridget. Sure, here is a work-box. That will fit me pocket like a glove. *(She pockets it.)* When a poor gairl is abused and chated as I have been, it is fair to defind herself.

*Enter **Mr. Manly**.*

Mr. Manly. There is your money. I have borrowed it. Begone!

Bridget. It's not Bridget Killmallybone will hurry for the likes of you! I wahnt my chist,—'twill not be safe to lave it in such kaping.

Mr. Manly. Well, take it, and leave the house this instant!

Bridget. Sure, and I cannot carry that same alone! If you will cahl the omnibus, and pay for the ticket, I will go; and, sure, no genthilman will refuse a ticket to a poor gairl!

Mr. Manly. There's a ticket. Stop that omnibus, and go to—

Bridget. It's not I will travel that road yet! Chowther, is it? *(She goes out.)*

Mr. Manly. Well, this is a brave beginning! No cook! Then I must call the chambermaid. *(He calls at the door.)* Kitty! Kitty! *(Enter* **Kitty**.*)* Kitty, I have dismissed Bridget, and you must take her place to-day, and do her work.

Kitty. It is not I could cook the asiest dish in the cook-book. And if I could, who would make the beds, and swape the room, and dust the things, and——

Mr. Manly. You can do it for one day, until I get a cook.

Kitty. It is not the likes of me will do another gairl's worrk! You may get a chambermaid, too, while you are about it. I have engaged to go with Bridget, and only wait for me wages.

Mr. Manly. How much is due you?

Kitty. Ten weeks, at nine shillings a week.

Mr. Manly. I will give you an order on my store.

Kitty. I wahnt no orthers,—the money is what I wahnt; and you may give me it in gold, if you plase, as the law requires, for I can't rade the dirty bills.

Mr. Manly. Get out! Leave the house, and come to-morrow.

Kitty. *(She sits down on an ottoman, with determination.)* It's here I'll *set* till I'm paid! Sure, no genthilman will drive a poor gairl into the street, and not pay her her hard airnings!

Mr. Manly. Myrtilla! Myrtilla! *(He goes out to find her.)*

Kitty. Sure, it will be a week or more that I shall be saking another place, and paying me board. Here is a gold pencil-case and spectacles. Sure, a poor gairl cannot be blamed if she pertects herself when she is wronged. *(She puts them in her pocket.)*

Mr. Manly. *(Entering with* **Myrtilla**.*)* There is your money. Now, leave the house this instant, or I will have an officer here!

Kitty. Sure, it is I that nades the officer! Hard times, if a pacible gairl must be abused in this manner! *(She goes out very slowly.)* I'll never do another gairl's worrk—not I!

Mr. Manly. Well, Myrtilla, if you had not happened to have the money, I should have been turned away by my own servants. A pretty pickle we are in! No servants, and no dinner!

Myrtilla. Don't be concerned. We will have a cup of tea for dinner, and I can make the beds. But what is this? Sister returned! Pray what can be the matter now?

Enter **Mrs. Manly.**

Mrs. Manly. Well, here I am! *(She plumps down on the ottoman the girl has just left.)*

Mr. Manly. I am glad you have come, wife! I want some money sadly.

Mrs. Manly. You may want, for all me! Money, huh!

Mr. Manly. But I must have it; and I have nobody to look to but yourself. Now you are lord of the treasury, we shall expect to see some liberality. I tell you I must have five-and-thirty dollars!

Mrs. Manly. I tell you you shall not have a cent! O, dear! O, dear!

Myrtilla. What is the matter? Has any accident disturbed you?

Mrs. Manly. Accident! Husband, go this instant to the store!

Mr. Manly. What is the matter, pray?

Mrs. Manly. Matter, huh! What isn't the matter? I had hardly entered the counting-room, before the clerk laid before me half a dozen bank notices of notes to be paid to-day!

Mr. Manly. Well, you prepared for them, of course?

Mrs. Manly. Prepared with a vengeance! How did you prepare for them?

Mr. Manly. As you did for the dinner, I suppose. What did you tell him?

Mrs. Manly. To go and pay them. He asked for the money, and expected me to furnish it. There was not a hundred dollars in the trunk. He then looked at the bank-book, and said you had overdrawn. I told him to let the banks wait. He said it would ruin your credit, and I had better borrow the money.

Mr. Manly. Well, you borrowed it, of course?

Mrs. Manly. Of course, I didn't! Borrow! Whom could I borrow five thousand dollars of? I never saw so much!

Mr. Manly. We have to pay as much every day.

Mrs. Manly. What do you pay with?

Mr. Manly. Money.

Mrs. Manly. Money! Where do you get it? Do you beg, borrow, or steal it? I saw no money in the drawer, or trunk, or safe.

Mr. Manly. You should have borrowed a check.

Mrs. Manly. I got one without borrowing,—an effectual check. Good gracious, Manly! tell me if this is the sort of life you lead?

Mr. Manly. You have a very fair specimen of it since the banks have been so tight.

Mrs. Manly. Bridget! Bridget!

Mr. Manly. Bridget has walked out.

Mrs. Manly. Walked out! What! in the forenoon? Kitty! Kitty! *(Calling.)*

Mr. Manly. Kitty has walked out, too.

Mrs. Manly. What do you mean? Why did you allow it? Pretty doings!

Mr. Manly. I proposed it.

Mrs. Manly. Proposed it! Manly, what do you mean?

Mr. Manly. I mean that your two girls have dismissed themselves or me. I am not sure which way it stands.

Mrs. Manly. Then, what has become of the dinner?

Mr. Manly. Nothing; we had none to become of.

Mrs. Manly. Husband, you know no more about housekeeping——

Mr. Manly. Than you do about storekeeping!

Mrs. Manly. Provoking! Myrtilla, you must think us a pretty pair of fools.

Myrtilla. Very well matched, I must acknowledge. But, sister, I am not surprised at the result of your experiment. The hen was never made to swim.

(**Mr. and Mrs. Manly** *look each other in the face, at first with determination; but at last they relax, and burst into laughter.*)

Mrs. Manly. You had better run to the store.

Mr. Manly. You know I am very ill of an illness you pronounced perpetual! How can I venture out?

Mrs. Manly. Begone, or I will be the death of you!

Mr. Manly. I will go; but, first, you will please to pay me "me wages."

Mrs. Manly. Put mine against yours, and let us pass receipts.

Mr. Manly. Agreed! Good bye to the empty kitchen!

Mrs. Manly. Good bye to the empty safe! When I complain again—— What will you have for dinner?

Mr. Manly. I must have a chowder; and Myrtilla must tell you why, while I run to the store and get an appetite. "A chowther, is it?"

CURTAIN

THE
SPIRIT OF
SEVENTY-SIX;

or, THE COMING WOMAN, A PROPHETIC DRAMA, Followed by A CHANGE OF BASE, and DOCTOR MONDSCHEIN

[ARIANA R. W. CURTIS AND DANIEL SARGENT CURTIS]

Boston: Little, Brown, and Company. 1868, pp. 1–73.

NOTE

This play was not written for the stage, nor with any view to publication, but simply for amateur performance; and therefore all scenery, stage-properties, &c., were purposely dispensed with, and the action limited by the resources of a drawing-room.

The other little pieces were written two years ago, with the same object, and under the same restrictions.

CHESTNUT HILL, March, 1868.

CHARACTERS _____

Tom Carberry.
Mr. Wigfall.
Wolverine Griffin.
Mrs. Badger.
Victorine.
The Judge.

The supposed period of this play is in the year 1876.

ACT I

SCENE I

A Waiting-room in a Railway Station; hung with Time Tables for 1876 of Pacific Railroad, direct route to Alaska, Walrussia, and Nootka Sound &c. &c.—Enter **Carberry.**

Carberry. Provoking! to wait here an hour when I'm in a hurry to get back to Boston! I arrived from China yesterday, after ten years' absence,—took the first train,—and just as I am almost in sight of the State House, the engine breaks down here at Newton Corner!—However, I must make the best of it. . . . Luckily I have this morning's paper. (*Lights a cigar, and takes out a newspaper.*) "Boston Daily Advertiser, September 25, 1876." It is incredible that I have lived ten years without the "Daily"! I have heard nothing about Boston since I left it, so I suppose I shall find some changes. I wonder who the Bank Presidents are now. (*Reads.*) "Merchants' Insurance Company,—President, Julia Backbay." *Julia?* Misprint, I suppose. "*Fire-women's* Insurance Company." Pshaw! what a careless compositor! . . . (*Reads.*) "*Wanted, as Porter in a store, a good, stout. . . .* WIDOW-WOMAN." . . . What a very extraordinary thing! . . . (*Reads.*) "*The Free-masons' secret divulged by a lady.*" . . . Some fool told his wife, I suppose. . . . (*Reads.*) "*The Boston Independent Cadets paraded yesterday on the Common. A new feature was the introduction of the Parasol Bayonet to shield the complexions of our fair and gallant Militia from the sun. The parasol is of blue silk, attached to the point of the Bayonet, and the effect on the march is exceedingly neat and imposing.*" . . . I never heard anything equal to that! Soldiers with sunshades! One would think they were a parcel of girls! It's time for another war.

Enter **Mrs. Badger** *in Bloomer costume. She nods;* **Carberry** *bows politely.*

Mrs. Badger. How are you, sir? Cigar, please.
Carberry. Madam, I'm sorry you object to smoking, but I took this for the gentlemen's waiting-room.
Mrs. Badger. Object. What do you mean? I want a light.
Carberry. Oh, I beg your pardon. I was not aware. (*Aside.*) Queer-looking female!

[*Gives her a light and returns to his paper.* **Mrs. Badger** *also takes out a newspaper.*]

Mrs. Badger. Bad accident to the "Amazon," sir.

Carberry. What's that?

Mrs. Badger. Portland Steamer,—Captain a particular friend of mine,—Jane Smith,—lost her reckoning, and ran aground on Cape Cod. Jane always *was* a hen-headed thing!

Carberry. I don't think I quite understand you.

Mrs. Badger (*reading*). But the "Transcript" says, "*No blame attached to the lady-like Captain, who was suffering under a severe attack of neuralgia. At the time of the accident our informant was talking to the woman at the wheel.*" . . . Ah! *that* was the trouble.

Carberry (*aside*). I don't know what she means. (*A pause.*)

Mr. Badger. Bad business that of the Boston City Government. It has all come out, you know,—Shameful misappropriation of the public money!

Carberry. What did they do?

Mrs. Badger. Voted themselves each a Cashmere shawl, worth a thousand dollars. Tax-payers must see to it at the next election.

Carberry. What on earth should the City Government do with Cashmere shawls?

Mrs. Badger. Do? Wear them, of course. (*Reads her newspaper.*)

Carberry (*aside*). They must look very ridiculous! Middle-aged men in fancy shawls! Dear me! I hope it isn't the fashion here for everybody. I should feel like a fool.

Mrs. Badger. We manage these things better at the Centre. No bribery and corruption there.

Carberry. What centre? Washington?

Mrs. Badger. Newton Centre, Stupid.

Carberry. Oh, I beg your pardon. (*A pause.*)

Mrs. Badger. Going to Boston, sir?

Carberry. Yes, madam. I am returning after an absence of several years.

Mrs. Badger. Going to live in Boston, sir?

Carberry (*aside*). Inquisitive! (*Aloud.*) No, madam, I am only going to see some old friends. After that, I shall live in the country.

Mrs. Badger. Where?

Carberry. At Chestnut Hill, if you must know.

Mrs. Badger. Chestnut Hill!—that's in my district.—I'm your assessor.

Carberry. I beg your pardon?

Mrs. Badger. What's your name?

Carberry. Thomas Carberry, if you desire it.

Mrs. Badger (*taking out a note-book*). What's your income?

Carberry. Madam!

Mrs. Badger. Professional, or derived from property?

Carberry. Excuse me, madam, if I question your right to ask me.

Mrs. Badger. Right! of course I've a right. What's your income?

Carberry. I decline to answer.

Mrs. Badger. O, you must, you know,—the law compels you.

Carberry (*aside*). This woman is certainly deranged.

Mrs. Badger. You'll be fined or imprisoned if you refuse to answer my questions.

Carberry (*aside*). She's mad,—I see it in her eye,—unpleasant to be shut up with her here.

A Voice (*without*). Cars coming for Worcester! (*Bell rings.*).

Mrs. Badger. That's my train. I'm off to the Convention. Good bye. I'll see you again about it, Carberry,—there's my card.

[*Exit.*]

Carberry (*reading the card*). "Mrs. Barbara Badger,—Newton. Assessor of Internal Revenue for the 5th District."—Singular delusion for a woman. . . . She certainly must have been crazy, and yet . . . I can't explain these extraordinary things in the newspapers. . . . Here they all are in black and white, and I can't understand a word of them. . . . Good Heavens! what if I were a little out of my head myself? . . . an effect of the voyage. . . . I have heard of such things. . . . (*Walks up and down in great agitation,—feels his own pulse,—goes to the other end of Waiting-room.*)

Enter **Victorine Wigfall** *in a shooting-dress, with gun, game-bag, &c.*

Victorine. O! how tired I am! Tramping all the morning through bogs and briers, carrying this horrid gun,—and I'm afraid of it too!

Carberry (*coming forward*). Pray let me relieve you of it, madam. (*Taking it.*)

Victorine. Oh, thanks. I've been dragging it about since sunrise, because some of my friends persuaded me it was good fun. But I think it's a downright humbug, and I'll never do it again.

Carberry. Is it not something new for ladies to indulge in field sports?

Victorine. New? Oh no; all the girls do.

Carberry (*putting down the gun and seeing her name on it*). "Victorine Wigfall!" Why, it must be Joe Wigfall's daughter! Allow me to introduce myself . . . an old friend of your father's . . . Mr. Carberry.

Victorine. Oh yes, indeed,—papa will be delighted. He often talks of you. You have been in some out-of-the-way place, haven't you?

Carberry. In China.

Victorine. Are there many curious spiders in China?

Carberry. Spiders?

Victorine. Yes. I 'm passionately fond of spiders . . . are you? I've got a beauty here. I found him this morning for my collection. (*Opens a box and produces a large black spider.*) Isn't he lovely?

Carberry (*recoiling*). Ugh!

Victorine. He's an *Epeira Diadema*. Do you want to take him? . . . No? . . . Why, are you afraid of spiders?

Carberry. I thought ladies were. I'm quite surprised to find a young lady interested in insects.

Victorine (*wearily*). One must be interested in something, you know,—and, to tell you the honest truth, horse-racing and dog-fighting bore me, and I'm not much of a club-girl, and no sportswoman,—so I've gone into spiders.

Carberry (*aside*). There's something very odd about all this. (*Aloud.*) When I was here last, young ladies interested themselves chiefly in society. Is there no gaiety in Boston now?

Victorine. Parties, you mean? I really can't tell you; I've hardly been to a party since my Sophomore year. I don't like them. It is so unpleasant asking gentlemen to dance . . . they make such a favour of it, and the nicest ones are engaged ten deep. . . . And then they always want so much supper! Really, after I've done helping my partner, I'm *so* tired, that when I get home I've hardly strength to turn the latch-key. So I don't often go. . . . And yet I'm fond of dancing too. . . . Are you?

Carberry. I have no doubt I *should* be, with such a charming partner,—but I'm afraid I haven't much experience.

Victorine. Oh doesn't your father let you dance round dances?

Carberry (*puzzled*). *My father?*

Victorine. Why, that's what so many young men say. But I think it is only an excuse, because they are too lazy.

Carberry. Society seems to have changed very much, for, when I left Boston, the gentlemen always asked the ladies.

Victorine. Oh, can you remember as far back as *that?* I think it must have been pleasanter then for the girls,—but mamma and Aunt Wolverine say I don't appreciate the blessings of emancipation. I *don't.* I should hate to vote . . . and I'd a great deal rather keep quiet, and *be* asked to dance, or to . . . anything.

Carberry. Miss Wigfall, such sentiments do you honor. A lady is never so charming as when adorned with modesty, of which I see the emblem in your *violet* eyes.

Victorine. How pretty! Is that the way gentlemen used to talk? Do go on.

Carberry (*aside*). It's not so easy for a shy man to go on.

Victorine. I don't know anything about the old ways, for mamma says lovers were frivolous, and won't tell me, . . . and I don't believe Aunt Wolverine ever had any, . . . so I can't get much out of *her.*

Carberry. The novels of the period would perhaps give you some idea.

Victorine. But all the old novels were burnt, you know, by order of the Ladies of the Legislature, because they represented Woman in her degraded state. They say there used to be a few at Loring's Library once, but he only keeps philosophical and scientific works now, and *Mr.* Putnam's Cookery Book.

Carberry. Do you mean to say you never read a novel?

Victorine. Only "The Imperial Votress" and "The Maid of Saragossa."

Carberry. No novels! . . . no parties! No poetry, perhaps,—that would be a good thing. Miss Wigfall, did you never hear of Tennyson?

Victorine. O yes, indeed! I have a beautiful song of his,—"*Come into the garden, George.*" I'll sing it to you some day. But now *do* tell me about old times,—for the train may be here any moment, and perhaps I shall never have another chance. I want to know whether gentlemen really cared anything for ladies then?

Carberry. Certainly, I knew a great many fellows who were over head and ears in love with pretty girls.

Victorine. In love! There! I knew there *was* such a thing! And what did they do and say?

Carberry (*aside*). What an embarrassing girl! (*Aloud.*) I dare say you know from experience, Miss Wigfall.

Victorine. I!—no, indeed,—I never made an offer to anybody.

Carberry. *You!* Of course not. What did you think I meant?

Victorine. Were you ever in love yourself?

Carberry. Never, *never*, I assure you.

Victorine. Oh, I wish you had been, for then you could have told me all about it. . . . But "those fellows" you spoke of, who were "over head and ears,"—what did they say? I only want to know what it sounded like. . . . Can't you *sigh?*—just once! . . .

Carberry (*very much embarrassed*). Really, Miss Wigfall. . . .

Victorine. Were they so very awkward? Come now,—what *did* they say?

Carberry. Well, then . . . they said . . . they said . . .

A Voice (*without*). Train starting for Boston—All aboard!

[**Victorine** *and* **Carberry** *snatch up guns, bags, shawls, and rush out.*]

ACT II

Drawing-room in Mr. Wigfall's house in Boston. **Mr. Wigfall** *sitting with a large work-basket, trying to darn his own stockings.*

Enter **Carberry.**

Carberry. WIGFALL, old fellow, I am delighted to see you again.

Mr. Wigfall (*not recognizing*). Whom have I the honour, sir, to see? . . .

Carberry (*aside, looking at the stockings*). What on earth is he about there? . . .

can he have gone mad like the rest? (*Aloud.*) So you don't know Tom Carberry after ten years?

Mr. Wigfall. Tom! my dear fellow,—where? when? how?

Carberry. From Shanghae,—a sudden idea,—arrived yesterday,—took the first train, and here I am. I met your lovely girl, what's her name? Glycerine—Bandoline—Kerosene—*Victorine!* at the Railway station,—didn't she tell you?

Mr. Wigfall. I haven't seen her. She dined at the Club, I believe.

Carberry. Indeed! And how is your wife,—charming as ever?—the only woman I was never afraid of.

Mr. Wigfall. Ah, my dear fellow,—don't speak of her.

Carberry. Why, you haven't had the misfortune to lose poor Susan? . . .

Mr. Wigfall. No; no such good—no such *bad* luck. She's well in health, but . . .

Carberry. It isn't her mind, I hope?

Mr. Wigfall. Yes, Tom, it's her mind, though not in the way you mean.

Carberry. You haven't separated, surely?

Mr. Wigfall. Oh, not at all,—though I don't see much of her now. (*Cries of a baby heard*). Excuse me, Tom, I must run,—there's that strong-minded baby!

Carberry. *You?* Why, where's the nurse?

Mr. Wigfall. The nurse has gone to a primary meeting! [*Exit.*]

Carberry. What on earth can he mean?

Re-enter **Mr. Wigfall**, *carrying the baby, and singing "Bye, Baby Bunting."*

Mr. Wigfall. Hush . . . sh. . . . She's going off . . . I'll be with you presently. . . . (*Puts the baby in a cradle at the back of the room.*) I keep her cradle down here, lately, because it is election time, you know, and the women can't attend to her.

Carberry. Wigfall, one of us two is either drunk or crazy,—and I'm afraid it's I. *What do you mean* by nursery-maids and elections?

Mr. Wigfall. Didn't you know the ladies had gone to the front in America?

Carberry. I'll be hanged if I understand you.

Mr. Wigfall. Didn't you read our papers out there in Shanghae?

Carberry. Never; nothing they said was true when they got there.

Mr. Wigfall. My dear fellow, you're behind the age. You went away in '66, before this infernal business of women's voting came up. That was the beginning of it all. At first they voted for their favourite generals and ministers,—they got that idea from the Fairs they used to have in the war-time,—but they soon gave *them* up, and began to elect each other. And now we are overrun by them. They're lawyers, ministers, tax-gatherers, —everything that's disagreeable!

Carberry. How appalling!—I can't comprehend it, for when I went away, the trouble was, that the women were entirely given up to extravagant dressing.

Mr. Wigfall. I know,—but times are changed. Then we lived under a Millinery Despotism. I wish we had it back!

Carberry. We used to complain a good deal about it, I remember.

Mr. Wigfall. Tom, the present state of things is a judgment on us,—we did not know when we were well off. Now the Ballot-box has crushed the Band-box flat.

Carberry. You don't mean to say women no longer care how they look?

Mr. Wigfall. Well,—not quite that,—even my wife tries to get herself up like the Lord Chancellor,—but it's nothing to what it used to be. It's cheaper now,—but still, I regret old times, when women were women.

Miss Griffin (*speaking to the servant behind the scenes*). Now, Bridget, be sure you vote the way I tell you to, and persuade all your friends, and I'll give you a pair of real imitation gold ear-rings.

Mr. Wigfall. Hang it, here's my sister-in-law! She's the worst one I know.

Enter **Miss Griffin.**

Miss Griffin. Joseph, I've come to stay till Saturday, as I speak on Thursday in Faneuil Hall.

Mr. Wigfall (*introducing*). Let me introduce Mr. Carberry, of Shanghae,— Miss Wolverine Griffin, Selectwoman of Newton, Mass.

Miss Griffin. Happy to see you, sir. I've just got back from Worcester, Joseph. Great rally. All the distinguished women of the state were there.

Carberry. Was it a baby-show?

Miss Griffin (*indignantly*). A baby-show! Sir, it was the Female Areopagus of the Modern Athens. Heard the news, Joseph? Glorious nomination!

Mr. Wigfall. No,—not I. Gentlemen don't understand politics.

Miss Griffin. But you should *try* to, Joseph, if they interest your wife and your sister. Overwhelming majority for Hon. Charleyanna P. Fillebrown for Governess of the State. But nine against her, and they were only men. You'll support her, won't you, Joseph?

Mr. Wigfall. It's as much as I can do to support myself. I sha'n't make any promises.

Miss Griffin. You want some man, I suppose! As if we hadn't had enough of them!

Mr. Wigfall. By no means, my dear Wolverine. I am only disappointed that they didn't nominate *you*.

Miss Griffin. Well, you needn't flatter yourself that it's of the slightest consequence how you vote,—for Sister Susan, and I, and Bridget, and the cook, and the parlour-maid, will make five to one against you in *this* house alone. But I can't waste my valuable time arguing with you, Joseph,—

one might as well talk to the winds. Men have such frivolous minds,—they don't care for anything but dress and company.—I don't mean you, Mr. Carberry; I dare say you are an exception.

Carberry. Everything seems to be exceptional, madam, so I suppose I am, too.

Miss Griffin. Pray, sir, what are Mrs. Carberry's political convictions?

Carberry. Madam, I have the misfortune to be unmarried.

Mr. Wigfall. Stick to it, Tom,—stick to it! *Returns to his baby.*

Miss Griffin. Unmarried! That will never do. No doubt you feel the isolation of your lot,—unfitted as you are by nature to struggle with the rude world alone.

Carberry. So far, I have got along pretty well, thank you, ma'am.

Miss Griffin. But now you feel the need of female guidance and support. I understand you perfectly. Leave it to me.

Carberry. Madam, you are very kind, but I shouldn't think of troubling you with my affairs.

Miss Griffin. It is not the least trouble, I assure you. Am I not bound to help the weaker sex? I could find you a wife immediately. I know exactly what you want.

Carberry. That's more than I do myself.

Miss Griffin. You want a guide, philosopher, and friend; so of course you wouldn't marry a baby. Then, as to mere wax-doll beauty, of course you don't care for *that.* You want a woman of majestic presence (*Drawing herself up*),—mind,—experience,—heart,—and, above all, *sound political principles*, which are the only sure foundation on which to erect the fabric of connubial bliss.

Carberry. That's a new sort of foundation, isn't it?—like pile-driving,—are you quite sure it won't "slump"?

Miss Griffin. Oh, my dear sir, believe me, the *first thing* in choosing a wife is to ascertain her political principles. Be sure they are sound, and then go ahead. By the way, perhaps you would like to hear my little speech before the Areopagus, published this morning in that admirable paper "The Revolver." (*Producing it.*) Not very long, you see . . . thirteen columns and a half.

[**Carberry** and **Wigfall** *look at each other and groan.*]

(*Reads.*) "The Hon. Wolverine Griffin then rose, and said: 'Fellow-Sisters. Woman now stands on the apex of the social Pyramid. Man is a mummy. The successful agitation of the Great Idea of Woman's Rights has worked results far transcending the fondest hopes of its originators. They demanded for Woman simple Equality with man, but Equality conceded, became the point upon which, resting the lever of her intellect, Woman has moved the world. She has succeeded where old Archimedes broke down. A hundred years ago it was thought a fine thing for a few American men to throw off the British Tyrant's yoke,—but that was a trifling achievement, compared to the new Revolution, in which twenty millions of ladies have thrown off *all* restraint, and now plant their victorious feet on the neck of the Male Oppressor! (*Immense cheering.*) Yes, fellow-sisters, the tocsin has sounded, the Great American Principle of Female Supremacy is spreading like wildfire, and the bloated old potentates of Europe shake on their rotten old thrones. (*Applause.*) Woman's pre-eminence is conspicuous in every department of literature and art. Poetesses, painteresses, sculptresses, triumphantly bear away the palm,—and all admit that as an oratress she has never been surpassed. (*Cheers.*) A distinguished lady-antiquary has recently discovered that the immortal Shakespeare was a woman,—and this fact, while it settles the numerous controversies as to who and what he, or rather *she*, was, is confirmed beyond the possibility of doubt by the ample internal evidence contained in his, or rather *her*, immortal pages.

Mr. Wigfall. Thanks,—don't tire yourself by reading any more.

Miss Griffin. How you interrupt, Joseph! Men never listen,—they always want to talk themselves! (*Resuming.*)

" 'Ancient Woman had immense opportunities, but unhappily she did not know it. Bowed to the earth as a sex, the few individuals who stood up were very conspicuous. Semiramis and Cleopatra both stood up in their day, and might have accomplished much, if they had kept clear of entangling alliances with men. Boadicea stood up, in her chariot (which by the way undoubtedly originated the idea of the modern mowing-machine, refuting those cavillers who assert that woman has invented nothing). Joan of Arc stood up in her day, in armour, *cap-a-pie*, and it worked well, till they made it too hot for her. Glancing rapidly at Queen Elizabeth, Mrs. John Milton, Christina of Sweden, Madame Roland, Joanna Southcote, and Mrs. Fry, who all stood up in their several departments,—I come down to modern times, and close the list of Ante-Revolutionary Heroines with the illustrious name of Mrs. Bloomer,—the last of her sex who stood up entirely alone. She sowed the dragon's teeth which produced armed women from Cape Cod to Alaska. To-day *all* stand up, and notoriety is getting to be next to impossible.' "

That is only the commencement. But I must leave you now, as I am one of the committee appointed to take our Nominee by the hand,— otherwise I'd read you the whole. . . . Good bye.

[*Exit.*]

Carberry *and* **Mr. Wigfall** (*together*). Thank Heaven!

Miss Griffin (*returning*). I forgot to say,—I am on the Finance Committee,

—great need of funds for the campaign. We want to circulate portraits of Charleyanna P. Fillebrown all over the State. . . . No use asking *you*, Joseph?

Mr. Wigfall. Not the slightest,—but here is Mr. Carberry rolling in riches . . . they call him the "China-Astor!"

Carberry (*aside to* **Wigfall**). Confound you, Joe! (*Aloud*). Madam, I never refuse a lady.

Miss Griffin (*aside*). Rolling in riches, and never refuses a lady,—I'll make a note of that. (*Aloud, graciously.*) Shall I say $500? . . . Thank you. Perhaps you would like to give a little something towards the purchase of a steam fire-engine to be presented to Queen Emma of the Sandwich Islands by her admirers in this city,—names of the subscribers to be elegantly engraved on the machine?

Carberry. Excuse me, ma'am,—but I hope Her Majesty won't be put out, if I prefer objects less remote.

Miss Griffin. Ah, then perhaps you would rather subscribe to the new statue, about to be erected in the Public Garden, after an original and comprehensive design by the gifted Miss Sculpin,—sometimes called the Phidias of the West. The group consists of a Colossal Bronze *Egg*, burnished like gold, which, cracking open, reveals Woman,—lovely Woman,—clad in complete armour, spreading her new-fledged wings. The inscription is simply "INCUBATED AT BOSTON." Imagine the effect at sunset! Could anything be finer!—Not to mention the *beautiful* bas-reliefs of myself and other great lady reformers, in bronze pantalettes, around the base.

Carberry. Bronze? I should think brass might be more appropriate.

Miss Griffin. Ah! my dear sir, *tin* is what we want. Shall I say $300?

Carberry. But, madam, I assure you I am wholly indifferent to . . .

Miss Griffin. . . . to money, in such a cause,—I knew that would be your characteristic reply. So I will say $300. . . . Thank you. *Good* evening! . . . good evening, Joseph. [*Exit.*]

Mr. Wigfall (*solemnly*). Are you aware, Carberry, of the awful fact, that there are *two hundred thousand* more women than men in Massachusetts alone?

Carberry. Oh, horrible,—most horrible!

Mr. Wigfall. Yes, and every year it gets worse and worse,—all the children now are girls. I've seven myself. (*The baby cries.*) "Talk of the angel."—There's my youngest now.

[*Goes to the cradle and hushes the baby.*]

Enter **Judge Wigfall** *in robes, ermine, and long powdered wig, with a brief in her hand.*

Carberry (*astonished*). Who can this be? Joe!

Mr. Wigfall (*sitting down with the baby*). Tom, this is Her Honour, Judge

Wigfall, of the Massachusetts Supreme Judicial Court. She's hen of the walk, now.

Carberry. Good Heavens!

Mr. Wigfall. My dear, do you recognize an old friend?

Judge (*to* **Carberry**). Pardon me, sir, if I do not at once recall you. In what case did you appear before me?

Carberry. Case? Susan! Judge! Don't you remember Tom Carberry?

Judge. Carberry,—Carberry,—*versus* whom?

Mr. Wigfall. Stuff and nonsense, my dear. . . . You recollect Tom,—went off to China ten years ago,—don't be a goose.

Judge. Mr. Wigfall! Respect this Court!

Mr. Wigfall. You can't have forgotten our cosy evenings together,—he and I smoking, and *you* darning the children's stockings.

Judge. I remember nothing before I was called to the Bar.

Mr. Wigfall. And that famous pigeon-pie you made us yourself the day we . . .

Judge. Mr. Wigfall! (*To* **Carberry**.) Sir, I dimly recall you now, and I welcome you back to this regenerated land.

Carberry (*bowing*). And permit me to congratulate you on your singular elevation.

Mr. Wigfall (*rocking the cradle*). Well, my dear, how was it to-day?—Plaintiff or defendant?

Judge. Pardon me, Mr. Wigfall, if I decline to make my grave judicial duties a subject of merriment for you.

Mr. Wigfall. How often did you change your mind to-day?

Judge. Mr. Wigfall, I never change my mind.

Mr. Wigfall. Oh, fie, fie! Judges shouldn't tell fibs. Didn't I go to hear you try your first case?

Judge. I take no notice of idlers who hang round the Court-room.

Mr. Wigfall. And didn't you first charge the jury to be sure and let the poor devil off,—and when they had been out ten minutes, didn't you send for them back, on second thoughts, and charge them all over again to convict him?

Judge. Mr. Wigfall, you cannot be expected to understand the intricacies of the law. During the interval you allude to, I was informed by Mrs. Attorney-General Talker that the prisoner in question had been a noted and violent opponent of the Emancipation of Women.

Mr. Wigfall. And so that was your reason for having him convicted of forgery, eh?

Judge. Mr. Wigfall, Chief Justice Mansfield held that Judges should never give their reasons. Moreover, it is perfectly competent for me to change my mind without any reason,—and had I done so twenty years ago, in *your* case, Mr. Wigfall, it would have been a wise decision.

Mr. Wigfall. From which I should never have appealed!

Judge. Are you in one of the learned professions, Mr. Carberry?

Carberry. No, madam, I am a tea merchant.

Judge. The Male mind, as a rule, is unfitted for the learned professions—the law especially—from its habit of jumping to conclusions. We are slow in forming a judgment, it is true,—but, once formed, it is unalterable. You agree with me, sir?

Carberry (*bowing*). I should never think of differing from a lady.

Judge. You mean that our opinions cannot fail to be correct, from the logical character of the Female mind?

Carberry. Exactly, madam,—I have always observed it to be so.

[During this conversation **Mr. Wigfall** *is playing bo-peep with the baby.]*

Judge. At the same time as one of a Conservative Judiciary, I shall always tolerate Man in his proper sphere, and never countenance . . . (*Suddenly changing her tone.*) Mr. Wigfall! I wish you'd take that child up stairs,— I can't hear myself speak . . .

Mr. Wigfall (*aside to* **Carberry**). Come, Tom, let's go and sit in the nursery.

[Exit **Mr. Wigfall** *with the baby, followed by* **Carberry.***]*

Judge. I say, I shall tolerate you in your proper sphere, and never countenance the popular doctrine of the complete Mental and Moral Inferiority of Man. I shall always be ready to guarantee your Equal Rights. (*Looks round and sees no one.*) Gone! While I was speaking! how extraordinary!

Enter **Victorine.**

Victorine. Oh, where's Mr. Carberry, mamma?

Judge. He is up stairs with your father,—minding the baby. (**Victorine** *is going.*) Stop, my daughter. I wish to speak to you. (*Seating herself.*) Have you read your Blackstone to-day?

Victorine. Yes,—no,—well, some of it.

Judge. And your Coke upon Littleton?

Victorine. Oh, I can't make head or tail of that nasty thing.

Judge (*mournfully*). Victorine, you will break your mother's heart! You have the finest opening of any girl in Boston,—and the best example,—and if you loved your Blackstone, and your Cruise's Digest, you might become, like me, the ornament of the Suffolk Bar. But who do you suppose would ever give *you* a brief? You don't deserve to be my daughter,—and the end of it will be, you'll have to marry,—you are not fit for anything better!

[Bursting into tears.]

Victorine. I don't want anything better!

Judge. Because you have never risen above the level of girls before the Revolution. I give you up, and I shall centre all my hopes upon your sister Portia,—a child of great promise,—who *cries* for Cruise's Digest.

Victorine (*clapping her hands*). Hurrah! then I needn't be a lawyer, after all!

Judge. But you must be provided for; and, since you are too lazy for the Law, and too giddy for the Church, and too pretty for a Family Physician,—I see but one resource.—What do you think of this Mr. Carberry?

Victorine. I think he's awfully jolly, mamma,—but do let me go!

Judge. I wish you to give up calling me "Mamma." It is unsuited to my present dignity. I wear my robes of office in private life, on purpose to inspire respect. The Lord Chancellor Erskine (though a man) most pertinently says, "Supreme Judges should always be seen in grave and suitable habits of distinction, to point out their stations, and continue the reverence inspired by their dignified appearance when administering the laws."— But to return to Mr. Carberry.—If I were you, Victorine, I should propose to him, immediately.

Victorine. Oh, mamma . . . Your Honour, I mean . . . I couldn't possibly. . . .

Judge. Why not? They say he has made a large fortune.

Victorine. Oh, I couldn't, indeed. . . . I should die of mortification.

Judge. Well, my daughter, if you don't secure him, he will certainly be snapped up by some of those maneouvring fathers, who are always on the lookout.

Victorine. I can't help it. I shall wait. Who knows? *he* might ask *me*.

Judge. Men never do now,—that custom is exploded.

Victorine. Besides, *I* believe there is such a thing as falling in love, after all.

Judge (*rising*). I tell you, love is as obsolete as a line-of-battle ship. Wives *rule* their husbands, and the memory of woman runneth not to the contrary. But do as you like. For my part, I disapprove of marriage altogether. I consider it a waste of time for any intelligent woman; but *you* will never be able to earn your salt in any decent calling, and you must either marry—or be sent to Congress.

Victorine. I don't care. *I* sha'n't ask *him*.

Judge. Just as you please,—but mark my words,—he'll be snapped up within twenty-four hours.

[*Exit* **Judge.**]

Victorine. It's a dreadful trial to a girl to have a Judge for her mamma! I don't like to go and look for Mr. Carberry, after what she said. Perhaps, if I sing something, he will hear it and come down. (*Sings.*)

> Come into the garden, George,
>   Don't sit there all night and drone,
> Come into the garden, George,
>   I am smoking here, alone,

And the smell of your Meerschaum is wafted abroad,
    And the scent of Cabañas blown.

For a breeze of evening moves,
    And the planet of Love doth rise,
I'm beginning to puff the weed we love
    In a smoky Paradise.
To puff in great clouds the tobacco we love,
    From a pipe coloured brown as your eyes.

Come into the garden, George, &c. &c.

[Enter Carberry *whilst she sings.]*

Carberry. Miss Victorine! Charmed to see you again. Do you come from the Opera?

Victorine. No, only from playing a game of billiards at the Club,—but all the jolly girls had gone to ride a steeple-chase, and there was only the marker to play with,—who's a horrid old woman,—so I came home.

Carberry. And how is your interesting reptile?

Victorine. Oh, you called him ugly, so I threw him out of the window.— Now I want to ask your advice about a profession. I have been thinking about it for a whole half-hour. I hate the law, and I think I'll be a doctor,—would you?

Carberry. A doctor! No, certainly not. What on earth should you know about doctoring?

Victorine. Oh, I know a good deal about it. I've skimmed over half a fat book on Rheumatism. And you know I've got to do something. Girls must earn their living, because there are two hundred thous . . .

Carberry (*interrupting her*). Yes, yes, I know,—but I advise you to retain your natural profession.

Victorine. What's that?

Carberry (*with a low bow*). Being a charming young lady.

Victorine. I never heard *any one* say such pretty things as you do! And, by the way, you were beginning to tell me something very interesting when that provoking train interrupted us. . . . About those friends of yours who were so much in love, you know.

Carberry. It would sound very flat at second hand.

Victorine. Yes, it is a pity you have not been in love yourself, for then you could describe it better;—but never mind,—do try. What did your friends do first?

Carberry. Well, first, I suppose they would tell the young lady she was charming.

Victoring (*aside*). Exactly what he said to me just now. (*Aloud.*) Well?—go on.

Carberry. Then they would perhaps send flowers, and go to church with her very regularly, and *say* they liked it.

Victorine. Yes,—and what next?

Carberry. Then, if they were *very* far gone, and she objected, *perhaps* they'd give up smoking,—but that was only in extreme cases.

Victorine. Oh, but is *that* all? didn't they say anything?

Carberry. Well,—yes,—if they got a good chance and could screw up their courage, perhaps they would take the young lady's hand (*taking* Victorine's) and say . . .

Victorine. Well,—what? Why do you stop? They would say . . . ?

Carberry (*tenderly*). They would say,—Dearest . . . what *lovely* weather!

[*Enter* Mrs. Badger.]

Mrs. Badger. How are you, fellows?

Carberry (*aside*). Thunder! what a bore! Just as I had almost made up my mind to go it! Why, it's that Infernal Revenue woman!

Victorine (*tartly*). If you have come to see Aunt Wolverine, she is out, Mrs. Badger.

Mrs. Badger. No, my business is with Carberry here. (*To* Carberry.) I saw you, just now, looking out of the nursery window, so I stepped in, to continue our little conversation about your income. I must trouble you to go away, Miss Victorine, as Income Returns are strictly confidential.

Victorine. Confidential? Yes, till *you* publish them in the newspaper. (*Aside.*) Provoking creature!

[*Exit* Victorine.]

Mrs. Badger. Now then! make haste,—for it's getting late, and you know you'll be taken up, if you are out after ten.

Carberry. Taken up! What for?

Mrs. Badger. New order of the Board of Alderwomen, "Any man, found absent from his home after ten o'clock at night, fined for a misdemeanour." The City Grandmothers mean to put a *stop* to men's staying out till cock-crow, and making their wives sit up for them.

Carberry. I shall go directly back to China.

Mrs. Badger. You made a large fortune out there, didn't you?

Carberry. It's the only country fit to live in,—they drown the superfluous females young!

Mrs. Badger. Come! don't shilly-shally. What's your income?

Carberry (*reluctantly*). Well, perhaps ten thousand dollars.

Mrs. Badger (*writing it down*). Married, or single?

Carberry. Oh, single, certainly.

Mrs. Badger. Age, then?

Carberry. Madam?

Mrs. Badger. Well,—age?

Carberry. Madam, I don't see what my age has to do with my income.

Mrs. Badger. Fiddle! Come, how old are you?

Carberry. Madam, permit me to say that it is none of your business.

Mrs. Badger. It is,—my very particular business, as long as you are unmarried,—"Special Income-tax for Bachelors over thirty years of age,—fifty per cent."

Carberry. *Fifty per cent!* Monstrous! I don't believe it.

Mrs. Badger. There's the printed form. (*Hands it to him.*)

Carberry. This comes of your infernal female legislating, I suppose! It's unconstitutional! It's anarchical! It's despotic! I won't submit to it!

Mrs. Badger. Large excess of women over men in the United States. Majority two hundred thousand in Massachusetts alone. Majorities are always right, you know.

Carberry. And am I to be the victim of your horrible statistic?

Mrs. Badger (*coolly*). If a man chooses to give himself the luxury of being a bachelor, he must pay for it, like other luxuries. All the men take it hard, at first, but they soon come round. So don't bother, but just tell me your age.

Carberry. Nineteen!

Mrs. Badger. Fiddle! if you don't tell the truth, I shall put you down as fifty. You're thirty-five, if you're a day. When was your birthday?

Carberry. Yesterday! I came of age.

Mrs. Badger. *Very well!*—(*Writing.*) "Thomas Carberry, Bachelor, age, fifty." It's a retrospective tax, you know,—takes in every year since you were thirty,—fifty percent on ten thousand dollars for twenty years . . . five times twenty. . . . One hundred thousand dollars, you will please hand over to the government, and I'll give you a receipt.

Carberry. Outrageous! I'm only thirty-two, I'll take my oath of it! It's an extortion,—a swindle,—an infamous swindle!

Mrs. Badger. If you are not satisfied, I'll call you sixty,—I've a right to make you any age I please.

Carberry (*getting more and more angry*). A right! And I've a right—an inalienable right—to life, liberty, and the pursuit of happiness! Are Men's Rights trampled underfoot? Is there no Antislavery sentiment left in Boston? No Society for the Abolition of Women? What are all the philanthropists about, now-a-days, I should like to know?

Mrs. Badger. It would be clearly unjust, in a Republican country, and contrary to the Spirit of the Age, if a great strong man, like you, were allowed to live in wealth and idleness, while *two hundred thousand single women* in your own State have to support themselves. If you won't marry, you must make it up to them in another way.

Carberry (*exasperated*). And do you pretend to say that fifty cents apiece is going to make up to them for not marrying me?—I never would have left China, if I'd had any conception of this! Women legislating, and robbing, and murdering!—It has no parallel in history! Draco and Robespierre were kittens, compared to them! It's enough to make George Washington turn in his grave! Madam! I . . . I . . . I wish you a good evening! (*Rushes out.*)

Mrs. Badger (*calling after him*). I'll send you the bill to-morrow.

ACT III

Drawing-room in Mr. Wigfall's house. **Carberry** *alone.*

Carberry (*pulls out a note and reads*). "Seven o'clock, . . . call here . . . important communication, . . . yours truly ever . . . Wolverine Griffin." . . . Well, that's beyond me! but I may get another look at Victorine by being here. I came home with the idea of marrying some nice pretty little wife, such as they used to have,—who would make much of me, and give me good dinners, and look pretty at the head of the table,— which is all a man wants in a wife. But they have all turned into such catamarans, that I feel discouraged . . . that is, all except Victorine. . . .

[Enter **Miss Griffin.***]*

Miss Griffin. Mr. Carberry, *how* kind! you were *not* uneasy? I *am* a little late. Excuse me,—sit down, and I'll explain. But, first, it may be proper to review the events of the past ten years.

Carberry. 'Hem. (*Looking at his watch.*) We might do five to-day, and the rest some rainy afternoon. Begin, madam; I am all attention.

Miss Griffin. You find a great change in our midst, my dear sir, on your return. Woman has taken her rightful place, and, no longer the Slave of Man, shares with you the duties and responsibilities of citizenship. A glorious change, Mr. Carberry.

Carberry. A very striking change, indeed, madam.

Miss Griffin. A *glorious* change, Mr. Carberry! The cruel Past is wiped out, with all its brutal, barbarous conventionalities, and the Female is free!

When you went abroad, my dear Mr. Carberry, she had no initiative,—positively *no* initiative. Her affinities were stifled, and her tongue was paralyzed. It was her humble part to silently await the Coming Man, who, perhaps, never came, or might better have stayed away.

Carberry. A trying position, certainly. (*Aside.*) Thunder! what a bore she is!

Miss Griffin. It was a cruel, cruel law which debarred us from the free exercise of our choice in the most important crisis of our lives. With perceptions, too, so much finer than those of Man, by which to detect the right person at once.

Carberry. Precisely. . . . But I think you spoke of wishing to see me on business?

Miss Griffin. Now, Woman, trusting to her unerring instinct, goes frankly to the man of her choice, and gives him her hand with her heart in it . . . *thus* . . . (*Offering her hand.*)

Servant (*at the door*). Miss Griffin, the Chairwoman of the Committee for the Suppression of Male Dinner-parties is down stairs,—says she *must* see you on business.

Miss Griffin. Provoking! But you sit perfectly still, and I'll be back directly.

[*Exit* **Miss Griffin.**]

Carberry (*alone*). Good Heavens! what a dreadful situation I am in! This woman is evidently going to make me an offer of marriage! What shall I do?—What can I say?—What on earth was it young ladies used to say in the good old times?—I am so upset, I can't even recollect what that pretty Fanny Slippery said to *me* in Shanghae! This is a thousand times worse than being refused one's self . . . Let me see . . . Fanny made at least a dozen excellent excuses . . . too young . . . short acquaintance . . . in-experience . . .

[*Re-enter* **Miss Griffin.**]

Miss Griffin. An unwelcome interruption, but you won't think the worse of me for putting public duty before private feeling. "I could not love thee, dear, so much, loved I not honour more." . . . Dear Mr. Carberry, you can't have mistaken me.

Carberry. Forgive me, Miss Griffin, but on so short an acquaintance . . . I assure you I never supposed . . .

Miss Griffin. Yes, it is short, as the world counts time,—but what of that, since henceforth our whole lives will be devoted to each other?

Carberry. Indeed, I never imagined that your feelings for me were more than a mere passing admiration . . .

Miss Griffin. That shows you have no comprehension of the transcendent Truthfulness of Woman. We should scorn to pay attentions to a young man, and win his timid affections, and then shy off, and mean nothing after all. Oh no, my dearest Thomas, I am deeply, terribly in earnest!

Carberry. I am most sorry, believe me, if any thoughtlessness of mine has encouraged these hopes. (*Aside.*) Thunder! how hard she is to refuse! (*Aloud.*) I have no idea of marrying, I assure you.

Miss Griffin. And why not? Why bloom a single rose?

Carberry. Oh, I'm too young!

Miss Griffin. I will wait.

Carberry. I am so ignorant, so inexperienced . . . I am not worthy of you. Forget me, I entreat you, and be happy with another!

Miss Griffin. Never! My happiness depends on your consent! I'll blow my brains out if you refuse! (*Goes down on her knees.*) I will *not* live without you! (*Seizing his hand.*)

Carberry (*trying to get away*). Don't,—don't,—my dear Miss Griffin! Get up, I beg of you! you distress me exceedingly!

Miss Griffin. No! I'll take root at your feet! I'll never get up till you give in.

Carberry (*in despair*). Well, well . . . I hear some one coming,—*only* get up, and I'll see about it,—I'll refer you to my father. . . .

[Enter Judge.*]*

Miss Griffin (rising). My dear sister, congratulate me; Mr. Carberry has promised to be mine!

Judge (*aside*). Just as I said! he is snapped up. *Quam celeriter!* (*Aloud.*) Wolverine, there are higher aims than marriage for the Women of '76,—and, from my own experience, I think a woman's career is hampered by a husband. But try it, if you like. Do you wish to be married immediately?

Miss Griffin. I'm all ready.

Judge. Then I will receive your declaration, which is all that is necessary to constitute a legal marriage.

Miss Griffin. You begin, dear Carberry.

Carberry. Oh, impossible! quite impossible! My conscience would never permit such a thing. I shouldn't feel married at all, unless it were in church.

Judge. Sir, religion has been reconstructed,—and such superstitions are out of date.

Miss Griffin. Yes, I wonder you should cling to those old-fashioned prejudices. However, if you really prefer it, we can send for the clergywoman. The Rev. Arabella Parsons lives next door.

Carberry. Oh no, you mustn't hurry me, indeed. I . . . I . . . (*Struck by an idea.*) I want at least three months to send to Paris for my trousseau. I couldn't think of having my wedding coat made in Boston. I won't be married at all unless I can have a proper wedding.

Judge (*indignantly*). A proper wedding! Sir, I would have you to know that a contract made before me is eminently a proper wedding. A simple declaration of your intention is all-sufficient in the eye of the law. In fact, I believe you have both already said so, and I shall proceed to make out the necessary certificate, without loss of time. (*Takes a pen.*)

Carberry (*seizing her arm*). No! I'll swear . . . I mean, I'm sure I didn't . . . you misunderstood me. I beg you, ladies, to give me a little time to recover myself. . . . This . . . happiness . . . has been so unexpected, I feel quite overcome. . . . I will give you an answer by and by . . . but now I have a severe headache . . . brought on by nervous excitement. . . .

Miss Griffin. Nervous excitement! Shaker Extract of Valerian is what you want. Lie down on the sofa, and put your feet up, and I'll bring you some in a quarter of an hour. (*Making* **Carberry** *lie down.*)

Judge (*looking at him with disdain*). Men are not like us, Wolverine. They have *no* strength of mind.

[*Exeunt* **Miss Griffin** *and* **Judge.** **Carberry** *covers his face with his handkerchief and groans.*]

Enter **Mrs. Badger,** *who goes to the sofa and peeps under the handkerchief.*

Mrs. Badger. Ah, Carberry! I thought I should find you here . . . about that little matter of the hundred thousand dollars, you know.

Carberry. Oh, *go away*—I'm ill . . . I'm very busy . . . I'm asleep . . . I can't attend to you now.

Mrs. Badger. I always like to be accommodating, and I've thought of a way to settle it.

Carberry (*reviving a little*). What?

Mrs. Badger. You must marry at once.

Carberry. I won't,—*I won't*,—I WON'T!

Mrs. Badger. That will exempt you from the Bachelor's Tax in future,—but the retrospective hundred thousand dollars will remain to be paid, *unless you marry the right person,—and there is* BUT ONE.

Carberry. Who? in the name of thunder!

Mrs. Badger. ME.

Carberry. You! You're married already! It says "Mrs." on your confounded card. . . . (*Pulling it out of his pocket.*) Where is Mr. Badger? I appeal to Mr. Badger for protection!

Mrs. Badger. Fiddle! Mr. Badger has been dead and buried these seven years.

Carberry. A widow! I never thought of that. (*Sinks into a chair.*)

Mrs. Badger. You see, if you marry me, I'll let you off paying the money to the government, and we'll spend it together.

Carberry. Venal and corrupt official!—is that the way you betray your trust! I'll denounce you! I'll publish it in all the papers! I'll have you turned out!

Mrs. Badger. Pooh! You wouldn't be so silly,—for then you'd have to pay up . . . twenty years from thirty to fifty . . .

Carberry (*furious*). I tell you I'm not fifty . . . I'll call the police! . . . Miss Griffin! Miss Griffin!

(**Miss Griffin** *running in.*)

Miss Griffin. What's the matter?

Carberry. Take away this assessor! She's offering herself to me!

Miss Griffin. You, Badger? How audacious! He's engaged to *me*.

Mrs. Badger. He has changed his mind,—he prefers *me*.

Miss Griffin. Badger, I'm ashamed of you! Annoying a poor young man in this way! What would become of him if he hadn't me to protect him?

Mrs. Badger. Nonsense! we were making a little business arrangement . . . you only bother us,—you haven't any head for business, Griffin,—you're too sentimental,—you'd better go away.

Miss Griffin. Yes, and it's precisely that delicacy of sentiment that Mr. Carberry admires in me. I hope I do my duty as a woman and a citizen, though I *haven't* sunk into a mere business hack, without a thought beyond money-making, like *you*, Mrs. Badger.

Mrs. Badger. Fiddle! Why don't you speak up, Carberry?—what are you thinking of?

Carberry. Madam, I was thinking of the Kilkenny cats, and the admirable end of their quarrel!

Miss Griffin. Barbara Badger, if you don't go directly away, I'll impeach you at the next Town Meeting for embezzlement of the public money.

Mrs. Badger. Well, I can't stop now to discuss it. I'll see you by and by. . . . But you haven't a chance, Griffin,—there are one hundred thousand arguments against you.—*You'll see* which way he makes up his mind!

[*Exit* **Mrs. Badger**, *nodding significantly.*]

Miss Griffin. You see, my dear Mr. Carberry, that it is absolutely necessary we should be married immediately, or you would be exposed to this sort of thing every day. I think we had better say to-morrow,—and, as you seem to fancy a showy wedding, I'll send word directly to the other Selectwomen, and the School Committee, to come in from the Centre, by the ten o'clock train, and walk in procession with us to the church.

[*Exit* **Griffin.**]

Carberry. There is something fatally attractive about me!

[Enter Victorine.*]*

Victorine. Here's a note for you, Mr. Carberry,—from a lady. (*Handing it to him.*)

Carberry. I won't read it! it may be another. (*Tears it up.*)

Victorine. Another what? It's an invitation to Mrs. Butterfly's ball. I'm going,—I'll take you. . . . What's the matter? Are you ill?

Carberry. Miss Wigfall, I'm on the brink of an abyss,—two abysses in fact. Your aunt intends to marry me.

Victorine. My aunt! You're joking! Why, she's a great deal older than you! It isn't possible that you . . . care for my aunt, Mr. Carberry?

[Enter Miss Griffin, *who listens unperceived.]*

Carberry. Care for her? I'm afraid of her! I am being dragged like a lamb to the altar! I said all I could,—I repeated every excuse that I remembered a young lady made . . . I mean, that I thought a young lady *would* make in such a case, but it was no use!—no use!

Victorine (*sighing*). Oh! how I wish I had minded mamma!

Carberry. I arrived here yesterday, so innocent and so happy,—and I find everything upset and topsy-turvy, with all this voting, and assessing, and judging,—and dreadful old maids swooping down upon one, like hawks,—and widows, like roaring lions! . . . You alone seem to me an innocent dove, a thousand times more charming by contrast . . . and . . . I've got to marry somebody . . . I mean, I love you passionately . . . only I shouldn't have told you so for months, under happier circumstances . . . I'm a shy man naturally . . . but now I'm goaded to desperation!

Victorine (*crying*). O! Mr. Carberry, why didn't you say so sooner?

Carberry. *Sooner!* I hadn't a chance! I'm a slow man naturally,—I'm not used to these railway methods,—and how could I ever have dreamed that your terrible aunt would mark me for her own!

(*Here* Miss Griffin, *who has heard all this, darts out again unperceived.*)

Victorine. Well (*Sob*), perhaps it's all for the best! . . . I'll try and take an interest in (*Sob*) politics . . . and forget it . . . but (*Sob*) I shall always love you . . . *as an uncle!*

[Re-enter Miss Griffin, *with two pistols.]*

Miss Griffin (*to* Carberry). Traitor! which will you have? *[*Victorine *shrieks.]*

Carberry. Neither, thank you.

Miss Griffin. No trifling, traitor! I have heard all, and I demand satisfaction.

Victorine. O aunt! please don't be angry,—I'll give him up!

Miss Griffin. There is but one reparation you can make me, Mr. Carberry, —take your choice.

Carberry. They have got over being afraid of pistols, too!

Victorine. O aunt! you shall have him indeed,—only *don't* hurt him.

Miss Griffin. No compromise with traitors! (*Sternly.*) Mr. Carberry, are you a gentleman?

Carberry. No! Are you?

Miss Griffin. Man! Would you rather be hanged? Don't you know Breach of Promise is a capital crime?

Victorine (*wringing her hands*). And the Governess will never pardon you!

Carberry. Well, if you *will* have it so, I'll name a friend to arrange the place of meeting. (*Aside.*) I'll take the first train to New York.

Miss Griffin. Mr. Carberry, I *never* lose time. Seconds and intermediaries would only cause delay. This quarrel is between you and me, and we will settle it this minute, in this apartment, without any more words. Victorine, have the goodness to walk twelve paces, taking as long steps as you can.

Victorine. I sha'n't! I won't! I'll call papa!

[Exit, crying "Papa! Papa!"]

(**Miss Griffin** *measures the distance herself, thrusts one of the pistols into* **Carberry's** *hand, and takes her place*).

Carberry. I wish I was back in Shanghae!

Miss Griffin. Now, are you ready? When I say *"three.".* . . . (**Carberry** *covers her with his pistol.*) Mr. Carberry! put that weapon down, sir! . . . When I say *"three"* . . .

Carberry. By Jove! I'll kill her! (*Covers her again.*)

Miss Griffin. *Will* you observe the rules, sir? . . . When I say *"three,"* we fire. . . . One,—Two—

[Enter **Judge,** *followed by* **Victorine,** *and* **Mr. Wigfall** *carrying the baby.]*

Judge. I arrest you both, in the name of the Commonwealth of Massachusetts!

Miss Griffin. Susan, why couldn't you have stayed away five minutes longer!

Judge. Mr. Wigfall, I appoint you Special Constable to secure these persons, discovered *flagrante delicto*, in the very act of breaking the peace of the Commonwealth.

(**Mr. Wigfall** *puts the baby down on the sofa, and takes hold of* **Griffin.**)

Carberry. I thank your Honour from the bottom of my heart.

Judge. Prisoners: It is my painful duty to remind you both, that, Whereas, the trial by wager of battle has long been obsolete, you have incurred a penalty of twenty years in the State's Prison, for duelling in Massachusetts. Where-fore, as guardian of the public morals, it also becomes my painful duty to send at once for the proper officers of justice, that you may be tried, and convicted for that offence.

Carberry. Nothing can hurt me now.

Carberry *and* **Griffin** *stand Right and Left with folded arms.*

Victorine. O mamma! forgive them this once! Punish aunt, if you will—

Carberry. Yes, punish aunt!

Victorine. It was all her fault, . . . but don't put Mr. Carberry in prison!

Judge. Child! he has violated the law.

Victorine (*imploringly*). But no one will ever know, if we don't tell. Don't say anything about it, that's a dear mamma.

Judge. And my own conscience, Victorine? Forbear, I am incorruptible.

Mr. Wigfall. That's right, my dear,—Smite 'em with the Sword of Justice!

Victorine (*aside to* **Mr. Wigfall**). O papa, how can you be so unkind? I thought you were on our side.

Mr. Wigfall (*aside to* **Victorine**). Be quiet, child. I haven't lived twenty years with your mother without finding out that the way to manage her is to give her her head.

Judge. Distressing as it is to my personal feelings, the Majesty of the Law must be vindicated.

Mr. Wigfall. Bully for you! *Fiat Justitia!* Don't let 'em off.

Judge. Mr. Wigfall! in this momentous crisis, I consider your remarks in the worst possible taste.

Mr. Wigfall. Why, I only said "*Fiat Justitia.*" Doesn't the learned Judge know what that means?

Judge. Silence, Constable!—As I said before, I stand here clothed in the Panoply of Justice, resolved to steel my heart, and execute the Law,—cost what it may.

Mr. Wigfall. Off with their heads! *Ruat Coelum!* Be a Spartan Mother! Be a Roman Father!

Judge. Silence!

Mr. Wigfall. Remember Brutus! Three cheers for the Boston Brutus! Hip, Hip . . .

Judge (*exploding*). Mr. Wigfall, you are perfectly unbearable! I don't care one pin for Brutus, and I *will* let them off,—just to spite you,—and to show you that I am independent of your sneers and innuendoes! Wolverine, I am thoroughly ashamed of *you*,—but this once I will overlook it, on condition that you never have anything more to do with any man—or men—whomsoever. Victorine, if you laugh, I'll commit you for contempt.

Victorine. O you dear little mamma! I knew you'd stop being an upright Judge, and turn out my own kind little mamma at last. (*Kisses her enthusiastically.* **Judge** *waves her off.*)

Judge. As for you, Mr. Carberry, I request you to inform the Court, whether you sincerely wish to marry my daughter.

Carberry. Most assuredly I do,—I declare it before your Honour with the greatest pleasure.—Is that enough? Are we married now? Are you my mother-*in-law?*

Judge. No. You may have your "proper wedding," and be six months about it.—Here, Victorine, take him, he's yours. Be firm with him from the first, and perhaps you may be happy. When you want a divorce, petition me, while you are yet in my jurisdiction. But don't delay too long, for at no distant day, the nation will rise, like One Woman, to turn out the man, Chase, and you will see ME Chief Justice of the Supreme Court of the United States.

[Retires majestically, followed by **Mr. Wigfall,** *to the back of the stage.]*

Carberry (*to* **Miss Griffin**). Madam, I hope you will forget the past, and believe me, I shall always regard you as a friend.

Miss Griffin. Man, don't speak to me.

Enter **Mrs. Badger.**

Mrs. Badger. There, Griffin, I told you so! You see he has made up his mind—

Carberry. Yes, to marry Miss Wigfall. So you and your tax may go to Jericho! (*Aside to* **Mrs. Badger.**) If you tell of me, I'll tell of you, but (*Aloud*), believe me, madam, I shall always regard you as a friend.

Mrs. Badger. Griffin, we're both jilted! Shall we go and drown ourselves in the Chestnut Hill Reservoir?

Miss Griffin. *For a Man?* No, Badger,—we are Stateswomen and Patriots. Let us rather renounce mankind and live for ourselves,—marching in the Van of the great Feminine Army of Progress, onward and upward forever! And when our mission is accomplished, and Woman of every colour, size, and shape reigns supreme from Pole to Pole,—*then* shall the names of Griffin and Badger be transmitted to future generations, as great and glorious examples of the new SPIRIT OF SEVENTY-SIX!

Curtain falls.

JUDGE'S CHARGE.

Addressed to the Audience.

Mrs. Forewoman, and Ladies of the Jury: You have now heard the facts, and it remains for you to find accordingly, divesting yourselves, as far as possible, of all individual bias, either for or against the defendant,— MAN,—and this Court will protect you in the performance of your duty.—The proper officer will now conduct the Jury to their room, and provide them with suitable refreshment.

Lords of Creation
Woman Suffrage Drama
In Three Acts

ELLA CHEEVER THAYER

Boston: Geo. M. Baker & Co., Publishers. 1883.

CHARACTERS _____

Dr. Endicott, a true Man.
Mr. Grovenor, the Head of his Family.
Eugene, his Son, taking Life easy.
Harold Doughlass, with more Money than Brains.
Jim, a Coachman, much in Love.
Kate Grovenor, who has a Mind of her own.
Lizzie, a young Seamstress.
Mrs. Grovenor, Mr. Grovenor's lesser half.
Alice Grovenor, anxious for a rich Husband.
Jennie, a Chambermaid who believes in Woman's Rights.

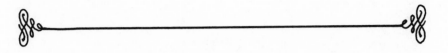

COSTUMES

Kate. Act I., handsome evening dress. Act II., house dress. Act III., black silk.

Alice. Act I., elegant evening dress. Act II., house dress. Act III., street costume, hat, etc.

Mrs. Grovenor. Act I., evening dress. Act II., house dress. Act III., wrapper.

Lizzie. Act I., plain street costume. Act II. and Act III., plain house dress.

Jennie. Pretty light calico and apron.

Dr. Endicott. Business suit.

Mr. Grovenor. Same.

Eugene. Elegant suit, rather flashy. Plain suit in Act III.

Doughlass. Elegant suit, not quite so loud as Eugene.

Jim. Handsome livery.

ACT I

SCENE

Elegant Drawing-Room. Door C., *Sofa,* R., *Chairs, etc. Table* L. C.

(Enter **Jennie**, C., *holding small bouquet in her hand.)*

Jennie. Here is Mr. Eugene's bouquet, and now where is Mr. Eugene? Not here, of course, and I must be running all over the house to find him. All a body has to do is to wait on him, that is what *he* thinks! For he is a lord of creation, he is! And he must have his buttonhole bouquet, and his hair parted in the middle, and his mustache waxed, and everybody must bow down and worship him! But after all, he isn't as bad as his father. Oh! isn't *he* just awful! Dear me, what a terrible thing it must be to think yourself so superior, all on account of your sex!

Jim (*looking in*, C.). May I come in?

Jennie (*looking over shoulder*). Oh! You are here, are you? I might have known you would be!

Jim (*coming down* R. *awkwardly*). Yes, because I always come where you are, if I can.

Jennie (L.). Too bad, ain't it, I don't appreciate it any better? You haven't seen Mr. Eugene anywhere, have you?

Jim. Seen him? No! That is, not since two o'clock this morning, when I helped him up-stairs, and he called me his darling Jim.

Jennie. How awful!

Jim. I guess you would have said so if he had hugged you the way he did me!

Jennie (*coquettishly*). Well, I don't know; perhaps that might not have been quite so awful either!

Jim (*walking about angrily*). Just let me catch him hugging you, or any other fellow, that's all.

Jennie. Dear me! And what business would that be of yours, I should like to know? This is a free country, sir, and I am a single woman, and hugging isn't a crime, and no man shall dictate to me. So! (*Stamps foot.*)

Jim. Who *is* dictating? How you do fly off! You know, Jennie, I think all the world of you!

Jennie. Yes, I dare say! Men always say so *before* they get married. I suppose that is what our master said to our mistress once, and now see the way he orders her about! And you would like to do the same by me, wouldn't you? But I am altogether too smart for that, sir!

Jim. But good gracious, Jennie, how you do fly off! Never thought of such a thing in my life!

Jennie. Oh, pshaw! Men are all alike! Now I will bet a pound of candy that you think you know more than I do, just because you are a man!

Jim. Well—I—of course about some things.

Jennie. Some things! just tell me one.

Jim. Well—I—you see it would take me some time to think.

Jennie. Yes, I guess it would! Well, I have my eyes open, and I haven't lived in this house going on a year for nothing, and seen the airs master and Mr. Eugene give themselves! Over Miss Kate, too, who knows more than both of them put together.

Jim (*gesticulating*). But, Jennie, a woman isn't *supposed* to know as much as a man. It isn't natural, you see! But a man likes them all the better for it, and he likes to be looked up to, you know.

Jennie (*drawing herself up*). You don't say so! How sorry I am I can't make you happy in that way. But the fact is, I'd rather have a man who likes me for what I know and not for what I *don't* know! So (*courtesying*) I'll leave you to find a woman with less brains than you have—*if you can.* (*Exit* c.)

Jim (*following*). Jennie! here, Jennie! She has gone and she is mad! How she does fly off! And oh, how I do love her! Good gracious, how I do love her! (*Comes down* c.) Now why on earth should she get mad about a little thing like that! Does she want me to say every man is a natural-born fool? Hang me if I don't believe they are, where a woman is concerned! Here for the last six months I've been a perfect slave to her. And all I get for it is to be told I belong to a tyrannical sex! But I won't stand it. No, I won't! (*Going. Stops at door* c.) I am afraid I can't help it, though. Oh, what an awful thing it is to be in love! And between me and the furniture, I do believe if a woman *is* the weaker sex, she always gets the best of a man somehow. (*Exit,* L. 2 E.)

(*Enter* **Mrs. Grovenor** *and* **Alice,** c.)

Mrs. Grovenor (*as she enters*). Well, no, my dear, Dr. Endicott is not a particularly good match. But Mr. Doughlass has an immense fortune, you know.

Alice (*sits* R. *on sofa*). Yes, But Mr. Doughlass is *such* a bore, ma.

Mrs. Grovenor (*sitting,* L.). Ah, well, a bore is better than a tyrant, child.

Alice. But there must be some men who are neither.

Mrs. Grovenor. That kind are very hard to find, and, by some strange chance, are usually poor in purse when found. Witness Dr. Endicott, for instance.

Alice. It would never do to marry a poor man.

Mrs. Grovenor. Do! With your extravagant tastes it would be madness. I have no doubt Mr. Doughlass would make you a very good husband, and it is time you were thinking of settling in life now.

Alice. But Kate is older than I am.

Mrs. Grovenor. I fear poor Kate will surely be an old maid, in spite of all I can do. Alas! There has never been one in the family yet, and to think one of *my* daughters should be first to bear that stigma is terrible to contemplate.

Alice. Isn't it strange that she *never* tries to be attractive to gentlemen?

Mrs. Grovenor. And she actually wants to vote. I am sure I cannot conceive where she obtained such thoughts. Certainly not from *me*.

(*Enter* **Kate**, c.).

Kate (*stopping at door*). You are mistaken, mother.

Mrs. Grovenor (*rising quickly*). *You* here, Kate? How you do startle one! What do you mean by that remark?

Kate (*coming down* c.). I mean, mother, that I first conceived my horror of occupying a dependent position from seeing how you were obliged to coax and manage, to bear cross looks and sarcastic remarks, whenever you asked father for money.

Mrs. Grovenor (*looking around alarmed*). Hush! Do not speak so loud; your father is in the library, and might hear.

Kate. I am not afraid to say to any one that I had rather earn *my* money than have it doled out to me as a favor grudgingly bestowed. (*Sits at table* L. C.)

Mrs. Grovenor (*sitting* L.). I will admit, Kate, that it has always been very hard to obtain money from your father; and now listen to reason. You are aware that we spend every cent of our income in order to keep up our style of living. The future of you two girls cannot be provided for by us, so there is but one thing for you to do,—to marry.

Kate. Are you sure that is the only thing?

Mrs. Grovenor Why, what else is there—for a woman?

Kate. Many women are independent by the fruit of their own exertions. Why could not I be?

Mrs. Grovenor (*with slight scream*). You quite shock me. Do you not know you would lose your position in society by such a course?

Kate. I am willing to lose it, if to keep it I must barter my own self-respect.

Mrs. Grovenor. Barter your self-respect! What *do* you mean?

Kate. I mean sell myself for the sake of being supported in idleness.

Alice (*languidly fanning herself*). The idea of a lady actually wanting to work!

Kate. *I* cannot live on husks, Alice.

Mrs. Grovenor. I cannot understand why you should be so opposed to marriage.

Kate. You mistake me very much if you think I am. Oh, no! I know well that the deepest and truest happiness in life is in love and marriage. It is against making marriage a trade, degrading it to a means of support, that I protest, with all my soul! (*Rises.*)

Alice. A trade! How absurd! Would you marry a poor man for love?

Kate. Without an instant's hesitation, and I would never be a dependent burden on him! Oh! mother, can you not see how much of the misery in the world is caused by the way girls are educated, in helpless dependence, often obliged to sell themselves to the first man who offers, because they cannot support themselves? Do not condemn me to such a fate. Give me a chance to be independent of all such considerations in my choice of a husband.

Mrs. Grovenor. (*with impatient gesture*). Nonsense. You are crazy.

Alice. The best thing you can do, Kate, is to set your cap for Dr. Endicott.

Kate. I am very much mistaken in Dr. Endicott if he would deign to notice a woman who had stooped to set her cap. (*Sits* L. C.)

Mrs. Grovenor (*sighing*). I am sure I do not know what will become of you with such ideas.

Mr. Grovenor (*outside*). Where is Eugene? I want him.

Mrs. Grovenor. Hush! here comes your father.

Alice (*starting up from reclining position*). Oh, mother! *do* try to get some money of him for a new ball dress. Mine are shameful!

Mrs. Grovenor. I will do my best, but it is hard work. I hope you may never know how hard when you have a husband of your own.

(*Enter* **Mr. Grovenor,** C., *his hands full of papers, bills, etc.*)

Mr. Grovenor (*very crossly*). Where is that boy? What do these bills mean? The expenses of this house *must* be cut down. Do you think I am made of money, Mrs. Grovenor?

Mrs. Grovenor (*timidly*). I am very sorry. I am sure I do the best I can.

Mr. Grovenor (*sitting* R. *of table and looking over bills*). I think you would find a way to be more economical if you had to earn the money you spent. It's a pity you women did not have to do it once in a while, and then you would know how good it was.

Kate (*leaning on table, earnestly*). That is just what I wish to do, father. Give me the chance and I will relieve you of the burden of my support.

Mr. Grovenor (*staring at his own papers*). You would do fine things I dare say. I do not believe you know exactly what you are talking about, but then a woman never does. Now, for instance, how long do you suppose it would take you to earn that dress you have on, at women's average wages?

Kate. I could wear a cheaper dress, if need be. I am aware that men, in whose hands now rests the power, show their boasted "chivalry" to the so-called "weaker sex" by paying her half they pay a man for the same work.

Mr. Grovenor (*dropping papers angrily*). What confounded folly you talk! If a woman did her work as well as a man she would get the same wages; but she does not. She isn't thinking of her work. When she is young she is thinking of getting married, when she is old she is mad because she can't.

Kate (*with dignity*). Pardon me, father, but I think it is you who are talking folly.

Mr. Grovenor. Humph! I suppose you would like to vote?

Kate. I see no reason why I should not.

Mr. Grovenor (*rises and looks her over, then looks at* **Mrs. Governor.**) What kind of sentiments have you instilled into your eldest daughter, Mrs. Grovenor?

Mrs. Grovenor. *I*, Mr. Grovenor! Do Kate's remarks sound like *my* teachings?

Mr. Grovenor (c.). Well, no, I will acquit you of ever having any tendencies towards doing anything to bring money into the family, Mrs. Grovenor.

Kate. Father, I have some artistic talent, I think; why may I not study and become an artist? All I ask is that I may not be a burden on you or any one (*going to him*). You will not refuse me this, father.

Mr. Grovenor (*putting arm around her*). There, there, Kate, you are a good girl, and if you was only a boy I would make something of you; but as you are not, the best advice I can give you is to go and marry some good man and forget these foolish ideas of yours about voting and all that stuff. (*Going, stops.*) Mrs. Grovenor, send that boy to me at once, do you hear? Here is a bill of his for champagne that is something frightful! He certainly has inherited your extravagant taste. (*Exit,* c.)

Mrs. Grovenor (*rising*). There, Kate, you heard what your father said. Perhaps you will take his advice if you will not take mine. Do you think you can find Eugene?

Kate. I will try. (*Aside.*) They all discourage me, but I will not be daunted! (*Exit,* L. 2 E.)

Alice. You did not say a word about my dress, mother.

Mrs. Grovenor. But he is in such a bad humor! However, I will go now and see what can be done. Talk about earning money! I am sure I doubly earn every cent I get from Mr. Grovenor, and always have. (*Exit,* c.)

Alice. I believe father grows more stingy every day. Oh, dear! I suppose I shall have to marry that dreadful Mr. Doughlass. What a strange girl Kate is! And yet I do not know, I am not sure but what it would be nice to be independent.

(*Enter* **Jennie,** c.)

Jennie (*coming down and handing card*). Are you at home, Miss Alice?

Alice (*takes it and reads*). "Harold Doughlass." Yes (*sighs*), I suppose so.

Jennie. Yes 'm. (*Aside.*) He is one of the superior sex, and he don't know so much as an idiot! (*Exit,* c.)

Alice. Now, were I independent, I should certainly have said I was engaged and I could not see him. How shall I be able to endure him for a lifetime, when he bores me so for an hour?

(*Enter* **Doughlass,** *eye-glass, cane, etc.,* c.)

Alice (*rising*). I am delighted to see you, Mr. Doughlass!

Doughlass (c.). Aw! thank you. You are looking more charwming than ever this evening, Miss Alice.

Alice (*aside*). He always says that. (*Aloud.*) You quite flatter me. Please be seated. (*Offers chair.*)

Doughlass (*sitting,* L.). Aw! this has been a fine day, hasn't it, now?

Alice (*sitting,* R.). Very fine indeed.

Doughlass. I hope we shall have as fine to-mowow.

Alice. I hope so, truly.

Doughlass. But I weally feaw we shall have wain.

Alice. You quite alarm me.

Doughlass. Aw! I do not like wain.

Alice. Nor I. (*Aside, yawning.*) Can't he talk about something besides the weather?

Doughlass (*adjusting eye-glasses*). I hope your pawents are both well!

Alice. Quite well, thank you.

Doughlass. I need not ask if you are, for you look more chawming than usual!

Alice. Ah! you are very complimentary. (*Aside.*) How many times is he going to say that?

Doughlass. Aw! yes, you are always chawming to me, you know! (*Aside.*) A fellow must flatter these girls. That's the secret!

Alice. You quite confuse me. (*Aside.*) Is he going to propose?

Doughlass. Aw! I—aw—I twust you do not dislike to be confused; because I think you chawming, you know? (*Goes and sits beside her on sofa.*)

Alice. Of course I am only too pleased to be so favored.

Doughlass. Yes—aw—and some day I shall tell you just how chawming I do think you. You are so different from your sister, you know. Why—aw— but weally a fellow is quite afwaid of her.

Alice. Afraid? What, you afraid of a lady?

Doughlass. Well, not—not exactly afwaid, of course, but you see—aw—I never know what to say to her. We fellows do not like these—aw—strong- minded ladies, you know. We like these—aw—gentle, clinging, soft girls, that do not know so much, you know, of whom you, Miss Alice, are such a chawming type!

Alice (*rising*). Indeed. Thanks for the implied compliment to my intellect, sir! (*Crosses to* C.)

Doughlass. Eh? (*Aside.*) What the deuce did I say to put her out like that? (*Aloud.*) I mean that you are vewy chawming, the style of girl we fellows pwefer, you know. (*Rises and bows low.*)

Alice (*aside*). It will not do to get angry with him yet. But if I marry him I'll let him know whether I have any brains or not! (*Aloud.*) Indeed, Mr. Doughlass? But really, I do not think Kate so very formidable. Ah! here she comes now. (*Goes to* R. C.)

Doughlass. I'm sorry—aw—to have our *tête-à-tête* interrupted, and I am sure I do not know what to say to her, nevaw do, you know!

Enter **Kate**, L. 2 E., *and bows to* **Doughlass** *coldly.*

Doughlass (*aside*). She looks at a fellow in a way that fweezes him all over. Aw—I'll flattaw her. (*Aloud.*) Aw—you are looking as chawming as usual, Miss Grovenor.

Kate. I am very glad if you have been so fortunate as to discover the fact.

Doughlass (*aside*). That always does please them, to be sure.

(*Enter* **Eugene**, L. 2 E.)

Eugene (*going to* C.) Well, Kittie, here I am; now where is the governor, and what's the row? Ah, Harold, my boy, how are you? Where were you last night? Jolly old time the boys had. But champagne does make a fellow feel like the deuce the next day.

Kate (L.). Is it worth while to drink it, then?

Eugene. Oh! come now! don't preach. Confound it, a woman is always preaching. If they had their way a fellow would have no fun at all, eh, Harold?

Doughlass. No—aw—that is, the ladies think so much of us, they want to make us saints, you know.

Eugene. Can't be done, though, eh? What is the use of living if a man can't have a good time? (*Sings.*) By Jove, I am glad I wasn't born a woman. They take things too seriously altogether. But they look up to us, for all their preaching, eh, Harold?

Doughlass (R.). To be sure—aw.

Kate. That must require quite a stretch of the imagination sometimes.

Eugene. Hope that isn't personal, Kittie. Never mind, you will be proud of me some time, only a fellow must have his fling, you know. Now I must go and get my dose from the governor. By by, Harold, see you again. (*Exit,* C.)

Kate. Poor Eugene.

Doughlass. I beg pardon. (*Aside.*) What the deuce ails her now? (*Aloud.*) Poor Eugene? Why, he is the liveliest fellaw I know. The boys nevaw think of having a champagne supper without Eugene, you know.

Kate. I am sorry if my brother is sought only for the purpose of gracing champagne suppers and disgracing himself.

Doughlass. Aw—weally now, weally, aren't you a little too severe.

Alice (C.). Of course she is. A young man must sow his wild oats.

Kate (L.). But I believe a young lady is not allowed that privilege. What is wrong for one must be for the other?

Alice. You shock me, Kate.

Doughlass. Aw—weally now, 'pon my honor, that is such a strange wemark, Miss Grovenor; a lady is of course above such things.

Kate. Then in that respect, at least, she must be superior to a man. I am glad to hear you acknowledge even so little.

Doughlass. Aw—now—aw—you quite confuse me. (*Aside.*) I must go wight away; never could stand these strong-minded ladies. (*Aloud.*) Aw—I—I never argue with a lady, you know. But I am afwaid I shall have to tear myself away, as I have a very particular engagement.

Alice. I am so sorry! But we shall see you again soon?

Doughlass. Aw—vewy soon—aw—I should only be too happy to wemain forever in your chawming pwesence. (*Kisses her hand, bows to* **Kate,** *and exit,* C.)

Alice. Well, you have driven him away. It will be very convenient to have you around *after* he and I are married, but previously the experiment is too dangerous, and I shall have to ask you to be kind enough to keep your strange ideas exclusively for our family circle. (*Exit,* L. 2 E.)

Kate. Strange ideas! Is it so strange to long to be independent? Is it strange to shrink from being a burden on an already over-burdened father, or dependent upon the whims of some unloved husband? Is it strange to wish to exercise the talents and energy God has given you instead of allowing them to rust out in darkness? Does the fact of my being a woman make me content to drift along aimlessly, in a stream that leads nowhere? No! a thousand times, no!

(*Enter* **Jennie,** C.)

Jennie. Dr. Endicott, miss.

Kate. Please ask him in.

Jennie. Yes'm. (*Aside.*) *He* is a man what *is* a man. (*Exit,* C.)

Kate. I wonder does he, too, think me strange?

(*Enter* **Dr. Endicott,** C.)

Dr. Endicott (*coming down* L.). At last I am with you once more, where I should have been long ago had not duty called me elsewhere.

Kate. I am delighted to welcome you. Father was saying yesterday he wished to see you.

Dr. Endicott. Oh, yes, there is a little business matter between us. And what have you been doing since I was last here?

Kate. Oh, nothing.

Dr. Endicott. Nothing? Really nothing?

Kate. Oh, I have embroidered a little, painted a little, and practised music a little. But it all amounted to—as I said—nothing.

Dr. Endicott. It served to pass away the time pleasantly, at least.

Kate. Yes. But is that what we are living for, to pass away time?

Dr. Endicott. You are right. Such a life is not suited to a woman of your temperament.

Kate. But what can I do? Father and mother object to my doing anything that is real. Because I seek some aim in life, because I seek an independent position, they call me unwomanly and strange.

Dr. Endicott. Is it indeed so? Alas that these old prejudices of a by-gone age should trammel a woman now!

Kate. I just frightened Mr. Doughlass away with my strange ideas.

Dr. Endicott (*laughing*). Poor Harold! But you cannot frighten *me* away, Miss Grovenor. It is just this free, untrammelled, independent woman we need in the world now.

Kate (c.). I can feel now that I have one friend who knows and sympathizes with me.

Dr. Endicott (*going towards her*). And who honors you above all women. Kate, may I add that this woman I have described is the woman I want at my fireside for my companion, friend, and my wife? There is one woman who is all I ask, one woman whom I love, but I dare not even hope for her favor. (*Enter* **Eugene**, c.) That woman, Kate, is—(*Takes her hand.*)

Eugene (*coming down* c. *between them*). That's right, doctor, shake hands with her, but after that keep at a discreet distance, for she hates men, you know. Wants to vote and smoke cigars, and wear bloomers and all that sort of thing, you know.

Kate (R.). Eugene! I am ashamed of you.

Eugene. Ah, never mind me, sis. The doctor won't take too much stock in what I say, will you, doctor. And as for you, Kit, you will get over all those notions of yours some day and acknowledge that we men are capable of taking care of the nation, eh, doctor?

Dr. Endicott (L.). Such very excellent care as we take of it!

Kate. And such pains as you take to elect none but honest men to office!

Eugene. Ha! ha! that isn't a bad one for you, sis, it's a pity you are a woman, for you would have been a smart man and no mistake. But what the deuce of a temper the governor is in! Making such a fuss over a little bill for our champagne supper last night as I never heard.

Kate. I wish you would let champagne alone, Eugene.

Eugene. Now don't preach. Say, can't you coax some money out of him some way? You women know how to do that sort of thing.

Kate. I fear I am deficient in that feature of our sex.

Eugene. Oh, hang it! but I must have the money some way.

(*Enter* **Lizzie**, c. *Looks at* **Kate**.)

Lizzie. Excuse me, but I was told I should find Mrs. Grovenor here. Are you the lady?

Eugene (*aside*). By Jove, Lizzie, and here! (*Goes to* L. *of* **Dr. Endicott**.)

Kate. Please come in and be seated. I will call mother.

Lizzie (*entering and going down* R.). I believe she advertised for a seamstress, and I—(*Looks at the gentlemen, screams, and sinks into chair,* R. C. **Dr. Endicott** *and* **Kate** *go to her.*)

Eugene (*aside*). This is devilish awkward. Hope she will know enough to hold her tongue. By Jove, I'm in a fix all around. (*Exit hastily,* C.)

Kate (*as* **Lizzie** *revives*). Are you better?

Lizzie. Yes—I—yes, thank you. (*Looking around. Aside.*) He has gone.

Dr. Endicott. The heat of the room overpowered her, doubtless. I will leave her to your care while I go and see your father.

Kate. You will find him in the library.

Dr. Endicott. I will soon return. (*Exit,* C.)

Kate (*aside*). She looked very strangely at the doctor before she fainted. What can it mean?

Lizzie. I—I beg pardon for troubling you so much. I cannot imagine what made me so dizzy.

Kate. I am very glad you have recovered.

Lizzie. Thank you. I—I will go now. (*Rises.*)

Kate. But I thought you wished to see my mother?

Lizzie. Yes—but I—I think I cannot attend to it now. (*Goes up* C.)

Kate (*aside*). There is something strange in her behavior. I will try and find out what is the matter. Perhaps I can help her. (*Aloud.*) Do not go until you are quite well. I thought you recognized the—the gentleman who was here just now. May I ask if it was so?

Lizzie (*coming down* R. *confusedly*). Yes—I—I have seen him before, in the country, where I lived. He boarded there one summer.

Kate (L.). Then you are acquainted?

Lizzie (C.). Acquainted? Have I not sat by his side hour after hour underneath the trees and—oh! what have I said?

Kate (*aside*). Why do I tremble? (*Aloud, going to her.*) Do not fear, child, have confidence in me and let me be your friend. I see you have some great trouble.

Lizzie. Forgive me for having said what I did, but his appearance took me so by surprise, and I have not yet recovered myself.

Kate (*putting arm around her*). Poor child, tell me all without fear, and I will do anything I can to help you.

Lizzie. You are good and kind, I know, and I will confide in you. He—he told me he loved me, and I—I—believed it. And I loved him with all my heart. Life was nothing to me without him. But one day, with promises to return soon and make me his wife, he left me and I never saw him again until to-day. Ah! it broke my heart! it broke my heart! (*Sinks sobbing on chair,* R. C.)

Kate (C., *aside*). And I, too, loved him. And he dared to speak of love to me, after having ruined the happiness of this confiding child. He whom I thought so good, so noble, who was my ideal of what a man should be. And how unmoved he was in her presence. (*Aloud.*) Poor girl (*goes to* Lizzie, *kneels and puts her arm around her*), you have my deepest sympathy. Be brave; he is not worth those tears. I will be your friend and comfort you all I can. Here (*rising*), go in this room; he will be back soon and I do not wish you to have the pain of meeting him. What you have told me shall be sacred. I will see you again soon. (*Takes her to* R.)

Lizzie. Ah! thank you a thousand times for your goodness. (*Exit,* R.)

Kate. Yes, he is coming back. Will he speak of his love again, trusting to her silence? His love? His noble words but now were decoys to catch the hand of a supposed heiress by pandering to her theories. Ah, heavens! is there no truth in the world? Unhappy, indeed, must the woman be whose whole life is dependent on the truth or falsehood of a man. Oh, woman's heart! who can escape the suffering its tenderness brings? Strong-minded let me be, and deal with him as he deserves!

(*Enter* **Dr. Endicott,** C.)

Dr. Endicott (*coming down* R.) I am happy to say your father and I have settled our little affair with mutual satisfaction; and now, Kate (*going to her*), may I finish the sentence so rudely interrupted? May I dare to ask the one woman in the world for me, to share my life?

Kate (*turning from him*). I should hardly think you *would* dare, sir. (*Goes to* L.)

Dr. Endicott. Kate, do I merit that strange tone of severity?

Kate. Sir, do you think you are worthy of such a woman as you have described?

Dr. Endicott. No, Kate, no man is. But I would hope by her aid and the influence of her pure example to make myself more worthy day after day.

Kate. Your hypocrisy deceives me no longer, Dr. Endicott. The man I marry I must honor as well as love. I cannot honor you. Farewell. (*Points to door,* C.)

TABLEAU.

Music. **Dr. Endicott**, R.; **Kate**, L.

ACT II

SCENE

Library in **Mr. Grovenor's** *House. Desk,* R., *Books, etc.* **Jennie** *discovered arranging Books at Desk. Chairs* R. *and* L.

Jennie. Now I wonder what it all means? Let me see. (*Counts on fingers.*) Mr. Grovenor is cross all the time, Mrs. Grovenor is frightened all the time, Miss Alice is nervous all the time, Miss Kate is sober all the time, and Mr. Eugene is drunk—I mean jolly—all the time. Dr. Endicott don't come here any more, Eyeglass Doughlass is here all the time, there is a sighing seamstress up-stairs, and Jim—but I know what the matter is with Jim—*he* is in love with *me, that's* what ails *him.* But what ails everybody else is more than I can tell.

(*Enter* **Mr. Grovenor**, L. U. E.)

Mr. Grovenor (*going to desk*). That will do, Jennie, that will do.
Jennie. Very well, sir. (*Aside.*) What a scowl he has on him! I do believe I should be tempted to marry Jim, if it wasn't for the awful example before me. (*Exit,* L. U. E.)
Mr. Grovenor (*sitting at desk,* R.). Nothing but debts, debts. What a fool a man is to get married and saddle himself with an expensive family! Well, there is one consolation, my girls will be off my hands some time. Not a bad bargain will the man make who gets Kate. It's a pity, a great pity she isn't a boy. A very different son she would have been to me from the one I have. If I had time to spare from money matters, Eugene would give me great anxiety. Here is that note of Brown's due next week; how am I to meet it? But it must be done or my credit is lost!
Jennie (*outside*). This way, sir; you will find him in the library.
Doughlass (*outside*). Aw—pwecisely. (*Enter* **Doughlass**, L. U. E.) Aw—good morning, sir. I twust you are well to-day.
Mr. Grovenor (*rising*). Not quite well, I am sorry to say. Will you be seated?
Doughlass (*sitting* L.). Aw—thank you, but you seem vewy busy.
Mr. Grovenor. We business men are always busy. (*Sits,* R.)
Doughlass. Aw, pwecisely. I will not twespass long on your valuable time. To pwoceed to business at once, I came to ask—aw—for your daughter's hand.

Mr. Grovenor. Indeed! Have you my daughter's consent?

Doughlass. Aw—not exactly, but I weally do not think there will be any twouble about that. (*Aside.*) Does he think *any* woman would wefuse *me?*

Mr. Grovenor. I was not aware matters had gone so far. But I have two daughters. Do you mean my eldest or—

Doughlass. Aw—no, no, your youngest. (*Aside.*) Does he take me for a woman's wights convention?

Mr. Grovenor. If my daughter is agreeable, then, you have my full consent. (*Aside.*) How little he knows what an expensive luxury he is about to indulge in.

Doughlass. (*rising*). Aw—thank you, I thought it was best to see you first, you know, and now I will not twespass on your valuable time any longer. Good morning.

Mr. Grovenor (*rising and shaking hands with him*). Good morning, and I wish you success. (*Exit* **Doughlass,** L. U. E.) Ay, that I do with all my heart. One burden less. Oh, if that note was only paid! (*Exit into anteroom,* R. 1 E.)

(*Enter* **Doughlass,** L. U. E.)

Doughlass. I beg pardon, but I believe I left my glove—aw—the old man has gone. Well, no matter, I'll just find my glove and depart. (*Looks for glove.*)

(*Enter* **Jennie,** L. U. E.)

Jennie. If you please, sir—oh!

Doughlass (*aside, looking at her through eye-glass*). Always thought she was devilish pwetty. (*Aloud*) Aw—do not be afwaid, my dear.

Jennie (*coming down* L.). Afraid of *you?* Oh, no, indeed, sir!

Doughlass. Aw—that is wight. Let me see, what is your name, my dear?

Jennie. Jennie, sir. (*Aside.*) Oh, what a fool he is!

Doughlass. Jennie—aw—vewy pwetty name, Jennie.

Jennie. Do you think so, sir? It *must* be if you do.

Doughlass. Aw—yes, and a vewy pwetty girl owns it, too.

(*Enter* **Jim,** L. U. E. Stops up stage listening.)

Jennie. You don't say so!

Doughlass (*getting closer to her*). Aw—didn't you know you were a vewy pwetty girl, Jennie?

Jennie (*imitating*). Aw—weally, sir!

Doughlass. You little wogue, I have a good mind to snatch a—

(**Jim** *comes down* C. *and throws him over to* R.)

Jim (C.). You have, have you?

Doughlass (R.). You vulgaw fellow, how dare you lay your hands on a gentleman!

Jim. Because you forgot to be a gentleman, sir, that's how, and I'll do it every time, too, so you needn't try to come any of them games here.

Jennie (L.). Ain't you ashamed of yourself, Jim? Suppose the gentleman did say I was pretty, what then? There was no occasion for you to show your superiority, and it's entirely out of place. (*Aside.*) Just as if I should have allowed that jackanapes to kiss me! What stupid things these men are!

Jim. He had no business to do it. He had no business to be so near you; I won't stand by and see it done.

Doughlass. Weally, this is a most extraordinary thing! Look here, fellow— (*Going towards him.*)

Jim (*crossing to* L.). Don't call me fellow, sir.

(*Enter* **Dr. Endicott,** L. U. E.)

Dr. Endicott (*coming down* R. C.). Oh, Mr. Doughlass, you here?

Doughlass. Aw—yes, happy to see you. (*Aside.*) Good gwacious! It will never do to have him catch me in a wow with the coachman. (*Aloud.*) Aw—I was about leaving. Here, my good fellow. (*Gives money to* **Jim** *and exit* L. U. E.)

Jim (*looks at money, then throws it after him*). There, sir! You will find money is not a plaster for everything.

Jennie. Ain't you ashamed of yourself, Jim! Is this the way you show your superiority, I'd like to know?

Dr. Endicott (C.). What does this all mean?

Jim. Excuse me, sir, it's nothing but a little quarrel that Jennie and I were having. Nothing uncommon, sir. She is like all women, the better a man likes her the worse he gets treated.

Jennie. Do not listen to him, please, doctor. It's all a bit of nonsense, any way. If that last you said is true, Jim, all I have got to say is that it shows a great weakness in the sex. (*Exit,* L. U. E.)

Jim. There you hear her, sir?

Dr. Endicott. Your sweetheart is a little wilful, I fear.

Jim. Sh! don't let her hear you say that, for she ain't my sweetheart, you know. That is, she won't acknowledge it. It's me who am a dangling and a dangling after her, and she laughing at me, or berating me for it all the time. Oh, sir! it is an awful thing to be in love. Why, sir, if this goes on much longer, I shan't have flesh enough left to keep my bones together with.

Dr. Endicott. Then why do you not insist on either yes or no from her and abide by it.

Jim. *Insist,* did you say, sir? *Insist?* Why, sir, I have to get down on my marrow bones, sir, and then she ain't satisfied!

Dr. Endicott. But what does she wish you to do?

Jim. I'll tell you what she wants, sir. She wants me to give up the dignity of my sex.

Dr. Endicott (*surprised*). I fear I do not quite understand.

Jim. She wants me to acknowledge that I am a fool, sir; nothing will content her but my admitting I am a perfect fool.

Dr. Endicott. That is very strange.

Jim. You see, she thinks it her duty to sit down on me! just to show she ain't inferior, you know.

Dr. Endicott. I am afraid she and you also have gone to the two extremes of an idea. Now I do not believe you would wish to exercise any undue authority over her.

Jim. Authority? over Jennie? No, indeed, sir, and to tell you the truth, I don't believe there is any fellow alive who *could* do it and live.

Dr. Endicott. I have more faith in Jennie than to believe she would really like a man who was inferior to herself. I think she adopts that tone as a safeguard because she has a misgiving that the masculine instinct is to assert itself over the feminine. But if you give her to understand that as far as you are concerned she is wrong, I think there will be no trouble.

Jim. Thank you, sir, I'll try. I suppose a man and woman *are* two halves, equal halves, but I have a feeling that Jennie won't be content with half; she will want two thirds at least. (*Exit*, L. U. E.)

Dr. Endicott. Poor fellow, I trust his Jennie will not be obdurate. As he says, it is an awful thing to be in love. Love! Is it a blessing or a curse? A week ago, and for me it meant happiness, and now—ah, Kate, what is it that stands between us? I can obtain no explanation from her; she refuses to see me alone. Is it what a man who has less faith in the sex than I would call a woman's caprice? No! Kate is a noble, a true woman, nothing can make me doubt that! "I must honor as well as love the man I marry." What can she have meant? What have I done? I am groping in darkness, but I will find my way into the light yet!

(*Enter* **Mr. Grovenor,** R. 1 E.)

Mr. Grovenor. Ah, my dear doctor, you are a stranger indeed. I sent for you to-day, as I am feeling far from well. I have had a great mental strain of late and I fear it has been too much for me.

Dr. Endicott. I can truly believe it. I am grieved to see you looking so ill.

Mr. Grovenor. My head troubles me sadly.

Dr. Endicott. You need rest.

Mr. Grovenor. Rest! Rest is impossible for me.

Dr. Endicott. Cannot your son—

Mr. Grovenor. Eugene! no! He is good for nothing except to sing comic songs at champagne suppers and talk soft nonsense to equally soft girls. No. I regret to say Eugene is not a son of whom I can be proud, or who is willing to be useful to me.

Dr. Endicott. But your daughter Kate. I am positive she could be of great assistance to you if you would allow her.

Mr. Grovenor. What! a woman meddling in my business matters? Absurd!

Dr. Endicott. I am sorry I cannot agree with you. I know Miss Grovenor has business ability, energy, and brains; what more do you want?

Mr. Grovenor. But she is a woman and that settles the matter. Let us not discuss this point. And now can you not give me something that will stop this burning in my head?

Dr. Endicott. I will try, but I fear, without rest, medicine will do you little good.

(Enter Kate, L. U. E.)

Kate *(coming down C.).* Father, I—Dr. Endicott!

Dr. Endicott (L.). Kate!

Kate. I thought my father was alone; excuse my intrusion. *(Aside.)* It is hard to remember how dishonorable he was when I see him as now. But I must.

Dr. Endicott. Do not go, I was about leaving. May I ask to be favored with an interview, at any time possible to you?

Kate. I regret to be obliged to say no to your request.

Mr. Grovenor. Why, what do you mean, Kate?

Kate. What I say, father.

Dr. Endicott. I appeal to your sense of justice. Is it right to refuse me all explanation?

Kate. Can you say you *need* one?

Dr. Endicott. I can.

Kate *(aside).* His eyes meet mine unfalteringly. Can there have been a mistake? But no, that is impossible. *(Aloud.)* As you will. I will see you to-morrow at this hour.

Dr. Endicott. I thank you. Pardon me, Mr. Grovenor, but as this is a matter that concerns me very nearly I could do no otherwise than speak in your presence—my only opportunity. I will send the medicine for you very soon. To-morrow at this hour, Kate, I hope to clear up all your doubts. *(Exit, L. U. E. Kate looks after him.)*

Mr. Grovenor. What cursed nonsense is all this?

Kate. Nothing, father, only Dr. Endicott asked me to be his wife.

Mr. Grovenor. The devil he did.

Kate. And I refused.

Mr. Grovenor. What! refused? why, you are a bigger fool than most women!

Kate. Thank you, father, But in a matter like that, you must allow even a woman has the right to choose.

Mr. Grovenor. And are you expecting a prince, that the doctor, a fine, handsome man, is not good enough for you? It is not every one who would want you, with your unfeminine ideas!

Kate. Well, father, I think I can manage to exist unmarried.

Mr. Grovenor. Exist? on what? I have no property to leave you.

Kate. Then at least I shall escape taxation without representation.

Mr. Grovenor. There you go again with your crazy ideas! I declare I have no patience with you. What was that he meant about an explanation?

Kate. That I am not at liberty to tell, as it is a secret that concerns others.

Mr. Grovenor. A secret? Ah, well, it will come out soon enough, then. No woman yet ever kept a secret.

Kate. We shall see.

Mr. Grovenor. Well, Kate, I will not deny you have always been a good girl; I believe you never teased me for money in your life, but you were a fool to refuse the doctor. However, there is no accounting for a woman's whims, and you may think better of it.

Kate. Let us dismiss that subject. I came here, father, to beg you to let me help you. I know you are ill and need rest. I know you are oppressed by many cares, while I—I have absolutely nothing to fill my time. I feel I could help you. Forget I am a woman, if need be, and let me try.

Mr. Grovenor. I know you mean right, child, but if I should agree to your proposition, you would be more bother than you were worth; don't you see you would, you goose?

Kate. At first I might until I learned your way. But that would not be long; at least let me try.

Mr. Grovenor. Well, some time when I have plenty of time, perhaps, I will see! (*Sits at desk*, R.)

Kate. You only say that to get rid of me. Is there no way I can induce you?

Mr. Grovenor. No, no. Now do not annoy me any more. (*Writes busily.*)

(*Enter* **Mrs. Grovenor,** L. U. E.)

Mrs. Grovenor (L.). Ah, Kate, you here? I would like to speak to your father alone a moment, my dear.

Kate. Very well, mother. (*Aside.*) Poor father so worn and harassed. I know I could lighten his labors. Why is he so obstinate? (*Exit* L. U. E.)

Mr. Grovenor (*without looking at her*). Well, Mrs. Grovenor, what is it— money? You can't have it.

Mrs. Grovenor. Not for myself. But Eugene is in great distress. He says he must have five hundred dollars at once, and goes on in a way that is frightful.

Mr. Grovenor. (*looking over shoulder*). Five hundred dollars! Do you see that note, due next week and not a cent raised to pay it with? Do you see these bills? Go back and teach your son to earn his money.

Mrs. Grovenor (*putting handkerchief to eyes*). Oh, would I not if I could! But alas! I am helpless and Eugene is going to ruin!

Mr. Grovenor (*writing*). There, do not snivel. You have an easy time enough. So spare a man at least your everlasting whimpering!

Mrs. Grovenor. An easy time? Bound, fettered, helpless, is that easy?

Mr. Grovenor (*turning in his chair and staring at her*). You are in an extraordinary mood to-day, Mrs. Grovenor! Bound, fettered—clothed, fed, given all the luxuries of life without lifting your own white hands, you mean. Helpless? To raise five hundred dollars to pay Eugene's—gambling—debts—doubtless. Who has been talking such stuff to you? Kate?

Mrs. Grovenor. Sneer if you will, but it is true that of Kate I have learned to think upon things I never did before, and to believe that, had I been differently educated, had my life been broadened instead of narrowed, had I been taught to be independent, and to make my matrimonial choice from love alone, I might have been a better mother to my daughters, and guided the steps of my son away from ruin and dishonor. (*Exit,* L. U. E.)

Mr. Grovenor (*staring after her*). Have all the women gone crazy? I have been married twenty-five years and I never knew my wife to speak in that way before. It's all Kate's fault! I must forbid this radical talk or my household will be utterly demoralized. But she was right in saying that Eugene is going to ruin. This constant struggle with money matters has given me no time to attend to my son, and now, what shall be done? (*Rises and walks back and forth.*)

(*Enter* **Eugene,** L. U. E.)

Eugene. Father!

Mr. Grovenor. Ah! have you come to tell me what you mean by your disgraceful conduct, sir?

Eugene. Disgraceful conduct? You are talking in enigmas to me; I'm all right. I have been a little jolly sometimes, to be sure, but that is no more than all the boys are. You had your fun when you were young, I suppose, so why shouldn't I?

Mr. Grovenor. How dare you, boy, insinuate that I—

Eugene. Ah! come, come, father, you know you wasn't a milk-sop any more than I am. It's all very well for the girls, but it won't do for us men, you know. So, now, let me have that five hundred, that's a good old dad.

Mr. Grovenor. Five hundred dollars! Do you know that I am on the verge of ruin?

Eugene. The deuce you are!

Mr. Grovenor. Nothing but a steady hand will save me. While I am struggling with all my might—sick enough to be in bed—to pull through, you all, not content with being dead weights on my shoulders, run into extravagance and profligacy. (*Takes bill from desk.*) The bill for my daughter Alice's last ball dress is here, $500. Here are two of your champagne bills, $100. I tell you this must be stopped. Your debauchery must be stopped. You have not the strength of mind to go through profligacy and come out solvent; if you had Kate's brains you might, but you have not; so I tell you this must be stopped, or you will have the pleasure of sowing the remainder of your wild oats in a pauper's back yard, if you do not fill a drunkard's grave! (*Exit,* R. 1 E.)

Eugene. By Jove! he means it every word! I never saw him so worked up before! And to say I, a man, had not so much strength of mind as Kate, he must be crazy! But what a fix I am in! I never dreamed but I could get the money without any trouble before the time to take up the note came, and if I cannot—great heavens! what I did was a crime, a State prison offence! State prison? Bah! the idea is absurd, I shall get the money some way. I will not think of it. It annoys me, too, to have Lizzie under the same roof. I have avoided her so far, but—oh! I will go and get a glass of whiskey and forget it all.

(*Enter* **Lizzie,** L. U. E. *She gives a startled exclamation.*)

Eugene. Lizzie!

Lizzie. You!

Eugene. What are you doing here?

Lizzie (*up* L.) I came to look for Miss Kate; they said she was in the library. Heaven knows I would not have come had I known you were here!

Eugene. Now, Lizzie, what is the use of making such a fuss about nothing? Because we had a jolly little flirtation once, it is no reason why we should go into heroics now, is it? Come, let us be friends, Lizzie.

Lizzie (*coming down* L.). Friends with you, who broke my heart?

Eugene. Nonsense! broken hearts went out of fashion years ago. There, forgive me, Lizzie, but what *is* the use of taking things so seriously? Life was never made to be taken seriously.

Lizzie. Perhaps not for you, but for those who have hearts life is indeed serious.

Eugene. I know it's a way women have to make themselves miserable, if they can. Now be sensible. Suppose we were awful spoons once; it was very pleasant while it lasted, but, of course, it could not last forever.

Lizzie. And why?

Eugene. Why? Do summer flirtations ever last? Certainly not.

Lizzie. But you said you never could be happy without me, that some day I should be your wife.

Eugene. By Jove! was I so far gone as all that? Well, I did like you amazingly, Lizzie, but, of course, that was mere talk.

Lizzie (*looking at him earnestly and moving towards him*). You did not mean it when you asked me to be your wife?

Eugene. Of course not, and I did not suppose you thought I did.

Lizzie (C.). And you call yourself a man, you who thus trifled with the heart of an innocent girl who loved you! Then if you are a type of a man, I thank heaven *I* am a woman.

Eugene. Now, Lizzie, don't get mad. I did not mean any harm, 'pon my word I didn't. (*Aside.*) By Jove, I believe I did treat the little girl confounded mean.

Lizzie. I loved not *you*, but the man I dreamed you were. *You* I despise.

Eugene. Lizzie, I am sorry it ever happened. You see, I am a thoughtless kind of a fellow. I—I—have done a great many things I ought not. (*Tries to take her hand.*)

Lizzie (C., *repulsing him*). Then cultivate a different disposition in amends for the past and to save yourself from ruin, to which thoughtlessness is too often a guide. (*Goes up* R.)

Eugene (L.). 'Pon my word, I—I believe I will try.

(*Enter* **Mr. Grovenor**, R. 1 E., *hastily, with paper clutched in his hand.*)

Mr. Grovenor. This—this is a forgery, and you, Eugene, do you—do you know—was it—can it have been you?

Eugene (L., *aside*). Heaven! that note to-day! I thought it was to-morrow. What shall I do?

Mr. Grovenor (C.). Answer and contradict if you can the guilt I see in your face.

Eugene. Father, forgive me. It was a debt of honor and I hoped to be able to pay the note before it came due. I—

Mr. Grovenor. Then it was you, my son. My curse upon you, ungrateful and miserable son. Go—to a prison. I will have no mercy on you.

(**Lizzie** *screams and comes down* R.)

Eugene. Oh! a prison! (*Staggers to* R., *and falls into chair.* **Lizzie** *leans over him.*)

Mr. Grovenor. Yes, a prison, and rot there. You have ruined me; do you hear, ruined me! What have I done that I should be the father of a son like this? A forger and a—(*Staggers.*) Ah, my head! how it burns! What was I saying? Mercy! I will have no mercy! Where is Kate? (*Rings bell over desk furiously.*) Yes, ruined! ruined!

(*Enter* **Mrs. Grovenor** *and* **Alice**, L. U. E.)

Alice (L. C.). Father, what is the matter?

Mrs. Grovenor (L.). What can I do? Are you ill? Speak to me.

Mr. Grovenor (*raving*). Yes, you have ruined me. (*Enter* **Kate,** L. U. E.) Who will pay these bills? I am ill, dying, dishonored; no one will straighten out my affairs. My son—no. I have no son. I—who will, who can help, save me? (*Falls,* C. **Kate** *comes down* L. C., *kneels and puts her arms around him.*)

Kate. Your *daughter*, father! (*Slow music.*)

TABLEAU.

> **Eugene** *in chair.* **Lizzie** *bending over him,* R. **Mr. Grovenor** *on floor.* **Kate** *kneeling beside him,* C. **Alice** *weeping, with arms around her mother,* L.

ACT III

SCENE

> *Same as First Act.* **Mrs. Grovenor,** *sitting on Sofa,* R. **Alice,** *Chair,* L. **Dr. Endicott,** R., *at Table, discovered.*

Mrs. Grovenor. Thank heaven, my husband is in his right mind once more, and after heaven we must thank you, doctor.

Dr. Endicott. I have done all I could, and I am happy to have been so successful.

Mrs. Grovenor. But since he has recovered his senses, his business affairs are worrying him. Would it not be better to explain everything?

Dr. Endicott. Yes, I think it will do to speak to-day, and, as a change of scene will be beneficial, get him up in his easy-chair and out here, if possible.

Mrs. Grovenor. And Eugene, that unhappy boy.

Dr. Endicott. I doubt not this experience will be the needed one to arouse him to better things. You had best leave him to Kate.

Mrs. Grovenor. Yes, I suppose so. Alas! I fear I have been much to blame for what has happened. I was too ignorant and helpless to be a wise mother. Dear Kate, what should we have done without her? (*Rising.*) But I must now go to my husband, who needs me every moment. I will follow your directions, doctor. (*Exit,* L. 2 E.)

Dr. Endicott. I am sorry to see you looking pale, Miss Alice, I hope you are not going to be ill also?

Alice. Oh, no! I have been anxious about father.

Dr. Endicott. But now all occasion for anxiety has passed.

Alice. Yes, and now I am to confess the truth somewhat out of sorts with myself.

Dr. Endicott. That is unfortunate, as we cannot easily get away from ourselves.

Alice. Too true.

(*Enter* **Doughlass**, c.)

Doughlass (*coming* L. *of table*). Aw—good afternoon, doctor. I thought I would come to take you out to wide, Alice.

Alice (*pettishly*). Why, you have been here once to-day.

Doughlass. Aw—yes—you cannot complain that I am not devoted, you know!

Alice (*aside*). I wish I could. (*Aloud.*) Well, I suppose I may as well go out to ride as anything else. (*Rising.*)

Doughlass. That is right; get your hat and we will go at once. (**Alice**, *exit*, L. 2 E.) You see I like to have her go out to wide, for it makes the fellows all envy me, you know. Alice is a devilish handsome girl, now, isn't she, doctor?

Dr. Endicott. Very handsome indeed.

Doug. Yes—aw—and it's weally wough on a fellow, you know, to have to pay his attentions in a lunatic asylum.

Dr. Endicott. A lunatic asylum!

Doughlass. Aw—yes—that is all I could think of whenever I have come here for the last two weeks, what with the old man waving wound, Eugene moping and tearing his hair, and Miss Kate having everything all her own way.

Dr. Endicott. Her father has cause to be thankful that his daughter does have everything her own way, at last. (*Rises.*)

Doughlass. You surprise me. Aw—I have no doubt my—aw—future sister-in-law is a very smart woman, you know, but you see a fellow is afwaid of these smart women.

(*Enter* **Alice**, L. 2 E., *with hat, etc.*)

Alice. Yes, it makes things too unequal, no doubt.

Doughlass. Aw—pwecisely. (*Aside.*) What the deuce does she mean? (*Aloud.*) Aw—if you are weady, my dear, we will bid the doctor good by.

Alice. Ah, yes. We will go. (*Aside, as they go up.*) I will teach him something about a woman's smartness after we are married. (*Exit with* **Doughlass**, c.)

Dr. Endicott (R., *looking after them*). Poor foolish couple! I pity you both. She is marrying him for his money, and he her for her good looks. And good looks fade, and money is powerless to satisfy the cravings of the heart, and then, what? (*Enter* **Jim**, c.) Well, Jim?

Jim. If you please, sir, will you want the carriage?

Dr. Endicott. Not yet. By the by, Jim, have you fixed everything all right with Jennie?

Jim. Not—not exactly, sir. To tell the truth (*comes down* L.), she has been going on worse than ever since the master has been sick, and Miss Kate has been, as it were, the head of the family. "There's a woman for you!" says Jennie, "and do you dare tell me you have any business to go and vote and Miss Kate stay at home?" says Jennie, and what can I say, sir? It's not for me to set myself up above Miss Kate!

Dr. Endicott. Poor Jim! Your love matters really do not glide along very smoothly. But they never do, Jim (*sighing*), they never do.

Jim. You're very right, sir. To be in love is the most wearing thing I know of.

Dr. Endicott. I fear Jennie is a sad tease.

Jim. Tease, sir! Why, she even teases me in my dreams!

Dr. Endicott. Then if she makes you so unhappy, why not give up all thoughts of her, and—

Jim. Give up all thoughts of Jennie! Never, sir! Why, I had rather be made that miserable that I am reduced to walking about in my bones than give up Jennie. No, sir! It's a curious fact. (*Enter* **Jennie**, c.) A strange weakness in the composition of a man is that the more unhappy a woman makes him the better he likes her!

Jennie (*coming down*, c.). You don't say so!

Jim. Gracious Peter! I have done it now!

Jennie. Yes, you are caught in a confession of great weakness!

Jim. I—I—take it all back.

Jennie. You can't; it's boarded.

Dr. Endicott. Right, Jennie. But what is this I hear about you?

Jennie (*confused*). About me, sir?

Dr. Endicott. Yes, about your great aversion to our unfortunate sex?

Jennie. Lor, sir, I don't know. I suppose Jim has been telling you some nonsense or other! (*Turns and makes face at* **Jim**.)

Jim. No, I haven't, Jennie, upon my soul I haven't. I only told him what you said about a man being inferior to a woman, that's all.

Jennie. Oh! that was *all*, was it? Well, Mr. Jim, you are a smart young man, you are! And besides, I never said anything of the kind. The fact is, doctor, I expressed my sentiments to him, that's all.

Dr. Endicott. And may I inquire what those sentiments are?

Jennie. Oh! it's only that I don't believe in getting married and being made a slave of and perhaps beat and told you don't know anything because you are a woman: those are the sentiments he objects to, sir.

Jim. Good gracious. Jennie! Did I ever do any such thing?

Jennie. Of course not; you never had a chance.

Dr. Endicott. But really, my good girl, I do not believe you think in your heart quite so meanly of Jim as your words would signify. In your zeal for your own sex, do not be unjust to ours, for remember that is the very thing you condemn in us. (*Exit,* c.)

Jennie (*half crying*). Well, Jim, I don't see what on earth you wanted to go and make me out so horrid to the doctor for. Just because I think a good deal of his opinion, I suppose.

Jim. There, now! oh, dear! how you do fly off, to be sure. Make you out horrid? I, who would think you was perfect if you would only let up a little once in a while on me about your rights.

Jennie. Yes, and you went and made the doctor think that I not only wanted my rights, which I do, but yours, too, which I don't.

Jim. You don't? I'm sure I thought you did.

Jennie (*stamping foot*). Oh! is there anything in the world so stupid as a man?

Jim. Stupid! I have a good mind to get mad.

Jennie (*turning her back to him*). I would if I were you.

Jim. Well, I— (*Goes up* c., *then returns.*) No, I can't get mad with you, Jennie. But won't you please just remember how you went on about the tyranny of the sex, and all that sort of thing, and then don't blame me if I thought you wanted to tyrannize a little. I am sure that wasn't stupid.

Jennie. It was absurd, then. I only want my share, that's all.

Jim. Is that all? Oh, Jennie (*gets down on knees*), if you will only marry me, you shall have your share, yes, and a little more.

Jennie. My share of being trampled on, do you mean?

Jim. Who said anything about being trampled on? Well, your share of trampling, if you must have it.

Jennie. I think it is just awful of you to say that I am a tyrant.

Jim (*jumping up*). Good gracious, there you go again! How you do fly off. When did I ever say any such thing?

Jennie. Well, Jim, supposing—just supposing, you know—that I should make up my mind to marry you—

Jim. Oh, Jennie! If you only would. The very idea makes me so happy, I—I could jump way to the ceiling. (*Holds out arms to embrace her, she runs under them.*)

Jennie. Could you? Well, don't be in too much of a hurry, because it might hurt you when you came down, for you know I was only *supposing.*

Jim. Jennie, do you want to see me pine to a shadow and blow away with love? I can't stand this sort of thing any longer. I will go away to California, that's what I will do!

Jennie (*coquettishly*). But, Jim, don't you think you had better wait until I get through *supposing?*

Jim. Wait! I will wait until I am bald if you will only promise to have me then.

Jennie. Dear me, I shouldn't want you *then*. In fact, I couldn't think of having you any way, if I thought you would *ever* be bald!

Jim (*very fast*). Oh, I never shall; no, indeed, we are not a bald family, there never was a bald man in it, the babies all are born with thick heads of hair. One of the family was scalped once, to be sure, but it was accidental, and his hair all grew out again in a few days. Look at mine. (*Sticks it up.*)

Jennie (*screams*). Oh, don't! Nature has made you homely enough without your trying to help her.

Jim. But I only wanted to settle this bald question forever. And now, Jennie, won't you go on *supposing?*

Jennie. Well, supposing I should marry you some time, would you find a minister who was willing to leave "obey" out of the marriage service?

Jim. If there is one in America I'll find him. For I shouldn't want to make you swear to a lie, Jennie.

Jennie. And then would you respect my rights and acknowledge equal rights for both of us?

Jim. Of course, your rights and equal rights,—principally your rights.

Jennie. Well, then, perhaps—but wait a moment; if there should ever be a balance over equal rights, it must come on my side, must it not? Because a man is apt to misuse his power, you know.

Jim (*going near her*). You shall have all the balances.

Jennie (*edging away*). I don't know but you are almost *too* willing.

Jim. Now she is off on another tack. What *can* a man do?

Jennie. However, I can get a divorce if you don't keep your word, so, as you are a pretty good fellow, Jim, I think I will condescend to try you as a husband.

Jim. Hurrah! (*Embraces her.*) But about this condescending—

Jennie. That is one of the balances, Jim.

Jim. Oh, well! (*Kisses her and is about to repeat when she stops him.*)

Jennie. No, Jim. Equal rights. I must give you half, you know. (*Kisses him and runs off,* C.)

Jim. Equal rights ain't so bad, after all. (*Goes after* **Jennie** *and runs against* **Eugene,** *who enters moodily,* C.) I beg pardon, sir, but I am so equal— happy. (*Exit,* C.)

Eugene. What is the matter with Jim? Happy! Well, I am glad some one is. I never shall be again. This is what my cursed easy disposition has brought me to. I have ruined myself and almost killed my father. If it was not for Kate I would blow my brains out—if I have any. (*Sits dejectedly,* R.)

(Enter Lizzie, c.*)*

Lizzie. Eugene!

Eugene. Lizzie, is it you? *(Aside.)* I am ashamed to look her in the face.

Lizzie. I have been trying to see you ever since that—that trouble, but I never have been able to find you alone. I thought perhaps it might be some little comfort to you to know that I sympathized with and pitied you, and that I had faith enough in you to believe you would redeem the past.

Eugene *(starting up)*. These words to me from you? Oh, Lizzie, I am a miserable wretch.

Lizzie. You have been gay, careless, reckless, but oh, I cannot believe you wholly bad. My share in your thoughtless past I freely forgive. I wanted to tell you this, and say I hope in the future to see you worthy the esteem of every one.

Eugene. I dare not hope that, Lizzie.

Lizzie. But you will try?

Eugene. Oh, yes! I shall try. But my father,—he will surely never forgive me, will banish me from his house.

Lizzie. Not if you tell him how penitent you are.

Eugene. He has not a heart like yours, Lizzie.

Lizzie. But Kate will intercede for you.

Eugene. Kate, heaven bless her, I know she will. What has she not done for me already? And to think that I once set myself up as so far above her, and plumed myself on being a lord of creation,—I, a poor, weak fool, not worthy to touch the hem of her garment.

Lizzie. Those words prove to me that you are no longer the Eugene you were.

Eugene. I hope, I trust not. As you say, I did not mean to be really bad. I was inexperienced, thoughtless, eager for the pleasures of life, and I never stopped to think of consequences. How could you have loved me—for you did love me once, Lizzie?

Lizzie. It was your best side you showed me, Eugene.

Eugene. At first, yes; but I showed you my worst afterwards.

Lizzie. The flaws in her idol cannot kill a woman's love.

Eugene. Lizzie, I did not mean to break your heart. Do you believe me?

Lizzie. I do; and, as I said, forgive you freely.

Eugene. For the first time I begin to realize the happiness that might have been mine, the value of the heart I threw away.

Lizzie. The heart that has always been yours, Eugene.

Eugene *(taking her hand)*. Mine! Mine now! What! Do you mean to say that you love me now, ruined and disgraced as I am, soon perhaps to be driven from my father's door, and go forth into the world penniless and alone?

Lizzie. How little you know of woman's love! Think you it endures only through the bright summer days of sunshine? No, Eugene. In the time of darkness and sorrow a woman's love never fails.

Eugene. And would you share my fate *now?*

Lizzie. Would I? Oh, how gladly! But you forget, I am a poor girl, a seamstress in your mother's house, and—

Eugene. I would indeed be unworthy of the blessing of your love should I think of *that.* Lizzie, your love shall raise me from the depths into which I have fallen. (*Embraces her as* **Kate** *enters,* C.)

Kate. Eugene! Lizzie!

Eugene (R. C.). Do not misapprehend, Kate. Let me explain before you judge.

Kate (*coming down* L.). Go on.

Lizzie (*aside,* R.). Dare I hope she will approve?

Eugene. Lizzie and I met—a year ago!

Kate. What! is it possible!

Lizzie. Do you not remember, I told you all the first day I came to your house?

Kate. What do you say? Do you mean (*staggers back against table for support*)—can it be that it was to him—to *Eugene* that you then referred?

Lizzie. To whom else? It was of course Eugene.

Kate. Eugene! Oh, what a cruel mistake! Oh, what a wrong I have done a noble man! Heaven forgive me!

Eugene (*going to her*). Dear Kate, what is the matter? what do you mean?

Kate. Do not ask me; dear, forget what I have said. It is all right now—yes! all right now! Eugene—Lizzie—you do not need tell me any more. I understand (*joins their hands*); I am very glad, and now will you please leave me? I—I would like to be alone.

Lizzie. You are not offended?

Kate. Offended? no indeed, child. I am sure you have both acted for the best.

Eugene. Dear Kate, with the help of my sister and my wife, I hope I may one day be what I once thought I was—a man! (*Exit,* C., *with* **Lizzie,** *who comes back to kiss* **Kate,** *then exit.*)

Kate. Can it be true? Has the heavy load that has lain on my heart, at the bottom of all the other loads that have lain there of late, really gone? Yes—gone—all gone! Will he, can he forgive me? I must see him at once! (*Rings bell.*) How could I for a moment mistrust him?

(*Enter* **Jennie,** C.)

Kate. Please ask Dr. Endicott to come here.

Jennie. Yes'm. (*Aside.*) They two would make another nice equal-rights couple. (*Exit,* C.)

Kate. What shall I say to him? Oh! if they could see me tremble, they would no longer call me "strong-minded."

(Enter Dr. Endicott, c.*)*

Dr. Endicott. You sent for me, Kate? At last we meet alone!

Kate. Yes, I sent for you to say, forgive me!

Dr. Endicott. Forgive you! For refusing me an explanation, do you mean?

Kate. For ever having doubted you. Oh! how can I say how bitterly I have wronged you?

Dr. Endicott. Wronged me? and how? Do not fear: tell me all. Whatever it may be, it is forgiven.

Kate. I doubted you. It seems impossible now that I could have done so, but I did; circumstances caused me to lay the wrong-doing of another at your door.

Dr. Endicott. If the cloud that has been between us so long has gone, I am too thankful to give anything else a second thought. So ask me not to forgive you, but rather let me ask you if you love me?

Kate. I love and honor you with all my heart.

Dr. Endicott. As I do you. (*Embraces her.*)

Kate. And please heaven our home shall be a happy one, if I *am* strong-minded!

Dr. Endicott. *Because* you are strong-minded, dear. And now we must prepare to relieve your father's mind of the anxiety that is growing greater every moment. Hark! they are bringing him in.

(**Mr. Grovenor** *is pushed in on chair by* **Mrs. Grovenor** *and* Jennie, c. Jennie *immediately exits,* c. Mrs. Grovenor *goes to* L.*)*

Kate (*going* R. *of him*). Dear father, I am so happy to see you out of your room once more.

Mr. Grovenor. Thank you, Kate. I—I hope to get back to business again soon.

Dr. Endicott (L. *of* Mr. Grovenor). Do not give yourself any uneasiness about your business. That has gone on well.

Mr. Grovenor. No, no, that cannot be. I remember—

Dr. Endicott. That you were on the verge of ruin. But the crisis has passed, and now all is well.

Mr. Grovenor. But—Brown's note.

Dr. Endicott. Brown has given you three months' time.

Mr. Grovenor. Strange—oh! but Eugene—

Dr. Endicott. That note has been paid.

Mr. Grovenor. Paid! can it be? But how, who has done all this—you, doctor?

Dr. Endicott. Not I, but one nearer and dearer, one more deserving of your thanks—your daughter. (*Indicates* Kate *to him, who is leaning over his chair.*)

Mr. Grovenor. What, my daughter! *You*, Kate, have done this?

Kate (*coming around to his side*, R.). Yes, dear father, my woman's wit has been equal to the occasion. I saw Brown myself. I had saved up a little money for the purpose of some day using in studying art, and with that I settled Eugene's debts. I have taken your place in the business as far as with my limited knowledge I could. So do not worry any more, dear father.

Mr. Grovenor. Ah! my daughter, how foolish, how blind I have been! But the scales have fallen from my eyes at last, and I thank God for the great gift of my daughter. (*Embraces* **Kate**.)

(*Enter* **Eugene** *and* **Lizzie**, C. **Eugene** *goes and kneels before* **Mr. Grovenor**. **Lizzie** *stops up stage*.)

Eugene. Father, can you overlook what has passed and let me try once more?

Mr. Grovenor. My boy, I have erred too much myself to condemn you. We will both redeem the past. (*Lays hand on his head*.)

Eugene. Father, your confidence will not, shall not be misplaced.

Kate (*bringing down* **Lizzie**, R.). And now, father, give your blessing, will you not, on his union with one who has long loved him, and who will help him to keep his word?

Mr. Grovenor. What! He wishes to marry Lizzie!

Kate. Yes, father, and she will make him a good wife.

Mr. Grovenor (*taking* **Lizzie's** *hand*). Let me look at you. You have a good, sweet face, child. Away with all false ideas of caste. Help my son to overcome his past errors and I will love you always. (**Lizzie** *kneels at* **Eugene's** *side and he joins their hands*.)

Eugene (*rising and taking* **Lizzie** L. *to* **Mrs. Grovenor**). And you, mother, do you consent?

Mrs. Grovenor. I will confess that once I might have said no, but now— now—now that I realize how false have been so many of my ideas, I dare trust myself only to say, may you be happy. (*Goes back of* **Mr. Grovenor's** *chair, leaning over it*.)

(*Enter* **Doughlass** *and* **Alice**, *followed by* **Jim** *and* **Jennie**, C.)

Doughlass (R.). Aw—quite a family gathering, I declare.

Alice. We are just in time to complete the circle.

Dr. Endicott (R. *of* **Mr. Grovenor's** *chair with* **Kate**). And now, Mr. Grovenor, will you give your blessing? For Kate has promised to be my wife.

Mrs. Grovenor. My dear Kate.

Alice. Can it be?

Doughlass (*aside*). Going to mawwy the strong-minded one? Good gracious!

Mr. Grovenor. Doctor, you have won a pearl of great price, but you are worthy of it. Heaven bless you both.

Alice (*aside*). My ideas have been all wrong, but my fate is fixed now.

Jim (*coming down* L. *with* Jennie). If you please, now, there is so much being said about getting married, I would like to mention that Jennie and I are going to get married, too.

Jennie. On equal rights.

Dr. Endicott. Equal rights to all.

Kate. And I wish to every woman in the land might come equal rights, independence, and last, but not least, love.

Music.

CURTAIN.

Alice, Doughlass, R.; Kate, Dr. Endicott, R. C.; Mr. Grovenor *in chair* C.; Mrs. Grovenor *at back of chair*; Eugene, Lizzie, L. C.; Jim, Jennie, L.

WHEN THE WOMEN VOTE
VOTE
A COLLOQUY

ELEANOR FREEMAN

Cincinnati: Standard Publishing Company, 1885.

CHARACTERS

Mrs. Van Arden.
Mrs. Rivers.
Mr. Van Arden.
Mr. Jones.
Bridget.

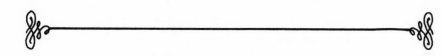

Mr. Van Arden (*seated, with paper in hand*). Ah, indeed! What's all this? Bill passed the House allowing Universal Suffrage to Women! *O tempora! O mores!* What's this world coming to? Now, here's my wife been on a lecturing tour for the last three weeks, using all her influence, I suppose, to get this Bill through, and leaving me to my devices. To be sure, I'm not so bad off as Jones, who has to mind the baby and go with half his buttons off, and his coat all frayed out. O pshaw! why can't my wife stay at home and let her sisters fight their own battles? I shouldn't care if all the women in the universe voted, if *she* would only—

[*Enter* **Bridget**].

Bridget. Och! Faith! an' ain't the misthress iver a comin' home from that lecturin' tower of her'n? The baby's been an' middled wid the elictric flour-sifter an' got an awful shock right on top of me a riscuin' of him from a sittin' on the stame hater! It's all blisthered to nothin' he is, and a howlin' as if he were a hurrahin' for Women's Suffrage.

Mr. Van Arden. Cicero Cæsar! That everlasting Woman's Suffrage! Will I ever hear the last of it?

Bridget. Begorrah an' it'll be the salvation of the country from the Mugwumps and sich like. Och, but the poor darlint's a bawlin' for me again—and— Howly Moses! I've lift the negative and what-ye-may-call-it batteries approachin' of one another an' in about a minute the dinner'll be quite gone up by spontaneous concussion! [*Exit* **Bridget.**]

Mr. Van Arden (*alone*). These little troubles are but the beginning of it all. Now the women will be rushing to the polls, but one thing is certain, *my* wife shall never be seen there.

[*Enter* **Mrs. Rivers**].

Mrs. Rivers. That depends on whether she wants to go or not, my dear brother.

Mr. Van Arden. Ah, Angela, is that you! You see I am still a deserted husband.

Mrs. Rivers. Yes, but a husband very well cared for, nevertheless. Your admirable wife has left her domestic arrangements in good condition, as you very well know. I have just seen the baby, who is in splendid health and crowing at the top of his lungs.

Mr. Van Arden. Why, Angela, Bridget has just told me that he has run the risk of his life twenty times this morning.

Mrs. Rivers. Bridget has drawn on her imagination a little and, besides, the poor girl is somewhat upset just now. She is divided between her duty to her mistress, whom she adores, and her affection for Dennis, who wants to marry her, but positively refuses to do so, if she ever dares to exercise the right to vote.

Mr. Van Arden. Hurrah for Dennis! I need a coachman and shall engage him directly.

Mrs. Rivers. That will be a difficult matter, as he is at present locked up in the station house on account of a drunken brawl with a fellow-voter, who can not write his own name, but who is, nevertheless, fully competent, in your opinion, to help make laws for us all.

Mr. Van Arden. Don't be sarcastic, my fair sister, your husband may like it, but I am afraid Mr. Vere de Vere would call it strong-minded; and a woman might as well hang up her fiddle as have that epithet tacked on to her. Even with *his* limited knowledge of the classics, the charming Oscar would quote:

> "Had she all the charms of golden Venus,
> Could she vie in skill with blue-eyed Pallas,
> Even so endowed, she were no bride for me."

Mrs. Rivers. I am not in a condition to be affected by such a quotation from Mr. Vere de Vere, unless, indeed, I should get a divorce, a thing which would be very easy under your man-made laws; but I assure you, that under the new regime, people will be much more careful about putting their necks into the matrimonial halter, unless they fully intend to remain there for better or for worse. Our first legislation shall have for its object, to guard the sacredness of home, to protect innocent children from the disgrace of having divorced parents, and Christian ministers from deviating so far from the teachings of their Divine Master, as to marry divorced persons.

Mr. Van Arden. You forget, Angela, that Divorce Laws are intended to protect women.

Mrs. Rivers. Then, in ninety-nine out of a hundred cases they have signally failed in their intention; for, pure-minded, refined, honorable women and *men*, too, will, if the ills of married life seem to surpass endurance, separate quietly, or, if that can not be done, they would die rather than appeal to the Divorce Court.

Mr. Van Arden. Still, I think there are cases in which divorce is conducive to the best interests of both parties; though I agree with you, that in most instances it favors only the wicked and shameless, and I think there would be fewer ill-assorted marriages, if the contracting parties were assured that it was a matter of a life-time.

[*Enter* **Bridget**].

Bridget. Plase, sir, the Lightnin' Flyin' Machine's just come in from Boston, and the misthress'll be here in the twinklin' of an eye. [*Exit* **Bridget**.]

Mr. Van Arden. So, now comes the tug of war. Excuse me a moment, Angela, and I will return with my wife. [*Exit* **Mr. Van Arden**.]

Mrs. Rivers (*alone*). Poor brother, he has heard so much of this twaddle about woman unsexing herself and dragging her unsullied purity through the mire of political corruption, that he actually fears for the peace of his own home. Strange that he should have married a so-called strong-minded woman, with whose lecturing propensities and rant about woman's bondage even *I* have no sympathy, though I am with her, heart and soul, in all her efforts to elevate humanity, whether in the form of man or woman; for, surely, whatever benefits one, can not be a detriment to the other, if their interests are, as the Creator evidently intended them to be, one and the same.

[*Enter* **Mr.** *and* **Mrs. Van Arden**].

Mrs. Van Arden. Let us congratulate each other, my dear Angela, the contest is ended, the victory over ignorance and prejudice is complete.

Mrs. Rivers. Yes, and better than all, you, my dear sister, are with us again, to remain at home, I hope.

Mrs. Van Arden. O, as for that I don't know. I don't consider it necessary to be a kitchen drudge, in order to have a well-managed household; and my husband has never complained of my house-keeping, though I *have* been guilty of the terrible enormity of appearing in public on the stage.

Mr. Van Arden. Perhaps that is owing to my unchanging good nature, and who knows but Jones may, at this very moment be speaking of *us*, as that *strong-minded* Mrs. Van Arden and her *poor hen-pecked* husband. I turn pale at the thought, I do worse; I return to my boyhood's "*dolor infandus*,"—like the pious Æneas, "*Obstupui. . vox faucibus haeret*" . . What's the rest of it? Angela, you used to know a little Latin; help a fellow out.

Mrs. Rivers. A little Latin! Just as if you could ever have gone through college without my help!

Mrs. Van Arden. That is true enough, Frank, but, whatever you do, don't quote the pious Æneas. If ever there was a mean hero, he is one, and I only wish Dido had burned *him* on a funeral pile instead of herself.

Mr. Van Arden. What a loss to literature that would have been! But to return to our subject, have you ever thought, my dear, what a *solemn*, what a *terrible* thing it is, to pose before the world as a strong-minded woman?

Mrs. Van Arden. I haven't thought anything about it, for the simple reason that I'm not posing at all. As for being called a strong-minded woman, I am not to be driven from my position by that taunt. I have heard it too often in the mouths of such men as Oscar Vere de Vere and your scarecrow Jones. The former, a poor, pitiful dandy, who, for years, has been seeking the position of son-in-law to a wealthy family, and the other, a great, brutal fellow, who thinks rudeness honesty, and who, having married a wife who pretended she thought women ought not to have any rights at all, is now getting just what he deserves—for she is a perfect tyrant at home, and only a modicum of peace is obtained by giving her everything she wants—for, if she don't get it, a fit of hysterics is the consequence, and even Jones is not proof against hysterics.

Mrs. Rivers. But then, Grace, she is so sweet *in public*—just the sort of woman gentlemen admire, for, she raises her hands in holy horror at the thought of a woman being anything but the echo of her husband or big brother.

Mr. Van Arden. Come, now, Angela, you are too hard on us. I'm sure I can't be called an admirer of the milk and water type, for, behold the proof of the contrary. Before you stands a perfect specimen of the other kind, whom I married with my eyes wide open; and, see, for three weeks she has been devoting herself to what she calls the *"Cause,"* leaving *me* to the tender mercies of Bridget and John, while Jones' wife is always at home, looking after her husband, children and servants.

Mrs. Van Arden. Yes, and the consequence is, the servants are driven mad by contradictory orders, the children are the terror of the neighborhood, and Jones himself, instead of improving, as he would have done with the companionship of a woman who had even a few ideas in her head, has grown to hate the whole sex, because he married a woman for her beauty, her wealth, and her *supposed* submission to the male sex. He is reaping just what he sowed, for his manly intelligence ought to have told him that, a beauty without mental charms can never grow old gracefully. She is forever seeking the ghost of her lost youth; and, not finding it, she becomes peevish and ill-natured, while her more cultured sisters rejoice in charms that grow brighter as the years advance, and make their homes centers of refined enjoyment for family and friends alike, while husband and wife look forward to that calm old age, whose pleasures Cicero has so eloquently described.

[Enter **Bridget.***]*

Bridget. If ye plase, sir, there's a craythur at the door that says it wants to see the masther, an' it was a goin' to march right in here, when I made bould to tell it the family was in the bosom of itself, and couldn't be disturbed by the loikes of it.

Mr. Van Arden. It! Who? What? Explain yourself, Bridget. Are you taking leave of your senses?

Bridget. Faith, an' it's me sinses that almost took lave of me when the craythur twirled a little cane—a sort of shillaly— in me face, an' says: "Bear me missage to the powers above." "An' is it a *madium* ye'd be afther makin' out of me, ye pore, wake little thing?" says I; "troth, an' if it's a missage ye want to send to the powers above, ye'd better fall on your own marrow bones, an' perhaps the Lord'll hear ye out of pity, for all ye do look so quare. Or, if that won't do, there's Father O'Nale, round the corner, as good a praste as iver lived; he'll help ye sind yer missage; but as for movin' of tables, or blowin' of horns, or any other spiritual doin's, ye've come to the wrong place for that, an' ye have." An' wid that, I was goin' to shut the door in its face, when it kind of gasped out: "Sind Mr. Van Arden down;" an' so, savin' yer prisence, sir, I thought I'd better come for ye.

Mr. Van Arden. Well, I should think so.

Mrs. Van Arden. Go quickly, Frank; I'm really afraid. [*Exit* **Mr. Van Arden.**]
(*To* **Bridget.**) Now, Bridget, what in the world is it?

Bridget. Well, mum, it's neither a man nor a monkey, but a kind of between.

Mrs. Rivers. The missing link! In other words, Oscar Vere de Vere!

Bridget. If ye hadn't towld me, I mustn't use slang, I'd of said it's what ye call a *dude.*

Mrs. Van Arden. That will do, Bridget. I think I understand now. [*Exit* **Bridget.**] Poor Oscar! he must have cut a sorry figure in the eyes of Bridget. John has let him in heretofore, and this is her first view of the *"craythur,"* as she calls him.

Mrs. Rivers. In truth, Grace, it is just such men as he that reconcile me to all you say in favor of woman's suffrage. The miserable affectation which *he* calls æsthetic culture, the rolling of his eyes and his mincing ways, almost disgust me with the race to which he belongs.

Mrs. Van Arden. There is a nobler type on which your eyes may dwell—the man who, conscious of his own strength, is yet willing to acknowledge the finer perception, the keener intuition of woman; who feels that her presence in the council halls of a nation would give added dignity to the gravest and most important deliberations. I speak now of woman in her highest and noblest development; for, of course, there will always be women for whom the kitchen and the laundry is the proper sphere, just as among men there always have been, and always will be, hewers of wood and drawers of water.

Mrs. Rivers. There you are, without meaning it, perhaps, the exponent of my husband's views. He has always labored for woman's suffrage, because he thinks it will raise the wife and mother out of the mere housekeeper. He maintains that well-trained servants under proper control, and treated with the consideration which every one owes to an employee, will perform the work of housekeeping perfectly, leaving to the mistress time for that which servants can not do.

[Enter **Bridget**.*]*

Bridget. Misther Jones, mum; shall I show him in?

Mrs. Van Arden. Why, I presume he wants to see Mr. Van Arden. Is he not in the library with Mr. Vere de Vere?

Bridget. Oh, no, mum; he wint out wid the craythur, but it's yersel an' Misthress Rivers that Misther Jones 'ud be afther seein'.

Mrs. Van Arden. Oh, well; show him in then. *[Exit* **Bridget**.*]* What can he want with us?

[Enter **Mr. Jones**, *bowing; the ladies salute him.]*

Mr. Jones. Delighted to see you, ladies; you are doubtless in the seventh heaven over the success of your little scheme. "Ce n'est que le premier pas qui coûte"—and one may safely conclude that your aspirations will now be limited by nothing short of the Presidential Chair.

Mr. Rivers. And why should they be? It would not be the first time that woman has held with steady hand the scepter of control. When was England more prosperous at home, more honored abroad, than in the golden days of good Queen Bess.

Mr. Jones. Oh, but you must admit, Mrs. Rivers, that *she* owed her glory to her statesmen.

Mrs. Rivers. Did she, indeed? What ordinary woman, or man either, could have rallied round the throne *such* statesmen! Had she been weak, unfit to govern, would such men as Burleigh and Walsingham have been ever at her side, eager to carry out her commands? It was the Queen herself, who, when beacon fires blazing from hill-top and tower announced the coming of the Spaniard, rode among her troops, exclaiming: "Though I have but the body of a woman, I have the heart of a king, and a king of England, too, and think proud scorn that Parma or Spain, or any prince of Europe, should dare invade the borders of my realm." And, inspired by her, you know how the British tars sent back to Philip the shattered remnant of his so-called *invincible* Armada.

Mr. Jones. I am willing to grant that Elizabeth *did* make a pretty good figure-head for England, but then what a weak, miserable creature she was as a woman.

Mrs. Van Arden. As far as that is concerned, historians who have striven in vain to belittle her public life, have turned to the miserable business of magnifying faults of character, which were, after all, but the natural outcome of her Tudor blood. Let her be placed in the same category with other rulers, judged by the laws that govern men in the same position, and how few will be found to excel her in their private lives, while none can claim to be her superior in the virtues that adorn a throne.

Mr. Jones. You do not mean to say that she did as much for the English people as other rulers?

Mrs. Van Arden. As much and more, according to the age in which she lived. What state-craft could have been deeper, what policy more far-reaching than that which induced her to gather in the exiled artisans whom the short-sighted policy of the French kings had driven from their native shores? With wise encouragement she stimulated their labors, until, as Richelieu said of France: "Throughout the veins of her vast empire flowed in strengthening tides, Trade, the calm health of nations."

Mr. Jones. Really, ladies, you seem to have studied up this case.

Mrs. Rivers. It is not the only one in point. History furnishes many an example in which women have accomplished undertakings, from which men have turned away in dismay. Need I cite the case of Columbus? Genoa treated him as a visionary, Portugal and England refused him aid, the crafty Ferdinand put him off from day to day, and, not until Isabella undertook the enterprise for her own kingdom of Castile, and pledged her crown jewels for its expense, did the world-seeking Genoese find himself able to start on that voyage which was to reveal a New World. When was the proudest period in Austria's history? Was it not when the Empress Queen, relying on herself alone, defied the allied powers of Europe? Never did a grander figure fill a throne, and yet she was only a woman, but a woman "who knew her rights, and knowing dared maintain."

Mrs. Van Arden. I think, Mr. Jones, we have given a sufficient number of examples, showing that women have been at the head of affairs without endangering public safety, to convince you that you need not fear rack and ruin, even *should* we aspire to the highest position in these United States. I presume that Mrs. Jones and Miss Arethusa are quite disgusted at the passage of the Bill.

Mr. Jones. No, indeed; and that is just what has brought me here to-day. My wife, who, you know, has always professed to detest the unfeminine proceedings of strong-minded women, has actually declared her intention of becoming a candidate for the Board of Public Works.

Mrs. Rivers. So she, like hundreds of her sex, is willing to profit by the rights, to obtain which her pioneer sisters have exposed themselves to the bitter shafts of ridicule. I am ashamed to think that I have sometimes laughed at the little peculiarities of these noble women, who by their self-devotion have done so much for our sex, especially in regard to property laws, which were formerly so unjust to women. But may I ask, Mr. Jones, what your wife's change of views has to do with your visit to us?

Mr. Jones. Simply this, I want you to help me to get this ridiculous notion out of her head, for I know that, notwithstanding your advocacy of woman's suffrage, you would never appear in public positions yourselves.

Mrs. Van Arden. Don't count too much on our modesty, Mr. Jones; both my sister-in-law and myself have aspirations, and the only thing we can promise you is that we will set up a rival candidate, so that Mrs. Jones, in order to secure her election, will have to imitate your sex and spend the greater part of your fortune in buying up votes.

Mr. Jones. My fortune! I'd like to see her get it.

Mrs. Rivers. A candid confession is good for the soul!

Mr. Jones. Well, ladies, there is one question I should like to ask you. Since you have taken upon yourselves to help to do the voting, do you propose to do the fighting also?

Mrs. Van Arden. We don't propose to have any fighting done. That is a relic of barbarism which we shall relegate to the Dark Ages. What is our boasted civilization worth, if we still resort to brute force instead of peaceful arbitration to settle the disputes which arise between nations as well as individuals?

Mr. Jones. I see I might as well take my departure, for you seem bound to have it all your own way. I won't try to keep my wife from voting, but one thing is certain, if, on my return home, I find that miserable dude, Oscar Vere de Vere, pouring his nonsense into Arethusa's ear, I shall just relieve my overwrought feelings by pitching *him* out of the window.

Mrs. Van Arden. Pray do, Mr. Jones, and a jury of ladies will certainly acquit you. [*Exit* **Mr. Jones,** *bowing.*] Really, Angela, Jones has been more polite than usual.

Mrs. Rivers. Certainly, and for the best of reasons, we are now independent voters. He thought that women of refinement would have nothing to do with politics, since even men have become so disgusted that many refuse to exercise the elective franchise. He is surprised to find that we have studied the subject and intend to vote—intelligently if we can—but vote at any rate. He knows well that men whose influence is on the side of justice, law and order, will gladly welcome a reinforcement of noble minded, intelligent, Christian women.

Mrs. Van Arden. It is undoubtedly true that women themselves are to blame for much of the contempt which men of weak or brutal minds regard the sex. It begins in childhood, when, instead of mutual deference and kindness, the boy is allowed to lord it over his sister, until she is made to treat him as a superior being, whose every fault is to be excused, while hers must receive the severest punishment. The same training warps the whole web of society, for there is a class of women who are merciless to their own sex, but smile sweetly on men guilty of greater offenses.

Mrs. Rivers. Well, I trust we are beginning to be more loyal to each other. You know it is a common belief that few women do their work as well as men. There is, no doubt, reason for this belief as far as some women are concerned, but as all work worth doing at all is worth doing well, the matter could be settled in a just way by fixing the value of the work done, and paying the price to whomsoever did it best, whether man or woman. But, begging your pardon for changing the subject, I am curious to know why Mrs. Jones has fixed her attention on the Board of Public Works.

Mrs. Van Arden. Well, I think Arethusa has probably ruined her best gown while promenading one of our filthy thoroughfares, escorted by the gentle Oscar. Mrs. Jones is quite right in supposing that if ladies were members of that Board, the subject of street cleaning would be taken up with a vigor hitherto unprecedented. And, after all, what is the use of Music Halls, Art Museums, or anything else of the sort, if we must wade through mire to get to them. Every person can not appreciate a fine painting or a sweet strain of music, but I defy you to find me one who does not enjoy a clean street. By all means let us have Music, Art and high, æsthetic culture, but if we must be deprived of something, pray let it be these rather than that "cleanliness which is akin to godliness."

Mrs. Rivers. I say amen to that, but really, Grace, I must be going, for I am expecting my husband who is to arrive from Washington this evening, where he has been for two weeks looking after the interests of his automatic *"Cooking Machine,"* which is to revolutionize the whole science of house-keeping.

Mrs. Van Arden. Good bye, then, but don't fail to be present at the primary meeting to be held in the Town Hall, the last week in September, to arrange a ticket for the October election.

CURTAIN

THE NEW WOMAN

A FARCICAL SKETCH
WITH ONE ACT, ONE SCENE
AND ONE PURPOSE

GEORGE RUGG

Boston: Walter H. Baker & Co. 1896.

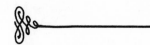

CHARACTERS

Darius Simpkins, married to the New Woman.
Mrs. Darius Simpkins (née Maria), attorney-at-law, and manager-in-chief of
the Simpkins household.
Mrs. Henrietta Dugald High-Mind, another New Woman.
Miss Betty Boston, A. B. C. Ph. D., M. D., X. Y. Z., ditto.

COSTUMES

Darius has coat off, sleeves rolled up, pants turned up at bottom, old carpet
slippers, hair in disorder, roller-towel pinned around body, an old apron on,
a faint moustache charcoaled on an otherwise beardless face. He wears a woe-
begone expression, and his "business" is to keep fussing around the tub till the
dénouement of the play.

Mrs. Simpkins is full of hustle. Speaks loudly and commandingly. Wears
an outlandish bonnet and affects a mannish dress.

Mrs. High-Mind carries her head high and speaks with decision.

Miss Boston wears glasses and is very distingué as well as literary.

PROPERTIES

Oil-stove, small table, wash-bench, tub, wringer, soap, a little water, a
few articles to wash, scrubbing-board, boxing-gloves (2 pairs), small mirror,
bell outside, three kitchen chairs, wash-stick to poke clothes, a dead mouse
back of the oil-stove.

SCENE

A kitchen interior on Monday morning.

Enter **Darius**. *He begins to scrub, tries wringer, etc. Wears a woe-begone expression, and speaks very slowly and with great feeling.*

Darius. Oh, dear me, dear me! My back is half broken! Maria says she can't afford a girl, and so here I am doing the washing for the family, to say nothing of cooking and taking care of the children. Well, thank heaven, Johnny is off to school at last, and the baby—bless its little heart— is asleep. I do wish Maria would be more considerate of a poor man's feelings (her husband at that). When she married me she swore to love, cherish and protect, but now all she seems to think of are clubs, lodge-meetings, bicycling and boxing. And she's so particular! I was always pretty good at plain cooking, but *she* even kicks at my doughnuts, and says they aren't "half so good as mother used to make." The other day she pulled my ears because I answered her back. We men ought to agitate for more privileges. Why, I haven't been out of an evening for two weeks. Let us rise in our might and throw off these shackles that—— Hush! she's coming. [*Scrubs assiduously.*]

Enter **Maria**. *She steps to glass and arranges bonnet.*

Maria. Well, Darius, busy at the bench? That's good. I must be off in a few moments to the Women's Monday Morning Club. We have a lecture by an educated high-caste Hindoo lady, Mrs. Rajput Rimkak Ragbag, on the "Occult Mysteries of the Fourth Dimension of Space." It will be highly inspiring.

Darius. Yes, I dare say it will. But say, Maria, please send up a pound of salt-pork for the beans, will you? It's time they were on. And, Maria, I haven't but eight cents in my pocket-book. Can't you give me a five-dollar bill? And say, Maria, my poor back is all but broken. Won't you stop a while and help me wring out the clothes, before baby wakes up?

Maria. Why, Darius Simpkins! To ask a busy woman like me to stop for a trifle like wringing out clothes! Besides, I expect Mrs. High-Mind and Miss Betty Boston every minute to accompany me to the Hindoo lecture. I am president of the club, you know, and must be there early. Why, just listen to my memorandum of the day's duties:—9:30 to 10:30—Monday Morning Club; 10:30 to 12—at the office, looking up the case of that pretty little Augustus Fairlove versus Georgiana Griggs, breach of promise.

Very interesting case; $10,000 damages claimed. *I* have been retained for the defence. 12 to 1—Dinner; and be sure you have it ready. 1 to 2—Bicycling on the park. 2 to 3—Political class at the Athenæum. At 3 I give my famous lecture on the "Rights of Married Men," before the Women's College of Law. At 5 I box four rounds with the *champion* at the gymnasium. This evening we have a smoke-talk at the Emerson Club. Miss Clementine Vere de Vere gives her ideas on the "Degeneration of Man." Now, be sure you take good care of baby, dear, and put a clean shirt on Johnny this afternoon before he goes to the party. (*Steps to mirror.*) How *nicely* my bonnet fits.

Darius (*kneeling before* **Maria**). Oh, Maria, please don't leave me alone all day. I am so lonely here and the baby is cross. Pity a poor young man! [*Blubbers and rubs his eyes.*]

Maria (*patting him on head*). There, there, hubby, I'll buy you a nice new Waterbury watch to-day.

Darius (*aside*). Yes, you will.

Maria (*continuing*). Come, dear, get to your work, for here are the ladies. I'll ask them into the kitchen here, as they're only neighbors.

Enter **Mrs. High-Mind** *and* **Miss Boston**.

Darius (*curtly*). Good-morning.

Maria. Ah, good-morning, ladies. Darius is hard at work, you see, like a good husband.

Mrs. High-Mind. Admirable! How well-trained you have him.

Miss Betty. Beautiful! I hope when I marry, I shall get such a sweet, docile husband.

Mrs. High-Mind. Are we ready for the lecture?

Maria. Yes; but wait a minute. Let us have one round with the gloves. I want to show you a new blow I learned at the gymnasium. Here are the pudding-bags, and Miss Betty will referee.

[*They put on the gloves.* **Miss Betty** *mounts a chair, takes watch in hand. The two boxers advance, shake, and* **Miss Betty** *shouts "Time." They box. After about thirty seconds* **Maria** *wheels clear around and delivers the famous "pivot" blow.* **Miss Betty** *shouts "Foul!" They take off the gloves.*]

Maria. Miss Betty, have you that poem completed for the Literary Circle?

Miss Betty. Only one verse. Shall I read it?

Both. Yes!

Miss Betty. The title is "The Heart of Man."

> "The heart of man, mysterious muscle,
>   How it moves us with its rustle;
>   Listen to its soulful beats,

How it chills us, how it heats!
Wondrous Heart of Man."

Both. Beautiful! Exquisite!

Maria. Mrs. High-Mind, let us hear the peroration of your address on "Courage," before the Culture Club, next Wednesday.

Mrs. High-Mind. Well, it's like this: "Courage! Virtue of Virtues! Concatenation of soulful strength! March on, oh Woman, to conquer the world. Tender, shrinking man must ever lean for strength upon the sturdy staff of female brains and courage. Woman knows no fear. She——"

Darius (*who has been poking around the stove for some time*). A mouse!

[*All three women shriek, jump into three chairs, and pull their dresses tightly around them.* Darius *calmly continues poking.*]

Maria. Help, Darius!

Mrs. High-Mind.
Miss Betty. } Help! Help!

Darius (*faces around on the three terrified women, stands erect, throws out his chest, and struts back and forth in front of them, flourishing the washstick*). Cowards! Poltroons! After all, you are only women! Darius is a man again, and revenge is sweet. Maria Simpkins, listen to me. (*Slaps stick on floor to emphasize.*) Will you help me wring out the clothes, or shall I set this ravenous beast upon you to fasten its fierce fangs in your quivering flesh?

Maria (*blubbering in fright*). Yes, yes, dear Darius; kill him and I'll wring out all the clothes.

Darius. And can I go out to call this afternoon?

Maria. Yes, but kill him. Oh!——

Darius. And can I have mother over to tea to-night?

Maria. Yes, yes!

Darius. I will now execute the marauder. [*Pokes around stove and finally brings out dead mouse by tail.*]

All the ladies (*in chorus*). Oh! oh! Is he dead?

Darius. Yes, his soul has departed for the happy hunting-grounds. Peace to his ashes, for he has been the means of showing up you three women in your true light. Henceforth the "Old Man" will divide honors with the "New Woman" in this household.

CURTAIN

A VERY NEW WOMAN

ALICE E. IVES

The Woman's Column IX, No. 11, March 14, 1896.

CHARACTERS

Miss Edith Parker
Mrs. Curtis Twillington
Mr. Arthur Twillington

Drawing-room of **Mrs. Curtis Twillington**. *A fireplace at right. Entrance to hall left. Easy chairs scattered about. All accessories indicating wealth and good taste. Discovered:* **Mrs. Twillington** *seated before the fire in easy chair.*

Mrs. Twillington (*looking at her watch*). Just in time (*putting back watch*). Arthur never would have forgiven me if I had been late. So I am to see my future daughter-in-law, Mrs. Arthur Twillington to be. Dear me, as the women in books, who are proposed to, always say,—this is so sudden! The courtship must have been a very rapid one. Why, I never dreamed there was anything in the wind, when, all at once, he informs me he is engaged, and is going to bring her to see me. Arthur certainly can't be old enough to marry. Let me see (*pauses, thinking*). Seventy-two—no, seventy-one. Good gracious! he's twenty-four (*sighing*). I suppose, then, he is of age (*sighing more deeply*). I'm to be a mother-in-law (*sighing more deeply still*). The next thing he'll be making me a grandmother. Ah, it's trying to be a mother. (*Door bell rings.*) There they are!

Enter **Edith Parker** *and* **Arthur Twillington** *from hall,* L.

Arthur. Mother, this is Edith.
Mrs. Twillington (*kissing her*). I am very glad to see Edith—I suppose I may call you that, too.
Edith. I wish you would.
Mrs. Twillington. Now, Arthur, take her to my room to lay off her wraps. You will find Maggie or the other maid somewhere to help her.

Exit **Arthur** *and* **Edith**, *hall door,* L.

Nice girl, I should think. Rather meek and quiet-looking, but pretty and stylish.

Enter **Arthur**, L., *having laid off his overcoat.*

Arthur (*to* **Mrs. Twillington**). I found Maggie in the hall, and put Edith in her charge. How do you like her?
Mrs. Twillington. My dear boy, how can I tell with just a glance? She's pretty.
Arthur (*enthusiastically*). Isn't she?
Mrs. Twillington. Yes. Dresses well, too. Is she a new woman?
Arthur (*stiffly*). You didn't suppose I'd marry an old woman, did you?

Mrs. Twillington. My son, will you be good enough to respect the presence of your mother, and not refer to age?

Arthur. Now mother, you know no one ever thinks of age in your presence.

Mrs. Twillington. Oh, that's all very sweet and nice of you, but you're evading me, and you know it. I want you to tell me whether she's a woman of to-day, whether she has advanced ideas and that sort of thing.

Arthur. Good Lord, deliver us! I hope not.

Mrs. Twillington. You hope not? Don't you know?

Arthur. Well, you see, Edith and I never talked about advanced ideas—we—we just—

Mrs. Twillington. Spooned!

Arthur (*looking a trifle foolish*). I suppose we did do a little at that. But not that all the time. Oh, I tell you, Edith is well read. We read Tennyson together.

Mrs. Twillington. H'm!

Arthur. Oh, yes. And she's such a dear, housewifely little thing. One of those womanly women so rare these days.

Mrs. Twillington. H'm! When did you get time to find out all these things? Never saw her till you met her at Bar Harbor, did you?

Arthur. No. But I saw a good deal of her there.

Mrs. Twillington (*grimly*). No doubt.

Arthur (*anxiously*). Mother, why do you speak so? You're not going to be prejudiced against Edith before you really know her?

Mrs. Twillington. Oh, no. But it's a bit natural that a mother should resent the wiping out, as it were, of her influence of twenty-four years by another woman's of twenty-four days.

Arthur. What do you mean?

Mrs. Twillington. I mean that I supposed I had brought you up to believe in the advanced woman, and here, all of a sudden, you veer about at the girl's bidding, and say "Good Lord deliver us" at the bare mention of the word.

Arthur. It is not at her bidding, mother. She never objected to my believing in the advanced woman; but I felt that she was such a dainty, delicate sort of a flower of a woman, and I knew her modest, retiring, womanly ways so well, that I never argued the point with her.

Mrs. Twillington (*grimly*). H'm!

Arthur. Then, too, I can't say I admire the "new woman" for a wife.

Mrs. Twillington (*coldly*). Having had before you such a dreadful example in your mother.

Arthur (*much hurt*). Mater! Don't say that!

Mrs. Twillington. Oh, well, there's no use dodging the point. You know very well I'm an advanced woman. I believe in a woman earning her own living, if she wants to, in any legitimate way under the sun. I believe in her privilege to improve herself physically and mentally up to the highest point of which any human being is capable. I believe in her right to the ballot, and to any office on the face of the earth to which a human being is eligible and which she is fitted to fill.

Arthur. Yes, mother, I know you believe that way.

Mrs. Twillington. And I thought you did. I never asked you in so many words, but I took it for granted. And to think—how have I brought you up after all—

Arthur (*apprehensively glancing toward door*). Mother, please don't! She may be coming in.

Mrs. Twillington. I hope she is. I want her to hear.

Arthur (*pleadingly*). For my sake, dear, don't shock her at the very outset. Get her to learn to love you a little before you upset her with your views.

Mrs. Twillington. Oh, then I'm not altogether unlovable?

Arthur. You know you're not. You are one of the most fascinating women in New York. Don't I hear it everywhere?

Mrs. Twillington (*sarcastically*). Oh, really!

Arthur (*coaxingly*). Now, dear, promise not to say anything about going out in the world and doing a man's work.

Mrs. Twillington. Nor holding office?

Arthur. Heavens, no!

Mrs. Twillington. Nor going into politics?

Arthur (*horror-stricken*). Not if you love me!

Mrs. Twillington. Nor the right to the ballot?

Arthur (*more horror-stricken*). Oh, Lord, no!

Mrs. Twillington. Very well; for your sake I'll dissemble and stultify myself. Did I ever think I should come to this?

Enter **Edith**, L.

Mrs. Twillington. Come in dear; sit right down by the fire. (*Places easy chair.*) Are you cold from your walk?

Edith. Oh, not at all. Did you think I had run away, I was gone so long? You see I had discovered I had caught my skirt facing somewhere, and it was all torn off. I had to send the maid for a needle and thread.

Mrs. Twillington. I see you are careful, and believe in the stitch in time. Arthur has been telling me how domestic and housewifely you are.

Edith. But I fear it was not entirely from choice. My mother died when I was twelve years old, and I had to be a mother to four little ones, all younger than myself.

Mrs. Twillington. Poor child! That was a severe lesson. To be faithful to such a trust must make one old before her time. But it certainly was a wonderful training for the position of wife. You haven't had time to run off after the fads of the *fin de siècle* woman.

Edith (*rather subdued*). No, I haven't had much time for fads; but I've had some time for good, serious work.

Mrs. Twillington. That's better than all. Being the head of a house and making a home seem to me about the most serious business any one can do.

Edith. Yes, but it's not altogether that, you know—(*hesitating*).

Mrs. Twillington. I suppose the care of the children, looking after their clothes, and seeing that they took their medicine.

Edith. Oh, of course. But I mean—I—I had to look to my own education— and the fitting of myself to—(*Aside.*)—Shall I ever get up the courage to tell them?

Mrs. Twillington. To be married some day. I see what you were trying to say. And the feeling does you credit, in these days, when women don't seem to think of fitting themselves for that honorable position.

Edith (*embarrassed*). Oh—I—I didn't mean that—I mean—(*Aside.*) Edith Parker, you miserable coward! Aren't you ashamed of yourself?

Mrs. Twillington (*taking her hand, kindly*). Now, never mind, dear, what you meant. I'm sure it was something sweet and unselfish and womanly. (*Kisses her.*)

Edith. You are too good to me altogether. You're just as Arthur said you were. (*Takes her hand from* **Mrs. Twillington's**, *gets up and goes to the other side of room, speaking aside.*) Am I going to cry like a great goose, or am I going to get up courage to tell them, as I know I ought to?

Mrs. Twillington (*fixing the fire*). Arthur, come here and raise that coal, won't you? (*Both being intent on arranging fire, do not see* **Edith's** *agitation.*)

Arthur. We are not very cold, mother. We had to hustle so to get here.

Edith. Yes; you see I did not get in just when I was expected. I was out at a meeting.

Mrs. Twillington. }
Arthur.   } A meeting!

Edith. Yes.

Mrs. Twillington. Oh, I suppose a missionary meeting.

Edith. No; a woman suffrage meeting.

Mrs. Twillington (*in amazement*). Suffrage?

Arthur (*same time*). What?

Edith. Yes. I belong to the League.

Mrs. Twillington. Belong to it?

Arthur. You don't mean——

Edith. Yes, I do mean it. I'm the recording secretary.

Arthur. Well!

Mrs. Twillington. Well! (*Laughs immoderately.*)

Edith (*distressed*). Oh, please don't laugh at me. I—I think I can bear anything but that. I was afraid you would combat me, perhaps hate me, but I can't bear to have you ridicule me. It has been so hard for me to tell you; oh, you don't know how hard it was.

Mrs. Twillington (*trying to stop laughing*). My dear girl—(*Breaks out again, laughing immoderately, as she catches sight of* **Arthur's** *distressed face.*) Oh, oh, oh! Ha, ha, ha!

Edith (*drawing herself up*). But, I assure you, this is no fad, no new amusement of mine. I've always felt that women should have just as many rights as men. I don't know when I didn't think that way. It's not mere talk with me. I have worked for it, and I mean to work harder still.

Mrs. Twillington. But, my dear——

Edith (*excitedly*). Oh, I know I should have spoken before; I should have told Arthur; but I saw that he was set against what he called "the new woman"——

Arthur. When did I say so?

Edith. Oh, ever so many times.

Arthur. I thought you didn't believe in her.

Edith. I know you thought so, and I know I should have undeceived you; but—but—I wasn't a new woman just then; I was weak—and—and——

Arthur (*coming to her*). Dear heart!

Edith (*drawing away*). Wait. There is something more dreadful still. I have been studying—law——

Arthur. Law!

Edith. Yes, and I am almost ready for examination. I thought I could give up all my ambitions and ideas, everything—for you—but I find I can't. I must tell you, and go away—if it breaks my heart. (*To* **Mrs. Twillington.**) I did find it hard shocking you, because—because——

Mrs. Twillington. There, now! You haven't shocked me at all, because I'm a new woman myself. You see Arthur made me promise not to shock you. He knew I belonged to a suffrage society.

Edith. You?

Mrs. Twillington. Yes, and if he doesn't want a new woman he can go and get an old one. You and I will keep house together. (*Drawing* **Edith** *to her.*)

Edith (*kissing her*). You are so good! But I—I—shouldn't want to part you. I would better go out of your lives entirely. If he feels that way, we could never be happy. Yes, yes; let me go. (*Breaks down, sobbing.*)

Arthur. Never, sweetheart! Forgive me for not knowing what a new woman really was. The fact is, I fell in with those ideas to please you, as I supposed. I'm not shocked; I'm only very much surprised. You must help mother to teach me.

Edith (*shyly*). Are you sure you won't want to teach me?

Arthur. Sure. I couldn't improve on you. You may think and do just what you like.

Edith (*mischievously*). And I may vote?

Arthur. Just as early and often as the inspectors will let you.

Edith. And the law?

Arthur. Hang out your shingle alone, or go in with me. I have a double office, you know. (*She hesitates.*) Speak, dearie. Don't keep me waiting so.

Edith. I—I think I'll go into the double office. (**Mrs. Twillington** *kisses her, and* **Arthur** *draws her head down on his shoulder.*)

Mrs. Twillington (*turning away*). I must go and see about dinner.

CURTAIN

SOMETHING TO VOTE FOR

A ONE ACT PLAY

CHARLOTTE PERKINS GILMAN

The Forerunner Volume II.
No. 6. June, 1911, pp. 143–153.

PEOPLE IN THE PLAY ——————————————————————

Mrs. May Carroll. A young, beautiful, rich widow; an "Anti"; President of Woman's Club; social leader.

Dr. Strong. A woman doctor, from Colorado, interested in Woman Suffrage and pure milk.

Miss Carrie Turner. Recording Secretary of Club; a social aspirant; agrees with everybody; "Anti."

Mrs. Reedway. Corresponding Secretary of Club; amiable, elderly nonentity; "Anti."

Mrs. Wolverhampton. Rich, impressive, middle-aged matron; "Anti."

Mrs. O'Shane. A little woman in black; thin, poor.

Louise. A maid.

Club Women. Mrs. Black, White, etc.

Mr. Henry Arnold. A Milk Inspector.

Mr. James Billings. Head of the Milk Trust.

TIME, 50 MINUTES. ——————————————————————

PLACE: A parlor, porch or garden, belonging to Mrs. Carroll. ——————————

PROPERTIES REQUIRED

Chairs enough, a small table, a small platform covered with a rug, a table bell, two pitchers, a glass, a vase; two milk bottles filled with water, starch and a little black dirt; a yellow-backed bill, some red ink, a small bunch of flowers, two large clean handkerchiefs, a small bottle of iodine, a teacup. Miss Turner has a bag for her papers, and Dr. Strong an instrument bag or something similar, also a large pocket-book.

Chairs arranged at right, platform, with table and three chairs at left front. Doors at left, right and center.

Enter **Miss Turner** *and* **Mrs. Reedway**, L.

Mrs. Reedway. Dear me! I was so afraid we'd be late!

Miss Turner (*Looking at watch.*). Oh, no! The meeting begins at three you know, and it's only quarter past!

Mrs. Reedway (*Drawing scarf about her.*). I wish it would get warmer! I do like warm weather!

Miss Turner. So do I!

Mrs. Reedway. What a lovely place Mrs. Carroll has! I think we are extremely fortunate to have her for our president.

Miss Turner. So do I! She's so sweet!

Mrs. Reedway. I hear she has asked Mr. Billings to this milk discussion.

Miss Turner. Yes—you're not surprised are you?

Mrs. Reedway. Oh, no! Every one is talking about them. He's been conspicuously devoted to her for some time now. I think it's her money he's after.

Miss Turner. So do I! But she's crazy about him!

Mrs. Reedway. I suppose she thinks he's disinterested—being so rich himself. But I've heard that he'd lose a lot if this milk bill goes through.

Miss Turner. So have I!

(*Enter* **Dr. Strong**, L.)

Dr. Strong. Sorry to be late. I was detained by a patient.

Miss Turner. Oh, you're not late, Dr. Strong. The ladies are usually a little slow in gathering.

Dr. Strong. I see! And about what time do your meetings really begin?

Miss Turner. About half past three, usually.

Dr. Strong. Next time I'll come then. I could have seen two more patients—I hate to see women so unpunctual.

Miss Turner. So do I! This is Mrs. Reedway, our corresponding secretary, Dr. Strong. (*They shake hands.*)

Mrs. Reedway. You must remember, Dr. Strong, that our members are not —as a whole—professional women.

Dr. Strong. More's the pity!

(Enter **Mrs. Wolverhampton,** L.*)*

Mrs. Wolverhampton. Well, well! Not started yet? But you're always on hand, Miss Turner. *(Fans herself.)* Bless me, how hot it is! I do hate hot weather.

Miss Turner. So do I.

Mrs. Reedway. Have you met our new member, Mrs. Wolverhampton? Dr. Strong, of Colorado. (**Mrs. Wolverhampton** *bows.* **Dr. Strong** *comes forward and shakes hands.)*

Mrs. Wolverhampton. Dear me! From Colorado! And I suppose you have voted!

Dr. Strong. I certainly have. You seem to think I look like it.

Mrs. Wolverhampton. Why, yes; if you'll pardon me, you do.

Dr. Strong. Pardon you? It seems to me a compliment. We're very proud of being voters—in my country.

(**Mrs. Reedway** *and* **Mrs. Wolverhampton** *draw aside and converse in low tones.* **Miss Turner** *fussily arranges papers; she has a large flat bag, and is continually diving into it and fumbling about.) (Enter* **Mrs. Carroll,** C.*)*

Mrs. Carroll. Pardon me, ladies! I'd no idea it was so late. *(Greets them all.)*

Miss Turner. Dear Mrs. Carroll! Would you accept these flowers?

Mrs. Carroll. How charming of you, Miss Turner! They are lovely. *(Sweeps toward* **Dr. Strong,** *both hands out,* C.*)* My *dear* Doctor! I feel so glad and proud to have you with us! *(Turns to others.)* You know, Mrs. Wolverhampton, Dr. Strong saved my mother's life! If she had come here sooner I'm sure she would have saved my baby! And she's going to be *such* a help to our club, aren't you, Doctor?

Dr. Strong. I'm not so sure of that, Mrs. Carroll. I'm afraid this isn't the sort of club I'm used to.

Mrs. Carroll. It's the sort of a club that needs you, Doctor! *(Takes* **Doctor's** *arm and sits down with her.)* Make yourselves quite at home, ladies, the others will be here presently. (**Miss Turner, Mrs. Reedway** *and* **Mrs. Wolverhampton** *go out,* C.*)* We've got everything arranged, Doctor. I'm going to have a bottle of the Billings Co. milk tested, and Mr. Billings himself is to be here.

Dr. Strong. That may be awkward.

Mrs. Carroll. Oh, no! The milk is all right—I've taken it for years. And I think he's a very fine man.

Dr. Strong *(Drily.).* So I hear.

Mrs. Carroll. You mustn't believe all you hear, Doctor.

Dr. Strong. I don't. But I hope it isn't true.

Mrs. Carroll. Hope what isn't true?

Dr. Strong. About you and Mr. Billings.

Mrs. Carroll. Never mind about me and Mr. Billings! The question is have you got the new Inspector to come?

Dr. Strong. Yes, he'll be ready on time—but the club won't, I'm afraid.

Mrs. Carroll. Oh, a few moments won't matter, I'm sure. It's a Mr. Arnold you said—do you know his initials?

Dr. Strong. His name's Henry T. Arnold. I believe he's honest and efficient.

Mrs. Carroll (*Meditatively.*). I used to go to school with a boy named Harry Arnold—he was the very nicest boy in the room. I think he liked me pretty well——

Dr. Strong. And I think you liked him pretty well—eh?

Mrs. Carroll. Oh, well! That was years ago!

Dr. Strong (*Suddenly.*). By the way, Mrs. Carroll, have you any red ink?

Mrs. Carroll. Red ink?

Dr. Strong. Yes, red ink—can you get me some?

Mrs. Carroll. Why, I'm sure I don't know. Let me see—I did have some—it's right here—if there is any. (*Goes out* R. *and returns with red ink.*)

Dr. Strong. Thank you. (*Takes out a yellow-backed bill, and deliberately marks it.*)

Mrs. Carroll. How exciting! What *do* you do that for, Doctor?

Dr. Strong. Just a habit of mine. Some day I may see that again and then I'd know it.

Mrs. Carroll. Do you mark all your money?

Dr. Strong. Oh, no. Only some of it. And now will you do me a real favor?

Mrs. Carroll. Indeed I will!

Dr. Strong. Please do not make any remark about this bill if you see me change it!!

Mrs. Carroll. How mysterious! I won't say a word.

Dr. Strong (*Putting away bill.*). You said I might bring along one of my patients, for evidence, and I have. I've got little Mrs. O'Shane here to tell them how it affects the poor people.

Mrs. Carroll. That will be interesting, I'm sure—where is she?

Dr. Strong. Waiting outside—I couldn't induce her to come in.

Mrs. Carroll. I'll bring her in.

(*Exit* **Mrs. Carroll**, L., *returns with a small shabby women in black, who shrinks into the chair farthest back and sits silent.*)

Mrs. Carroll. It's very good of you to come, Mrs. O'Shane; we're so much obliged!

(*Enter* **Louise**, L.)

Louise. Mr. Arnold, Ma'am.

Mrs. Carroll. Show him in, Louise.

(Exit **Louise.** *Enter* **Mr. Arnold,** L.*)*

Dr. Strong. Mrs. Carroll—Mr. Arnold.

Mrs. Carroll. It is Harry Arnold, I do believe! But you don't remember me!

Mr. Arnold. Don't remember little May Terry! The prettiest girl in school! I've never forgotten her. But I did not expect to find you here.

Mrs. Carroll. I'm glad to welcome you to my home, Mr. Arnold, as well as to our club. And how are you—getting on?

Mr. Arnold. Nothing to boast of Mrs. Carroll, if you mean in dollars and cents. I like public work you see, and the salaries are not high.

Mrs. Carroll. But some of our officials get very rich, don't they?

Mr. Arnold. Yes, some of them do,—but not on their salaries.

Dr. Strong. If you knew more about politics, Mrs. Carroll, you would think better of Mr. Arnold for not making much. And he an Inspector, too!

Mrs. Carroll. You don't mean that our public men are bribed, surely!

Dr. Strong. It's been known to occur.

Mrs. Carroll. Oh, I can't believe that such things go on—here! Did any one every bribe you, Mr. Arnold?

Mr. Arnold. Some have tried.

Mrs. Carroll. Not in this town, surely.

Mr. Arnold. Not yet.

Dr. Strong. He's only just appointed, Mrs. Carroll.

Mr. Arnold. Thanks to you, Dr. Strong.

Dr. Strong. Yes, I guess I did help.

(Enter **Louise,** L.*)*

Louise. Mr. Billings.

Mrs. Carroll. Ask him to come in. *(Exit* **Louise,** L. *Enter* **Mr. Billings,** L.*)* Good afternoon, Mr. Billings. Let me present you to my dear friend, Dr. Strong—our new member. And Mr. Arnold you probably know—the Milk Inspector. (**Mr. Billings** *approaches* **Dr. Strong,** *who bows stiffly. He shakes hands amiably with* **Mr. Arnold.**)

Mr. Billings. Well, Mr. Arnold, I think we're going to make an impression on these ladies. I trust you'll deal gently with me.

Mr. Arnold. I'll do the best I can, Mr. Billings. I didn't expect to have the head of the Milk Trust in my audience.

Mrs. Carroll. That is all my fault, Mr. Arnold. I have taken milk of Mr. Billings' company for years, and it's always good. And I want the ladies to know it. Mr. Billings can stand the test.

Mr. Arnold. I'm glad to hear it, Mrs. Carroll.

Mr. Billings (*Genially.*). You'll show up all of us rascally milk-men I don't doubt.

Mr. Arnold. I hope not. (**Mr. Billings** *goes to* **Mrs. Carroll.** *They talk apart.* **Dr. Strong** *confers with* **Mr. Arnold.**)

Dr. Strong (*To* **Mr. Arnold.**). Now Mr. Arnold watch me, and be sure you play up. Say you can't make change for this bill! (*Goes to* **Mr. Billings.**) Mr. Billings—can you—and will you—change this bill for me? Mr. Arnold here can't make it.

Mr. Arnold. I'm sorry, Doctor. But I haven't seen a hundred dollar bill in some time.

Mrs. Carroll. Perhaps I can—

Mr. Billings. No indeed, Mrs. Carroll! I shall be delighted, Dr. Strong,—if I have that much about me. (*Brings out bills from pockets and makes up the amount.*)

Dr. Strong. Thank you, Mr. Billings. (*Gives him her marked bill. The club members are seen arriving in background,* c. *Returning to* **Mr. Arnold.**) What figures have you brought, Mr. Arnold? I don't want to cross your trail. (*They confer apart.*)

Mr. Billings (*To* **Mrs. Carroll.**). Isn't it rather a new thing for you to interest yourself in public matters, Mrs. Carroll?

Mrs. Carroll. Oh, but milk is really a domestic matter—don't you think so? So many of our ladies are getting interested in it.

Mr. Billings. I suspect that is because you are! I do not think you realize your influence in this town.

Mrs. Carroll. I'm sure you overestimate it.

Mr. Billings. Not in the least! Look at the way you swing this club! And these are the society lights—all the other women follow. And the men are yours to command anyhow! I tell you such an influence as yours has Woman Suffrage beaten to a standstill!

Mrs. Carroll. Oh!—Woman Suffrage! (*With great scorn. Enter* **Mrs. Wolverhampton,** c.)

Mrs. Wolverhampton. Pardon me Mrs. Carroll, but it is half past three.

Mrs. Carroll. Dear me! yes, we must come to order. (*Ladies all come in and take seats. Some polite confusion.* **Mrs. Carroll** *in the chair.* **Mrs. O'Shane** *and* **Mr. Billings** *at extreme right, behind others but near front of stage. Platform, table, etc.,* L. *front.*)

Mrs. Carroll (*Rising.*). Ladies, and—gentlemen,—I—er—as you all know, I can't make a speech,—and I'm not in the least fit to be the president of a club—but you would have it you know! (*Murmur of approval; faint applause.*) I am very glad to welcome you to my home, and I'm sure I hope we shall all enjoy meeting here. (*More faint applause.*) I don't suppose it's very business like—but the very first thing I want to do is to introduce our new member, Dr. Strong of Col. (**Mrs. Carroll** *sits,* **Dr. Strong** *rises and bows.*) O do come forward to the platform, Doctor, where we can all see you.

Dr. Strong (*Coming to platform.*). Madam President—Ladies—and gentlemen! I did not expect to be sprung on you until after the reading of the minutes at least. But I am very glad to meet you and to feel that you have honored me with membership in what I understand is the most influential woman's club in this community. I have heard that this is a very conservative club, but I find that you are interesting yourselves in one of the most vital movements of our time—a question of practical politics—Pure Milk. (*The ladies cool and stiffen at the word "politics."*) It is a great question—a most important question—one that appeals to the mother-heart and housekeeping sense of every woman. It is a matter of saving money and saving life—the lives of little children! I do not know of any single issue now before us which is so sure to make every woman want to vote. The ballot is our best protection. (*Cries of "no!" "no!" Much confusion and talking among members. One hiss.* **Mrs. Wolverhampton** *rises ponderously.*)

Mrs. Wolverhampton. Madam President! I rise to a point of order! I move you that our new member be informed that all discussion of woman suffrage is forbidden by the by-laws of this club! There is no subject so calculated to disrupt an organization.

Mrs. Black. Madam President!

Mrs. Carroll. Mrs. Black.

Mrs. Black. I wish to second the motion! We decided long ago to allow no discussion of woman suffrage! I consider it to be one of the most dangerous movements of our time!

Mrs. White. Madam President!

Mrs. Carroll. Mrs. White. Won't you come forward, Mrs. White?

Mrs. White. O no, excuse me—no. I'll speak from here. I merely wish to agree with the previous speaker. Woman suffrage breaks up the home.

Mrs. Grey. Madam President!

Mrs. Green. Madam President.

Mrs. Carroll. Mrs. Grey I think spoke first. In a moment, Mrs. Green.

Mrs. Grey. I just want to say that I for one should feel obliged to resign if woman suffrage is to be even mentioned in the club!

Mrs. Green. Madam President!

Mrs. Brown. Madam President!

Mrs. &c. Madam President! (*There has been a constant buzz of disapproval.*)

Mrs. Carroll. Ladies! One at a time, please! (*Several ladies are on their feet. All speak together.*)

Mrs. Green. A woman's place is in the home, Madam President! If she takes good care of the home and brings up her children right—

Mrs. Brown. Women are not fitted for politics, they haven't the mind for it —and my husband says politics is not fit for women, either!

Mrs. Jones. This club decided long ago that it was against woman suffrage— et al. Who'd take care of the baby?

Our power is through our feminine influence—

Yes—a woman's influence.—(*Great confusion.*)

Mrs. Carroll. (*Rapping feebly on the table.*) Ladies, ladies, we will adjourn for some refreshments. Won't you please all come and have some tea? (*All go out,* c. *and* R. *still talking.* **Mrs. Carroll** *and* **Mr. Billings** *last.* **Dr. Strong** *and* **Mr. Arnold** *remain.*)

Mr. Arnold (*To* **Dr. Strong.**). Well, Dr. Strong, you did put your foot in it!

Dr. Strong (*Ruefully.*). Yes—that was unfortunate, wasn't it? I'd no idea they'd fly up like that.

Mr. Arnold. Never mind. I'll only talk milk to 'em—pure milk!

Dr. Strong (*Walks up and down, hands behind her, much perturbed.*). I'm right sorry to have annoyed those women. This is an awfully important occasion. Even if they can't vote, they could do something.

Mr. Arnold. Don't you fret, Doctor, we'll get them interested.

Dr. Strong. You don't know how important this is. The death rate among the babies here is something shameful—it's mostly owing to bad milk—and the bad milk is mostly owing to this man Billings. If this bill passes he's got the whole thing in his hands! And he's crooked!

Mr. Arnold. I'd about come to that conclusion, myself.

Dr. Strong. He's got her confidence you see—and she swings this town, socially. What's more, he means to marry her—and he's not a fit man to marry any decent woman. We've got to put a spoke in his wheel, Mr. Arnold!

Mr. Arnold. I'm willing.

Dr. Strong. You'll never get a better opportunity than right now! He'll try to fix you before you speak—I'll promise you that! and do you stick out for that hundred dollar bill—and take it!

Mr. Arnold. I guess not! What do you think I am?

Dr. Strong. I think you're man enough to see this game through. It's a marked bill, I tell you! You take that hundred and look at it—if there's a speck of red in the middle on the top—on both sides—you take it, and bring it out in evidence after you've shown up the milk!

Mr. Arnold. But the milk he sends here'll be all right.

Dr. Strong. Of course! But I've brought in another bottle in my bag—and I'm going to substitute it! It's his milk, all right—the common grocery store kind—you'll be safe with the iodine test. Sh! You take that bill!

(Re-enter **Mrs. Carroll** C. *bringing tea to* **Mrs. O'Shane**.)

Mrs. Carroll (*To* **Mrs. O'Shane**.). We are really much indebted to you for coming, Mrs. O'Shane—I hope you are quite comfortable?

Mrs. O'Shane. Thank you Ma'am, thank you kindly!

Mrs. Carroll (*Crossing to* **Dr. Strong**.). Now Dr. Strong, you mustn't be angry because our ladies are not suffragettes.

Dr. Strong. Not a bit—I'm only sorry I mentioned it—I'm here to talk milk —not suffrage.

Mrs. Carroll. That's so nice of you! Now do go out and get some tea, doctor. (*Exit* **Dr. Strong** R.)

Mrs. Carroll. I suppose you're going to be very impressive Mr. Arnold! You were as a boy, you know!

Mr. Arnold. Was I? I don't remember that.

Mrs. Carroll. Yes, indeed. You used to brush your hair,—when you did brush it—in a way I thought extremely fine.

Mr. Arnold. And yours was always brushed! Beautiful long soft curls! I used to wish I dared touch them!

Mrs. Carroll. My hair's grown so much darker since then, and I'm getting grey.

Mr. Arnold (*Drawing nearer.*). Grey! It's a libel! Not a single one.

Mrs. Carroll. There were—two or three—but, to speak confidentially, I pulled them out.

Mr. Arnold. It wasn't necessary. You will be still more beautiful with grey hair!

Mrs. Carroll. You didn't make compliments at thirteen.

Mr. Arnold. No—I didn't dare.

Mrs. Carroll. And how do you dare now.

Mr. Arnold. The courage of desperation, I suppose. Here you are, still young, more beautiful than ever—the richest woman in the town; the social leader; able to lift and stir all these women—and here am I, a lot older than you are—and nothing but a milk inspector!

Mrs. Carroll. You haven't had much personal ambition, have you?

Mrs. Arnold. No, I haven't. But I might—if I were encouraged.

Mrs. Carroll. Mr. Arnold! I am so glad to find you are my old friend. And to think that you do—perhaps—value my opinion.

Mr. Arnold. You're right as to that. That's what discouraged me when you married Carroll; and when I heard that you had become a mere society woman—You've got a good mind, always had, but you don't use it.

Mrs. Carroll. You do think I have a mind then?

Mr. Arnold. Indeed I do! A first-class one!

Mrs. Carroll. Then let me persuade you to speak for this milk bill, Mr. Arnold!

And I do hope in your speech—you'll mention the excellent influence—
on the milk, you know—of Mr. Billings' company.

Mr. Arnold. Why—I shall have to tell what I know, Mrs. Carroll; you want
the facts.

Mrs. Carroll. Of course we want the facts! But—having Mr. Billings' milk to
be tested—and Mr. Billings here—and he being a good friend of mine
—I'm particularly anxious to have his reputation thoroughly established.

Mr. Arnold. I see. And if I said anything against Mr. Billings, we should meet
as strangers?

Mrs. Carroll. Not at all, Mr. Arnold! It's the milk we're talking about—not
Mr. Billings.

Mr. Arnold. I beg pardon—I understand! (*Re-enter* **Mr. Billings** c. *Exit* **Mr.
Arnold** r.)

Mr. Billings (*Coming to* **Mrs. Carroll.**). I began to think I shouldn't have a
chance to see you at all!

Mrs. Carroll. Why I'm quite conspicuous, I'm sure,—in the chair!

Mr. Billings. Ah! But I like best to see you alone!

Mrs. Carroll. No one sees me when I'm alone!

Mr. Billings. You can joke about it, Mrs. Carroll; it is a very serious matter
to me. You must know how much I care for you—how long I have been
devoted to you. You know I'm an ambitious man, Mrs. Carroll. I must
be to dare hope for you! There are things I can't speak of yet—big chances
in politics—if I had you with me—with your beauty and fascinating
ways—By Heavens! There's no place I wouldn't try for. (*Walks up and
down excitedly.*) I never wanted anything so much in my life—as I want
you. When will you give me an answer?

Mrs. Carroll. Certainly not now, Mr. Billings.

Mr. Billings. When the meeting is over?

Mrs. Carroll. Perhaps—when the meeting is over.

(*Enter* **Miss Turner** c. *with bag and papers.*)

Mrs. Carroll (*rises, and goes to her.* **Mr. Billings** *turns away*). Well, Miss
Turner, are you going to set us to work again?

Miss Turner. I hope I don't interrupt——

Mrs. Carroll. Interrupt! Why this is a club meeting, Miss Turner! Are we ready
now?

Miss Turner. Perhaps, if you'd have the maid bring in the sample.

Mrs. Carroll. Oh, yes. (*Rings. Enter maid* r.)

Mrs. Carroll. Bring in the bottle of milk, Louise. (*Exit maid* r. *Re-enter* **Dr.
Strong** *and* **Mr. Arnold** c.)

Mr. Billings (*jocularly*). I'm to be the scapegoat for the sins of the whole
community, I see!

Mrs. Carroll. You are going to clear the good name of our milk supply, Mr. Billings.

(Re-enter maid R. *with bottle of milk, sets it on table* L. F.*)*

Mrs. Carroll. Here it is! The best milk in town. *(They all approach table.)*

Mr. Billings *(takes it up).* That's mine, all right. Name blown in the bottle, sealed with paraffine, air-tight from cow to customer, Mr. Arnold!

Mr. Arnold *(examining bottle).* Looks like good milk, Mr. Billings.

Mr. Billings. It *is* good milk, Mr. Arnold; there's none better in the market! We're not afraid of your examination.

Mr. Arnold. Do you send out a uniform quality?

Mr. Billings. Well, hardly that, of course. We have some with less butter fat, comes a cent or two lower—but it's all pure milk.

Dr. Strong *(to* **Arnold** *aside).* Get 'em to look at your papers—call 'em off!

Mr. Arnold. Have you seen our official cards, Mrs. Carroll? *(Takes out papers. They turn to him. The doctor whips out bottle of milk from her bag and changes it for the one on the table. Billing hears her and turns around. Comes over to the table and takes bottle up. Starts. Others turn also.)*

Dr. Strong. What's the matter?

Mr. Billings. Matter? Why—nothing.

Dr. Strong. Name blown in the bottle all right? Paraffine seal all right? *(All come to look.)*

Mr. Billings. Yes, yes, it's all right. *(Moves off evidently perturbed.)*

Mrs. Carroll. What is it? Anything wrong with the milk?

Mr. Billings. No, no, certainly not.

Mrs. Carroll. Well, Miss Turner, I think we must collect our audience. *(They go out.* C.*)*

Dr. Strong. Can I be of assistance? *(Follows with a meaning glance at* **Mr. Arnold** *who is by the table.)*

*(**Mr. Billings** with sudden determination walks swiftly to the table to take milk bottle.* **Mr. Arnold** *seizes it.)*

Mr. Billings. Excuse me, Mr. Arnold—but there's a mistake here! This is not the milk I sent Mrs. Carroll—by some error it's a bottle of our second quality. I'd hate to have her find it out. I've got my car here and I'm just going to run off and change this—it won't take but a minute!

Mr. Arnold *(holding the bottle).* I don't think you'd better, Mr. Billings. It would look badly. There's really no time.

Mr. Billings *(agitated).* I guess you're right. See here—this is a very important matter to me—more important than you know. . . . This bottle is not my *best* milk—but—but I'd be much obliged to you if it tested well——

Mr. Arnold *(drily).* I hope it will.

Mr. Billings. Look here, Arnold, confound it! They'll all be back in a minute! Here! Quick! (*Passes him a bill.*)

Mr. Arnold (*takes it. Looks at it, both sides*). I'm not in the habit of taking bribes, Mr. Billings.

Mr. Billings. Sh! I can see that—you are so stiff about it! For goodness sake, man, see me through this foolish hen-party and I'll make it well worth your while! Come, put that in your pocket for this one occasion, you understand!

Mr. Arnold. Well—just this one occasion! (*Puts bill in pocket.*)

(*Ladies all re-enter* R. L. C. *and take seats. Meeting called to order.* **Mrs. Carroll** *in chair as before;* L. F., *bustle, talk.*)

Mrs. Carroll (*rapping on table*). Will the meeting please come to order. I think, since it is already so late—and since we have such important—er—such an important—question to discuss, it will be as well to postpone the regular order of business until our next meeting. I'm sure you will be glad to have our discussion opened with a few words from Mr. Billings. Mr. Billings is the head of the milk business here, and knows more about it than any man in town. It is his milk which we are to have tested this afternoon—and he is proud to have it so—aren't you, Mr. Billings? (*Smiles at him.*)

Mr. Billings (*rather constrainedly*). Yes; yes.

Mrs. Carroll. Now, do talk to us a little, Mr. Billings. Won't you please come forward.

Mr. Billings (*rising in his place*). Madam President, and ladies, also Mr. Inspector: I feel it to be an honor to be here to-day to meet so many of the leading ladies of our community; to see so many fair faces—hear so many sweet voices—take the hand of so many I am proud to number among my friends. I wish to congratulate this club on its new president (*bows to* **Mrs. Carroll**)—a lady whose presence carries a benefaction wherever she goes. (*Applause.*) In these days, when so many misguided and unwomanly women are meeting together for all manner of unnecessary and sometimes utterly mistaken purposes, it is a genuine pleasure to find here so many true women of that innate refinement which always avoids notoriety. (*Takes out large white handkerchief and wipes face.*) The subject upon which I have been asked to address you is one which appeals to the heart of every woman—milk for babes! The favorite food of our children, the mainstay of the invalid, the foundation of all delicate cookery!

It has been my pleasure, ladies, and my pride to have helped in serving this community with pure and healthful milk for many years past.

Our new organization, of which there is now so much discussion in the public press, is by no means the evil some would have you believe. I speak as one who knows. This is not the place for dry financial statistics, but I assure you that through this combination of milk dealers which has been recently effected you will have cheaper milk than has ever been given here before, and a far more regular and reliable service. For the quality we must trust to the opinion of these experts (*waves his hand to* **Dr. Strong** *and* **Mr. Arnold**); but for the wish to serve your best interests, and for a capacity in service developed through years of experience, you may always count upon yours truly. (*Bows and sits. Stir and murmurs of approval. Applause.*)

Mrs. A. Isn't he interesting.

Mrs. B. Just what I think.

Mrs. Carroll. I'm sure we are all very grateful to Mr. Billings for giving us so much of his valuable time. It is so interesting, in this study of large general questions, to get information from the fountain head. And now we shall learn the medical side of it from a most competent authority. Ladies, I take pleasure in introducing my dear friend, Dr. Strong, who will speak to us on—what do you call it, Doctor?

Dr. Strong (*coming forward*). Let us call it The Danger of Impure Milk. (*Stands a moment, looking earnestly at them.*) We all love babies. We love our own babies best of all, naturally. We all want to feed our babies well, and some of us can't do it ourselves. Next to the Mother, the most important food supplier for our children is the Cow. Milk is the most valuable article of food for little children.

I suppose you all know that bottle-fed babies die faster than breast-fed—by far; they die mostly in summer, and from enteric and diarrheal diseases. (*Reads from notes.*) 17,437 babies under a year old died in New York in 1907; 1,315 died in Boston between June 1st and November 30th of that same year—in six months. In Fall River, at that time, more than 300 out of 1,000 died—nearly one-third. In New York, in five years, over 23,000 children of all ages died of measles, scarlet fever and diphtheria combined, and in the same time over 26,000 babies under two years died of diarrheal diseases. Out of 1,943 cases of these infantile diseases, in New York, only three per cent were breast-fed.

Now, ladies, this class of diseases comes from bacteria, and the bacteria come, in the vast majority of cases, from the milk. You see, the bottle-fed baby does not get its supply directly from the source, as when fed by its mother; between the Cow and the Baby stands the Milkman. The Milkman is not a mother. I really believe that if mothers ran the milk business they would not be willing to poison other women's babies even to make money for their own!

The producer and distributer of milk has small thought for the consumers' interests. To protect the consumer, the law now provides the Milk Inspector. But the Milk Inspector has on one side a few alert business men, often ready to pay well to protect their interests, and on the other the great mass of apathetic citizens, who do not take the trouble to protect their own.

The discussion to-day is in the hope of rousing this club to see the vital importance of pure milk for our children, and to urge its members to use their influence to secure it.

By the kind permission of your president I have brought with me a resident of a less fortunate part of the town, that she may give you a personal experience. Mrs. O'Shane, will you please come to the platform? (*The little woman in black rises, hesitates, sits down again.*)

Mrs. Carroll. Won't you please make room, ladies? (*She comes down and escorts* **Mrs. O'Shane** *to platform.* **Mrs. O'Shane** *much agitated.*)

Dr. Strong. Brace up, Mrs. O'Shane. It's for little Patsy's sake, you know. He's gone, but there are many more.

Mrs. O'Shane. Indade there are, thank Hiven! It's not too late for the others! The street's full ov thim! If ye please, ladies, did any of you ever lose a child?

Mrs. Carroll (*coming to her and taking her hand*). I have, Mrs. O'Shane. (*Sits again.*)

Mrs. O'Shane. There's many, I don't doubt. But ye have the consolation of knowin' that your children had all done that could be done for thim. An' ours dies on us every summer—such a many of thim dies—an' we can't help it. They used to tell us 'twas the Hand 'o God, and then they said 'twas the hot weather, and now they're preachin' it to us everywhere that 'tis the milk does it! The hot weather is bad, because thim things that's in the milk shwarms thicker and faster—thim little bugs that kills our babies. . . . If ye could have seen my little Patsy! He was the han'somest child, an' the strongest! Walkin' he was—and him hardly a year old! An' he was all I had—an' me a widder! An', of course, I took the best milk I could get; but all the milk in our parts comes from the Trust—an' sixteen cents a quart for thim fancy brands I could not pay. An', just think of it —even if I could, there's not enough of that sort *to go around!* There's so many of us! We have no choice, and we have no money to pay for the extras, an' we must give our babies the milk that is sold to us—an' they die! . . .

I know I should care most for the hundreds an' thousands of thim— an' for Mrs. Casey's twins that died in a week last summer, an' three of Mrs. Flaharty's, an' even thim little blackies on Bay street; but I care the most for my Little Patsy—havin' but the wan! Ladies, if you could have seen him! The hair on his head was that soft!—an' all in little rings o' curls! An' his cheeks like roses—before he took sick; an' his little feet was that pretty—an' he'd kick out so strong and bold with them! An' he could

stand up, and he was beginning to hold on the chairs like—an' he'd catch
me by the skirts an' look up at me with such a smile—an' pull on me he
would, an' say Mah! Mah! An' what had I to give him but the milk? And
the milk killed him. . . . I beg your pardon, ladies, but it breaks my heart!
(*She cries. Mrs. Carroll comforts her, crying too. Many handkerchiefs out.
Mrs. Carroll rises up, repressing emotion.*)

Mrs. Carroll. Ladies, we will now hear from our new Inspector, Mr. Arnold.
(**Mr. Arnold** *comes forward and bows.*)

Mr. Arnold. I fear cold facts will make but little impression after this moving
appeal. Mrs. O'Shane has given you the main points in the case. Most
people are poor. Most milk is poor. And the poorest milk goes to the
poorest people. The community must protect itself. The Inspector has no
power except to point out defects in the supply. Action must be taken to
enforce the law, and unless the public does its duty there is often no action
taken. (*Reads from paper.*) Dr. Strong has given you some figures as to
the mortality among babies. There is also a heavy death rate for adults
from contaminated milk, as in the case of the typhoid fever outbreak in
Stamford, Conn., in 1895, when 160 cases were reported in nine days,
147 of which had all used milk from one dairyman. In about six weeks
386 cases were reported; of these 352 took milk from that one dealer, and
four more got it from him indirectly. His dairy was closed, and in two
weeks the outbreak had practically subsided.

Typhoid fever, scarlet fever and diphtheria, as well as many less common diseases, are spread by infected milk.

The inspection service watches both the producer and distributor;
examining the dairy farm as to the health of the cattle, the nature of their
surroundings, the care given them, the methods of milking, bottling, and
so on; and looking to the milkmen in each step of handling, carriage and
delivery.

In judging milk there are three main questions to be considered: Its
comparative quality as good milk (the percentage of butter-fats, etc.); its
cleanliness (dirty milk is always likely to carry disease); and its freedom
from adulteration—from the primitive pump-water and starch down to
the subtler and more dangerous commercial methods of today.

I have been asked to show you a simple test or two—such as might
be used at home. These do not require chemical or bacteriological analysis,
a microscope or a lactometer; merely a fine cloth (*produces it*) and a little
iodine (*produces that*).

(*The ladies lean forward eagerly.* **Mr. Billings** *looks indifferent.*)

Mr. Arnold. Please understand, ladies, that neither of these tests proves anything absolutely harmful. I feel extremely awkward in testing a bottle of

the Billings Company milk in the presence of Mr. Billings. Please remember that the Billings Company has many supply dairies. If this one bottle should not prove first-class it is no direct reproach to your guest.

Mr. Billings. Ladies, I do not ask any excuses. The Billings Company is reliable.

Mrs. Carroll. We have every confidence in this milk, Mr. Billings; that is why I asked for the test.

Mr. Arnold. May I ask for another vessel—a pitcher or milk bottle?

Mrs. Carroll *rings. Enter* **Louise**, R.

Mrs. Carroll. Bring another pitcher, Louise, and an empty milk bottle—clean. (*Exit* **Louise**, R., *and returns with them*, R., *while* **Mr. Arnold** *continues.*)

Mr. Arnold. Only two things are to be decided by this little test—whether the milk is clean, and whether it has starch in it. If it is clean milk, according to our standard, there will be but a slight smear on the cloth when it is strained. (*He puts cloth over top of pitcher, pushing it down inside, and fastens it with string or rubber band; then solemnly pours in most of the milk. Buzz among ladies.*)

Mr. Arnold. While this is straining, I will apply the iodine test to what remains in the bottle. If there is starch in it, it will turn blue. (*Pours water from a glass into the bottle, adds a few drops of iodine, shakes it, holds it up before them. It is blue.*)

Mrs. White, Mrs. Black, Mrs. Grey (*together*). Oh! Look at that! Just think of it!

(**Mr. Billings** *much confused, but unable to escape.*)

Mr. Arnold. I'm afraid one of the supplying dairymen thins his milk and whitens it. Starch is not dangerous. Dirt is. We will now examine our strainer. (*Holds up cloth. A heavy, dark deposit is shown. There is a tense silence.*)

Mrs. O'Shane (*suddenly rising up*). That's what killed my Patsy! (*Points at* **Mr. Billings**.) An' 'twas him that did it! (*Commotion.*)

Mr. Billings (*rising*). Ladies, I demand to be heard! You have all known me for years. Most of you take my milk. You know it is good. There is some mistake; that is not the milk that should have been delivered here.

Mrs. Carroll. Evidently not.

Mrs. O'Shane. No! 'Tis not the milk for the rich—'tis the milk for the poor!

Mr. Billings. Ladies, I protest! My standing in this community—my years of service—ought to give me your confidence long enough to look into this matter. I must find out from which of my suppliers this inferior milk has come. We will have a thorough overhauling, I assure you. I had no idea any such milk was being handled by us.

Mr. Arnold. Then why did you give me this bill? (*Shows marked bill.*) This was handed to me a few moments ago by Mr. Billings to ensure my giving him a favorable test. It is the first time I ever held a bribe—even for evidence.

Dr. Strong (*coming forward*). Ladies, I wish to clear Mr. Arnold of even a moment's suspicion. I knew the Milk Trust would not bear inspection, so I urged Mr. Arnold to take the money, if it was offered, and bring it out in evidence. There it is.

Mr. Billings. I suspected as much! This is admitted to be a conspiracy between our new doctor and our new inspector. But I trust, ladies, that more than the word of two strangers will be required to condemn an old friend and fellow-citizen.

Dr. Strong. I gave you that bill, Mr. Billings; it's the one you changed for me just now. That much of a conspiracy I admit.

Mr. Billings. So you and your accomplice had it all framed up to knife me! And is your word and his—a man whose very admission proves him a venal scoundrel—to stand against mine? Do you think I had but one hundred-dollar bill about me?

Dr. Strong. I doubt if you had more than one with a red mark in the middle of the top—on both sides! (**Mrs. Carroll** *suddenly takes up bill and examines it. Rises.*)

Mrs. Carroll. It was a painful surprise to find the quality of milk which has been served to me, but it is more painful to see that it was evidently known to be bad. Ladies, I saw Dr. Strong mark that bill. I saw her give it to him in change for smaller ones.

Mrs. O'Shane. Sure, an' I saw him pass it to the man!

Mrs. Carroll. Ladies, if you will kindly move a little I think Mr. Billings would be glad to pass out. (*They make way for him and he goes out, turns at door and shakes fist at* **Mr. Arnold.**)

Mr. Billings. You'll lose your job, young man! I have some power in this town!

Mrs. Carroll. And so have I, Mr. Billings. I'll see that Mr. Arnold keeps his place. We need him. You said this club could carry the town; that we women could do whatever we wanted to here—with our "influence"! Now we see what our "influence" amounts to! Rich or poor, we are all helpless together unless we wake up to the danger and protect ourselves. That's what the ballot is for, ladies—to protect our homes! To protect our children! To protect the children of the poor! I'm willing to vote now! I'm glad to vote now! I've got something to vote for! Friends, sisters, all who are in favor of woman suffrage and pure milk say Aye!

(*Clubwomen all rise and wave their handkerchiefs, with cries of "Aye!" "Aye!"*)

CURTAIN.

Bridget's Sisters

or THE LEGAL STATUS OF

ILLINOIS WOMEN IN 1868

CATHARINE WAUGH McCULLOCH

Chicago: Illinois Equal Suffrage Association. 1911.

INTRODUCTORY NOTE

An incident very similar to the one shown in this play occurred in the life of Mrs. Myra Bradwell about the year 1868. She was garnisheed by a saloonkeeper to pay a debt due him by a drunkard whose wife had left with Mrs. Bradwell for safe keeping some of her hard-earned wages. When Mrs. Bradwell was forced by law to pay these savings to the saloonkeeper she and other public-spirited women secured the passage of a law making a wife's wages her own property and no longer the property of her husband. These same people were active in the organizing of the Illinois Equal Suffrage Association and the two matters are here linked together.

The Mrs. Bradley of the play is in no way like Mrs. Bradwell, for Mrs. Bradwell's legal education would have made it unnecessary for her to ask so many legal questions as did Mrs. Bradley and Mrs. Bradwell and her husband, too, had long been suffragists. Mrs. Bradley represents the home-loving type of woman.

The other women in the play represent the different types of women, who, with a common sisterly spirit, saw their own duty toward their helpless women neighbors. The men of the play are average men, no one of whom desires any harm to women in general. A discussion of the legal situation, however, arouses some of them to action. The legal condition of women before this time and the gradual changes which followed are briefly shown in a note at the close of the play.

C. W. McC.

PERSONS ————————————————————————

Mary Bradley, A Home-loving Woman
John Bradley, Husband of Mary
Bridget O'Flannigan, A Washerwoman
Patrick O'Flannigan, A Drunkard, Husband of Bridget
Mr. Summons, A Constable
Mr. Common Law, A Justice of the Peace, Talkative But Accurate
Mr. Vulture, A Saloon Keeper
Mr. Sharp, His Attorney, Only Insisting on His Client's Legal Rights

Mrs. Pious — *Allison*
Mrs. Adoremen — *Tarek*
Mrs. Takerights ⎬ Various Employers of **Bridget**
Mrs. Equity — *Kyra*
Mrs. Bitter — *Emily*
Miriam

TIME, November, 1868 ——————————————————————

PLACE: Chicago, Ill. ——————————————————————

ACT I

SCENE

In late afternoon in November. Front hall in the home of **Mr. and Mrs. Bradley.** *A large clock is in the hall.* **Mrs. Bradley** *enters talking with* **Bridget,** *who, with her shawl over her head, is ready to go home.*

Mrs. Bradley. You have had a hard day's work at washing, Bridget, and I will pay you more than your regular price of one dollar. I will make you a little present of fifty cents more.

Bridget (*Taking the money*). May all the Saints bless your swate soul! You are always so generous to a poor body, and I thank you kindly. (*She courtesies, then takes the money to the clock and puts it in an envelope there.*)

Mrs. Bradley (*Smilingly*). Well, Bridget, how much is there now in this bank of yours?

Bridget. This makes $15.00 here in the clock and I can soon get every one of my darlints some warrum shoes and woolen underclothes. I must buy yarn so I can knit some stockings for their father, too. Sure mum, I can not save much from my wages. I use every cent other people pay me for food to eat and for rent, and sometimes Pat gets away my pay when he is raging drunk, and that's pretty hard.

Mrs. Bradley. Your husband will never get that $15.00. The old clock tells no stories and you know you can trust me never to tell anyone.

Bridget. Yes, I know you are the truest friend I have, and I laugh inside every time I think about how old Pat is fooled.

Mrs. Bradley (*A sound of the baby crying a little startles her*). Oh, there is baby, not quiet yet. Excuse me, Bridget. Let yourself out by the front door. It locks itself. I must have baby fast asleep before his papa comes to dinner. Goodbye. (*She hurries out and is heard humming to the baby while* **Bridget** *talks.*)

Bridget. 'Tis a rich woman I am with $15; more than I have seen for many a day. Perhaps I might buy little Pat some shoes to-night on my way home. How cunning the little darlint would look. It might soften up the heart of old Pat himself. Mostly he has been a good husband and niver lays on me the weight of a finger or gives me a cross worrud when he is sober. But he is hardly ever sober. I have begged that old saloon keeper, Mr. Vulture, not to sell him another drop, but the tears of a poor woman don't count. (*Wipes her eyes.*) I could stand Pat's batings all right, for he says the law is, that a husband can bate his wife if he uses a stick no thicker than his thumb, and tho Pat has a thick thumb I must obey the law. But what I can't endure, and it's worse than the batings is to see the blessed children hungry or cold. Well, well, I ought to stop thinking about my troubles and remember my blessings. It is good I am strong and can work for the five children. Bless their bright eyes! How lucky I am to have five of them to love me. Yes, I will get those shoes for little Pat. (*She rattles some money out of the envelope into her hand and puts the envelope back into the clock. She goes out.*)

Mrs. Bradley *is humming more softly, then stops.* **Mr. Bradley** *enters a moment later.* **Mrs. Bradley** *runs in to meet her husband.*

Mr. Bradley. Good evening, Mary. Has this been a blue Monday for you? Or is washday one glorious carnival of rest? (*He takes off his outer clothes, combs his hair and brushes his clothing while talking.*)

Mrs. Bradley. Well, not exactly a day of idleness, John, but a happy day. Baby is in bed and dinner is ready and I am at peace with the world. We can have a lovely evening with our music and that new book. You can read to me while I wash up the dishes. Washday is never a hard day for me, because Bridget is so competent, and so very grateful, too, for all I try to do to help her. Poor Bridget! I am so comfortably situated here, looking after this pretty little home, with a chance to enjoy the baby every day, and all day long, and knowing that you are coming home at night, cheerful, ready to help me if I am tired. When I compare my lot with poor Bridget's, who works away from home day after day, to earn enough to feed and clothe her family and yet can not be with them to enjoy their cunning ways, I think I am the most fortunate of women, and through the gratuity of my generous and loyal husband. (*At the last of this sentence she takes him by his coat lapels and gazes fondly at him.*)

Mr. Bradley. But, Mary, you legally deserve all you get. (*Laughing.*) The law only provides that I furnish you with clothing, shelter and food, and that is about all you do get. You put in all your time, bring up the baby, and make this home so delightful, that you do not really receive any gratuity. You only receive what the law would really force me to give you. (*He puts on his slippers.*)

Mrs. Bradley. It is lovely of you to say that; but poor Bridget deserves it just as much as I. It's a pity that the law don't bring her the things you say the law brings me. I believe you put in a lot of extras that no law would mention. Bridget's case, of course, is an exception. Most of us women are taken care of tenderly by devoted husbands and we need never bother our minds about law or rights. I have all the rights I want, with my dear baby, my chivalrous husband and my comfortable home. Other women are also contented.

Mr. Bradley. Oh, Mary, I have my doubts about that. What about those suffrage women in New York and Massachusetts. Have they not been discontented for the past twenty years? There must be some trouble some-where.

Mrs. Bradley. I have read about some women who are talking about their rights all the time, just like men. Yes, some are even so foolish as to want to vote. I can not imagine how any woman with a loving husband like mine could ever have any use for the ballot.

Mr. Bradley. I am afraid you will make me egotistical if you keep praising me for the few little things I do. (*Patting her on the shoulder.*)

A knock is heard at the door. **Mrs. Bradley** *goes to the door, a hum of voices is heard and she comes in followed by* **Constable Summons**.

Mrs. Bradley (*Distressed*). Oh, John, dear! This man is a constable. He says that he has some papers to serve on me. I am being sued somewhere, and I tell you I don't owe anybody a cent. My books are in perfect order and I always pay cash.

Constable. Excuse me, ma'am; you don't quite understand. You are merely garnisheed in a case where Mr. Vulture has sued Bridget O'Flannigan's husband.

Mrs. Bradley. But what in the world have I got to do with a saloon keeper, Mr. Vulture? I never drank a drop of intoxicating liquors. You know I didn't, John. Tell him, John, that I never touch the stuff.

Mr. Bradley. Why, Mr. Summons, of course my wife never drinks. What is this all about anyhow?

Constable. Why, I think I heard the Justice say when he issued this summons that O'Flannigan owed Vulture $50.00 for drinks, and that there is some money due him from Mrs. Bradley.

Mrs. Bradley. Indeed there is not, for Patrick O'Flannigan never did a stroke of work for me. If he was like his hard-working, industrious wife he might be of some value to somebody; but he is so good-for-nothing I do not believe anybody ever owed him a cent.

Constable. This was something about Mrs. O'Flannigan, I think. You have some of her wages here.

Mrs. Bradley. But this is not his. He will never touch a cent of Bridget's wages. I have given her my word of honor, and he will never have her money as long as I live. Will he, John?

Mr. Bradley. Certainly not.

Constable. Well, I can't say how the case will come out, Ma'am, but you will have to come to court and explain things to the Justice. Sorry to trouble you. Good evening. (**Constable** *goes out.*)

Mrs. Bradley. Did you ever hear of such an outrageous, wicked constable! The idea of thinking he could threaten me into paying over Bridget's money! That money is saved in the clock and will stay saved. Must we have a lawyer?

Mr. Bradley. No, I think not. My poor little wife, I will go down with you to court and see what there is to this. I know the Justice. He is a kind-hearted man and wants to do the fair thing. We need no lawyer to see the legal rights of the question. It is plain enough that Bridget's money is her's and not Pat's.

Mrs. Bradley. Of course. There cannot be any legal right for Mr. O'Flannigan and Mr. Vulture to take the money that Bridget earned here. It would be wicked. I am perfectly disgusted with that justice and the constable and the saloon keeper, and, of course, with Patrick O'Flannigan. It is terrible. Only a minute ago we were so happy together, looking forward to our lovely quiet evening by ourselves, and now this trouble comes. Why is it that innocent people get mixed up with other people's troubles? If we behave ourselves that ought to keep us free from outside suffering. But come on out to dinner and you can think up something, I know. You are so clever. You can argue with the judge and explain what is right. You can save that $15.00 for Bridget and her children.

ACT II

SCENE

Court room of **Mr. Common Law**, *a Justice of the Peace. The* **Justice** *sits behind a table which has a half dozen large calf-bound law books.* **Mr. and Mrs. Bradley** *are near one end of the table, and at the other end are* **Mr. Vulture**, *the saloonkeeper, and* **Mr. Sharp**. *Woman patrons of* **Bridget** *sit behind the* **Bradleys**, **Mrs. Adoremen**, *daintily dressed in the height of style for 1868,* **Mrs. Pious** *in Quaker clothing,* **Mrs. Equity**, *sensibly dressed,* **Mrs. Bitter**, *plainly dressed, and* **Mrs. Takerights**, *plump, handsome and richly dressed.* **Bridget** *is seated near them, knitting a stocking, and throughout the proceedings seems peacefully unconcerned. The people come in one by one and the constable hunts up chairs for them.*

Justice Common Law. Case No. 1209, Vulture vs. O'Flannigan. Mary Bradley, garnishee. Are the parties present?

Mrs. Bradley *and* **Mr. Vulture** *rise.*

Both. Yes, your honor.

Justice. Well, put on your case. Who are your witnesses, Mr. Sharp.

Sharp. My only witnesses are Mr. Vulture and Mrs. Bradley.

Justice. You may rise and be sworn. Lift up your right hands. (*Repeats rapidly.*) You do solemnly promise by the everliving God, that the testimony you shall give in the cause now on trial shall be the truth, the whole truth, and nothing but the whole truth, so help you God.

They both bow the head and sit down.

Mr. Sharp. I offer in evidence the record of the judgment in favor of Mr. Vulture against Patrick O'Flannigan, case No. 1167 on your Honor's docket and the execution which was issued thereon, with the constable's return upon said execution showing no property found and no part satisfied. Now, Mr. Vulture, you may take the stand and tell the court about this case.

Vulture. Well, your honor, Mr. O'Flannigan has been buying drinks for a long while at my saloon and the bill ran up to $50.00 and I sued him, your honor remembers, and got a judgment.

Mr. Sharp. That's all right, but tell now about the garnisheeing of Mrs. Bradley.

Mr. Vulture. Well, I heard one of the O'Flannigan children say on the street one day: "My mother is going to buy us all some new shoes when she gets her money from Mrs. Bradley," and so I says to the youngster, "How much money has Mrs. Bradley got of your mother's?" and she said, "Oh, lots—maybe a million dollars. Enough to buy shoes, anyhow." So I guess she may have enough to pay this bill.

Sharp. That is all Mr. Vulture.

Just then the door opens and **Patrick O'Flannigan** *stalks in. He is sober but mad.*

Patrick. And what is a respectable woman like Bridget O'Flannigan doing here.

Justice. Order, please; your wife is interested in this law suit and you must not disturb the proceedings.

Patrick (*with a reverential bow*). Excuse me, your honor but cannot some one tell me what a court has to do with Bridget.

Justice. Yes. This is a suit to secure some of Bridget's wages to pay a liquor bill due Mr. Vulture.

Patrick. Is that ould sneak after Bridget's wages?

Justice. Yes, that is what it means.

Patrick. Well, he isn't her husband I guess and he will find I am the only one who owns Bridget and her wages. He's an old varmint.

Justice. You must not talk that way or I shall fine you for contempt of court. Sit down and be quiet. (**Pat** *sits meekly down across the room away from* **Bridget**.) Do you wish to cross-examine the witness, Mr. Bradley or Mrs. Bradley?

Mr. Bradley. Did Mrs. O'Flannigan ever buy any thing to drink in your saloon?

Mr. Vulture. No.

Mr. Bradley. Has not Mrs. O'Flannigan been to you frequently and asked you to refuse to sell any liquor to Mr. O'Flannigan?

Mr. Vulture. Well, yes, I suppose she has, but he is the head of the family and is the best judge whether he wants to drink. How could we ever make money if we stopped for crying women?

Mr. Sharp. That is all; you may step down. Now, Mrs. Bradley, you may take the witness stand.

Mrs. **Bradley** *goes to the witness chair vacated by* **Mr. Vulture.**

Mr. Sharp. Do you know Patrick O'Flannigan and his wife Bridget?

Mrs. Bradley. I know Bridget O'Flannigan; I never have such acquaintances as Patrick O'Flannigan. (*Very stiffly.*)

Mr. Sharp. You know that he is her husband?

Mrs. Bradley. Yes, she has told me so.

Mr. Sharp. Does Mrs. O'Flannigan wash for you on Mondays?

Mrs. Bradley. Yes.

Mr. Sharp. Have you paid her all you owe her?

Mrs. Bradley. Well, in a way, yes. (*Evasively.*)

Mr. Sharp. Explain what you mean. Have you not in your possession money belonging to her?

Mrs. Bradley. Well, not exactly in my possession.

Sharp. Is there not some in your house?

Mrs. Bradley. Well perhaps there may be some in our house belonging to her, but I would not attempt to have any control over it. I have never touched it or counted it so I really do not *know* anything about it.

Mr. Sharp. Do you know where it is?

Mrs. Bradley. Well, I suppose I do.

Mr. Sharp. How much is it and where is it?

Mrs. Bradley (*To the* **Justice**). Judge, do I need to tell all these things to this man?

The Justice. Yes, you will have to answer and tell the truth.

Mrs. Bradley. But, Judge, that money was earned by Bridget belongs to her, and these people have no right to it. She has worked so hard to keep the children fed. Her husband does almost nothing for them, and she needs this money for the children's clothes. All these other women give washing to Bridget. (*The other women stand as though eager to testify.*) They are ready to testify how industrious and honest she is.

Justice. Bridget's character has nothing to do with the case. You must answer the question, Madam.

Mrs. Bradley (*Tearfully*). Well, then what was the question?

Mr. Sharp. How much of Bridget O'Flannigan's wages is now in your house and where is it?

Mrs. Bradley (*Faintly*). I suppose about $15.00 and it is in the clock.

Mr. Sharp. Louder, please.

Mrs. Bradley. Fifteen dollars, I suppose, and in the clock.

Mr. Sharp. That is all, Mrs. Bradley. Thank you. That is our case, your honor.

Justice. That is all, Mrs. Bradley. You may step down. Have you any witnesses, Mr. Bradley?

Mr. Bradley. No, your honor, but I wish to discuss the question of justice and law and protest against this attempted outrage.

Justice. Very well. You shall have an opportunity in due time. Now, Mr. Sharp, do you wish to make an argument?

Mr. Sharp (*Rising*). Your honor, I have proved that O'Flannigan owes us $50.00, that we have a judgment for that amount and that the execution issued thereon has been returned no part satisfied. We have also proved that Mrs. Bradley has $15.00 of Mrs. O'Flannigan's wages now in her control and in her house. (**Bridget** *motions* **Pat** *to come over where she is. She whispers something to him at which* **Pat** *slaps his leg and bursts out laughing.*)

Justice. Order there, Mr. O'Flannigan.

Mr. Sharp (*Continuing*). The good old common law, which was the protection of our fore-fathers, still protects the rights of creditors in Illinois. A man cannot purchase drinks, refuse to pay and then cheat an honest merchant when he has sources of income like this. Mr. Vulture is only doing what any businessman would. He is trying to make his customers pay their bills.

Mrs. Bradley. How can you say this when Bridget was never a customer? She never bought a thing there!

Mr. Sharp. You do not understand, Madam, the glorious principle of the unity of the married pair. When they go to the marriage altar they are made one. If Patrick is a customer Bridget practically is also, for she must pay the bill. They are one now in the eyes of the law. In this marriage between Bridget and Patrick they are one. Bridget's wages are Patrick's.

Mrs. Equity (*Calmly*). Are Patrick's wages also Bridget's?

Mr. Sharp. Well hardly, madam.

Mrs. Equity. Why not when they are one?

Mr. Sharp. Because Bridget is not that one. Patrick is it. So your honor, as this $15.00 of wages earned by Bridget belongs to Patrick, I ask that it be turned over by Mrs. Bradley towards the payment of a part of this judgment. We can garnishee others later for the rest of it.

Justice. Mrs. Bradley, have you anything further to say?

Mrs. Bradley (*In tears*). My husband will speak for me.

Mr. Bradley (*Stepping forward to the Judge*). Your honor, this is a case which must appeal to the heart of the Court. One of the greatest attainments of a Judge is to know when not to be too severe. This hard working devoted mother is trying single-handed to save some money for her children's winter necessities and even for her husband's stockings. With no help from her husband, she is trying to keep the wolf from the door. Every cent she

earns from these other patrons of hers, she must spend daily for food and
fuel and rent. She has only this little ahead for the cold winter. I have
read about a wife's separate estate being hers and surely Bridget's wages
ought to be her separate estate. The law of 1861 helped things, some, I
have heard.

Justice. You mistake the meaning of separate estate. This term does not apply
to a case of wages. The law of 1861 only made some changes in the so-
called separate estate which a father might put into a trustee's hands for
the benefit of the daughter before the daughter's marriage. Other states
are trying the same experiment but it amounts to little except as to the
saving of the principal. All the income a wife will use anyway in her home.
That law of 1861 did not even change the old rule that the produce of a
wife's lands belonged to the husband. You know the law of curtsey gave
to the husband the use of his wife's lands during his life, if a living child
was born. So when the husband can still control the wife's products and
income from land, he must continue the ownership of the more personal
and intimate produce of her toil, her wages.

Mr. Bradley. But Judge, look at it from another point of view. This $15.00,
earned by many days of hard work, is a trust fund which my wife has held
sacred for the use of this noble, self-respecting woman. You would put
my wife in a very uncomfortable position and force her to be untrue to
her trust. Decide this case solely with the thought of doing righteousness.
Let this poor woman have her $15.00, and your decision will be approved
in the highest court of morals. (**Mr. Bradley** *sits down.*)

Justice. Have you, Mr. Sharp, anything to say in closing?

Mr. Sharp (*Rising*). Your Honor, this is not a court of morals. This is a court
of Law. Your honor needs no reminder that we must not be swept away
by emotional appeals. You understand better than these kind-hearted but
misguided people, that even a justice-court must be run according to legal
principles, like a court of law and not like a soup kitchen. There is no
precedent in law for the forcing of a charitable contribution from my client
out of money legally belonging to him. (*He sits down.*)

The Justice. I must say that this is a very difficult question to decide. I wholly
agree with Mr. Bradley that as a question of righteousness and morals the
wages earned by this hard-working woman ought to continue to be hers,
to be used by her for whatever cause, or whatever necessity she has, but
I am reminded by the plaintiff in this case that I cannot allow my decisions
to be governed by sentiment. I must decide this question according to law.
At this time of the century, 1868, there is scarcely a state in this union
where the judge would not hold as I am about to hold, that a wife's wages
absolutely belong to her husband. The wife's wages belonged to the husband from the time of the old English common law. There is no method

except by changing that law, whereby we could prevent these wages from coming into the hands of the husband's creditors.

Mrs. Bradley. May I interrupt, Judge? Not all of the $15.00 is really wages, what I agreed to pay her, but some of it is presents. Sometimes I made her a gift out of my pin-money and that was not wages. Surely this part you can save her away from the saloon keeper.

Justice. I am very sorry to hurt the feelings of gentle and tender-hearted ladies like Mrs. Bradley, and I shrink from giving over to Mr. Vulture the money Mrs. O'Flannigan planned to use for winter clothes. It is edifying to see the motherly affection bestowed on offspring, even in the lowest walks of society. But, Mrs. Bradley, even if the whole of the $15.00 had been a gift from you to Bridget, my ruling must be the same. I must administer the law as it is, and not as it ought to be. All the wife's personal property, her clothing, even her wedding gifts, everything of this sort, whether coming to her by gift or bequest or her own personal labor, belongs to the husband. In return for this the husband, of course, is expected to support the family. In this very case the law presumes that Patrick is supporting the family, a very violent presumption, I see, and one evidently incapable of legal enforcement. Even the children are absolutely his in all our States and in most of them he can will the guardianship of children away from the mother to strangers. The father is legally the sole parent when it comes to the question of rights. The mother is only allowed duties in connection with her children.

Mrs. Bitter. Judge, do you not think these are very wicked laws?

Justice. As a man and a human being, I might agree with you, but as a justice, I am not called on for opinions of what ought to be. I must enforce law as I find it. This matter about Bridget's wages I cannot evade. I must enforce this law as it stands. The Legislature is the only power to change laws. Women cannot control their own property until the Legislature removes some of their legal disabilities.

Mrs. Equity. How can we get the Legislature to change those wicked, immoral laws?

Justice. Well, that's a conundrum. When I have been obliged to enforce these unjust laws, I have often wondered why the wronged women did not resort to riot and bloodshed as men have often done to avenge their wrongs. Perhaps it is because the blow comes to each woman singly and she is ignorant that she has companions in misery. Then, too, ages of masculine domination has broken the spirit of most women, and, with due respect to you generous women, many women are too selfish and narrow to care for sister women's sufferings.

Mrs. Bradley. We never imagined before that any law could be so cruel or any man mean enough to take advantage of it.

Mrs. Adoremen. No, indeed, all the men I ever knew were so chivalrous. They would pick up your handkerchief, open doors, give you compliments, stand up when you entered the room, kiss your hand, and always show such delicate attention.

Mrs. Bitter. I wager that when Bridget begged Mr. Vulture not to sell whiskey to Pat, Mr. Vulture never kissed Bridget's hand.

Mrs. Adoremen. Well, perhaps not. Of course God made different orders of society and we should not all expect the same treatment. Some women don't have tact. They don't know how to handle men. You must not ask men to do things which interfere with business or pleasure. If you don't antagonize men I have always thought men were so nice.

Mrs. Pious. Perhaps some men were foreordained to be nice, but I am positive some of them elected to be otherwise. Now, Judge, the thing for us Christian women to ask in this situation is: What ought we to do to help Bridget in this and future calamities? We must help other women as well, for many others will be in similar trouble.

Justice. These laws ought to be changed and I do not quite see how you women can make changes now. If you had a vote, the Legislature would be quick to listen to the petitions of women constituents. Then they would hurry to make necessary changes in the old common law to please women voters. You really need the ballot if you are in earnest. If you only want to play at philanthropy, never mind about voting, for without the ballot you can play at it longer.

Mrs. Adoremen. But Judge, I have always felt that the men know best what we women needed, and that we would show lack of faith in our own husbands if we insisted on controlling our own property. (*Sentimentally.*) I felt perfectly willing to trust my husband to control my property when I had already given myself to him.

Mrs. Bitter (*Aside*). She had nothing when she married.

Justice. Very touching, I am sure, Madam, but Bridget's husband seems hardly worthy of such confidence and devotion. Great masses of women voters could not fail to inspire more Legislative respect for women than any one woman, however beautiful and charming, could gain through chivalry. Chivalry is good for poetry and during courting days, but alas, it is poured out most freely on those who need it least. In the eyes of her Creator, Bridget needs not only justice and rights, but chivalry also, and yet—well, Mrs. Bitter explained it pretty well when she said Mr. Vulture did not kiss Bridget's hand. Those honest hands, roughened with heavy work, deserve the greatest honor, but do not get it. Those who receive no favors need the ballot to secure for them the barest rights.

Mrs. Equity. I suppose Abigail Adams had some such thoughts when she asked her husband, John Adams, to secure the rights of women in the new

United States government. A class politically disfranchised must be legally, socially, and industrially helpless.

Justice. To protect the negroes, the ballot will soon be given them by a fifteenth amendment to the United States Constitution. Naturalized foreigners too are seeking the ballot for the same reason. When women are voters, I shall not be obliged to enforce such unjust laws, for the great mass of women will be so true to their sex that some of these iniquities will be changed. (**Bridget** *and* **Pat** *whisper and motion to* **Mr. Bradley** *and then tell him something while* **Mrs. Bradley** *and the* **Judge** *continue to talk.*)

Mrs. Bradley (*Hopefully*). Judge, you see the right so clearly you surely will not make me give this money over?

Justice (*Sadly*). I must be true to my oath of office and administer the law as I find it, though I am sorry to grieve these kind women. I must decide against you. Even should Mr. Vulture garnishee the rest of Bridget's employers for her daily pittance, I should be forced to decide the same. You must give Mr. Vulture the $15.00.

Mr. Bradley. Your Honor, I should like to call Bridget O'Flannigan as a witness as she has some important evidence which might change your opinion as to the practicability of such a decision.

Justice. Well, this court is always ready to change opinions if the law and evidence justify a change. We will hear from Bridget.

Mr. Sharp. I object, your Honor. Bridget has not been sworn and besides the case is closed.

Justice. Well, Sharp, you are a stickler for the fine points of the law. I did not say the case was closed. If, before I enter judgment, I hear of other evidence, on my own motion, I will call the witness. Bridget, you may be sworn. Hold up your right hand.

Sharp. I object, your Honor, to receiving the testimony of this witness. She is admittedly the wife of the defendant in the original proceeding and she is legally incompetent.

Mrs. Adoremen (*In amazement*). Why, Mr. Sharp! Are you not a little inconsistent? A moment ago you did not want the judge to believe Bridget because she had not been sworn and now you won't let her be sworn.

Mr. Sharp. I am only standing on my legal rights to protect my client's interests. Your Honor knows the benefit of this good old common-law rule that wives should not be allowed to testify in suits where their husbands are parties. The sacredness of marital confidences must be respected.

Mr. Bradley. But this evidence was in the possession of Bridget alone. Patrick never told her. There is no marital confidence about this.

Mr. Sharp. Your Honor knows that I am merely stating the rule of law, well established in hundreds and thousands of cases. The wife cannot testify in such a case, can she?

Justice. Well, Sharp, you have the law with you and I cannot let Bridget testify.

Bridget. It's all the same to me, your Honor. (**Mr. Bradley** *whispers to the constable and gives him a large key. Constable goes out.*)

Justice. I can see no other way out of this, Mrs. Bradley. You will be obliged to pay that money. (**Mrs. Bradley** *sobs and turns to* **Mrs. Adoremen** *and* **Mrs. Pious** *who weep also.* **Mrs. Bitter** *and* **Mrs. Takerights** *whisper vigorously as though angry.* **Bridget** *remains placid. A knock at the door is answered by* **Mr. Vulture.** *He returns.*)

Mr. Vulture. Your Honor, a man wants to speak to you a moment in the next room.

Justice. Excuse me, I will just step to the door a moment. I will enter judgment when I return. (*As the* **Justice** *leaves* **Vulture** *and* **Sharp** *follow and the women are much excited.*)

Mrs. Bitter. That's the way men always stand up for men. The Judge's soft words are nothing but bosh. He is against us. For ages men have humiliated and domineered over women legally or illegally. They all defend each other in being cruel and selfish to women. When I think of the wrongs women suffer I almost feel as Caligula did when he wished his subjects had one neck, so he could enjoy wringing it at one time. I feel like revenging myself on the whole sex.

Mrs. Pious. Dear sister, do not be uncharitable. Remember that unlimited power in the hands of anyone is liable to abuse. If women had unlimited power over men, they, too, might have become equally unjust. Remember, too, that our martyred Lincoln said he favored those sharing in the government's privileges who assisted in bearing its burdens, and he included women. He said, too, the nation could not be half slave and half free. He was a prophet of God and a man, and he believed in women suffrage. So do not hate all men. Pray for your enemies.

Mrs. Bitter. My whole life has been a struggle to forgive my personal enemies, but I feel no call of conscience to forgive the enemies of my whole sex.

Mrs. Takerights. How would the ballot help us? Don't you think women themselves are to blame for not taking what they want instead of humbly begging?

Mrs. Bitter. A lot you know about it, with that jolly husband of yours. You lead him around by the nose. Most of us are worms of the dust, ground down under man's heel, with not enough spirit left to do more than wish we were serpents with fangs. You know how hard I work and my husband is in comfortable circumstances, partly through my hard work on the farm and yet I cannot get the clothes I should have. Why, I take things, too, but it makes me feel mighty mean. I can hardly ever have my own butter and egg money, and I absolutely must pick my husband's pockets of a quarter every night to get money for new baby clothes.

Mrs. Takerights. I did not mean taking our rights that way. If I needed money out of my husband's pockets, I would help myself in broad day-light, right under his nose. I go to the same cash-box he does without any timidity and I never hear a grumble from my husband.

Mrs. Pious. Sister. God has certainly given you a good husband, but is he quite normal? How did you ever learn to manage him?

Mrs. Takerights. I never would manage him, but I gave him to clearly understand in our first year of married life that I was a real partner and would expect the rights of a partner. Father trained me in the economical use of money and talked over his business with me. So when I married his young partner I expected just as much respect, and I got it.

Mrs. Bitter. Well, your ownership of your father's two-thirds of the place doubtless raised the market value of your opinions. Those who have, receive more, and those who don't have, get their crumbs stolen away just as Bridget's scanty savings must go to Vulture. And to think that whenever the rest of us hire Bridget, we shall see the constable on our door steps with his hand outstretched for that day's wages. We can all take our turns at being garnisheed. (*Scornfully.*)

Mrs. Adoremen (*Sweetly*). What was it that kind old Justice said about our voting? If some of the men believe in it, I should not feel so timid about it. Men see so clearly. They have such logical minds. Sometimes they like to talk with women of good sense better than with butterflies.

Mrs. Equity. He said the suffrage was what we needed to protect the moral rights of women which were as yet unrecognized by law. The question of money, wages, share in family income which we are discussing, is, to my mind, only one phase of the whole question. That brilliant Myra Bradwell never had trouble with her noble husband and his expenditures, but I am told that our Illinois Supreme Court will refuse her admission to the bar. Miss Doctor has just been refused entrance to the medical school and there is not a college in the State which will admit women. I sent my girl to Oberlin College in Ohio. The equal rights of women in every department has long appealed to me, and I believe woman suffrage will help us.

Mrs. Pious. You are right about there being other wrongs to women. Our women's church society tried to help Mrs. Mater get her two little children. She was the one whose husband took the children and deserted her to live with that bad woman in the next town. This Justice told our committee the father was the sole guardian of the children, could choose the family home and had a legal right to do this cruel thing. He said if she did not want to be parted from the children she must tag along, and if she did not, her husband could get a divorce on the ground of her desertion. But the husband had the children.

Mrs. Bitter. I know another thing worse. You remember little Maggie Mueller whose parents died of cholera two years ago. Well, she is ten years old and for these two years has been out at the poor house. I knew her mother and go out about every six months to take her something. This time I found she had been wronged by the poor-master and the child does not know enough to appreciate her condition, nor had she ever complained to any one. She is so young. I went to old Judge Precedent for whom Maggie's father had worked. If Maggie had a father or a brother, that poor-master would have been shot, and as Maggie was the ward of the State, the State should do a father's part. I wanted that poor-master legally hung. The old Judge was polite enough and sorry, but he said that Maggie was past the age of consent, which was ten years and as I had no proof that she had protested or complained, the law presumed that ten-year-old Maggie consented to her own ruin. So there could be no punishment for the man who wronged her. The old Judge has a heart, though, for he went out to the store with me and bought a handsome fifty-cent doll for me to give her. This was as bad as asking bread and getting a stone. I asked justice and got a doll.

Mrs. Equity. We women should raise that age of consent. We cannot save Maggie, but we can save other girls.

Mrs. Bradley. That is the very worst thing I ever heard. Yes, we women ought to vote to help the women and children. I am ashamed to say I have criticised Miss Anthony, Lucy Stone, and the other women who went around lecturing and organizing women suffrage societies. I feel now that we must all be Bridget's sisters and help her.

Mrs. Pious. We ought to follow the example of Miss Anthony and Lucy Stone. My time has been so limited to religious work I have neglected God's suffering ones here, but I have learned how to work in an organized way. Tho my parents were Quakers, I have been in the regular woman's mission work of this church here and have there learned the strength which can come from organized womanhood. Let us now and here organize ourselves to get the ballot for Illinois women. We can pay $1.00 a year dues just as we do in our foreign missionary society. The foreign heathen are not much worse off than poor Mrs. Mater and Maggie and Bridget. We should have an Illinois Equal Suffrage Association. The Legislature will meet in January next, 1869, and we must have changes made.

Mrs. Equity. That's right, and we will all join if you will be president. Here is my dollar.

Mrs. Pious. All right, just to get a preliminary organization started. We must call a meeting for a permanent organization next February in Library Hall and have some of these brilliant women of the east help us. Here is my dollar.

Mrs. Bitter. I want to join this, too, and here is my dollar. Don't ask me how I got it. I am afraid my husband won't like it, but I shall have to endure that. You tenderly sheltered women, who have kind husbands, good education, money or experience in other organizations, you are for the most part the only ones who will dare to belong to this Equal Suffrage Association. Mrs. Bradley, you helped Mrs. Livermore in starting the Sanitary Commission here in Chicago. You be the treasurer. Stop crying, now is the time for work.

Mrs. Bradley. Well, if you insist, but I am not worthy to be a treasurer of anything. To think of me being obliged to go to that clock and hand over Bridget's $15.00 to that Vulture! Oh, Bridget, will you ever forgive me?

Bridget (*Cheerfully*). Oh, yes, indeed, there is no trouble between you and me.

Mrs. Bradley (*Still tearfully*). How can you keep so self-controlled. I am wondering what you will do for your poor children.

Bridget. The Lord will provide, mum.

Mrs. Takerights. Well, she is religious. Here, Bridget, is a little money the Lord probably provided me to give you. Here is my dollar, Mrs. Bradley for the new society. I believe after all I ought to help the other women who haven't my nerve. My father's training and money has helped me and I'll pass on the help to others. No one beats me and I wonder now why I never used my own freedom for anyone but my ownself. It's nothing but ignorance of such possibilities which keeps us women quiet.

Mrs. Adoremen. Let me be a member for the humblest work. I never before realized that we women must stand together like sisters. I thought each one of us as individuals could ogle out of men anything we wanted. I did that with poor dear papa when he lived and when my husband did not please me, I wept sweetly. That brought him around. I could tell how long to keep it up by peeking around the corner of my handkerchief. But now when I hear you brave women talk about our duties to other women, I am ashamed of having selfishly played the baby-act. I must try from this day to be a grown-up woman, and be of some real use. Bridget must be the sister of all of us. Poor Mrs. Mater and poor Maggie are also sisters. They could not cajole men as I have.

Mr. Bradley. May I join, too?

Chorus. Yes, indeed! A man's dollar is as good as a woman's. We will take every man we can get. We call it equal suffrage.

Mrs. Equity. You men already have political influence and so you will be the most valuable members to help change laws.

Patrick. Then I'll join, for I think the law and this court is beneath contempt. It's bad enough the way I treat Bridget, but I am her husband and have some rights, but I'll be bumped before I have every saloon keeper in town jumping onto Bridget's wages. I'll help stop it by joining. I can help stop Bridget's suffering by joining the equal "sufferin" people myself.

Mrs. Bradley. But you cannot afford to pay your $1.00 dues, Patrick.

Patrick. The lawyer said I had resources in an industrious wife and she will help out on the dues, I know.

Bridget. Indade, Patrick darling, I will, and here's a dollar I earned from Mrs. Equity yesterday. Here, Mrs. Bradley is Patrick's dues. Just as soon as I can afford it I shall join too.

Patrick. Bridget, I will get to work and the first dollar I earn I will pay back, and as far as one man can help, I will help to make things better. I will settle that Vulture bill myself and then keep out. Yes, we will both be members, Mrs. Bradley.

Mrs. Bradley. Poor Bridget, you cannot afford it with the loss of the $15.00 too. How brave you are, Bridget. That awful lawyer Sharp will keep on getting your wages and that $15.00 is gone. (*She weeps.*)

Bridget. Don't cry another drop out of your swate eyes.

The **Judge** *comes on and stands looking at the group silently. The women's backs are turned.*

Mrs. Bradley. But do you not understand? You are a great loser by the Judge's decision. He is coming back in a minute to enter judgment, and that means Vulture will get your money. You are very brave.

Bridget. Them's brave who are in no danger. Vulture will never get that money.

Mrs. Bradley. But the Judge said he would.

Bridget. The Judge don't know what he is talking about. I defy the Judge or Vulture to ever get it.

Justice (*Going on the bench*). Here, my poor woman, you must not talk that way in a court room against the judge. I am forced to decide against you.

Bridget. I was not talking against the Judge, but only saying Vulture would never get that money.

Justice. But he must have it, for I am going to write down in this big book, my docket, that Mrs. Bradley must pay that $15.00 over to him. We have spent a good deal of time on this little case.

Mrs. Equity. Yes, Judge, but the time has been well spent. While you were out we talked over what you said and made a preliminary organization of the Illinois Equal Suffrage Association.

Mrs. Pious. Yes, Judge, you showed us our duty as Christian women and had it not been for the peril which threatened Bridget and which will threaten her every time she washes for anyone of us until that $50.00 liquor bill is paid, if it had not been for you we would not now be bound together like sisters to have these laws changed. We want the ballot given to women so we can with our ballots help protect our helpless sisters. You are the one who has influenced us to be bound to each other for this great task, and we thank you.

Justice. I appreciate, Madam your kind words. I must unofficially congratulate your new organization and ask to be a charter member. But officially I must enter judgment ordering Mrs. Bradley to pay over the money. Vulture is legally entitled to it.

Bridget. How does your honor think he will get it?

Justice. Just as easy as can be. He will walk along to the Bradley home, Mrs. Bradley will go to the clock and get the money.

Bridget. Begging your Honors pardon. You are mistaken. Mrs. Bradley will not get any money out of the clock. She can't find any. Won't that be a joke on Vulture?

Mrs. Bradley. What do you mean?

Mr. Bradley *and his wife whisper and she smiles.*

Justice. Where then has Mrs. Bradley kept your money?

Bridget. She hasn't it anywhere.

Justice. Stop your nonsense and tell me plainly who has your money and what does this all mean?

Bridget. It's no nonsense, but the truth. Well, that night before the constable came, I took out the money to get little Pat new shoes and when I got to the store I decided to spend it all. Clothes and shoes are a safer investment than money. Lucky I did.

Patrick. Good for Bridget.

Justice. Where are those clothes?

Bridget. On the bodies of the youngsters, your honor. With the yarn I bought I am knitting socks for Pat.

Justice. Why did you not say this long before?

Bridget. Well, first Mr. Sharp wouldn't let me and then I wanted to enjoy a little Irish joke on Vulture and him a stealing the information from my children. I did not want to be talking much before learned men.

Justice (*Dryly*). You do not seem much abashed now. Well Mr. Sharp, this puts a different face on the whole matter.

Sharp. I cannot see that it alters the legal situation. We have no evidence but what the money is still in the clock.

Mrs. Bradley. But Bridget says it is not there and that she took it.

The constable enters and gives **Bradley** *the key.*

Constable. I can tell your Honor. I ran to Bradley's home just now to look and the envelope with Bridget's name on it is empty.

Women. Oh, thank you, Mr. Summons.

Sharp. Still we have no evidence.

Justice. Constable, you be sworn. You cannot object to him Sharp.

Sharp (*Angrily*). Oh, I don't care. (*He and* **Vulture** *go out slamming the door violently.*)

Justice. You solemnly promise by the ever living God that the testimony you shall give in the cause now on trial shall be the truth, the whole truth and nothing but the truth?

Constable. I do.

Justice. Tell what you found.

Constable. I searched carefully in the hall clock and found no money. I found this envelope with Bridget's name, but it was empty.

Mrs. Bradley. So, Judge, you can't make me pay over the money can you, when I havn't it?

Justice. No, Mrs. Bradley, I can legally discharge you now and make all of Bridget's friends happy. Altho this case, by reason of the peculiar circumstances, is decided in your favor, I should have been obliged to decide otherwise if Mrs. Bradley had had the money in her possession. Of course, your new association will help change the laws, but until it does everything stands as I have previously stated. It's a pity tho we have wasted so much time on this suit.

Bridget. Oh, your Honor, it was not really wasted. You showed these comfortable richer women how we poorer ones needed the help. The grand ladies that they are, they have been just like sisters to poor old Bridget. Then your Honor, I never get much fun in life and I enjoyed the whole trial beyond words. For once we got ahead of old Vulture.

Patrick. I'll help you better after this, Biddy darling. A good wife and mother deserves the best any man can do for her. You shall have a little pin money for your own. When you want independent money all your own to spend just as you please for me and the children, why you shall have it. I shall make you a grand present. No matter what the law says, after this, I will make you a present of your own wages.

Chorus of Women. Generous Patrick.

Justice. Court is adjourned. Now on to the State House.

CURTAIN

CHRONOLOGY OF THE WOMAN'S RIGHTS MOVEMENT IN ILLINOIS

The old English common law relating to woman's rights was practically unchanged in Illinois during the first half of the nineteenth century. Under it, married women had no right to their children, to their earnings, to their personal property, to the income from their real estate, or to their own personal liberty. Husbands had full control. Women were not admitted to the professions nor to higher schools of learning. They did not vote or hold office. Not only were these rights of women denied by law, but what was worse, many wrongs against women were not recognized nor redressed. The age of consent was ten years. No holier crusade ever enlisted nobler heroes than this which sought to gain the denied rights of women and to redress their wrongs. Many exhausted workers have died in the ranks but their places have been filled by younger women of unflinching courage and the cause moved on. Although the early progress was heartbreakingly slow, notice, that there have been no backward steps. No law giving women greater liberty has been repealed. Illinois men believe that Illinois women deserve all they have received up to date

1855   First local suffrage Association in Illinois organized at Earlville. Moline, our oldest living club, was not organized until 1877.

1860   Dr. Hannah Tracy Cutler and Mrs. Frances D. Gage campaigned Illinois asking for suffrage and equal property rights.

1861   Mr. Pickets of Rock Island introduced in the Legislature the property rights bill. A petition about woman's rights resulted in an indecent report from a committee of the Legislature. Dr. Cutler asked the Legislature to make mothers joint guardians.

For several years the abolition of slavery engrossed the attention of many woman's rights workers. They were promised their freedom if they would help free the slaves. The Sanitary Commission also absorbed much time and money. Double agricultural, industrial and financial burdens were borne by women whose husbands, sons and brothers went to war. The negroes were finally freed, but Illinois women were left in the same legal position they were before the war. Their improved abilities, their sharpened wits, their successful achievements made their desire for liberty greater.

1868   In the fall, preliminary state organization effected.

1869   February in the Library Hall, Chicago, The Illinois Equal Suffrage Association was organized with Mary A. Livermore, President. Myra Bradwell was refused admission to the Illinois bar. She appealed to U.S. Supreme Court. A wife's wages were secured to her own use by Illinois law.

1870   Although the Constitutional convention refused to submit a woman's suffrage proposition, Judge J. B. Bradwell and Judge C. B. Waite secured the omission of a clause forbidding women to hold office. Ada H. Kepley of Union College of Law, Chicago, now the Law Department of Northwestern University, was the first woman in the world to be graduated from a law college.

1872   Catherine V. Waite filed a petition for mandamus to compel election officers to allow her to vote, but she was refused. Fathers and mothers were made equal in inheritance from a deceased child. As Myra Bradwell was held by U.S. Supreme Court to be ineligible to practice law, she and Alta M. Hulett then secured the passage of the law admitting women to all occupations and professions.

1873   The statute was passed recognizing women's eligibility to hold school offices.

1874   Ten women were elected County Superintendents of schools. "Curtsey" was abolished. Spouses' interests in each other's real estate were made a dower right for each.

1875   Women were allowed to be Notaries Public. Myra Bradwell secured the word "persons" in the law concerning notaries.

1876   Elizabeth Boynton Harbert was elected President of Illinois Equal Suffrage Association; re-elected until 1884, and then later, twice, one year each. Mrs. Harbert's idea for a "Sane Fourth" carried out at Evanston was the forerunner of the present Sane Fourth reform. Dr. Sarah Hackett Stevenson was the first woman admitted to American Medical Association.

1877   Woman's Kingdom in Inter Ocean with Mrs. Harbert editor for seven years, helped woman's cause. Mary H. Krout later was editor.

1879   The mammoth petition for suffrage for women was signed by 180,000 persons, but it was kicked about scornfully in the Legislature. This made Frances E. Willard more zealous for suffrage. The W.C.T.U. had many suffrage workers. Ten small Illinois cities allowed women a straw vote on the license question, but the men who elected the aldermen controlled. Helen Schuhardt was held by the lower court ineligible to be Master in Chancery, but the Supreme Court later reversed this decision; a Master's position was appointive.

1884   Mary E. Holmes was elected President of Illinois Equal Suffrage Association for five years and again for seven years, 1890 to 1897.

1887   Age of consent was raised from 10 to 14 years. Catherine V. Waite the Superintendent of Legislative work, sent her resolution for suffrage amendment to Speaker Elijah M. Haines. She was Superintendent until the election of Mrs. McCulloch in 1890.

1888   Large suffrage conventions were held in the northern half of Illinois by Senator M. B. Castle, for twenty years Chairman of Executive Committee, Mary E. Holmes, Julia Mills Dunn, Helen M. Gouger, and Judge C. B. Waite. Many organizations were effected in this year and during the rest of Mrs. Holmes's presidency.

1891   Senator Charles Bogardus fathered a measure for full suffrage in the Senate. Hon. G. W. Curtis, of Lena, in the House, secured 54 votes, a majority of those voting, but not enough. Mrs. Zerelda G. Wallace, Mrs. Holmes and Mrs. McCulloch held six weeks of conventions in southern Illinois, even to Cairo. Senator Thomas C. MacMillan secured 29 votes in the Senate for the School Suffrage Bill and Dr. H. M. Moore got 83 votes in the House. It passed. Four times the Supreme Court has decided what are its various constitutional limitations.

1893   The Child Labor Law passed.
        Senator Charles Bogardus made an excellent report to the Senate on the petitions, saying that there were more for woman suffrage than for all other subjects put together. Twelve anti-suffragists signed a petition. Mrs. Altgeld, the wife of the Governor, came on to the floor of the Senate and personally thanked the Senators who on second reading had voted for our bill. Senator R. W. Coon secured the necessary 26 votes in Senate for the passage of the township suffrage bill.

1894   Dr. Julia Holmes Smith was appointed to fill an unexpired term on the Board of Trustees of State University, the first woman. Mrs. Lucy L. Flower, who had been elected before, took her seat second. Mrs. Florence Kelley was appointed Chief Factory Inspector. No other State has thus honored women. Governor Altgeld appointed several women to important positions.

1895   First big suffrage hearing with twenty women speakers. Senator R. W. Coon secured 23 votes for the township suffrage bill.

1897   Senator George W. Munroe labored faithfully to pass our bills.

1898   At special session about taxation Senator Munroe introduced bill to exempt women's property from taxation until they could vote.

1899   Governor Tanner appointed Mary M. Bartelme Public Guardian of Cook County. She was reappointed by Governors Yates and Deneen.

Senator Isaac M. Hamilton forced two of our bills to a vote. Suffrage petitions from 25,000 labor union men of Chicago were well received.

1901   Joint Guardianship Bill passed Senate with 34 votes and House with 119. Senator Niels Juul and Rev. John Hughes fathered the bill. Rev. Kate Hughes worked for it constantly. Supreme Court decided tax cases in favor of Teachers' Federation.

At this session and the many following sessions suffrage amendments, township suffrage bills and larger suffrage bills were introduced every session by different Senators, among them being Senators D. A. Campbell, O. T. Berry, E. C. Curtis, John McKenzie, and James Gibson. Petitions were presented, literature mailed, letters poured in from constituents, eloquent speeches were made and the tone of Illinois newspapers grew more friendly. At one hearing Iva G. Wooden had pasted the petitions on muslin a yard wide and draped 75 yards of them from the galleries and through the aisles of the House.

1902   Illinois Federation of Woman's Clubs endorsed a tax-paying woman's suffrage bill.

1903   At an Executive Mansion reception, Mrs. Yates, the wife of Governor Yates, asked two of the suffrage officers to stand by her in the receiving line. Since then Governor Deneen's wife has often invited the suffrage officers and speakers to her receptions following the suffrage hearings.

1904   Illinois Federation of Woman's Clubs endorse municipal suffrage bill.

1905   Age of consent raised to 16 years. Ella S. Stewart was elected President of the Illinois Woman Suffrage Association.

1906   Illinois Federation of Woman's Clubs endorsed woman suffrage in the proposed Chicago charter.

1907   Ellen M. Henrotin, chairman of delegates from women's organizations aggregating a membership of 100,000 women urged municipal woman suffrage in the Chicago charter. It was defeated in convention by only one majority. Though this charter passed the Legislature no woman worked for its approval and it was defeated by the voters.

1909   Jane Addams was chairman of the committee which went before the charter makers the second time. They agreed to submit a separate woman suffrage measure which in the Legislature received more votes than most of the separate measures. Senator Charles Billings secured twenty-five votes for the full state wide municipal suffrage bill. Ten hour law, law against pandering and law as to providing seats for women employees passed both houses.

1910   Ella Flagg Young elected Chicago Superintendent of Schools and later President of National Educational Association. At special legislative session Senator Martin Bailey and Representative R. P. Hagen introduced bills to allow women to vote at primary elections and under a commission form of government. Summer suffrage auto tours covered seven-eighths of Illinois counties. Jane Addams was elected President of National Conference of Charities and Corrections.

1911   Municipal Suffrage bill passed the Senate with a vote of 31 to 10; thanks to Senator Wm. M. Brown and other friends. Representative Homer Tice secured two roll calls in the House, on the first of which we had 74 friends and on the last 67. We needed 77 there to pass the bill. This is the first time in many years that the House has gone on record. Ten hour law for women extended to more occupations. Automobile tours in the counties not touched in 1910 find similar enthusiasm.

1913   What will be done by this Legislature? Will it do as well as did five other State Legislatures in 1911? Wisconsin, Kansas, California, Oregon and Nevada submitted the question to the voters. Six states already have fully enfranchised their women: Wyoming, Colorado, Utah, Idaho, Washington and California. Illinois will continue her progress when the voters demand it insistently.

CATHARINE WAUGH MCCULLOCH

ILLUSTRATIONS

John Leech, *Two of the Fe'he Males*, 1851. Early anti-feminist caricatures on both sides of the Atlantic showed women as bold and impudent creatures in Bloomer costumes, smoking cigars in public. (Courtesy of Culver Pictures.)

Selwyn's Theatre.

MANAGER .... MR. J. H. SELWYN

(May 2 - 1868)

THIS AFTERNOON,

Will be presented (by permission), a prophetic drama, in three acts, entitled

THE SPIRIT OF '76;

Or, THE COMING WOMAN.

TOM CARBERRY.. MR. FREDERIC ROBINSON
MR. JOSEPH WIGFALL.. MR. G. H. GRIFFITHS
HER HONOR THE JUDGE..................................... MRS. MARIE WILKINS
VICTORINE WIGFALL.. MRS. F. S. CHANFRAU
  [In which character she will sing "Come into the Garden, George," and "I'll Follow Thee."]
MISS WOLVERINE GRIFFIN................................... MISS AMILIE HARRIS
MRS. BARBARA BADGER... MR. HARRY JOSEPHS

PERIOD 1876.

NEW SCENERY . . BY . . MR. GEORGE HEISTER

Act 1—Railroad depot at Newton Centre. Acts 2 and 3—Mrs. Wigfall's house at Boston.

THE ORCHESTRA,

Consisting of the most celebrated artists, and acknowledged the finest in the United States, will perform, during the evening, a varied and brilliant selection of music, under the direction of

Mr. CHARLES KOPPITZ.

The performance will commence with

Who Speaks First?

CAPTAIN CHARLES.. MR. FREDERIC ROBINSON
ERNEST MILITANT... MR. G. W. GARRISON
POTTER.. MR. G. F. KETCHUM
MRS. MILITANT.. MISS LOUISE ANDERSON
SMART... MISS MARY CARY

Saturday evening.. LIGHT AT LAST

Playbill for *The Spirit of Seventy-Six*, performed at Selwyn's Theatre, Boston, from April 20 to May 9, 1868. The part of Mrs. Badger was played by a male actor to emphasize the lack of femininity of woman's rights leaders. (Courtesy of the Boston Athenæum.)

Currier & Ives, *The Age of Iron, or Man as He Expects to Be,* 1868. This lithograph shows the reversal of traditional public and private spheres. It illustrates the common fear that female emancipation would result in a world turned upside down. (Courtesy of the Museum of the City of New York.)

Currier & Ives, *The Age of Brass, or the Triumph of Women's Rights,* 1869. One of the most common claims of anti-feminists was that once they were granted the vote, women would spend all their time at the polls. The Currier & Ives lithograph satirizes not only the bold and immodest woman candidate, Susan Sharp-Tongue, but also shows that husbands would actually have to hold the baby while mother casts her vote. (Courtesy of the Museum of the City of New York.)

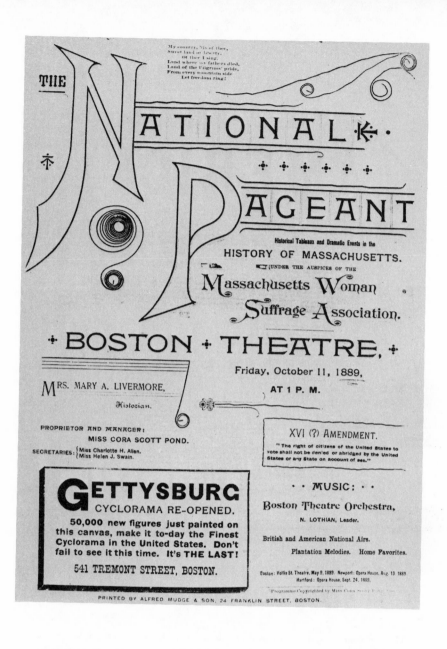

THE NATIONAL PAGEANT

My country, 'tis of thee,
Sweet land of liberty,
Of thee I sing:
Land where our fathers died,
Land of the Pilgrims' pride,
From every mountain side
Let freedom ring!

Historical Tableaux and Dramatic Events in the
HISTORY OF MASSACHUSETTS.
UNDER THE AUSPICES OF THE
Massachusetts Woman Suffrage Association.

BOSTON THEATRE,

Friday, October 11, 1889,
AT 1 P. M.

Mrs. MARY A. LIVERMORE,
Historian.

PROPRIETOR AND MANAGER:
MISS CORA SCOTT POND.

SECRETARIES: Miss Charlotte H. Allen.
Miss Helen J. Swain.

XVI (?) AMENDMENT.
" The right of citizens of the United States to
vote shall not be denied or abridged by the United
States or any State on account of sex."

GETTYSBURG
CYCLORAMA RE-OPENED.
50,000 new figures just painted on
this canvas, make it to-day the Finest
Cyclorama in the United States. Don't
fail to see it this time. It's THE LAST!

541 TREMONT STREET, BOSTON.

·· MUSIC: ··
Boston Theatre Orchestra,
N. LOTHIAN, Leader.

British and American National Airs.
Plantation Melodies.   Home Favorites.

Boston: Hollis St. Theatre, May 9, 1889. Newport: Opera House, Aug. 13, 1889.
Hartford: Opera House, Sept. 24, 1889.

Programme Copyrighted by Miss Cora Scott Pond.

Retrospective and Prospective

AMERICA!

GRAND

SPECTACULAR ENTERTAINMENT.

Under the Auspices of the

INDEPENDENT WOMEN VOTERS and WOMAN'S PUBLISHING CO.

MUSIC HALL, BOSTON,

THURSDAY, APRIL 26TH, AT 7.45 P. M.

TABLEAUX AND VIVID ILLUSTRATIONS

Of the Prominent Scenes in American History,

Represented by 100 Different Characters.

MRS. MARY A. LIVERMORE

will be the Historian of the occasion.

These pageants usually consisted of a series of tableaux vivants while texts or long descriptive poems were read aloud to illustrate the scene. Mary A. Livermore, the temperance and suffrage leader and lecturer, successfully organized both local and national pageants that toured the country. (Courtesy of the Boston Athenæum.)

Studio photograph of architect and suffragist Florence H. Luscomb as an "Indian Hod Carrier" in a pageant (April 1913). Throughout the suffrage movement, pageants remained a popular form of presentation to celebrate women's achievements. (Courtesy of the Schlesinger Library, Radcliffe College.)

Charlotte Perkins Gilman (1860–1935) devoted her life to writing and lecturing on many social ills. She was especially identified with the labor movement and the woman's movement. The photograph shows her in her silk lecture gown. (Courtesy of the Schlesinger Library, Radcliffe College.)

Catharine Waugh McCulloch (1862–1945) practiced law in Chicago
and in 1890 became legislative superintendent of the Illinois Equal Suffrage
Association. The photograph was taken in 1907 when she was elected
Justice of the Peace of Evanston, Ill. (Courtesy of the Schlesinger Library,
Radcliffe College.)

Suffrage parades became an annual event in New York City after 1910. This photograph of women in academic gowns was presumably taken during the parade on May 6, 1911, which went down Fifth Avenue from Fifty-seventh Street to Union Square. Catharine Waugh McCulloch can be seen marching on the extreme right. (Courtesy of the Schlesinger Library, Radcliffe College.)

Besides pamphlets, a wide variety of suffrage paraphernalia like this calendar for 1912 were sold for propaganda purposes. (Courtesy of the Schlesinger Library, Radcliffe College.)

Emily Sargent Lewis (1866–1931), author of *Election Day* and a suffrage pageant called *Dream of Brave Women*. Philadelphia society was shocked when some of its leading members became active in the suffrage movement. (Courtesy of Mrs. Millicent Lewis Pettit.)

Actress Mary Shaw (1854–1927) became an ardent supporter of the woman's movement in the 1890s. She acted in *Votes for Women!*, a play written by her friend Elizabeth Robins. Shaw also wrote and produced suffrage plays of her own. (Courtesy of Harvard Theatre Collection, Harvard College Library.)

Suffrage paraphernalia became more imaginative and humorous as the fight for the vote went on. The idea for this
suffrage parakeet, made of yellow and blue tin and distributed
for the Massachusetts referendum on November 2, 1915,
might have been inspired by Mary Shaw's play *The Parrot
Cage*. (Courtesy of the Schlesinger Library, Radcliffe College.)

The seriousness and moral fervor of the early woman's rights campaign gave way to lighthearted suffrage carnivals and operettas as the end of the movement came into sight. The photograph shows three women performing a Butterfly Dance during a suffrage ball in New York City, January 31, 1914. (Courtesy of Bildarchiv Preussischer Kulturbesitz, Berlin.)

Mrs. O. H. P. Belmont (1853–1933), one of the best known
society women in New York City, supported the woman's
movement not only by financing the New York headquarter
of the National Suffrage Association, but also by buying a
house on Capitol Hill for the National Woman's Party.
(Courtesy of UPI/Bettmann Newsphotos.)

A VOTING DEMONSTRATION

or AN ELECTION IN PRIMERVILLE

(A FARCE IN ONE ACT)

KATE MILLS FARGO

[Redlands, Calif.] privately printed. 1912.

CHARACTERS

Mrs. Frances Adelaide Clark, Voter.
Mrs. Rachel Emeline Somers, A Business Woman.
Mrs. Mary Elizabeth Brown, Fashionable Lady.
Miss Gertrude May Pratt, Would-be Voter.
Mrs. Wilkins, Politician.
Mrs. Sarah Edgerton Phelps, Foreigner by Marriage.
Miss Pauline Peters, English Spinster, uneducated.

Board of Electors { Two Judges.
Two Inspectors.
Two Clerks.
Two Ballot Clerks.

Police Officer.

TIME, six o'clock in the morning.

PLACE: Primerville, small unfurnished cottage.

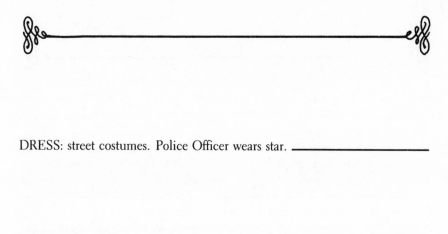

DRESS: street costumes. Police Officer wears star. ———————————

TIME, 20 minutes. ———————————————————————

NOTE

The election laws governing this play are those of the State of California. When presented in other states, the election laws governing such states can be compared with California laws. Naturalization laws are the same, of course, for all states.

When this play is given before womans' clubs and civic classes, the parts of the Board of Electors can be taken by women.

SCENE

> *A room fixed for polling votes. Index of Precinct Register on wall. Voting booth with ink pad, rubber stamp, cards of instructions to voters and blotting paper on table. Ballot box, guard rail, large table, chairs, register for clerk and voting roster. Clock on wall set at one minute of six. Board of Electors in their proper places. Police officer stationed near guard rail.*
>
> *Enter a group of women from the door in rear. They look anxiously at clock and walk about nervously.*

Teacher. This demonstration of voting is given to illustrate the mistakes which can be made by those ignorant of the laws governing the polls. Please bear in mind that this exercise is intended to be purely an instructive one, and is not meant merely for entertainment. *Reads cast of characters to audience. (When the teacher is addressing audience, all action by those taking part in play ceases.)*

First Clerk (*in loud voice*). The polls are now open. (*For dramatic effect, this should be repeated three times.*)

> **Inspector** *opens ballot box and shows it to be empty. Closes box.*

Mrs. Clark (*Looks at Index Register on wall, finds her number and advances to the guard rail. She gives her name, address and number to clerk*). Mrs. H. M. Clark, 334 Ninth St., Primerville, No. 5.

> **Clerk** *hands her voting roster.* **Mrs. Clark** *writes her name, Mrs. H. M. Clark, also her address and number.*

First Clerk (*Turning to clerk at register, repeats*). Mrs. H. M. Clark, 334 Ninth St., Primerville, No. 5.

> **Second Clerk** *looks in register to verify name and number. He turns to* **Judge** *who is seated near him, and calls his attention to the register.*

Judge (*Addressing Mrs. Clark*). But there is no Mrs. H. M. Clark on the register. The name Frances Adelaide Clark is opposite your number.

Mrs. Clark. Well, that is the same. That is my name.

Judge. But you must give the same name at the polls that you gave when registering, and it must be your full Christian name.

Mrs. Clark. Oh, dear, I didn't suppose it made any difference.

Mrs. Clark *is given another chance; writes her name again and it is verified by clerk at register.*

Teacher. Mrs. Clark made a mistake at the beginning of her voting. The name given at the polls must be the same as that given when registering and it must be the full Christian name. This is an important thing to know.

Mrs. Clark *starts to enter the place enclosed by the guard rail, taking a friend with her.*

Police Officer (*Stopping the friend, addresses* **Mrs. Clark**.). You must go in the booth alone, Madam. You cannot take your friend with you.
Mrs. Clark. Oh, I'd never dare go alone!
Police Officer. You will have to.

Mrs. Clark *passes through the guard rail.* **Ballot clerk** *gives her a blank ballot and she takes the ballot ticket to the booth.* **Clerk** *at the register writes the number of the ticket opposite* **Mrs. Clark**'s *name.*

Second Clerk (*As* **Mrs. Clark** *passes to booth*). Use the rubber stamp in marking your ballot.
Teacher. Mrs. Clark has made another mistake you see, in attempting to take her friend in the booth with her. These two women are bosom friends, and have shopped together and have gone from counter to counter in each other's company. They very naturally thought they could do their voting together. Here is a point not to be forgotten. The person voting *must be alone* in the booth.

Mrs. Clark *prepares her ballot by stamping X opposite the answer she desires to give. She folds her ballot ticket so that the number of the ballot on the strip, separated from the ticket by a perforated line, shall appear on the outside. She steps out of the booth and gives her ballot, folded, to the* **Inspector** *and gives him her name.*
Frances Adelaide Clark.

Inspector (*Repeats name*). Frances Adelaide Clark. (*also number of her ballot ticket in loud voice.*)

Second Clerk *at register verifies the number of the ballot ticket opposite the name on the register, and writes the word "voted" opposite name. He repeats in loud voice.* Frances Adelaide Clark, voted.

Inspector *tears off perforated slip, drops ballot in box and destroys number.*
Exit **Mrs. Clark**.

Mrs. Somers, *a business woman with long lead pencil sticking in her hair, next votes.*

Mrs. Somers (*Looks on Index Register for number, gives name and address to clerk*). Rachel Emeline Somers, 710 Breeze Ave., Primerville, Number 15.

Clerk *repeats name, address and number to clerk at register. Her name is found on register. She passes inside guard rail.* Ballot clerk *gives her a blank ballot.* Clerk *at the register writes the number of the ticket opposite* Mrs. Somers' *name.* Mrs. Somers *passes hurriedly to booth.*

Second Clerk (*Calling after her.*). Use the rubber stamp in marking your ticket.

Mrs. Somers *enters booth. Instead of using stamp she draws pencil from her hair and marks her ballot. She folds ballot, steps from booth with pencil in her hand. She hands ballot to* Inspector.

Judge (*Stopping her.*). Madam, did you mark your ballot with that pencil in your hand?

Mrs. Somers (*In brisk, business-like tone.*). Why yes, of course.

Judge. Don't you know you ought not to do that?

Mrs. Somers (*In surprise.*). Why, what should I mark it with?

Judge. There is a stamp and an ink pad in the booth for that very purpose.

Mrs. Somers. Well, how was I to know that?

Judge. You were told as you went in.

Mrs. Somers. I didn't hear anything said about it.

Judge. If you had attended some of the classes that were formed to teach women how to vote, you might have learned about it.

Mrs. Somers (*Indignantly.*). I did not have time for any such nonsense. I am a working woman.

Judge. Well, you can read, can't you?

Mrs. Somers. Yes, indeed.

Judge. The newspapers were full of instructions to voters before this election and a little study would have made it all plain.

Ballot Clerk *hands* Mrs. Somers *another blank ballot. She returns to booth and stamps ticket noisily. If rubber stamp will not make noise enough, something should be placed in booth, with which she can pound her ticket. She does this several times in quick succession.*

Mrs. Somers *steps from booth, hands ballot to* Inspector.

Inspector (*Frowning.*). Madam, your ticket is folded wrongly. This is the way. (*Shows her how ballot should be folded.*)

Inspector *repeats name, Rachel Emeline Somers to clerk at register, also the number on her ballot ticket.*

Clerk (*Writes "voted" opposite her name and announces*). Rachel Emeline Somers, voted.

Inspector *tears off perforated slip, destroys number.*

Mrs. Somers. Well, I think you are awfully particular. (*Exit, jerking her shoulders.*)

Teacher. The knowledge that the stamp must be used may seem a small thing in itself, but any irregularity in marking will render the ballot void for the question voted upon. It is the attention that is given to all these little details before voting that is going to make the casting of votes by women an easy and pleasant service. (**Teacher** *shows class how to fold ballot.*)

In folding the ballot ticket, the number of the ballot on the slip, separated from the ballot by a perforated line, should appear on the outside.

Miss Pratt (*Looks up number on Index Register, goes to guard rail, gives name*). Gertrude May Pratt, 415 Sweet Briar Ave., number 16. (**Clerk** *hands her voting roster. She writes her name.*)

Clerk (*Turning to clerk at register.*). Gertrude May Pratt, Sweet Briar Ave., number 16.

Judge (*Looking her over politely.*). How old are you, Miss Pratt?

Miss Pratt (*Blushing.*). Eighteen.

Judge. Don't you know you have to be twenty-one before you can vote?

Miss Pratt. Why, no. I just thought I had to be of age.

Judge. What age did you give when you registered?

Miss Pratt. Why, I told the man I had just come of age, and I supposed he put it down eighteen.

Judge. I am sorry, Miss Pratt, but you can't vote.

Miss Pratt (*Beginning to cry*). Its all that horrid man's fault anyway, and I *did* want to vote so. (*Exit* **Miss Pratt.**)

Teacher. In the State of California and in some other states, a girl is of age at eighteen years, but she cannot vote until she is twenty-one.

Enter **Mrs. Brown.** *She is dressed in the extreme of fashion and leads a little dog by a chain. She advances smilingly and with great sang froid* (*announces her name to the clerk*). Mary Elizabeth Brown, Snob Hill, Primerville, number 23. (*She very elaborately writes her name on roster.*)

Clerk (*Turning to clerk at register.*). Mary Elizabeth Brown, Snob Hill, Primerville, number 23.

Judge. We do not find your name on the register. I challenge your vote. It is now 12 o'clock. Have you come direct from your home, here, Mrs. Brown?

Mrs. Brown. Oh, no, indeed. I have been away all morning.

Judge. Have you been in any other voting place?

Mrs. Brown. Oh, yes, several.

Judge. Mrs. Brown, have you voted before coming here this morning?

Mrs. Brown. Why,—yes.

Judge. Don't you know it is against the law to cast more than one vote?

Mrs. Brown. Why, I thought we could vote all we wanted to. I thought that was what Woman's Suffrage meant when they were talking so much about it. *It is such fun to vote! (Exit, giggling and simpering.)*

Teacher. There are a great many women to whom the privilege and responsibility of voting will not appeal very seriously. Mrs. Brown is evidently one of this class.

Mrs. Wilkins *is noticed standing apart with another woman, to whom she is talking earnestly.*

Police Officer (*Going up and laying his hand on* **Mrs. Wilkins'** *shoulder.*). Madam, I am obliged to arrest you.

Mrs. Wilkins (*Terrified*). Why, what have I done?

Police Officer. I heard you trying to influence this woman's vote. You will have to come with me. (*Leads* **Mrs. Wilkins** *away.*)

Teacher. Mrs. Wilkins has committed a very serious offense. The law states distinctly:—"No person shall solicit a vote or speak to a voter on the subject of marking his ticket within one hundred feet of the polling place." It states further:—"No person shall ask another at a polling place for whom he intends to vote." The extreme penalty of the law in this State for wilfully violating any of the laws relating to elections, is a fine of one thousand dollars, or imprisonment in the State's prison for five years, *or both.* As Mrs. Wilkins is evidently ignorant of these laws she *may* get off easier.

Mrs. Phelps *finds her number on Index Register; goes to guard rail, gives name.* Sarah Edgerton Phelps, 307 Broad Street, Primerville, number 19.

Clerk *presents voting roster and she writes name and address.* **Clerk** *passes her name on to clerk at register.* **Second Clerk** *finds her name in register.*

Judge. Wait a moment, please. Were you born in the United States?

Mrs. Phelps. Yes.

Judge. Are you married?

Mrs. Phelps (*Sighing*). Yes.

Judge. Was your husband born in the United States?

Mrs. Phelps. No, in Germany.

Judge. Has your husband been naturalized?

Mrs. Phelps (*Languidly.*). I am sure I don't know.

Judge. Well, you will have to find out before you can vote.

Mrs. Phelps. Why, what difference would that make?

Judge. When you married, you assumed your husband's citizenship and unless he has been naturalized, you are neither of you American citizens. Didn't they ask you about these things when you registered?

Mrs. Phelps. I told them I was American born. They didn't ask me anything about my husband and I didn't mention him. I don't like to talk about him.

Judge. Well, they should have been more particular.

Mrs. Phelps. Supposing my husband is not naturalized and refuses to be; how *can* I vote?

Judge. You can take out naturalization papers yourself, become an American citizen, and then you can vote.

Mrs. Phelps (*Wearily*). Here I was born and brought up in the United States and now I have to be born again in order to vote. I don't understand this.

Judge. Neither do I. (*Exit* **Mrs. Phelps.**)

Teacher. This seems a little difficult for anyone to understand. In the State of California the legislature has changed the law under which women were disfranchised by marrying aliens. Under the new law a Native Daughter of California is a citizen regardless of whether she weds a foreigner or not, her marriage not affecting her right of suffrage.

A new amendatory law has also been passed in California which does not require women voters to give their age when registering.

Miss Peters *looks up number, goes to guard rail, gives name and address.* Pauline Peters, 112 Angelica St., Primerville, number 2.

Clerk *presents voting roster. She signs name.* **Clerk** *passes name, address and number to clerk at register.* **Second Clerk,** *looking in register, turns to* **Judge.**

Judge. Pauline Peters? Are you married?

Miss Peters (*Severely*). I, married? No!

Judge. Where were you born?

Miss Peters. In England.

Judge. How long have you been in this country?

Miss Peters. I'll not answer that question. I came here when I was a baby.

Judge (*Smiling*). Didn't you give your age when you registered?

Miss Peters. The man didn't ask me. He was a gentleman.

Judge. Didn't he ask you if you had been naturalized?

Miss Peters. Naturalized! What's that? It was dinner time, and the man was hungry and wanted to go home, and he didn't ask me anything.

Judge. Have you any papers to show that you are a citizen of this country?

Miss Peters. I have the deed to the house and lot I own.

Judge. That won't do. If you want to vote you will either have to marry (**Miss Peters** *starts*). a citizen of the United States or take out naturalization papers.

Miss Peters (*Anxiously*). Which would be the worst?

First Clerk (*Proclaims in loud voice*). The polls are closed.

CURTAIN

Teacher. To recapitulate—we find there are five essential points in voting which should be carefully borne in mind.

> First—Look up number opposite name on Index Register.
> Second—Write same name when voting that was given when registering.
> Third—Enter booth for marking ballot alone.
> Fourth—Use rubber stamp found in booth for marking ballot.
> Fifth—Fold ballot correctly.

It is essential for us all to learn what we can about these details, in order to pass along our knowledge to those who can not attend classes. The thought of voting will be a positive burden to the majority of women until they have learned how. Then it will be a pleasure.

Another thought for women to carry and spread is this: That the polls are as legitimate a place for women to appear in as the church. The polls are as sacred a place as the church. We go to church to learn the principles that work for righteous government. We go to the polls to put these principles into practice.

A Suffragette Baby

A Comedy in One Act

ALICE C. THOMPSON

Philadelphia: The Penn Publishing Company. 1912.

CHARACTERS ——————————————————————————————

Anna Spence ⎫
Helen Moore ⎬ Suffragettes
Sybil Henderson ⎪
Susan Trimble ⎭
Mrs. McGinnis, The landlady.
Miss Harriet Driver, A reporter.
And **The Baby**, who has not a speaking part, but is very important.

TIME OF PLAYING, Thirty-five minutes. ——————————————

COSTUMES ————————————————————————————————

Anna. Simple indoor dress, and small work apron. Wears hat and coat on
  second entrance.
Mrs. McGinnis. A "widdy woman" of forty or over. Rather stout. Wears
  gingham dress and large apron. Hair rolled up in a tight knot. Bare
  arms.
Helen. Street costume, with hat, coat, gloves, etc.
Sybil. Simple street costume.
Susan. Should be rather taller and more severely dressed than the others.
  She is a very neat, "tailor-made" type. On first entrance wears street
  suit, and across shoulder a broad sash with words "Votes for Women"
  in large yellow letters, and carries banner.
Harriet. A stylish young woman, in street costume. She carries a smart
  shopping-bag, and wears large suede gloves.

PROPERTIES ——

A baby's white lawn dress, some pieces of white lawn, lace and silk. A paper pattern; scissors; baby's bonnet done up in parcel; a dollar bill; a white banner on a wooden pole, with the words "Votes for Women" in large yellow letters; a shoe-box; white cloth; five cups and saucers, spoons, knives, tray, plate of bread, teapot, cream pitcher, and covered dish; note-book and pencil; shoe-box, wrapped up; roll of paper.

STORY OF THE PLAY

Susan Trimble and her "bachelor girl" friends, all suffragettes, live together. A baby is left an orphan in their boarding-house. Each of Susan's three friends secretly adopts the baby, and pays the landlady to look after it. Susan thinks that she and her friends do not care for children, but when a charity officer tries to take the child to an orphanage, it is Susan who rescues her. Each girl puts in her claim. "She'll belong to all of us, and we'll bring her up a suffragette!"

SCENE

The bachelor girls' sitting-room. At R. C. is a table covered with scraps of white lawn, lace and silk; two chairs beside table. At L. C. an armchair and two others. At L., back, a shelf or square table holding five cups and saucers, five plates, spoons, knives and a white cloth. Entrances R. and L. At rise **Anna Spence** *discovered sitting at table L. C., with a pair of scissors in her hand. She holds up and examines, first, a baby's white lawn dress, then the paper pattern. A knock is heard R.* **Anna** *starts and covers the dress with her hands.*

Enter **Mrs. McGinnis** R. *She is a stout, cheerful, good-natured woman wearing a big gingham apron.*

Anna (*with relief*). Oh, it's you, Mrs. McGinnis. I'm so glad. I thought it was one of the girls, and that I was caught for sure.

Mrs. McGinnis. I see ye're busy, Miss Anna.

Comes down C.

Anna. Yes, trying to make the baby's little dress. I came home early on purpose. Do you think this will fit her? (*Holds up dress.*) How do you like it?

Mrs. McGinnis. 'Tis purty enough fer a princess, and the very thing she's a-wantin'. I do hev that manny in the tub for her ivery day.

Anna. How is she? I haven't seen her since last night.

Mrs. McGinnis. Bright as a button, and happy as the marnin'. Shure, she's the very picter of contintmint. (*Noise heard* R. **Anna** *starts.* **Mrs. McGinnis** *goes up* C.) 'Tis nothin'. Don't be scairt.

Anna. But the girls will be in any minute now. (*Gathers up work.*) They mustn't know on any account that I've adopted the baby, Mrs. McGinnis. They wouldn't understand, you know.

Mrs. McGinnis (*with an air of great confidence*). Sure, 'tis our secret, Miss Anna. Troost me.

Anna (*giving her the dress*). Please try it on her, and let me know how it fits.

Mrs. McGinnis. I do be wishin' the darlint had a new pair of shoes. Her poor little feet is almost nixt the bare ground.

Anna (*reproachfully*). Oh, why didn't you tell me before? My poor child! What size does she take? For a two-year-old, I suppose. I'll go out at once and get her a pair. (*Puts on hat.*) I hope she doesn't give you much trouble, Mrs. McGinnis.

Mrs. McGinnis. She kapes me a-movin', Miss Anna. But sure 'tis a pleasure to tend the loikes av her. I raymimber how I sez the very day her poor mother died, and she only a roomer and a stranger to me, savin' that I knowed her for a decent widdy woman like meself, and I sez, "Now, what's to become av the poor choild she's afther lavin' in this harrd worrld?" I sez. And then down you come and offers to pay for the kape av her. (*Wipes her eyes.*)

Anna. Take this dollar, Mrs. McGinnis. It will help to buy something for her. (*Gives bill.*)

Mrs. McGinnis. 'Tis the good hairt ye have, Miss Anna. Indade, no one wad be takin' ye for one of these suffergette ladies at all, at all.

Anna. Oh, don't say that, because I am one, and proud of it. (*Earnestly.*) When *we* women get votes, Mrs. McGinnis (*speaking in oratorical tone*), the world will be a happier, better place to live in. There will be provision made for orphan children without the need of applying to charity, and every widow will have a pension.

Mrs. McGinnis. Think of that, now! I wisht I hed the givin' of the votes to ye, Miss Anna. You'd git one to-marrow.

Anna. It will come in time. It must. Now I'll go out and get the shoes. Don't let any one suspect (*finger on lips*) the baby, you know——

Mrs. McGinnis. Mum's the word, miss.

Exit **Anna**, L. **Mrs. McGinnis** *puts the baby dress in a large pocket under her apron. She then tidies table, picking up all the tiny scraps of lace and silk overlooked by* **Anna**, *and puts them also in her pocket. Enter* **Helen Moore**, L.

Helen. Oh, Mrs. McGinnis, you're the very one I want to see. How's my baby?

Mrs. McGinnis. Bright as the marnin', and happy as a new button. No, I mane——

Helen. Never mind. (*Runs down* R. *and* L., *cautiously looking about. Returns* R. C.) Is she well?

Mrs. McGinnis. The very picter of health.

Helen. Thank you for your kind care of her, Mrs. McGinnis. I don't know what I'd do without you. Of course the girls have no suspicions. You've never given them a hint that I have adopted the baby?

Mrs. McGinnis. Niver a soul av 'em. I well raymimber the day her poor mother died. Just a month agone to-day. I sez to myself, "Now who will look after the poor, helpless craythur? And much I'd loike to kape her meself, but bein' only a poor, hard-worrkin' woman, and sometimes rooms not let——

Helen. Yes, I know. And I love to feel that she's all mine; no father, no relatives to claim her. Of course the others wouldn't understand. Here's something

I bought for her to-day. (*Unties parcel and holds up dainty bonnet.*) Won't she look sweet in this?

Mrs. McGinnis. Now what good angel put it into yer head, Miss Helen? 'Tis the very thing she's a-wantin' most.

Helen. I'll try to look in to-morrow on my way down-town. I wish I could see her to-night, but I'm going out and must go and change my dress now. Take good care of her, Mrs. McGinnis.

Exit **Helen**, R. **Mrs. McGinnis** *puts bonnet in pocket.*

Enter **Sybil Henderson**, L., *wearing hat.*

Sybil. Oh, Mrs. McGinnis, I'm so glad you're up here. Are any of the girls in, do you know?

Mrs. McGinnis. Just Miss Helen.

Sybil. Oh! (*In a whisper.*) How's my baby?

Mrs. McGinnis. She's bloomin' like a rose.

Sybil. Don't let any one know she belongs to me, Mrs. McGinnis.

Mrs. McGinnis. Troost me, Miss Sybil. 'Tis a sacret betwixt us and no others.

Sybil. You see, they don't care for children. You've noticed that.

Mrs. McGinnis. Poor dears! 'Tis the way they was raised.

Sybil. Well, I must say I never did until I came across my baby. And now she's everything to me.

Mrs. McGinnis. And there's that Mrs. Clancy acrost the street was a-sayin' the suffergette ladies had no hearts. "They make me tired," sez she, "with their clamorin' fer votes when they'd oughter be home mindin' the children. But the truth is," sez she, "they can't abide thim." A lot she knows about suffergettes, I'll tell her.

Sybil. No, no. You mustn't give away my secret.

Mrs. McGinnis. No, not that, Miss Sybil. 'Tis as safe as a church wid me. (*She is fumbling nervously in pocket and drops the bonnet.*)

Sybil. Yes, I can depend upon you, I'm sure. (*Smiles sweetly and exits* R.)

Enter **Susan Trimble**, L.

Susan. Good-afternoon, Mrs. McGinnis. How is your little charge? (*Comes down and puts banner down* R.)

Mrs. McGinnis (*a little in awe of* **Susan**). Thank you, ma'am, she's hearty.

Susan. I suppose there have been no relatives to claim her.

Mrs. McGinnis. Not a one. I'm just a-wishin' some kind lady like yourself, ma'am, would adopt the pore lamb and give her a home.

Susan. Oh, dear, no. I don't care for children. And what should I do with a child? I'm far too busy. She would be better off in an institution. Have you made an application for her?

Mrs. McGinnis. What! Give her up to one av thim there orphin homes! Not me. There's them as will have a worrd to say to that, Miss Susan.

Susan. Now, be sensible, Mrs. McGinnis. The child will be well fed and well cared for. She will be taught to be self-supporting.

Mrs. McGinnis (*squaring her shoulders*). Let 'em come and thry for to take her, that's all I say.

Susan. I spoke to the Charity Organization Society about the case. They could help us to place the child in good hands, I'm sure. One of their officers may call and see you about her.

Mrs. McGinnis. I'll give him a pace av me moind.

Susan (*calmly*). An orphanage would be best. In time all children will be brought up by the state. You'd better be prepared.

Mrs. McGinnis. Oh, I'll be praypared all roight—wid a shtick.

> **Mrs. McGinnis** *exits* L. **Susan** *looks after her and smiles, then sees bonnet lying on floor.*

Susan. Why, what's this? (*Picks up bonnet and holds it before her.*) It's the baby's. Mrs. McGinnis must have dropped it. The poor little thing! (*She puts bonnet impulsively to her lips.*)

> *Enter* **Anna**, L., *carrying shoe-box, wrapped up.*

Anna. Why, Susan, what have you there?

Susan (*with great show of indifference*). It's some trifle of the ba—of that child's, I believe. Mrs. McGinnis must have dropped it. (*Goes* R. *and calls.*) Mrs. McGinnis! (**Mrs. McGinnis** *re-enters.*) Here, I believe you dropped this.

Mrs. McGinnis (*taking bonnet*). The saints preserve us, I did that. (*Stands* C., *embarrassed.*)

Susan. You're back early, Anna. (*Comes down* R.)

Anna. I—I hadn't much to do to-day. The work was light. (*As she passes* **Mrs. McGinnis**, *she puts the box in her hands.* **Susan** *watches her. Exit* **Mrs. McGinnis**, R.) Did you have a good meeting, Susan?

Susan. Splendid. I wish you had been there. It was so enthusiastic, and the speeches were the best I have ever heard.

Anna. I must try to go next time.

Susan. It is worth making an effort to go, it seems to me. You'll join the monster parade on Friday, I hope?

Anna. Oh, of course.

> *Enter* **Helen**, R.

Helen (*going to* **Susan**). Congratulations, Susan! You were wonderful. I never heard anything more to the point than your speech. Did you hear me shout "Hooray!" from the back of the hall?

Susan. I did not distinguish any individual voice among the general applause. I am very glad, however, that you liked my speech. (*Grows oratorical.*) The time is coming when all women will——

Anna puts white cloth on table and places cups and saucers, etc.

Anna (*laughing*). Hurray! Them's my sentiments, Susan. Go on!

Enter **Sybil**, R.

Sybil. Oh, Susan, how did you do it? You were wonderful. What a leader you are! (*She throws herself into chair down* R.) Oh, you missed it, Anna. Susan never faltered for a moment.

Helen helps **Anna** *set table, bringing knives, forks, etc., from table or shelf up* C.

Susan. Falter! Why should I falter? The glorious cause is almost won. All we need now are a few more devoted women free from cares of children and——

Anna and **Helen** *look at* **Susan** *and she pauses.*

Anna (*laughing, as she goes* R.). That's it, Susan. Excuse me, I must cut the bread. But go on; I can hear you. Free from cares of children——

Exit **Anna**, R. **Sybil** *leans forward looking at* **Susan**.

Susan (*resuming, but not so forcefully*). Yes, when we have a few more real women leaders we shall—— Good gracious, Sybil, don't stare at me so. What is it?

Helen goes on setting table.

Sybil. Oh, Susan, I was just remembering what you said this afternoon about the man and the home.

Susan. Yes.

Sybil. Surely you believe in the home, Susan?

Susan. Certainly. Isn't this a home? Aren't we perfectly happy here, we four free and independent women, responsible to no man for our actions, dependent upon no man for our necessities, glad to work for our daily bread? I think it is an ideal condition.

Helen. But the children——

Susan. What children?

Helen. I mean there should be children, or at least a child, in an ideal home.

Susan. Not necessarily. Children are a serious drawback to a career.

Sybil. Or a great incentive.

Susan. See here, Sybil, are you getting interested in some young man? I never heard you talk like that before, Sybil.

Enter **Anna** *carrying a tray on which are a teapot, cream pitcher, plate of bread and a covered dish.* **Susan** *removes her sash.* **Sybil** *places chairs at table.*

Anna. Come to table, girls. Supper is ready. What was that you were saying about children?
Susan. I said children were a serious inconvenience.
Anna. Oh!

All sit at table, **Susan** *at left end,* **Anna** *at right end.* **Helen** *and* **Sybil** *are on side facing audience.*

Helen. But it would be nice to have a bright, happy child in the house.
Susan. Nice, but not at all practical.

Anna *pours tea and passes it. All take bread.*

Anna. Like that dear baby down-stairs.

A knock heard L. **Helen** *rises and opens door* L. *Enter* **Miss Harriet Driver.**

Harriet. Oh, I'm afraid I have come at an inconvenient time.
Susan (*rising*). Not at all.
Harriet (*giving card from bag*). I represent the "Morning Telegraph."
Susan (*reading card*). Miss Harriet Driver. Sit down, Miss Driver. Of course you are interested in woman's suffrage?
Harriet (*sitting down* L.). Yes—impersonally. I have come to see you about your meeting this afternoon. You had one, didn't you?
Susan. Had one! Why, we're the talk of the town. It was splendid! Were you not there?
Harriet. No. I must explain that I am the society reporter. Mrs. Barnes, who has charge of the woman's page, had something else on and couldn't come, so she asked me to take this. (*Seats herself.*) I do the weddings, teas, receptions, and so on.
Anna. Do have a cup of tea, Miss Driver.
Harriet. Thanks; I've had my supper, but I'll join you in a cup of tea if I may just sit here and not disturb you. Please go on with your own and don't mind me.

Anna *brings* **Harriet** *tea and resumes seat.*

Susan. Society reporter. Hm. Rather frivolous work, I should say. Doesn't it bore you?
Harriet. Oh, never. I love to describe pretty clothes. (*Swallows tea hurriedly, returns cup to table and goes back to chair, taking pencil and note-book from bag.*) Now, please tell me what you wore this afternoon.
Susan. My usual suit, a tweed.

Harriet (*writing, and then reading aloud*). "Miss Trimble looked very handsome in a well-tailored tweed suit and——"

Susan. I was not there to look handsome, but to carry conviction!

Harriet (*looking up*). Certainly. But good clothes are always convincing. "And a hat——"

Susan. Black straw with a white wing; perfectly plain and unpretentious.

Harriet (*writing*). "And a smart little black hat trimmed with a white feather mount."

Susan (*with grim earnestness*). Elastic side shoes.

Harriet. I'll skip that.

Susan. Cotton gloves.

Harriet. Not necessary to mention gloves. (*Writes and reads.*) "She carried——" What kind of flowers did you carry, Miss Trimble?

Susan. Flowers! What do you think it was—a wedding or a pink tea? I carried my banner and my speech.

Harriet. Oh, I'll skip that, too.

Susan. The most important of all. Miss Driver, you are concerning yourself altogether with trivialities. What do clothes matter?

Harriet. A great deal.

Susan. Not to us.

Harriet. Not to any of you? Your friends—— (*Looks around.*)

Susan. Are with me heart and soul. We share all our thoughts; don't we, girls?

Helen
Sybil } *hastily and guiltily*). Yes. Oh, certainly.

Harriet. And they belong to the suffrage movement?

Sybil. Indeed, yes.

Helen. It is our life. We care for nothing else—almost.

Susan. Speak up, Anna.

> **Anna** *rises suddenly*.

Anna (*loudly*). Votes for women! (*Sits down promptly.*)

Susan. Nothing matters but the one, the all important thing. Oh, if I could but convince you.

Harriet (*earnestly*). I see. Er—— Can you remember what any of the other ladies at the meeting wore? I mean the leaders.

Susan. Certainly not. They were clothed, that is sufficient. (*Rises and walks about.*) To us who have such a glorious end in view, clothes are nothing. Anything apart, anything inimical to our places, we brush aside. A sheltered home, children,—let other women take them. To us they do not count. We stand alone. Am I not right, Helen?

Helen (*faintly*). You are, Susan.

Sybil (*boldly*). Hear, hear. (*Rises.*) Oh, listen.

Anna. What is it?

Sybil. I thought I heard the baby—that is, I thought somebody was crying.

Susan. Who would give up so enthralling a vocation for the ordinary duties of a domestic life, or for the frivolous pleasures of an effete society?

Harriet (*rising*). Well, I think I have all the copy I need. Thank you so much for your kindness. (*Goes up* C.)

Susan (*rushing to her*). But the speech, the speech! (*Grasps her arm.*)

Harriet. Oh, yes. I'm afraid I haven't time to copy it. Couldn't you lend it to me?

Susan. Here it is. Take care of it, please, and see that it is copied correctly. (*Gives roll of paper.*)

Harriet. I'll give it to Mrs. Barnes; she'll attend to it. Now I must run. I've got two weddings and an "at home" to do this evening. (*Drops paper.*)

Susan. There, you've dropped it already. I think I'd better mail it. (*Picks it up.*)

Harriet. No, no, I'll take care of it. (*Takes paper.*)

Susan. And tell Mrs. Barnes I'll be pleased to see her at our next meeting, if she's not too busy.

Harriet. Oh, poor Mrs. Barnes! If you had her work to do you'd find excuses, perhaps.

Susan. I—I! The hardest working woman in the city, who could be busier than I? I earn my own living, Miss Driver—I——

Harriet. Yes, but you have only to feed and clothe one. Mrs. Barnes is a widow with three small children dependent upon her for everything. Good-bye; so pleased to have met you all. (*Exit,* L.)

Helen. Three children!

Sybil (*sighing*). Something to work for.

Susan. Children—or clothes. There goes a butterfly! And she makes her living by describing the colors of other butterflies. What a life!

Anna. And yet she is a necessary part of our social system. But one would almost rather be—Mrs. Barnes—I think. Oh, was that the baby crying, Sybil?

Mrs. McGinnis *is heard off weeping and wailing in a loud voice.*

Helen (*jumping up*). Good gracious! What's the matter?

Enter **Mrs. McGinnis,** L.

Mrs. McGinnis. Och, whatever shall we do? The charities is got her!

Sybil }
Anna } The charities! What do you mean?

Helen. Not my—not the baby!

Mrs. McGinnis. Och, 'tis that same. 'Tis dishtracted I am, entoirely. The swate lamb, to be took off widout even so much as if ye plase——

Anna (*going to her*). What has happened, Mrs. McGinnis?

Susan. Quick! Tell us! They haven't taken the baby——

Mrs. McGinnis. Yes, the love. 'Tis a bowld man has taken her off this minute, under me very nose; he sez he's a charity officer, and she's to go to an institution to be brought up proper, having no mother or father. (*Shakes her fist at* **Susan.**) Miss Trimble, 'tis yourself's at the bottom of this.

Susan. No, no. I never told him to take her. I only mentioned the case. Oh, I'll bring her back. (*Exit* L., *hastily.*)

Mrs. McGinnis. And what shall I do now widout her? 'Tis a sorry day fer me. The poor lamb!

Helen (*wringing her hands*). My poor baby!

Sybil (*putting her hands over her face*). My darling child!

Anna. My precious little one! (*Weeps.*)

Mrs. McGinnis. And her not three years old. (*Sobs loudly.*)

Helen. An orphan asylum. It's horrible. I will never permit such a thing. To steal my own darling child!

Sybil. Your darling child! I adopted her!

Anna. Oh, no. She is mine. I adopted her the day her mother died.

Helen. You are both mistaken. She belongs to me. Isn't it so, Mrs. McGinnis?

Mrs. McGinnis (*bewildered*). Why, sure, Miss Helen. You——

Sybil. Haven't I been paying you for her board? Answer me that.

Mrs. McGinnis (*wringing her hands*). Och, yis; och, yis, Miss Sybil.

Sybil (*triumphantly*). There! I guess——

Anna. Why—why—so have I—and making clothes for her, haven't I, Mrs. McGinnis?

Mrs. McGinnis (*sitting in chair and throwing apron over her head, wailing*). 'Twas out of the kindness of yer swate heart. Ochone!

Anna. There!

Sybil. Mrs. McGinnis, how dare you sit there and say that? She's mine.

Helen. How dare you allow any one else to support my child?

Mrs. McGinnis. (*rocking back and forth, apron over head*). Och, I'm a poor widdy woman. I'm a poor widdy woman, with nobody to——

Anna. Mrs. McGinnis, I solemnly call upon you to declare that that baby is mine.

Mrs. McGinnis. Yours she is, miss, if ever ye see her swate face again. (*The girls all look at one another.*)

Sybil (*tragically*). Oh, how I have been deceived!

    Mrs. McGinnis *goes up* C.

Mrs. McGinnis. Hark! I do belave as they're a-comin' back. (*Opens door* L.) Och, praise be! Here's Miss Susan with the baby. (*All go up* C.)

Enter **Susan,** L., *carrying a baby girl of about two years of age, daintily dressed. She comes down* C., *the rest following.*

Susan (*caressing child*). There, dear; there, dear lamb, don't be frightened. The naughty man shan't have you, shall he?

Anna. Why, Susan!

Susan. Girls, that man didn't even know how to carry her!

Helen. Why, Susan Trimble!

Susan (*sheepish, but defiant*). Well, Helen Moore! Do you think I'd let a man carry her off like that without so much as by your leave? We insist on our rights. If the child is to be taken to an institution it shall be done decently and in order.

Anna. No, no. Give her to me!

Susan (*doubtfully*). I know of a very good orphanage——

Sybil. She shall never go to one.

Helen. Never.

    Susan *puts the baby on floor.*

Sybil (*going to her*). She is mine. (*Drops on her knees.*) I have been paying for her board and clothes ever since her mother died.

Susan (*amazed*). What!

Anna (*going to baby and kneeling on the other side of her*). And so have I. And I love her.

Susan. You, too, Anna!

Helen. And I. Oh, Mrs. McGinnis, I thought I could trust you.

Mrs. McGinnis. Sure, what was I to do wid an orphan choild on me hands, and three rale ladies all clamorin' to be her mother, and ivery blissed one av ye a-comin' to me and sayin', "Mrs. McGinnis, don't let the others know." Sure I hadn't the heart to refuse ye, and how could I go back on me worrd, once after givin' it?

Susan. It is perfectly absurd, girls. I'm afraid the child would be better in an institution. Besides, we—that is, you all have your work. And what about our mission? Oh, don't let us forget that. Let us be faithful. (*Seizes banner.*) Girls, you must choose between them. (*Stands beside baby holding out the banner with "Votes for Women" on it, and looks sternly ahead as if seeing into the future.* **Helen** *picks up the baby.* **Anna** *and* **Sybil** *rise and stand beside her, each putting an arm around her.*) Alas! Divided interests!

Sybil. No, no; united interests. Come, Susan.

Mrs. McGinnis (*going toward* **Susan**). That's right. United we shtand pat, divided we fall. (*Trips over banner and nearly falls.*) Let them have her, Miss Susan, darlint.

Susan (*holding banner and facing front, sternly*). No!

Helen (*holding up baby*). Only look at her, Susan. Isn't she a darling?

    Susan *glances around, and thrusts banner into hands of* **Mrs. McGinnis**, *who carries it up* C.

Susan. Helen Moore, give me that child. You're squeezing her to death. (*Takes baby from* **Helen**, *and caresses it.*)

Mrs. McGinnis (*waving banner*). Glory be!

The girls all laugh. Knock heard L. **Mrs. McGinnis** *opens the door. Enter* **Harriet**, L., *and comes down* C.

Harriet. Excuse me, what color did you say—why, Miss Trimble, I thought you didn't care for children?

Susan (*calmly*). You were mistaken. We stand for the rights of womankind— old, or—young.

Anna. And the younger they are, the better we like them. And this one, Miss Driver, belongs to—— (*She hesitates.*)

Susan. She belongs to all of us. We've adopted her. We're going to bring her up in the true faith. She's going to help us to win——

Anna.
Sybil. } Votes for women!
Helen.

Mrs. McGinnis (*waving banner*). Glory be—she's a suffergette baby!

CURTAIN

ELECTION DAY

A SUFFRAGE PLAY

(A COMEDY IN ONE ACT)

EMILY SARGENT LEWIS

Philadelphia: privately printed, 1912.

DRAMATIC PERSONNEL ————————————————

Mr. Richard Gardner, A Golf Enthusiast.
Mrs. Richard Gardner, his wife, An Anti-Suffragist.
Dorothy, aged twenty-one, Their daughter.
Dick, aged ten, Their son.
Mrs. Carter, sister of Mrs. Gardner, A Suffragist.
Mr. Thomas Randolph, A suitor for Dorothy.
Katy Casey, A woman who goes out to work by the day.
Augustus White, A negro who takes charge of the Gardner's furnace.
Mary, A waitress.

TIME: The Present. ————————————————

PLACE: An American City. ————————————————

SCENE

The scene is laid on election-day in the breakfast room of the Gardner household, at eight o'clock in the morning. **Mary**, *the waitress, is putting the finishing touches to the breakfast table.*

Enter **Mrs. Gardner** *in picturesque morning dress.*

Mrs. Gardner. Good-morning, Mary. Nobody down yet? I'll just glance over the paper until some one else comes. (**Mary** *gives her paper and continues arrangement of table.*)

Mrs. Gardner (*sits on sofa and unfolds paper, reads*). The usual sensational headings—"Typhoid epidemic threatened." Shocking! Fortunately it's not in our part of town. (*Turns to* **Mary**.) Mary, be sure to serve only bottled spring water, for the *family* I mean, of course.

Mary. Yes, ma'am.

Mrs. Gardner (*still reading*). "Another strike!" I never read about those silly labor troubles. "Demand for better public schools"—that doesn't interest me; fortunately, we've always been able to send the children to private schools. "Suffragists hope for victory at the polls to-day"—well they certainly will be disappointed. After the magnificent speeches made by our anti-suffragist leaders last week, the "Yellow Peril," as our dear president so beautifully names the movement, is trampled under foot.

Enter **Dick**, *runs to his mother and kisses her.*

Dick. Good morning, mother.

Mrs. Gardner (*kissing him*). Good morning, darling. How rosy you are this morning.

Dick (*looks over mother's shoulder at paper and reads aloud*). "Votes for Women!" Oh, mother, one of our teachers wore a pin with that on it, and I asked her why she didn't have "Votes for Monkeys," too.

Mrs. Gardner (*laughs and goes toward table, followed by* **Dick**). An excellent question, Dick, what did she say? (*With sudden change of tone*) Why don't you pull out my chair for me? Don't you know that a gentleman always shows respect for ladies? (**Dick** *seats her, then sits down himself.* **Mary** *passes fruit, etc.*)

Dick. Say, mother! Honestly, don't you wish you could vote to-day?

Mrs. Gardner. No, indeed. I am quite willing to put all my political burdens upon my husband's shoulders.

Enter **Dorothy** *with* **Mr. Gardner,** *who is in golfing clothes.* **Dorothy** *kisses her mother.* **Dick** *seats his father, etc.*

Mrs. Gardner (*to* **Mr. Gardner** *tenderly*). I was just saying, my dear, that I am so glad to lay all my political burdens upon your strong shoulders.

Mr. Gardner. Very nice of you, my love! May I have my coffee right away? I've just time to catch my train for the country-club. (**Mrs. Gardner** *pours coffee,* **Mary** *passes it.*)

Dorothy (*to her father*). It's fortunate that we have such fine weather for election-day, isn't it, father? They say it makes such a difference.

Mr. Gardner. Yes, indeed, the links will be crowded.

Dorothy. I was thinking of the polls. You know you will have to bear my political burdens, too, to-day, father, since I am twenty-one.

Dick. When I'm twenty-one I'll bear my own burdens. You won't have to worry about me, Dad. Girls haven't enough sense to vote, poor things!

Mrs. Gardner (*to* **Dick**). Don't be rude to your sister. (*To* **Mr. Gardner**) You won't vote until late this afternoon, I suppose?

Mr. Gardner (*embarrassed*). I'm afraid I can't manage to pull off a vote to-day. The Committee on Golf is going to stay at the Country Club to dine. There are some highly important matters to decide, and I shall not get back to town until late this evening.

Mrs. Gardner. Oh, I'm sorry, dear. I did want you to vote against the Woman's Suffrage Amendment.

Dorothy (*shyly*). I think that I wanted you to vote in favor of it, Father.

Mrs. Gardner (*to* **Dorothy**). Dorothy, I am surprised at you.

Mr. Gardner (*rising*). Well, I wish that you women would attend to your own politics. I'm going to play golf. I refuse to have the burden of the vote thrust upon me against my will. Good-bye, don't wait up for me. (*Kisses wife.* **Dick** *gets him bag of golf-sticks, etc. Exit* **Mr. Gardner.**)

Dorothy (*teasingly to mother*). Now who is to represent us at the polls to-day, Mother? Father's playing golf, Jim is away, and Dick is not of age.

Mrs. Gardner. Tom Randolph would represent you, if you would only accept him. As for me, I must use indirect influence somehow. (*To* **Mary.**) Has Augustus gone?

Mary. No, ma'am, he is scrubbing the steps.

Mrs. Gardner. Tell him to come here at once. (*Exit* **Mary.**)

Mrs. Gardner *leaves table, sits on sofa. Enter* **Augustus.**

Augustus (*bowing*). Good day, ma'am, good day, Miss. Good day Marse Dick. Please, 'scuse my pussonal appearance, ma'am. I was just doing down the stepses.

Mrs. Gardner. Have you voted yet, Augustus?

Augustus. No, ma'am, not yet ma'am, I haven't. Jus' as soon as I'se put the coal on Mrs. Jones next door, and turned the hose on Dr. Parks, I'se going to the polls, yes, ma'am.

Mrs. Gardner. Do you understand about this Suffrage Amendment?

Augustus. Yes, ma'am. Indeed, I do. All the ladies has been talking about that Sufferin Commendment. I'se going to vote for it, sure, ma'am.

Mrs. Gardner. Why?

Augustus. Well, ma'am, not for pussonal reasons. My wife lives down in Virginia, and dat Commendment won't do her no good, no, ma'am. But you see I'se an old man now, and I remember how it felt when President Lincoln, he told us black people we might vote just the same as other folks. It do make you feel fine somehow to be treated like *folks*. You feel sort of 'spectable, you do so. I'se sure you ladies would like to feel that way, ma'am.

Mrs. Gardner (*rising*). Augustus, you are talking nonsense. How dare you imagine that anything could make me feel more respectable than I do now? I wish you to vote against this Amendment. It is a danger to the country. Unless you do as I tell you you need not come here to work any more.

Augustus (*alarmed*). 'Scuse me, ma'am. I didn't know you ladies was dangerous, I did not. I jus' thought you'd like to feel like folks. Jus' as you say, ma'am, jus' as you say. (*Backs out.*)

Mrs. Gardner (*proudly to* **Dorothy**). Now you see the power of Indirect Influence.

Dick (*jumping up from table*). Hurrah! When I'm grown-up I'll have a factory with a thousand men, and if they don't vote the way I like I'll bounce them. Hurrah!

Mrs. Gardner (to **Dick**). Go to school at once or you'll be late. (**Dick** *collects school-books with* **Dorothy's** *help, exit.*)

Dorothy. I think I'll go out, Mother. I want to take some books to the hospital.

Mrs. Gardner. My dear! You can't go over in that part of the town on Election Day. When I was a girl ladies never went out at all on Election Day. There were always so many drunken men.

Dorothy. But I promised to leave the books to-day, Mother.

Mrs. Gardner. Oh, very well. Mary can take them over this evening when she has finished her work. (*To* **Mary**, *who is clearing table.*) It will be a nice little outing for you, Mary.

Dorothy. But, Mother, Mary is younger than I am, and surely the streets will be more dangerous after dark.

Mrs. Gardner (*stiffly*). If Mary behaves herself properly she will be perfectly safe. Pray, what are the police for? (*Exit* **Mary**.)

Mrs. Gardner *takes sewing from bag and sits on sofa.* Dorothy *sits at desk and does up a parcel of magazines.*

Mrs. Gardner. Darling, I wish that you had heard my anti-suffrage speech yesterday. I flatter myself that some of the phrases were very telling. In one place I said: "Why turn the sewer of American politics into the sanctity of the home?"

Dorothy. What does that mean, Mother? Is it an argument?

Mrs. Gardner. No, my child. We have no arguments, but we know that we are right. Women have such wonderful intuition about right and wrong!

Dorothy. Wouldn't that intuition be helpful in politics?

Mrs. Gardner. Whoever heard of intuition in a sewer? By the way, speaking of politics, we must give a dinner to Senator Grant in the holidays. It is most important to get him interested in Jim's appointment to West Point. (*Sentimentally.*) I do want one of my dear sons to serve his beloved country.

Dorothy. Can one serve it only by fighting?

Mrs. Gardner. What foolish questions you ask, Dorothy. You must have formed the habit at college.

Dorothy. I'm sorry that I was tiresome, Mother. Tell me something more about your meeting.

Mrs. Gardner. Well, two of the speakers were men, both very distinguished in their professions. One of them said that the women of the Orient are the ones who have real influence, because they are truly feminine.

Dorothy. Why, Mother! I thought that they got sewed up in sacks and thrown into the Bosphorus, and that sort of thing.

Mrs. Gardner. Oh, very few, I fancy. Only the suffragists, probably. Then the other gentleman told us wonderful truths. He said that no woman is ever born a suffragist.

Dorothy. How does he know? New babies can't talk.

Mrs. Gardner. Oh, he is very clever about statistics and all those things about being born come under the head of statistics, of course. He said, too, that if we should get Woman's Suffrage, the State would relapse into barbarism.

Dorothy. Surely, he was joking.

Mrs. Gardner. Not at all. He was most serious, and it made us all feel very sad. I wish that your Aunt Madeleine could have heard him. She is always so cheerful!

Dorothy. I'm afraid that Aunt Madeleine is the exception, for she is sure that she is a *born* Suffragist.

Enter Mary. *Announces* Mrs. Carter. *Enter* Mrs. Carter. Mrs. Gardner *and* Dorothy *rise; all embrace, then sit down again.*

Mrs. Gardner. How are you today, Sister? I was afraid that you would be too busy to drop in this morning.

Mrs. Carter. My turn as watcher at the Polls comes later. Everything is going splendidly, and I feel that I can give myself an hour's rest.

Mrs. Gardner. You suffragists have wonderful energy. Now, I feel quite exhausted after my speech of yesterday.

Mrs. Carter (*sweetly*). I don't wonder, dear, after what I've heard of it.

Mrs. Gardner (*melodramatically*). But how can one give one's strength better than in defending the sacred traditions of home?

Mrs. Carter. Woman's enfranchisement will be a sacred tradition of home for future generations.

Mrs. Gardner. Madeleine, I admit that you and I might use enfranchisement well, but (*impressively*) how would you like your *cook* to vote?

Mrs. Carter. He does.

Mrs. Gardner (*in confusion*). How stupid of me. I forgot that you have a chef now. Well, consider then what it would mean to enfranchise an ignorant woman, like Kate Conner, the washerwoman, for instance.

Enter **Mary.**

Mary. Please, Mrs. Gardner, may Katie speak to you for a moment?

Mrs. Gardner. I suppose so. Send her in.

Exit **Mary.** *Enter* **Katie.**

Katie. Good morning, ma'am. Good morning, Miss Dorothy. Oh, good morning, Mrs. Carter. Was the last week's wash all right, ma'am? Miss Polly's nightgowns is pretty enough to wear outside, I always tell my girls. (*Turns to* **Mrs. Gardner**) Sure, it was about the laundry stove I wanted to speak a word. Since the stove man put it in perfect order I can do nothin' with it at all.

Mrs. Gardner. I'm sorry, Katie, but I don't think we could get anyone to look at it today, on account of its being Election Day, you know.

Katie. I suppose so, ma'am. The men act as if it took 'em all day to vote. Anything for a holiday, I'm thinking. Well, I'll just have patience with the stove, and maybe the cook will give me a fling at the range (*turns to go*).

Mrs. Gardner. One moment, Katie. When you came in Mrs. Carter and I were talking about Woman's Suffrage—you know what that means, I suppose?

Katie. Yes, ma'am. I often hear my girls talking about it with their friends.

Mrs. Gardner. Of course, you would take no interest in enfranchisement. You have, I suppose, no education?

Katie. Awful little, ma'am. My girls could do better with their books when they was ten years old than myself at any age. When I was young it was terrible hard for the poor to get any schooling. My mother, God rest her soul, was always saying I had no need of edication, I had so much sense. (*Apologetically.*) You know the way mothers do be talking about their own.

Mrs. Gardner. I see. You acknowledge, then, that you are illiterate. I suppose that you never even heard of the Tariff, for instance?

Katie. Indeed I have, ma'am. That's what they tell about at the store when they do be asking a fancy price for their things. Sure, somebody ought to keep an eye on it, for it's cruel hard on the poor when it gets to going on so.

Mrs. Gardner. Of course, you have no ideas at all about Finance?

Katie. No, ma'am. None of my aunts was ever fine at all, just poor people like myself.

Mrs. Gardner. Not fine aunts, Katie, but Finance. That means—er—banking and that sort of thing.

Katie. Ah, the savings-bank, you're meaning. All a poor woman like me knows is to put her bit of money in it and then pray God on her bended knees that it won't bust up on her.

Mrs. Gardner. Then, have you ever heard of Civil Service Reform?

Katie. Civil Servants' Reform, is it? I'm thinking it would be best to reform them that ain't civil—the butlers, now—some of them will be giving themselves the airs of the blessed Holy Father himself.

Mrs. Gardner (*aside to* **Mrs. Carter**). You see, Madeleine, she does not even know the meaning of the names of these important issues.

Katie. If they'd be after asking me such hard questions on Election Day, I'd have no luck at all with my voting. I'd better go back to my tubs, I had, and not be showing my ignorance to you ladies (*turns to go*).

Mrs. Carter. Wait, Katie. If you had the vote is there anything that you would care to help about—anything that especially concerns you and your neighbors, the other women, I mean?

Katie (*slowly*). That concerns us women? Ah, we're alike, rich and poor, I'm thinking, in what lies nearest our hearts. We want to keep our husbands working steady, and have decent food and shelter that don't cost too dear, and give our children a better chance than we had ourselves.

Mrs. Gardner. Your own husband is dead, is he not?

Katie. That he's not, ma'am. He's just across the river in the next State enjoying himself. He left me when my baby was a week old, and there were three other children to look to.

Mrs. Gardner. Why didn't you have him arrested and brought back?

Katie. Sure, I said to John Kelly, the officer on our block, a great friend of my husband's he was. I sez to him: "It's an arm of the law you call yourself, John Kelly. Can't you get the body of it to slip across the line and fetch Mike back to his children, for it's near starving we are?"

Mrs. Carter. What did he say?

Katie. "I'm sorry for you all, Mrs. Conner, indeed I am," he sez, "but the law can't fetch Mike back to the State, for it's just a misdemeanor, his leaving you, it is. Sure, if you'd have us chase after all the deserting husbands that clear out of the State we'd have no time at all to catch the really important criminals, and the expense would be terrible," he sez, "and that's a thing you women don't consider."

Mrs. Carter. What did you say to him, Katie?

Katie. "What's the law for, John Kelly?" I asked him, "if it's not to protect the helpless and innocent and keep 'em from being a public charge?" "You don't understand matters of state," he sez; "go home and mind your baby." "My baby's dead—they do die most ways when their mothers are starving," I sez, "and I'm working my fingers to the bone to keep the others alive while their father's but a few miles away, earning good money and spending it to get some other poor girl into trouble." (*She wipes her eyes with her apron.*)

Mrs. Carter. Poor Katie, how did you manage to get along?

Katie (*cheerfully*). Well, I got washing and cleaning to do, and you don't have to buy awful much food when there's no man to feed. Then when my Annie got old enough she went into a mill and helped me keep the others. She's a good girl, but delicate like.

Mrs. Gardner. It's only the lazy poor that don't get on.

Katie. May be, may be, but I think that there's such a thing as too hard work for the young. Many a night Annie would come home a-crying with her poor back and her sore feet after the twelve hours' standing in rush times. What with the small pay and the fines and the weeks the girls get laid off between seasons, it's more than laziness keeps 'em from getting rich. Many a one has slept on my kitchen floor when there was no other place for her but the street, and you know what that means.

Mrs. Gardner. I've been told that an honest, industrious girl could always find work.

Katie. May be so, may be so, ma'am, but you may be thankful that your own is safe at home with her pianny, and not out in the cold with a sore heart, looking for a job, and some divil a-following her up.

Mrs. Gardner (*shocked*). Really, Katie, you must not use such language.

Katie. You must excuse me, ma'am, but you asked me, like. I'll go back to my wash now or I'll not have a rag out on the line before mid-day (*turns to go*).

Mrs. Carter. Katie, I believe that if we women get the vote that you and your neighbors will help us to understand your troubles and try to improve conditions for women and children.

Katie (*simply*). I'm ignorant, indeed, as Mrs. Gardner has a right to be saying, but as for knowing about husbands that beat you up and leave you, and boys that get led away in the saloons and gambling places, and the tenements where the babies die like flowers that have got no water, and the young girls that go to the bad because they're cold and hungry—why, I understand all that as you'd understand a tea-party—I'd be dumb enough if I didn't when I live in the midst of it (*turns to go, but adds*). My girls aren't ignorant like me. My Maggie's in the High School, she is, and she's going through it if I have to work till I drop to keep her there. She's going to have her chance. (*Exit.*)

Mrs. Carter. Well, Genevieve, the illiterate woman isn't such a bug-a-boo as you Anti's picture her.

Mrs. Gardner. Katie really has unusual intelligence for a woman in her position, and she's an excellent laundress, too. I don't know whether I approve of her sending her youngest girl to the High School. She'd much better go out to service. Still, one must help the poor. I shall give Katie her carfare after this—she often stays after hours when the wash is very large. Dorothy, you might send her girls that blue hat of yours that is so hideously unbecoming and your black muff that the moths got into last summer.

Dorothy. Mother, dear, I think I'd rather send them something really pretty and new.

Mrs. Gardner. That's very generous of you, darling, but you'd better send the muff, too, for after the moths have once been in a thing I'm glad to get it out of the house.

Mrs. Carter (*rising*). I must take my turn as a watcher now. Good-bye, Genevieve; good-bye, Dorothy.

Dorothy (*embracing* **Mrs. Carter**). I wish I could go with you, Aunt Madeleine; I really am a Suffragist at heart.

Mrs. Gardner. Dorothy, you astonish me. You know how conservative Tom Randolph is. If you mix yourself up in this unfeminine movement his feeling for you will surely change.

Dorothy (*exasperated*). Then let it change! I haven't promised to marry him, and I never will marry any man who looks upon a wedding ring as a muzzle.

Mrs. Gardner (*turning to* **Mrs. Carter**). Now you see, Madeleine, what your example has done. Tom Randolph is the most desirable young man in our set.

Mary announces Mr. Randolph. Enter **Tom Randolph**, *pulling off gloves.*

Randolph. Good morning, Mrs. Gardner. (*shakes hands*). Good morning, Mrs. Carter (*shakes hands*). Good morning, Dorothy (*shakes hands*). (*To* **Mrs. Gardner**) Awfully early for a visit, I'm afraid. I suppose you are fearfully busy—with housekeeping and all that.

Mrs. Gardner. Oh, not at all; we're always delighted to see you. Do sit down and tell us the news from the great masculine world.

Randolph. Well, really, it's rather early in the day for news. I've just come from the Polls, and it was rather jolly there. An awfully pretty girl gave me this (*points to a pin marked "Votes for Women" on his coat*).

Mrs. Gardner. How exceedingly forward in her! It was very kind in you to take it, I'm sure.

Randolph. Oh, really, Mrs. Gardner, she wasn't forward at all. She had the manners of a princess. She handed this to me like a cotillion favor, and I just said: "Thanks, awfully." Then she said: "Put it on, please, and vote for the Suffrage Amendment" (*pause*)—so I did.

Dorothy. Oh, I'm so glad, Tom!

Mrs. Gardner. But you've always talked against Woman's Suffrage, Tom.

Randolph. Just sentiment, Mrs. Gardner. I'm so jolly sentimental I never reasoned about it. I just thought I wouldn't want my wife to talk politics to me, because I've always been rather stupid about them, and I wouldn't want my wife to know just what an ass I am, but (*cheerfully*) she'd probably find it out, anyway.

Mrs. Carter. You are too modest, Mr. Randolph. Let me thank you for your support.

Randolph. Not at all, Mrs. Carter; don't mention it—always a pleasure to do anything for you. (*More seriously.*) Besides, I was jolly glad to be on the other side from the gang that have been working against the Amendment. I never saw a tougher lot in my life—of course, I don't mean you, Mrs. Gardner (**Mrs. Gardner** *bridles at this*), but the men who are opposed to it—most of them want a wide open town all the time. While I was waiting for my turn I saw Sykes, the chap who keeps the worst saloon in this ward, talking to a policy-shop friend of his. Then there was Smith, that man the Consumer's League is always getting after, and that chap Jones that fights against child labor reform. They weren't wearing any "Votes for Women" buttons, not they! I was rather proud of mine when I saw how those fellows glared at it.

Mrs. Gardner. But the sanctity of the home, Tom?

Randolph. Well, I guess that the home's all right with the right woman in it (*looks at* **Dorothy**). Perhaps next year I'll go to the Polls with my wife— now wouldn't that be jolly? What do you think, Dorothy?

Dorothy (*shyly*). I think it would be rather nice.

He goes over and sits by her and they talk.

Mrs. Carter. Yes, I am sure that next year the Polls will look like Noah's Ark with all the couples approaching. (*Turning to* **Mrs. Gardner.**) And how will you feel then, Genevieve?

Dorothy (*goes over to her mother*). They shan't tease you, darling, if it happens. We'll just slip out quietly and vote and not bother you about it.

Mrs. Gardner (*indignantly*). Not bother *me* about it? Do you suppose that if you other women vote I shall stay at home doing nothing? I think that I know what I want as well as anyone, and if I can't get it any other way I'll just go and vote for it. Let me see. I think that about three o'clock in the afternoon would probably be the *nicest* time at the Polls.

Randolph. Hurrah then for next Election Day! I'll meet you at the Polls at three o'clock, Mrs. Gardner. (*Kisses her hand.*)

She smiles and nods assent.

Dorothy and Mrs. Carter (*together*). Oh, mother! Oh, Genevieve!

CURTAIN

A Suffrage Rummage Sale

MARY WINSOR

Haverford P.O., Penn.: privately printed. 1913.

TO BE SOLD AT PUBLIC AUCTION

A choice lot of prejudices, superstitions, fallen idols, curios, second hand costumes, worn-out ideals, cast-off toys, antique furniture and Anti-quated notions.

ARTICLES TO BE AUCTIONED

An image of Buddha, a Turkish flag, a pair of Chinese shoes or an Oriental veil, a screen, a spinning wheel, home-made preserves or fancy work, a set of china, a suit of armor, a shillalah or big stick, and a vacuum cleaner.

PREFACE

SOME PRACTICAL SUGGESTIONS

All the articles sold at the auction should be donated. Business firms and department stores are generally willing to donate if promised that their names will appear on the Program as having contributed the goods. As the public may not realize that this is to be a bona-fide auction, it is wise to enclose in each invitation the Program with a list of the articles for sale. At the time of the auction the articles to be sold should be put on exhibition in a conspicuous part of the theatre and the aids or ushers be instructed to exhibit the articles. When the sale is about to begin, they should be arranged on the stage in the proper sequence for the auctioneer to take them up in order. As each is sold it should be handed over the footlights by the auctioneer so as to leave the stage clear for the entrance of Mrs. Grundy, etc. A certain article should be agreed upon as Mrs. Grundy's cue, and she should enter after that article has been auctioned off.

THE AUCTION
INTERRUPTED

DRAMATIS PERSONAE ⸺⸺⸺⸺⸺⸺⸺⸺⸺⸺⸺⸺⸺⸺⸺

(In the order of their appearance.)
The Auctioneer
Mrs. Grundy
Mrs. Partington
The Mad Hatter

SCENE

*There is a small table in the centre of the stage. One chair to left of stage—one to right, but none near the table. The **Auctioneer** is finishing the last sale.*

*Enter **Mrs. Grundy**, Right. She is a small, "well-preserved" woman, with ringlets and rosy cheeks, rather tightly laced, wears a gaily colored poke bonnet with a wreath of roses under the brim, crinoline, lace shawl, white stockings with black slippers, lace mitts, and with fan dangling from her waist. Her manner is mincing, honeyed, patronizing, very determined and dictatorial, occasionally spiteful. She is quite aware of her own importance.*

Mrs. Grundy (*Right Centre*). I am here to register a protest against the modern point of view. It is an outrageous assault on womanhood. Let those of us who belong to the privileged classes be content with our privileges and not join in this vulgar clamor for "rights." We must never forget that *man* is *man* and *woman* is *woman*. Ah! Let us leave woman where Heaven has placed her—on a pedestal! Don't let us drag her down into the mire. I am scandalized at the indecorum of the present day,—especially the bold young girls of the present day, who demand a college education just as if they were men, and some of them actually want to earn their living in horrid masculine ways—typewriters, or doctors, or lawyers, or farmers, or gardeners. Why, in my time, if a girl did not marry she was quite content to stay at home and do a little sewing in a state of genteel starvation. That was the proper thing for a well-bred woman.

Auctioneer. Is this Mrs. Grundy?

Mrs. Grundy *curtsies.*

Auctioneer (*Advance to the Audience*). Ladies and gentleman, this is the celebrated Mrs. Grundy—the arbiter of fashion—the mould of form—the guardian of propriety. (*Crosses to **Mrs. Grundy**, lays a hand on her arm confidingly.*) Mrs. Grundy, are you a Suffragist?

Mrs. Grundy. I—a Suffragist? (**Auctioneer** *quickly retreats.*) Oh, no indeed. How could I be anything so promiscuous? Why if I could vote, my cook could vote, and I might meet my cook at the polls. How vulgar! Suffragist? No, no!

Auctioneer. Then may I ask what are you doing here?

Mrs. Grundy. I have come here to protest against the brazen woman who makes herself conspicuous on a public platform. May I have the doubtful

pleasure of saying a few words of rebuke to the unmanly men and unwomanly women whom I see before me?

Auctioneer. Certainly, our platform is always open to Anti-suffragists, for we
believe in free speech. (*Back centre.*)

Mrs. Grundy (*Advancing to the front of the platform centre, looking penetrat-
ingly at the audience with a winning smile*). Do you ladies really think
you *need* the vote? Look at me. I have never had the vote, and yet I ask
you, doesn't Mrs. Grundy rule the world? I am sure there are a great many
persons who would like to come out openly for woman suffrage, but they
don't dare! Why? They are afraid of me. I am proud to think that my
influence is keeping millions of women in their proper sphere. (*Back to
left as* **Mrs. Partington** *enters.*)

Enter **Mrs. Partington** (*Right*) *with a large broom. She is tall, gaunt,
respectable, middle-aged, muscular, belligerent, with a gruff voice and
determined manner. Costume—that of a scrub woman.*

Mrs. Partington (*Centre. To the audience*).

> The Woman Movement must be stopped!
>   I'm here to stop it.
> And Woman Suffrage must be dropped—
>   I tell you, DROP IT!
> Though like the sea you fume and fret
> With my good broom, I'll stem you yet.

(*Looks around the audience—Sweeps—*)

> Fie on your brazen faces—
> You suffragettes may fume and frown,
> But if you rise, I'll put you down
> And keep you in your places.

(*Brandishes the broom.*)

Mrs. Grundy (*Crosses to* **Mrs. Partington**). Dear Mrs. Partington, I am glad
to meet such a womanly woman. In this violent age of unsexed females
it is a pleasure to see a gentle creature like yourself who believes in quiet
lady-like methods.

Auctioneer. Ladies, really the rummage sale must go on. (*Centre between
them.*) If you insist on remaining, I shall have to auction you off as curios.
(*Seizing the auctioneer's hammer from the table. Front.*) We have for sale
two very valuable pieces of antique furniture—slightly shop-worn and
somewhat moth-eaten, to be sold to-day at greatly reduced prices.

(*From behind the right scenes are heard shouts.*)

I protest! Shame! Stop! Stop!

Mrs. Grundy *and* **Mrs. Partington** *look alarmed and withdraw to one side, back to left.*

Auctioneer. Oh! What is that? Did any one speak?

Enter **Mad Hatter**. *Costume as described in Alice in Wonderland.*

Mad Hatter (*Rushing on the stage*). Yes, I spoke, and I intend to go on speaking. It's my business to speak and women should listen respectfully. Woman's place is in the Home. She should stay there and attend to her children. Her domestic duties should occupy her entire attention. No matter what calamities befall the nation, like Werther's Charlotte she should go on cutting bread and butter.

Auctioneer. Is that a slice of bread and butter I see in your hand?

Mad Hatter. Yes; and it's the best butter.

Auctioneer (*To audience*). Ladies and gentlemen, permit me to introduce that celebrated character—the Mad Hatter.

Mad Hatter (*Tosses the bread and butter into wings, takes off hat, makes low bow. Oratorically*). I have come here this afternoon to represent the silent woman.

Auctioneer. The silent woman? I don't know the lady.

Mad Hatter (*Vociferating*). Of course, you don't know her—none of your friends are silent. Suffragettes talk all the time. I represent women like Mrs. Grundy and Mrs. Partington—the quiet stay-at-home kind that never appear in public.

Auctioneer. They seem to be here, and this is a public meeting.

Mad Hatter (*Not paying the slightest attention*). There is nothing so horrid, so disheartening to a manly man like me as the sight of a female on a public platform. Shocking! Real women are domestic, demure and reticent. As for speaking in public, Mrs. Grundy and Mrs. Partington would rather die than do such a brazen deed.

Auctioneer. Mrs. Grundy and Mrs. Partington are both present. (**Mad Hatter** *much embarrassed crosses Right.* **Mrs. Grundy** *and* **Mrs. Partington** *look displeased and haughty.*) And both ladies have put aside their reticence and favored us with a speech.

Mad Hatter. They had to do it. Their sense of duty compelled them to speak. The Anti's are obliged to talk all the time in order to keep the other women quiet.

Mrs. Grundy *and* **Mrs. Partington** *bow and smile, cross Right to* **Mad Hatter.**

Mrs. Grundy. The Anti-suffragists are like Thomas Carlyle—we preach the virtues of silence—in forty volumes.

Mrs. Partington. We do not wish to appear in public. I speak for all good housekeepers when I say we would rather remain in the Home.

Mad Hatter. The Anti-suffragist never leaves her home. She never goes to the theatre, or the opera, or concerts, or lectures, or bridge-whist parties. No, never! Nor luncheons, nor dinners, nor suppers, nor teas, nor bargain counters, nor white goods sales. She remains in the Home hermetically sealed there like a fly in amber.

Mrs. Partington (*Fanning herself with her broom. In a sepulchral tone*). Woman's place is in the Home.

Mrs. Grundy, Mrs. Partington and **Mad Hatter** (*in chorus*). Forever in the Home.

Auctioneer. Then all the hundreds and thousands of women whom we meet in the theatres, the opera, the department stores, the railroad stations, the streets and the churches—are they all Suffragists?

Mad Hatter. Every one of them.

Auctioneer. How the cause is growing! (*Crosses Right to* **Mad Hatter**, *very close to him, looking into his eyes.*) Don't you think that all nations will soon grant their women the franchise?

Mad Hatter. If Woman Suffrage were adopted, it would bring about—it would bring about—the down-fall of civilization. (**Auctioneer** *backs toward left;* **Mad Hatter** *follows.*) It would take us—it would take us—straight back to the caves of our primeval ancestors. (**Auctioneer** *backs to a chair, Left, falls into it exhausted.*)

Mrs. Grundy (*Right. Loftily*). I would have you know *my* ancestors were too aristocratic to live in caves. The very first one of them was born in a palace. That's why I don't want the ballot. Women of wealth and social position can get along very comfortably without it. I don't want it myself, and I don't intend other women to have it.

Mrs. Partington (*Centre*). No good housekeeper wants it. I would rather scrub the floors forever than undertake the heavy and burdensome task of voting once a year.

Mrs. Grundy. Mrs. Partington, you are the greatest living authority on house-cleaning, and I would like to inquire, do you approve of this nasty new-fangled Vacuum Cleaner?

Mrs. Partington. No, madam. Like Nature, I abhor a vacuum. With my broom I scour the seas and sweep away modern inventions.

Mrs. Grundy. The restless women who want to gad abroad claim that a Vacuum Cleaner would save them time and trouble.

Mad Hatter (*Left*). A mere pretext to escape their Home duties. What's their time worth? I agree with the farmer who was asked to buy an incubator because it would save the hens so much trouble. "Pshaw!" said the farmer, "what's a hen's time worth anyhow?" That's what I say about the women.

Let them go on toiling and moiling—scrubbing and sweeping—in the good old-fashioned way.

Mrs. Grundy (*Approvingly*). As their great-grandmothers did before them.

Mrs. Partington. We want no change.

Mrs. Grundy. We need no vote.

Mrs. Partington. We have all the rights we want.

Mrs. Grundy. With the immortal poet, Alexander Pope, we say, "Whatever is, is right." Conservatism—that is the key-note of the Anti-suffrage movement.

Mrs. Partington. But it is *not* a movement. It is a concerted and organized effort to stop movements—to sweep back movements. (*Sweeps furiously.*)

Mrs. Grundy (*Right*). Our mission is to make these restless, modern women cultivate repose of manner and true decorum—to teach them how to say, "Prunes and Prisms"—how to sit—(*Sits*)—and how to rise gracefully—(*Rises*)—how to receive a gentleman visitor—(*Greets the* **Mad Hatter** *who skips across the stage to bow and scrape before her*)—how to tread a minuet—(*Dances a few steps with the* **Mad Hatter** *as partner*)—(**Mrs. Partington** *beats time with her broom*)—how to manage a fan bewitchingly and how to attract men—That is more important than to vote. And of course, no woman can do both. (*Coquettes with antiquated graces.*)

The **Mad Hatter** *becomes very gallant. Takes her hand, slips his arm around her waist and chucks her gently under the chin.* **Mrs. Partington** *shows signs of impatience and disapproval.*

Mrs. Grundy. But we old-fashioned women know how to repel a forward suitor whose attentions are too pressing. (*Repulses the* **Mad Hatter**, *who falls on the floor.* **Mrs. Partington** *comes forward clearing her throat. Centre front.*)

Mad Hatter (*From the floor*). One of the "silent women" wishes to speak again.

Mrs. Partington. Man is always Woman's superior. No matter what position he occupies, Woman should look up to Man and treat him respectfully. (*Plants her foot firmly on the prostrate form of the* **Mad Hatter**.) Women can not vote because they can not fight.

Mad Hatter (*Jumping to his feet and almost upsetting* **Mrs. Partington**). Can not fight? But what about Mollie Pitcher in the Revolutionary War, who manned her husband's gun?

Mrs. Partington (*Angrily*). Women can not fight.

Mad Hatter. Well, of course, ladies, I am an Anti-suffragist. In my capacity of *Mad* Hatter (*rolls his eyes and taps his forehead*) I couldn't be anything else; but I must take exception to the physical force argument. (*To* **Mrs. Grundy.**) Think of the Maid of Saragossa! Think of Joan of Arc! Think of Boadicea and the Amazons! Just think!

Mrs. Grundy (*With intense concentration*). I won't think! And you can't make me think! If I thought, I wouldn't be an Anti-suffragist. But I know that Woman's place is not on the battle-field.

Mad Hatter. What about Clara Barton and Florence Nightingale?

Mrs. Partington (*Threatening him with her broom*). WOMEN CAN NOT FIGHT! We are too weak, I tell you! (**Mad Hatter.** Weak? Ha! Ha!) Woman's strength is her weakness. We are miserable timid things. We are not strong enough to force our way to the polls. (*Chases him around the table.*) We can't defend our vote. Ballots and bullets go together. I am a poor, weak woman, and I need protection. How dare you say that women can fight? It's a libel on the sex. Women can not vote because they can not fight. (*Beats him with her broom.*) I am now using the physical force argument.

Mad Hatter. Yes, madam, I feel the force of your arguments. I assure you that they make a deep impression on me. (*Rubbing his shoulder. Gets the broom away from her. Holding up the broom.*) With this domestic implement you have conquered me. (*Front. Apostrophizing the broom.*) Ah, broom! Symbol of Domesticity! How well you grace a woman's frail and trembling hand! (**Mrs. Partington** *shakes her fist at him.*) How much better you look clutched in the female paw than that monstrosity, the ballot! Ah! Ladies, promise me that your lily-white fingers will never be contaminated by sordid contact with politics. (*Murmurs of "We promise" from* **Mrs. Partington** *and* **Mrs. Grundy.** *In a sermonizing voice to the* **Auctioneer.**) If the housewives of this city, instead of clamoring for that vain bauble, the ballot, would only grasp the broom and go out into the streets and sweep, and sweep, like our friend, Mrs. Partington, how soon the streets would be nice and clean, in spite of politics and politicians.

Auctioneer (*Taking the centre of the stage*). Suffragists think the vote in the hands of women would be a broom with which we could make a clean sweep—not only of the streets, but of all unclean things. Therefore, the last thing I have to offer you to-day is the most precious of all—the ballot. (*Holding up a sample ballot.*) Look on it with hope, for Heaven willing, it will soon be yours. Look on it with reverence, for it is the symbol of power. When it comes to you, may you use it well; but before it will come to you, you must be willing to bid for it, and bid high. Not only money must you bid, but courage, and devotion, and self-sacrifice. You must be ready to contribute your youth, your charm, your ability, your name, your personality and your heart. And I will ask those who are ready to lay this great price on the altar of their country to give their assent by a rising vote.

CURTAIN

AN ANTI-SUFFRAGE
MONOLOGUE

MARIE JENNEY HOWE

New York: National American Woman Suffrage
Association. 1913.

Please do not think of me as old-fashioned. I pride myself on being a modern up-to-date woman. I believe in all kinds of broad-mindedness, only I do not believe in woman suffrage because to do that would be to deny my sex.

Woman suffrage is the reform against nature. Look at these ladies sitting on the platform. Observe their physical inability, their mental disability, their spiritual instability and general debility! Could they walk up to the ballot box, mark a ballot, and drop it in? Obviously not. Let us grant for the sake of argument that they could mark a ballot. But could they drop it in? Ah, no. All nature is against it. The laws of man cry out against it. The voice of God cries out against it—and so do I.

Enfranchisement is what makes man man. Disfranchisement is what makes woman woman. If women were enfranchised every man would be just like every woman and every woman would be just like every man. There would be no difference between them. And don't you think this would rob life of just a little of its poetry and romance?

Man must remain man. Woman must remain woman. If man goes over and tries to be like woman, if woman goes over and tries to be like man, it will become so very confusing and so difficult to explain to our children. Let us take a practical example. If a woman puts on a man's coat and trousers, takes a man's cane and hat and cigar, and goes out on the street, what will happen to her? She will be arrested and thrown into jail. Then why not stay at home?

I know you begin to see how strongly I *feel* on this subject, but I have some reasons as well. These reasons are based on logic. Of course I am not logical. I am a creature of impulse, instinct, and intuition—and I glory in it. But I know that these reasons are based on logic because I have culled them from the men whom it is my privilege to know.

My first argument against suffrage is that the women would not use it if they had it. You couldn't drive them to the polls. My second argument is, if the women were enfranchised they would neglect their homes, desert their families, and spend all their time at the polls. You may tell me that the polls are only open once a year. But I know women. They are creatures of habit. If you let them go to the polls once a year, they will hang round the polls all the rest of the time.

I have arranged these arguments in couplets. They go together in such a way that if you don't like one you can take the other. This is my second anti-suffrage couplet. If the women were enfranchised they would vote exactly as their husbands do and only double the existing vote. Do you like that argument? If not, take this one. If the women were enfranchised they would vote against their own husbands, thus creating dissension, family quarrels, and divorce.

My third anti-suffrage couplet is—women are angels. Many men call me an angel and I have a strong instinct which tells me it is true; that is why I am anti, because "I want to be an angel and with the angels stand." And if you don't like that argument take this one. Women are depraved. They would introduce into politics a vicious element which would ruin our national life.

Fourth anti-suffrage couplet: women cannot understand politics. Therefore there would be no use in giving women political power, because they would not know what to do with it. On the other hand, if the women were enfranchised, they would mount rapidly into power, take all the offices from all the men, and soon we would have women governors of all our states and dozens of women acting as President of the United States.

Fifth anti-suffrage couplet: women cannot band together. They are incapable of organization. No two women can even be friends. Women are cats. On the other hand, if women were enfranchised, we would have all the women banded together on one side and all the men banded together on the other side, and there would follow a sex war which might end in bloody revolution.

Just one more of my little couplets: the ballot is greatly over-estimated. It has never done anything for anybody. Lots of men tell me this. And the corresponding argument is—the ballot is what makes man man. It is what gives him all his dignity and all of his superiority to women. Therefore if we allow women to share this privilege, how could a woman look up to her own husband? Why, there would be nothing to look up to.

I have talked to many woman suffragists and I find them very unreasonable. I say to them: "Here I am, convince me." I ask for proof. Then they proceed to tell me of Australia and Colorado and other places where women have passed excellent laws to improve the condition of working women and children. But I say, "What of it?" These are facts. I don't care about facts. I ask for proof.

Then they quote the eight million women of the United States who are now supporting themselves, and the twenty-five thousand married women in the City of New York who are self-supporting. But I say again, what of it? These are statistics. I don't believe in statistics. Facts and statistics are things which no truly womanly woman would ever use.

I wish to prove anti-suffrage in a womanly way—that is, by personal example. This is my method of persuasion. Once I saw a woman driving a horse, and the horse ran away with her. Isn't that just like a woman? Once I read in the newspapers about a woman whose house caught on fire, and she threw the children out of the window and carried the pillows downstairs. Does that show political acumen, or does it not? Besides, look at the hats that women wear! And have you ever known a successful woman governor of a state? Or have you ever known a really truly successful woman president of the United States? Well, if they could they would, wouldn't they? Then, if they haven't, doesn't that show they couldn't? As for the militant suffragettes, they are all hyenas in petticoats. Now do you want to be a hyena and wear petticoats?

Now, I think I have proved anti-suffrage; and I have done it in a womanly way—that is, without stooping to the use of a single fact or argument or a single statistic.

I am the prophet of a new idea. No one has ever thought of it or heard of it before. I well remember when this great idea first came to me. It waked me in the middle of the night with a shock that gave me a headache. This is it: woman's place is in the home. Is it not beautiful as it is new, new as it is true? Take this idea away with you. You will find it very helpful in your daily lives. You may not grasp it just at first, but you will gradually grow into understanding of it.

I know the suffragists reply that all our activities have been taken out of the home. The baking, the washing, the weaving, the spinning are all long since taken out of the home. But I say, all the more reason that something should stay in the home. Let it be woman. Besides, think of the great modern invention, the telephone. That has been put into the home. Let woman stay at home and answer the telephone.

We antis have so much imagination! Sometimes it seems to us that we can hear the little babies in the slums crying to us. We can see the children in factories and mines reaching out their little hands to us, and the working women in the sweated industries, the underpaid, underfed women, reaching out their arms to us—all, all crying as with one voice, "Save us, save us, from Woman Suffrage." Well may they make this appeal to us, for who knows what woman suffrage might not do for such as these. It might even alter the conditions under which they live.

We antis do not believe that any conditions should be altered. We want everything to remain just as it is. All is for the best. Whatever is, is right. If misery is in the world, God has put it there; let it remain. If this misery presses harder on some women than others, it is because they need discipline. Now, I have always been comfortable and well cared for. But then I never needed discipline. Of course I am only a weak, ignorant woman. But there is one thing I do understand from the ground up, and that is the divine intention toward woman. I *know* that the divine intention toward woman is, let her remain at home.

The great trouble with the suffragists is this; they interfere too much. They are always interfering. Let me take a practical example.

There is in the City of New York a Nurses' Settlement, where sixty trained nurses go forth to care for sick babies and give them pure milk. Last summer only two or three babies died in this slum district around the Nurses' Settlement, whereas formerly hundreds of babies have died there every summer. Now what are these women doing? Interfering, interfering with the death rate! And what is their motive in so doing? They seek notoriety. They want to be noticed. They are trying to show off. And if sixty women who merely believe in suffrage behave in this way, what may we expect when all women are enfranchised?

What ought these women to do with their lives? Each one ought to be devoting herself to the comfort of some man. You may say, they are not married. But I answer, let them try a little harder and they might find some kind of a man to devote themselves to. What does the Bible say on this subject? It says, "Seek and ye shall find." Besides, when I look around me at the men; I feel that God never meant us women to be too particular.

Let me speak one word to my sister women who are here to-day. Women, we don't need to vote in order to get our own way. Don't misunderstand me. Of course I want you to get your own way. That's what we're here for. But do it indirectly. If you want a thing, tease. If that doesn't work, nag. If that doesn't do, cry—crying always brings them around. Get what you want. Pound pillows. Make a scene. Make home a hell on earth, but do it in a womanly way. That is so much more dignified and refined than walking up to a ballot box and dropping in a piece of paper. Can't you see that?

Let us consider for a moment the effect of woman's enfranchisement on man. I think some one ought to consider the men. What makes husbands faithful and loving? The ballot, and the monopoly of that privilege. If women vote, what will become of men? They will all slink off drunk and disorderly. We antis understand men. If women were enfranchised, men would revert to their natural instincts such as regicide, matricide, patricide and race-suicide. Do you believe in race-suicide or do you not? Then, isn't it our duty to refrain from a thing that would lure men to destruction?

It comes down to this. Some one must wash the dishes. Now, would you expect man, man made in the image of God, to roll up his sleeves and wash the dishes? Why, it would be blasphemy. I know that I am but a rib and so I wash the dishes. Or I hire another rib to do it for me, which amounts to the same thing.

Let us consider the argument from the standpoint of religion. The Bible says, "Let the women keep silent in the churches." Paul says, "Let them keep their hats on for fear of the angels." My minister says, "Wives, obey your husbands." And my husband says that woman suffrage would rob the rose of its fragrance and the peach of its bloom. I think that is so sweet.

Besides did George Washington ever say, "Votes for women?" No. Did the Emperor Kaiser Wilhelm ever say, "Votes for women?" No. Did Elijah,

Elisha, Micah, Hezekiah, Obadiah, and Jeremiah ever say, "Votes for women?" No. Then that settles it.

I don't want to be misunderstood in my reference to woman's inability to vote. Of course she could get herself to the polls and lift a piece of paper. I don't doubt that. What I refer to is the pressure on the brain, the effect of this mental strain on woman's delicate nervous organization and on her highly wrought sensitive nature. Have you ever pictured to yourself Election Day with women voting? Can you imagine how women, having undergone this terrible ordeal, with their delicate systems all upset, will come out of the voting booths and be led away by policemen, and put into ambulances, while they are fainting and weeping, half laughing, half crying, and having fits upon the public highway? Don't you think that if a woman is going to have a fit, it is far better for her to have it in the privacy of her own home?

And how shall I picture to you the terrors of the day after election? Divorce and death will rage unchecked, crime and contagious disease will stalk unbridled through the land. Oh, friends, on this subject I feel—I feel, so strongly that I can—not think!

CINDERELLINE
or, THE LITTLE RED SLIPPER

FLORENCE KIPER [FRANK]

Chicago: Dramatic Publishing Company, 1913.

CHARACTERS _____

Sylvius Sylvester, a rich young poet.
Mrs. Sylvester, his practical mother.
Grazielline Smith, a young lady of the world.
Isabelline Smith, a "home" woman.
Cinderelline.

SCENE

The apartment of **Sylvius Sylvester**. *It is studio, library, reception room in one. It contains a grand piano, an easel with an unfinished portrait, plaster casts, etchings, prints, etc. A large arm chair with a tiny footstool is in the center of the stage. To the left stands a small sofa with cushions. To the right is a rickety cobbler's bench with bits of bright colored leather scattered about it. The entire room is in pleasant confusion.*

The act is played in bright morning sunlight.

The curtain rises to the strains of the Wagner Wedding March. Discovered **Sylvius Sylvester** *seated on the end of the cobbler's bench, working on a red slipper. He is a handsome youth in white flannels, over which he has tied a heavy leather cobbler's apron.*

For a few moments after the rise of the curtain the music continues playing. When **Sylvius** *speaks the music stops.*

Sylvius.
A pretty little slipper! Red—heart's red!
Bring me my bride!—It's queer, now, how the Spring
Strives in a man. The woods are all awake,
And every glistening pond and stream is stirred
By the swift dip of little mating birds.

Enter **Mrs. Sylvester.** *She is fat, and garishly dressed.*

Mrs. Sylvester.
Sylvius Sylvester, what's the matter now?
You're moonstruck!

Sylvius.
　　　　Moonstruck, yes—dear little mother,
And sun-struck, wind-struck, rain-struck, Spring-struck, too.

Seats himself on the bench, and again works on the slipper.

Mrs. Sylvester.
Why did your father ever have his way!
He always argued, "Let the boy alone!"
And see now—! Well, thank Heavens, the fault's not mine.
There's never been a poet in our family.

Sylvius.
But I'm a cobbler now. I'm making shoes.

Mrs. Sylvester.
O my poor boy, why don't you stick to verse!
That's bad enough. But every day to change
Your occupation—sculpture, fiddling, shoes,
The milk-supply, the rings around the moon!
I'm fairly dizzy!

Sylvius.
        I must see the world.

Mrs. Sylvester.
You've money—lots of money. Take a trip.

Sylvius.
Why should I lug my body all about!
I sit within this room, and bring the world
Here to my doors.

Mrs. Sylvester.
        But something less—less common
Than making slippers!

Sylvius [*Mysteriously*].
        Mother, can you keep
A secret!

Mrs. Sylvester.
        If it's some new scheme of yours,
I'd really rather not a soul should know.

Sylvius.
Well, then, I'll tell you. See this little slipper!

Mrs. Sylvester.
O, yes, I see it plainly.

Sylvius.
        Say the truth!
This slipper doesn't differ from its kind—
Now, does it?

Mrs. Sylvester.
        Yes, the heel is crooked.

Sylvius.
Ah, but I mean one scarcely would suppose
That in this little piece of colored leather

Shaped to the semblance of a human foot—
There's magic power!

Mrs. Sylvester.

The boy is off his head!

Sylvius.
You don't believe it? You shall see yourself.
They're coming here to try it on.

Mrs. Sylvester.

Who's coming?

Sylvius.
The ladies who would like to be my wife.

Mrs. Sylvester [*Excitedly*].
The hussies—running after you!—I'll tell them
They're talking to a lunatic. No wife
Would stand the things I've stood.—The bold-faced chits!
There's not a one that's good enough for you.

Sylvius.
She whom the slipper fits shall be my bride.

Mrs. Sylvester.
The slipper fits! The slipper! If I'd used
A slipper oftener when you were young——

Sylvius.
Into the seams I've sewed my very soul.

Mrs. Sylvester.
It wouldn't fetch a nickel at the store.

Sylvius.
One woman is there—one! And she shall come.
I shall kneel down and fit the slipper on her.
Then I shall know! And we two shall step forth
Into God's sunshine, out across the world.
I've made a poem on it. I shall read it.
    *He pulls from his pocket a sheet of paper, places an arm affectionately
    about his mother, and walks with her toward rear of stage, reading aloud
    as he does so:*

        "That one in whom I find my life fulfilled
        Shall find complete fulfillment but through me.

Two souls of equal radiance shall we be
With the same joy of inner wonder thrilled."

Mrs. Sylvester *and* **Sylvius** *exeunt rear, he still reading his poem. His voice dies away in the distance.*

There is a moment of silence, and then, after a knocking on door, to which there is no answer, enter **Grazielline** *and* **Isabelline**. **Grazielline** *is elaborately and beautifully,* **Isabelline** *plainly, gowned.*

Isabelline.
This is the place.

Grazielline.
           His room?

Isabelline.
                  His little workshop.
Isn't he odd?

Grazielline.
          Yes, but he's very rich.

Isabelline.
He's very messy. If I tidied up,
Do you think 'twould make a good impression on him?

Grazielline.
Do, my dear girl! And dust the pictures, too,
And plump the cushions! 'Tis your stock-in-trade.

Isabelline [*As she attempts to put cobbler's bench in order*].
I know that you despise me. Never mind.
Men *do* like comfort.

Grazielline [*Seating herself in large armchair, center*].
                Isabelline dear,
I despise no one. It brings ugly lines
About the mouth.

Isabelline.
             Do you suppose it's here—
The slipper? O, if we could try it on
Before he comes!

Grazielline.
            He mustn't see us looking.
Men dislike curiosity in women.

Isabelline [*Plumping herself on footstool at* **Grazielline's** *feet*].
Do you think all men are very much the same?

Grazielline.
All men, my dear, are very much the same
In liking to be thought distinct and different.
The secret is to follow where each leads.
To adapt oneself—that is the woman's business.

Isabelline.
But it's the men that follow you!

Grazielline.
                                    O yes,
That is the finish of the little game.
I know the sex's secrets. I can twist
The best of them about this tiny finger.

Isabelline.
Did it take you long to learn?

Grazielline.
                              I knew from birth.
My intuitions are straight, subtle, sure.

Isabelline.
Still, men love artless women, such as me.

Grazielline.
They like good cooking.

Isabelline [*Jumping up, half sobbing*].
                        You are very cruel!

Grazielline.
Don't cry! There's no one here but me to see you.

Isabelline.
Sh! Here he comes!

    Grazielline *rises, as* **Sylvius** *enters with* **Mrs. Sylvester** *trotting at his heels.*

Sylvius [*With a low bow*].
                        Ladies, my compliments!
You honor and illumine this poor dwelling.

Isabelline [*To* **Grazielline**].
Isn't he handsome?

Grazielline.
     Sh! Affect indifference!

Sylvius [*Introducing*].
My mother—Miss—Miss——

Grazielline.
        Grazielline Smith.
This is my younger sister, Isabelline.

Mrs. Sylvester.
I'm pleased to meet you. Are there only two
In the family?

  Isabelline *and* **Grazielline** *glance meaningfully at each other.*
Isabelline.
    Yes.

Grazielline.
  Yes, there are only two.
Unfortunately, daughters both.

Sylvius.
       No, no,
Most fortunate! To be a splendid woman,
Why, that's a great thing—wonderful——

Isabelline.
          We saw
Your ad——

Grazielline [*To* **Isabelline**].
Sh! You'll spoil everything—

  [*To* **Sylvius**].

        You think
All women, then, so wonderful?

Sylvius.
       All women
Have something mystic, like the sap of a tree
In the young May, because with them is life.

Isabelline [*To* **Mrs. Sylvester**].
What does he mean?

Mrs. Sylvester.
    Nothing. He is a poet.

Grazielline [*Very close to* **Sylvius**].
A woman is not wonderful alone.
Till she is loved, her soul is not awake.
She but exists. Man gives to her, her life.

Sylvius.
Most flattering! I wonder if it's true.

Grazielline.
I do not flatter. See, within my eyes
Deep wells of truth.—O, you're not looking at them.

Sylvius.
I always use a telescope for stars.

Isabelline.
We saw your ad——

Sylvius.
                    Ah yes, about the slipper.
You wish to try it on?

Isabelline.
                    Yes, if you please.

Mrs. Sylvester.
I'm sure you'd never like it. It's a cheap thing.
I'm sure you'd do much better at the store.

Sylvius.
Mother!

Grazielline.
        Mr. Sylvester scarcely wishes,
To make so crude a test. A man must know
The woman at first sight—the destined one.

Isabelline [*To* **Mrs. Sylvester**].
She's said that to a dozen men before.

Mrs. Sylvester.
O, my poor boy! She's drowning him again
In those wells of truth.

Sylvius [*Gazing at* **Grazielline** *as if spellbound*].
                    You think so? It may be!

Grazielline.
I know so. Love draws love across the world.

Sylvius.
That's a good line. I'll have to put that down.
Excuse me just a minute.

[*Draws out pad and pencil, and writes.*]

Grazielline [*Stamping her foot*].
                              Pshaw!

Sylvius.
                              There now!

[*Looks up brightly.*]

What were you saying?

Grazielline [*Vexed*].
                    I was saying love
Draws love—O yes, you wrote that! But you think
She cannot tell—the woman? When I came
Into your presence I was conscious of
A something—shall I say it?—from afar.

Isabelline [*To* **Mrs. Sylvester**].
She'll tell him they were lovers in Assyria.

Mrs. Sylvester [*Wringing her hands*].
O, can't you stop her?

Grazielline.
                    From some other clime
An odor wafts, and all the world is dim.

Sylvius.
I knew you when the armies streamed afar
Along the plains of sunlit Troy—O Helen!

Grazielline.
Since man has loved I—I—have been his lure.

Sylvius.
Phyrne!

Mrs. Sylvester [*To* **Isabelline**].
        O Heavens, what shall we do?

Grazielline [*Passionately*].
                              My poet!

Isabelline [*Stepping determinedly forward*].
Please, sir, my sister quite forgot to mention
You may have met me, too, in ancient Greece.
I used to scrub the armour.

Grazielline.
                    Silly thing!

Isabelline.
Please, sir, since the beginning of the world
I've done the work and she has had the praise.
I'm getting tired of it.

Mrs. Sylvester.
                    Lord, I thought
That she, at least, was not a lunatic.
"The beginning of the world! The——"

Sylvius [*To Isabelline*].
                            You have stayed
At home and minded children, have you not?—
Woven the cloth and tended the red fire?

Isabelline.
And waited patiently my lord's return.

Grazielline.
While I with music soothed his wearied soul.

Isabelline.
He liked my cooking better, just the same.

Grazielline.
Pah! What else can you do?

Sylvius [*to Grazielline*].
                        What else can *you*?

Grazielline [*Radiantly*].
I can dance till life is rhythmic. I can sing.
I can be beautiful!

Sylvius.
                No more than that?

Grazielline.
I can be beautiful. That is enough.

Isabelline.
She can spend money, too.

Mrs. Sylvester.

I'll warrant she can.

Sylvius.
To dance till life is rhythmic and to sing,
To glow with beauty in a darkened world,—
That is enough. You brought your beauty down
Into foul places till the air was sweet.
You sang to hopeless women, who had hope
Straightway. You taught pale children how to dance
Till their life, too, was rhythmic.

Grazielline [*Embarrassed*].

No—I—I——

Sylvius.
Surely the earth is fairer that you live.

Grazielline.
I can't stand poverty and dirty brats.
My sister does the family's charity work.

Isabelline.
O, I adore the poor!

Sylvius.

Adore? Adore?

Isabelline.
I mean, of course, it makes one feel so good
To comfort them and feed them.

Sylvius.

And to teach
Freedom, unrest—until the very name
Of poverty becomes a curse——

Isabelline [*Pedantically*].

I always
Teach them they should submit to the will of God.

Sylvius.
Um—hm! And let God's sunshine in their rooms,
And breathe God's air a little. You, of course,
Know that the building code——

Isabelline.
The building code?

Sylvius.
If only 'twere enforced! But Sloth and Greed—
To attack, besiege them—that's a difficult task.
Their own fortress they build well. Still, I have faith
That if a valiant woman army stormed
Against the entrenchments—women such as you,
Who love, adore the poor—a glorious fight!
I see them stretching out before me now,
The army of free women, unafraid—
Whose battle-cry is "Strength unto the weak!"
Whose battle banner bears aloft the sign,
"We fight for justice for the unborn babes!"
Why, there's a clash and clamor worth the pains!——

Isabelline.
O sir, you frighten me! A woman's place
Is never in a battle——

Sylvius.
It is then—?

Isabelline.
Why, in the home and tending to the babies.

Sylvius.
The babies! O, of course, the babies! Surely!
They couldn't take their babies into battle.

Isabelline.
No, sir.

Sylvius.
Still, they must teach them how to fight—
Fight well, and having fought, to govern well
Their territory won—the boys, I mean.
And women wish for boy babes, do they not?
Do you think large families preferable to small?

Isabelline [*Embarrassed*].
I—I——

Sylvius.
Would you yourself, for instance, choose
Say, two well-born and healthy ones?

Isabelline.

O please!

Sylvius.
Some curious questions this Eugenics raises.

Isabelline.
Eugenics?

Sylvius.
Yes, the science that attempts
To give a human child as good a chance
As a well-bred horse or pig.

Isabelline.
O, if you please—
I think that's very vulgar.

Grazielline.
Really now,
This conversation is most interesting,
But I've a thousand things to do today—
Massage, a luncheon, matinee, a dance!
I can't spare a moment more——

Sylvius.
Madam, my pardon.
We shall fit the little slipper on at once.

He goes to armchair center and draws it forward. **Grazielline** *seats herself,
with the grace of an empress.* **Sylvius** *kneels, with the slipper in his hand.
Suddenly there are sounds outside of a mob hooting and jeering. All start,
and listen attentively.* **Sylvius** *half rises. Then there bursts into the room
a young girl in a dirty gray cape which envelopes her from head to feet.
Her cape is spotted with ashes. She is breathless and panting.*

Cinderelline.
Pardon me! Pardon! May I rest a moment?

Sylvius [*Springing up*].
My house is at your service.

Mrs. Sylvester.
Who is she?

Isabelline *and* **Grazielline** *confer excitedly in whispers.*

Isabelline.
How did she get here?

Grazielline.
>Coming in that dress!

Isabelline.
What shall we do?

Grazielline.
>Don't lose your head. Stay calm.
We must act as if she were a stranger to us.

Cinderelline.
O, I am breathless! They were jeering at me!
They hooted! They——

Sylvius.
>But now you are with friends.
Don't flutter like a little, wounded bird.
We shall protect you——

Mrs. Sylvester [*To Sylvius*].
>Find out who she is.
Maybe she is a burglar in disguise.

>Sylvius *gently draws* Cinderelline *to the large armchair and seats her.*

Sylvius [*To Mrs. Sylvester*].
Be quiet, mother.
Sylvius [*To Cinderelline*].
>There! Don't talk! Don't move!
Close your poor eyes and rest. There now! Now there!

Cinderelline [*As she closes her eyes*].
O, you are very kind!

>Isabelline *and* Grazielline *again confer.*

Isabelline.
>Look at the ashes
Stuck to her cloak.

Grazielline.
>To come in at this moment!
If he finds out that she belongs to us,
He may not wish to take me as his bride.

Isabelline.
Perhaps it's me the slipper fits, not you.

Grazielline.
Don't be ridiculous! With that big foot!

Isabelline.
I think we ought to go before she sees us.

They attempt to slip out.

Mrs. Sylvester [*Comes up to them confidentially*].
Who is she? She looks like a chimney sweep.
She's here for no good purpose, I'll be bound.
I think she is a burglar in disguise.

Grazielline.
Really, I've never seen the girl before.

Isabelline.
I haven't either.

Grazielline [*With a malicious glance at the exhausted* **Cinderelline,** *over whom
hovers the solicitous* **Sylvius**].
Mr. Sylvius
Is evidently busy. We'll return
This afternoon at three.

Isabelline.
Tell him we hope
He'll not let anybody try it on
Till we come back.

Cinderelline [*Opening her eyes—looking dazedly at* **Sylvius**].
Who are you? Who are you?
O, I have never seen this room before.
Who are those ladies? Grazielline—you!
And Isabelline with you!—Why, how strange!
I ran in here. They hooted me and jeered me——

Sylvius.
You know my guests?

Cinderelline.
Oh yes, they are my sisters.

Sylvius.
Your sisters?

Mrs. Sylvester.
Why, you said there were only two
In the family!

Cinderelline.
They are not proud of me.

Grazielline.
I never saw the silly girl before.

Isabelline.
She looks as if she sat among the ashes.
Our sister!

Cinderelline.
      No, they are not proud of me.
But it is half, I think, because they fear me.

Grazielline.
Fear her!

Isabelline.
     Fear Cinderelline!

Sylvius.
            Cinderelline?
Then you *do* know her?

Isabelline [*Confused*].
      No—I——

Grazielline [*Quite at ease*].
           No, indeed!
My sister, I presume, thinks that she looks
Like Cinderella in the fairy-tale,
And so she called her——

Cinderelline.
         By her rightful title.
My name is Cinderelline, if you please.

Sylvius.
But who are you?

Cinderelline.
      I'm not as old as they.

Sylvius.
No, no—you are a young thing.

Cinderelline.
        Tell me, please,
Why they should hate me. All my arduous toil
Is but for them. I do it willingly.
I do it willingly, to bring them joy

And freedom—but they laugh at me and jeer me,
As did the mob that drove me to your door.

Sylvius.
What mob?

Cinderelline.
          A motley throng—all sorts of folk.
Men for the most part, but some women, too.
I think they do not know me, but they jeer
Because my costume is yet strange to them.

Grazielline.
They jeer at her because she wants the vote.
And goes about and tells men that she wants it.

Isabelline.
And says her home is larger than her house.

Grazielline.
And, heedless of her sisters' reputations,
Works, and earns money by it.

Isabelline.
                   Goes to college.

Grazielline.
Lectures in public places on a platform
Without a tremor.

Isabelline.
            She's not womanly.

Grazielline.
She's proven it by intruding here today.
I all but had the slipper on my foot.

Cinderelline.
Intruded! I am sorry! But you saw
I did not know whose house it was I entered.

Sylvius.
Perhaps Miss Cinderelline will herself
Do me the honor to try on the slipper.

Isabelline [*To* **Grazielline**].
That's what she came here for!

Grazielline.

How very bold!

Cinderelline.
The slipper? Pray, what slipper?

Sylvius.

She whose foot
This slipper fits is destined for my bride.

Cinderelline.
O, thank you! I'm not looking for a husband.

Mrs. Sylvester.
Yes, but your sisters are—and they've been waiting
Some time—to try the slipper on, I mean.

Cinderelline.
O, I shall leave immediately!

Sylvius [*Intercepting her*].

No,
You must stay.

Cinderelline.

But they don't want me.

Sylvius.

And I do.

Cinderelline.
O!

Sylvius.
Now, Miss Grazielline, if you wish
We'll put the little slipper on your foot.

Same business as before, of arranging arm-chair. **Grazielline** *sits, and pettishly kicks off her own elegant slipper.* **Sylvius** *kneels and places the red slipper on her foot.*

Grazielline.
It fits exactly.

Sylvius.

Hm! A trifle large!

Sylvius [*To* **Isabelline**].
What do you think?

Mrs. Sylvester.
It's falling off her foot.

Isabelline.
She's always squeezed herself in little shoes.

Grazielline.
Really, the slipper's not a stylish shape,
And red is such a very garish color!
I don't think that I care to——[*Rises haughtily*].

Isabelline [*Slipping hastily into her place*].
Well, I do!

Sylvius *attempts to fit the slipper on her foot, but the slipper is evidently too small.*

Mrs. Sylvester.
Look out—don't break her toes!

Sylvius [*Struggling valiantly*].
It—it's a trifle
Small, don't you think?

Isabelline.
It fits me perfectly.
Ouch—perfectly! I never had a shoe
That felt more comfortable—ouch!

Mrs. Sylvester.
Stand up and walk.
Stamp in it first. That's a good way to tell.

Isabelline.
Of course—perhaps for working in the house——

Mrs. Sylvester.
I always like real roomy shoes for that.

Isabelline.
If I were idle, like *dear* Grazielline,
'Twould be a perfect fit—but——

Sylvius.
O, of course!
I understand.

Removes slipper from her foot, and turns to **Cinderelline.**

                    Then there remains but you!

Cinderelline.
Truly you wish that I should try it on?

Sylvius.
Truly I wish it.

Cinderelline.
                    What have you to give,
That you dare ask a woman for herself?

Sylvius.
I have my lands, my houses, all my wealth.

Cinderelline.
Already I possess a dwelling place
Richer than yours. The round earth is my home.

Sylvius.
I have my homage and my fealty.
I give her loyal faith throughout this life.

Cinderelline.
A noble gift to give. Still, she may tire
Of lifelong fealty alone. What else?

Sylvius.
I have desires and dreams and aspirations,
An eager interest in the teeming world
Of men and women—love for music, books——

Cinderelline.
That's jolly, comrade. Are you a good friend
To little kiddies? Are you one of them?

Sylvius.
They always tumble me about the place.

Cinderelline.
One question more. I hesitate—and yet—
Do you come pure in thought and pure in deed?

Sylvius.
Pure as my bride I come to her pure heart.

> *She seats herself in the arm-chair.* **Sylvius** *kneels at her foot with the little
> red slipper. The other three look on, breathless.* **Sylvius** *fits the slipper to
> her foot.*

Isabelline.
It's on!

Grazielline.
        It fits her!

Mrs. Sylvester [*Throwing up her hands*].
            I'm a mother-in-law!

> **Cinderelline** *springs up triumphantly. With a quick gesture, she throws off her dingy gray cape, and reveals herself robed in glistening and sparkling white. There is a moment of silent amazement.*

Cinderelline [*Simply—to* **Sylvius**].
My dress is not so ugly as my cloak.

Sylvius [*Draws her to him in rapt adoration*].
My comrade and my bride! My perfect woman!

> *The curtain falls to the strains of the Wagner Wedding March.*

CURTAIN

THE WOMAN OF IT

or OUR FRIENDS, THE ANTI-SUFFRAGISTS (A SATIRICAL COMEDY IN ONE ACT)

MARY SHAW

Chicago: The Dramatic Publishing Company. 1914.

CAST OF CHARACTERS

Mrs. Allright—President of an Anti-Suffrage Club.
Mrs. Grundy—A Member of one of our "oldest families."
Mrs. Pure-Drivel—The Poetess of a "Lost Cause."
Mrs. Sweet—An Ideal Wife and Mother.
Mrs. Grouch—A Dyed-in-the-Wool "Womanly Woman."
Miss Noodle—Just a beginner at the "Womanly Game."
Miss Moore—A Guest of the Club.
Miss Berry—A Guest of the Club.
Miss Foster—A Guest of the Club.

SCENE

The Club room of an Anti-Suffrage Club. A table for the President to preside—with a gavel, paper, pencil and note book. Chairs for members and guests. Any number of club women can be used—only the six antis and three guests are necessary. President's table centre, with chair behind it. The six antis are seated on right after they enter. Guests on left. If more women are used, they can sit on either side of President—in a semi-circle facing audience. The audience represents the imaginary men on the Legislative Committee and all the cajolery is addressed to them.

At rise of curtain the stage is empty. Noise of women talking is heard outside. In a few seconds, **Mrs. Allright** *enters, goes to table; busies herself arranging things for meeting.* **Miss Noodle** *enters with sketch of club motto in her hands.*

Miss Noodle. Dearie—[*Kisses* **Mrs. Allright** *effusively on both cheeks*]. Here's the finished sketch of the motto. [*Hands her drawing.*]

Mrs. Allright [*Admiringly*]. It's perfectly lovely! So sweet of you! Oh, you darling! [*Kisses her again gushingly.*]

Enter **Miss Moore, Miss Berry** *and* **Miss Foster.**

Miss Moore. Well, Fanny, here we are.

Miss Allright [*Embracing* **Miss Moore**]. Oh, you dear; how sweet of you to come. How do you do Miss Berry! [*Shaking hands.*] And Miss Foster, too—how well you are looking! This is our new club room. We think it is just too sweet. Oh, allow me—Miss Noodle, may I present—Miss Moore—Miss Berry—Miss Foster. [**Miss Noodle** *shakes each lady's hand effusively.*] Sit here, please [*Indicating chairs to left of table*]. There will only be a few here this afternoon. It's a sort of rehearsal for the ladies who are to speak at the Hearing before the Legislative Committee. I thought it such a good chance for you to hear our most brilliant speakers give their reasons for opposing woman's suffrage. [*Goes to door and speaks off.*] Ladies, will you please come right in now. We must begin.

The women enter, chattering noisily—greet **Miss Noodle** *and continue to laugh and chatter till* **Mrs. Allright** *calls them to order with the pounding of the gavel.*

Mrs. Allright [*Rapping several times before she can get silence*]. Ladies, ladies,

ladies, please. Here are three ladies who ought to join our Club. Miss Moore, Miss Berry, Miss Foster—ladies. [*Introduction acknowledged by mutual bows.*] They say they do not know whether they are anti-suffragists or not. But I know they are—for they are dear friends of mine—and lovely women. So I have invited them to hear the rehearsal for the Hearing before the Legislative Committee. [*Women begin to chatter as soon as she stops speaking.*] And, ladies, ladies, ladies, please. [*Rapping vigorously with gavel.*] Before we begin—Miss Noodle has designed our motto for us. [*Takes up sketch and shows it.*] She has taken our watchwords "I Love You," and "Oh, My Dear Baby," and placed them over two intertwined hearts, symbolic of the husband and the child. This is to be framed and hung in our clubroom.

Mrs. Sweet. Isn't that sweet of Miss Noodle?

Mrs. Grouch. She is such a dear!

Mrs. Pure-Drivel. How lovely of her!

Mrs. Allright [*Rapping for order*]. Ladies, all rise, please, and repeat the pledge. "I pledge myself to remember each day and remind other women every hour—"

Women [*Repeat in unison*]. "I pledge myself to remember each day and remind other women every hour—"

Mrs. Allright. "—that there are only two great moments in a woman's life—"

Women [*In unison*]. "—that there are only two great moments in a woman's life—"

Mrs. Allright. "—One, when she gives her first kiss to her lover—"

Women [*In unison*]. "—One, when she gives her first kiss to her lover—"

Mrs. Allright. "—the other when she gives her first kiss to her own little baby—"

Women [*In unison*]. "—the other when she gives her first kiss to her own little baby—"

Mrs. Allright. "—And, no matter what else she may have, what else she may gain—"

Women [*In unison*]. "—And, no matter what else she may have, what else she may gain—"

Mrs. Allright. "—the woman who misses these two great moments is still a failure."

Women [*In unison*]. "—the woman who misses these two great moments is still a failure."

Mrs. Allright. Our Motto:—First great moment—"I LOVE YOU." Second great moment—"OH, MY DEAR BABY."

Women [*In unison*]. First Great Moment—"I LOVE YOU." Second Great Moment—"OH, MY DEAR BABY."

Miss Foster. There are no old maids in this club, I judge.

Miss Berry. Oh, yes; while there's life—there's hope, you know.

Mrs. Grouch [*Rising*]. Mrs. President—

Mrs. Allright [*Rapping for order*]. Ladies, ladies, ladies, please—[*When talking stops*]. Mrs. Grouch.

Mrs. Grouch. I am a loyal anti-suffragist—and a firm believer in our pledge. But it just makes me tired to see how many "failures" among women, who never had the two great moments—manage to get so much credit. Yes, and from men, too, while we poor things who are busy doing our duty are taken as a matter of course—and hardly get a "thank you."

Mrs. Sweet. Yes, that's so. It isn't fair.

Miss Noodle.—Why is that, Dearie?

Mrs. Grouch. Look at that terrible old maid—Queen Elizabeth of England! I never heard any man say she was a failure. And in our own time—see the sickening gush over those old maids, Florence Nightingale—and Clara Barton—and Jane Addams—and Susan B. Anthony— [*Women cover their faces and groan.*]

Mrs. Grundy. These women are exceptions, my dear. They may get praise— but they do not get reverence as we do.

Mrs. Grouch. Well—we may get reverence, tho' I have my doubts about that. But we don't get any statues erected to us, outside of the cemeteries, and they do.

Miss Noodle. Well, I think that a woman who stands being an old maid all her life, deserves a statue. [*Women laugh and chatter.*]

Mrs. Allright [*Rapping for order*]. Ladies, ladies, ladies, please. We don't want statues nor praise. We only want to be loved. To lavish love on some-thing—even if the object is unworthy. To waste love if need be. For only when we love are we truly womanly.

Mrs. Grouch. You say we must waste love on the unworthy? Does that mean we must love those suffragists? [*Folding arms and looking cross.*]

Miss Allright. No, decidedly not. A true woman cannot love unworthy women. She can only love unworthy men.

Miss Berry. Isn't that odd?

Mrs. Allright. No, Miss Berry, it is not odd. It is woman's mysterious nature.

Mrs. Pure-Drivel. Mrs. President—

Mrs. Allright [*Rapping for order*]. Ladies, ladies, ladies, please. [*After quiet is restored.*] Mrs. Pure-Drivel.

Mrs. Pure-Drivel. Perhaps you ought to select someone in my place to speak at this Hearing. I am divorced, you know. I did not waste any time or love on Duncan Pure-Drivel after I found out he was unfaithful. Of course, I did not know then that it was unwomanly to be indignant.

Mrs. Grundy. My dear, I am permitting divorce now. Strictly among the very rich. Many of our best families are using it. But we selected you for your appearance. Unfortunately, there are so few womanly women who are stylish.

Miss Noodle. Well—did you hear that?

Mrs. Sweet. My word! I like that!

Mrs. Grouch. What a knock! [*Women protest to each other.*]

Mrs. Allright [*Rapping for order*]. Ladies, ladies, ladies, please. Mrs. Grundy only means that womanly women spend all their time loving and trying to be good.

Mrs. Grouch [*Angrily jumping up.*] I never had to try to be good. I always was good.

Miss Noodle. So was I. The idea! Did you ever?

Mrs. Pure-Drivel. I never was so insulted in my life! Telling me to my face that because I am stylish I am not good. [*Very indignantly.*]

Mrs. Grundy. My dear Mrs. Pure-Drivel, you are that rarest thing on earth —a woman who is both good and stylish. [**Mrs. Pure-Drivel**, *soothed by compliment, sits down.*]

Mrs. Allright. Ladies, please—we must get to business. We are here today to listen to what our members are going to say to the Legislative Committee at the Hearing on the Question of Suffrage for Women. After the Suffragists have finished I shall make my opening speech. It's the same one I make every year. [*Throwing sheep's eyes at the audience, who are the committee.*] Gentlemen: A woman's proper place is at home. No true woman would ever leave it to come here and wrangle about politics. [*Applause.*]

Miss Moore. Don't these men think it's funny that you do not stay at home, then?

Mrs. Allright [*Annoyed*]. Not at all. They know I am dragged here to uphold the cause of true womanhood.

Miss Foster. Why, who drags you here, Fanny?

Miss Noodle. Yes; I'd like to know, too, who it is makes us do this unwomanly thing. My brother asked me why we Antis didn't stay at home and practice what we preach—and I couldn't tell him.

Mrs. Allright [*With a superior air*]. I have no time to go into that now.

Miss Moore. Why do you bother about these other women voting, anyway?

Mrs. Allright. Because if they get the suffrage we will have to vote. And we'd rather die than vote.

Miss Moore. Why will you have to vote if you do not wish to?

Mrs. Grundy. Obey laws that women make? Never!

Mrs. Grouch. Not on your life! If they vote, we'll vote.

Women [*Together*]. Yes, indeed. If they vote—we'll vote.

Mrs. Allright [*Beguilingly*]. Gentlemen, love is our religion. Husband— home—child. That is our Trinity. All the ladies opposed to Suffrage for Women, that I shall present to you today, are wives and mothers. Ah, those holy words—wives, mothers. They are all man's ideal woman. The utterly womanly. [*Women applaud as* **Mrs. Allright** *finishes.*] Gentlemen, this is Mrs. Sweet—an ideal wife and mother. [*Women applaud as* **Mrs. Sweet** *rises.*]

Mrs. Sweet [*Embarrassed and giggling*]. Oh, dear! I am so nervous. I shall act like a fool.

Mrs. Grundy. That's all right, my dear. Men expect women to act like fools. Mrs. President, I suggest that we all repeat the first commandment of the "womanly law," to encourage Mrs. Sweet?

Mrs. Allright. A splendid idea, Mrs. Grundy. Ladies, repeat the first commandment of the "womanly law," please.

Women [*In unison*]. "Have as little brains as possible and don't use all you have."

Mrs. Grundy. You'll make a great hit with the men, Mrs. Sweet.

Mrs. Sweet [*Flattered*]. Oh, do you think so?

Miss Moore [*To* **Miss Berry**]. She acts to me as if she had the smallest brain in captivity.

Mrs. Sweet [*Putting on her sweetest manner, speaking to audience who represent committee of men*]. Gentlemen, I don't know anything about this old suffrage thing—and I don't want to know anything about it. [*Women applaud.*] But I do know that I have the best husband that ever lived. He loves me to distraction, and honestly, he thinks I am the only woman in the world. My babies are the cutest, dearest babies alive. My home is simply a paradise. So, why should I want to vote? What good would it do me?

Mrs. Moore. Mrs. Sweet would not be compelled to vote, would she, Mrs. Allright?

Mrs. Allright. No, no, of course not. Go on, Mrs. Sweet.

Mrs. Sweet [*Looks viciously at* **Miss Moore**, *then changes to sweet manner*]. Women were just made to be loved and protected by the strong arm of a loving husband.

Miss Berry. Protected from what, Mrs. Allright?

Mrs. Allright. Well, um—er—er— I don't know exactly. But men are very sensitive on that point, Miss Berry. They all say that woman needs protection by the strong arm of man—and they know.

Miss Moore. But don't they usually leave the job to the ordinary policeman?

Mrs. Grundy. But the idea is very beautiful, don't you think so, Miss Moore? It is called Chivalry. Men say that they can't feel it if a woman claims to be their equal.

Miss Berry. And the more inferior to them a woman is the greater they feel the chivalry—is that it?

Mrs. Allright. Yes.

Miss Berry. Then a man feels more chivalrous towards a scullery maid or scrub woman than he does to a society lady?

Mrs. Allright. Oh, no; I hardly think so.

Miss Berry. Why not? The scrub woman is very much more his inferior than the society woman is.

Miss Moore. Perhaps his chivalry extends a couple of notches below himself and then stops working.

Mrs. Allright. How very clever of you, dear, to figure it out for us.

Miss Noodle. Why, I thought Chivalry was raising hats to women, carrying their wraps, and rising when a woman comes into the room!

Mrs. Grouch. Heavens, no! Those are just parlor tricks—like not eating with your knife.

Mrs. Grundy. Ladies, you had better accept this ghost of a beautiful idea and ask no questions. Men are very sentimental, you know.

Mrs. Allright. Go on, Mrs. Sweet, please.

Mrs. Sweet. Real women don't want to think. They just want to bloom beside man in the home and shed the fragrance of their womanhood over his troubled life—as The Ladies Home Twaddle so beautifully expresses it. [*Sits amidst great applause.*]

Mrs. Grundy. Why she is positively inspired! Ladies, I predict that Mrs. Sweet is going to be one of our finest speakers.

Mrs. Allright. I agree with you, Mrs. Grundy. But may I suggest, dear, that you leave out the question—"What good will it do me to vote?" Never give those suffragists a loophole to get in their old statistics. We find it far safer to keep to mossgrown platitudes about husband, home and children. Then they can't corner us.

Miss Noodle. Oh, Mrs. Sweet, aren't you going to tell your lovely story?

Mrs. Sweet. Oh, Mrs. President, I forgot my lovely story!

Mrs. Allright. Oh! Do tell it, Mrs. Sweet.

Mrs. Sweet [*Rising, beguilingly*]. Gentlemen: I knew a suffragist once. Like all of them, she neglected her husband and home. Sometimes she never saw her baby girl for weeks together. An ignorant nursemaid took entire charge of her. The woman spent all her time at suffrage clubs. One day, as she was crossing a park, she saw a baby carriage with a baby in it tipped up against a tree. A jar would have thrown it over. The poor little frightened cherub was crying piteously. She righted the carriage and tried to soothe the poor, frightened darling. A nursemaid, who had been talking to a policeman, came running towards her. She was just about to demand the address of the mother to report what she had seen— Oh, gentlemen, it was her own nursemaid. And that miserable, neglected, angel baby was her own child. [*The six antis are weeping.*] She had seen it so seldom that she did not recognize it. Think of it, gentlemen—a mother not to know her own baby! That is what will happen in every home if these women get the suffrage. [*Sits.*]

Mrs. Allright. That is a terrible story, Mrs. Sweet, and only too true.

Miss Moore. Have the men on the committee any sense of humor?

Mrs. Allright. I really can't say. I'm afraid I do not know what a sense of humor is. Does any anti know what a sense of humor is?

Women [*In turn*]. No—no—no—no. What is it?

Mrs. Allright. You see, nobody here knows what it is, Miss Moore.

Miss Moore. Yes, I see.

Mrs. Allright. Gentlemen, our youngest anti, who will plead with you for the "Girl of the Future," Miss Noodle, gentlemen.

Miss Noodle [*Rising, beginning shyly and gradually getting very modern and familiar*]. Gentlemen, I am a girl—so I want to say a word for the "Girl of the Future." Her fate is in your hands. Men will not marry when women claim to be their equals, and pretend to think and try to earn real money. So there will be no husbands nor homes for the poor girls of the future if these suffragists get what they want. I think it's real mean and selfish of women who have had the two great moments to try to do us girls out of them. It's just pure spite—that's what it is. My brother says there isn't a woman a man would look at twice who wants to vote. He says these suffragists are all disappointed old maids or "gone to seed" married women. You men are wise to them, my brother says. Please don't take any stock in their saying they are going to do fine things for the future race. Why, there will not be any future race if they keep on. What's the use of girls anyway except for men to make love to? Oh, gentlemen, gentlemen—please fix it so the girl of the future will have a show. [*Great applause as she sits down.*]

Mrs. Allright [*In a very solemn tone*]. Ladies, Miss Noodle's appeal is like an agonizing cry from the cradle of the human race. And now, ladies—before I forget it—I must warn you against mentioning, this year, a dear old platitude which we have used with telling effect a hundred thousand times. Please, please do not say anything about the vast hordes of disreputable, immoral women who will rush to the polls and contaminate the pure wives and mothers while they are voting.

Miss Moore. But I understood you to say that the pure wives and mothers will never vote.

Mrs. Allright. Please, Miss Moore, this is very important. Ladies, it seems that in those dreadful places where women vote now—[*Women cover their faces with their hands and groan.*] The disreputable women are as bitterly opposed to woman suffrage as the womanly women are.

Mrs. Pure-Drivel. Infamous! How dare a disreputable woman pretend to have a womanly feeling!

Miss Noodle. Why is that, Dearie?

Mrs. Allright [*Coughing, embarrassed*]. Ahem! Ahem! I'd rather you didn't hear the reason they give, child. Please stop up your ears. [**Miss Noodle** *puts fingers in her ears.*] They say it will hurt their business—which is to please men.

Miss Moore. Why, that is your business, too—isn't it, ladies? [*Laughing heartily.*] Well, I must say that is a good joke on you! [*All three visitors laugh uproarously. Antis look at one another amazed.*]

Mrs. Grundy. Oh, it's too bad we must give up that lovely pipe-dream! It was such an effective argument.

Miss Moore. You Antis all seem so satisfied with things as they are. Isn't there one right as a woman that any of you would like to claim?

Mrs. Grouch. Yes; there's one right I'd like to have—

Miss Moore. Good! What is it, Mrs. Grouch?

Mrs. Grouch. The right to look just as God made me. I'd like to be as fat and bald and homely as men have the right to be—and not be expected to apologize and do penance for it all my life. With all the rights these suffragists are digging up—it's a wonder to me they never thought of the right to be homely. I wish we women could unite and go on strike on this "beauty" business! I believe it would settle the whole "woman" question.

Mrs. Sweet. Oh, Mrs. President, if women did that—there wouldn't be any "Beauty Column" on the woman's page of the newspapers. And I just dote on the beauty column.

Miss Moore. Why, Mrs. Sweet, those "How I Keep Myself Beautiful" articles in the papers are all written by men. They pay the "Beauties" who are supposed to write them a hundred dollars a week for the use of their names. The "Beauties" never even see them. It is a conspiracy between the druggists and the newspaper editors.

Mrs. Sweet. Now, that isn't true! My sister-in-law has a neighbor who met a woman at an afternoon tea who told her that she had a cousin who knew a lady once who had a friend who talked with a girl who was a maid to Lillian Russell.

Mrs. Allright [*Rapping for order*]. Ladies, ladies, please. Mrs. Grouch says she does not care to speak at the Hearing, so I am going to excuse her. But I do hope she will tell us what she intended to say if she had decided to go.

Women. Oh do, Mrs. Grouch—please.

Mrs. Grouch [*Rising*]. Ladies, I know men through and through. I've had eight brothers, two husbands and four sons. Fourteen men in the family has given me all the practice I need in fooling and palavering men. If a woman has only one or two men to practice on she should seize every opportunity, like these Hearings, to keep her hand in. That's how you become experts at the game. Those suffragists are all on to your tricks—

but what do you care? If those deluded women think they are going to get anything that men want to keep themselves—let them go ahead and try to get it. You and I know that the way to get things out of men is to throw dust in their eyes by wheedling, coaxing and flattering them. The moment I put my eye on a woman I can tell just how much she knows of the game. You antis are all more or less expert bluffers. That's why I am an anti. I have only one reason for opposing Woman Suffrage. And it is this: I never found any work a man didn't want some woman to help him do —especially the uninteresting, drudgery part of it—never one single thing except voting. And I say—if there's one thing on earth that men want to do all alone, for Heaven's sake, let them do it. Encourage them. [*All the women laugh heartily, but as if* **Mrs. Grouch** *was joking.*]

Mrs. Allright. Dear Mrs. Grouch, you are always so amusing! [*To visitors.*] Mrs. Grouch is one of our stanchest members, but she must have her little joke. [*Changing her tone to one of deep significance.*] And now, gentlemen, I have the honor to present to you Mrs. Duncan Pure-Drivel, the Poetess of our Cause.

Mrs. Pure-Drivel [*Rises—amidst great applause. Takes attitude of deference to imaginary men—rolls languishing eyes at them—keeps through her speech the Circe tone and manner of luring men through sex attraction. The manner sexual, the matter she speaks supposedly intellectual, is what brings out the humor of the role*]. Gentlemen, I am a woman. [*Pause.*] Have always been a woman. [*Pause.*] And I pray God, may always remain a woman, so I can tell you how a woman feels. A woman cannot reason—so she can never understand nor help to make laws. But she has something far higher than reason—a Divine intuition. This Divine intuition is of no use to women outside of the kitchen and nursery, for, infinitely above reason as it is, it cannot comprehend the affairs of state. Yet its discovery by men was a stroke of genius, for it enables them to lay the burden of the morals of the universe on women. This is the spiritual essence of it. A baby girl has within her at the moment of birth the intuitive knowledge of good and evil. So any sin a woman commits is done deliberately, defiantly against the law of her nature. That is why there should be no pity for erring women. Man, it seems, has to learn slowly and painfully by reason what sin is. That is why it is just that men should escape punishment while they are learning the lesson of life. Why the same moral laws cannot be made for men and women. Why a man must be forgiven again and again—even unto the end.

Miss Moore [*Aside to* **Miss Berry**]. Well, for a divorced woman, I call that triumphant nerve!

Miss Berry. She's looking for number two, remember.

Mrs. Pure-Drivel [*Arraigning, with extended finger the imaginary suffragists*].

Those women, for they seem to be women, tho' it is hard to believe it—declare that our morals and our stupidity have been forced on us by men for their own comfort and convenience. I deny it—in the name of womanhood. Our morals and stupidity were given us by God. They are our mysterious lure which no man will ever fathom, yet does not wish to escape. Before Time was—it was decreed by Heaven, that man should speak of woman as his superior, treat her as his inferior. So no more talk of ballots and of laws. We are satisfied with our empire over the hearts of men. We are content to be queens by Divine right of sex. [*Applause.*]

Miss Noodle. Wonderful!

Mrs. Allright. Splendid!

Mrs. Grundy. Marvelous!

Mrs. Grouch. Perfectly magnificent!

Mrs. Allright. Mrs. Pure-Drivel, I almost wish I might have put you down to speak last—your effort is so poetical, so original, so irresistibly convincing. But Mrs. Grundy always has the last word—and she is the bulwark of our cause. So, gentlemen, our best beloved leader and supporter, Mrs. Grundy. [*Applause.*]

Mrs. Grundy [*Rising*]. Gentlemen, I have been your good old friend from time immemorial. The Mrs. Grundys have worked faithfully through all the ages to keep women in their proper spheres. You men couldn't have done it without Mrs. Grundy's help. Don't rise, gentlemen, you overwhelm me with your homage. Keeping women in their proper sphere has never been an easy task, but during the last ten years I have been several times on the point of giving it up as a bad job. Of course, I have kept up a splendid bluff, pretending nothing unusual was happening, but deep within me I know this abominable heresy of woman suffrage is going to be the death of men. And that last news from California—87,000 more women than men registered to vote—has put a crimp in me that never will come out. Now, gentlemen, I have heard all your reasons why women are cutting these capers, but none of you have hit on the right one. It is not education, nor industrial conditions, nor any of the things you lay it to. The trouble began way back in the fourth century, when some misguided Fathers of the Church met together in solemn conclave and decided by a bare majority vote—just one vote, gentlemen—think of it—that woman had a soul. That she was responsible to God—not men—for the deeds done in the flesh. How did such an idea ever come into their heads, you ask? Very simple. They wanted women to support the church and had to offer them a soul to get them interested. Of course, they did not give woman a soul of her own. They gave her only as much of a soul as it was safe and convenient for her to have. The kind of one they could take back if it didn't work right. They knew the innate stupidity of woman. They were perfectly sure she would go on piling up the power and glory and profit of men in the church and never once think of sharing in it. And so she did for fifteen centuries, when suddenly a woman arose, alone and unaided, who, without asking permission of any Pope, or offering to share any power or glory with men, put herself at the head of a new religion—Mary Baker Eddy. Now, what has happened in the church is going to happen in the state. If you give women the ballot—if you make them mayors, judges and governors—where will it end? There are a million more women than men. They'll outvote you, finally. Set up a new code of morals. Oh, I know—women are not creative. But oh, they are splendidly imitative. They will give you an imitation of yourselves that will paralyze you. Punish men for sin and let women escape. Give you their names at marriage, so you lose all your identity. Pay you for your work, with love and flattery and keep the hard cash. In short, gentlemen, turn the tables on you. There is only one remedy. You must use it and use it quickly. Take away women's souls! Giving women souls was the cause of all the trouble. If you can't do that gentlemen, it is utterly hopeless. [*All the antis are greatly excited over the end of this speech and moaning as if in the face of some great calamity.*]

Mrs. Allright [*Weeping, slightly hysterical*]. Gentlemen, I can hardly control my feelings sufficiently to close our testimony after Mrs. Grundy's awful warning. But dear, dear gentlemen, please do not let them make us sheriffs and aldermen—

Antis [*Going down on knees, with outstretched arms, pleading*]. Oh don't, gentlemen, please—

Mrs. Allright. Do not let them make us mayors and governors—

Women [*Still on knees, pleading*]. No, no, gentlemen, please don't, don't.

Mrs. Allright. Save us—oh save us from this awful fate!

Women [*Crying out agonizingly*]. Save us, oh save us, gentlemen!

Mrs. Allright. For we will die—yes, gladly lay down our lives—before we are forced to become senators and presidents. [*Shrieks of horror from the antis.*]

Miss Moore [*After excitement has calmed down a little goes to console* **Mrs. Allright**]. Oh nonsense, Fanny, there isn't any danger of women being forced into high political offices.

Mrs. Grundy. Yes there is, young woman. At the rate these suffragists are gaining ground—I should not wonder if some one here lived to see a woman president. [*More shrieks from antis and hysterical weeping.*]

Miss Berry [*Shaking hands with* **Mrs. Allright**]. Good-bye—we must go now. Thank you very much, ladies.

Miss Foster. Yes; we have enjoyed it very much.

Mrs. Allright. Wouldn't you like to join our club?

Miss Berry. We cannot.

Mrs. Allright. Why, haven't you decided after what you have heard?

Miss Berry. Oh yes; we have found out we are suffragists.

Women. Suffragists!

Mrs. Grouch. I knew they were suffragists the minute I put my eyes on them.

Miss Moore. The other night I told a friend I was going to a suffragist meeting to find out whether I was a suffragist or not. "Don't" she said. "Go to an anti-suffrage meeting; they'll make a suffragist of you at short notice." Everybody says you make more converts to equal suffrage than the suffragists do.

Miss Berry. Do you always do it so quickly? It is wonderful!

Mrs. Allright. What are you talking about?

Miss Moore. Well frankly, ladies, we have discovered your secret.

Mrs. Allright. Our secret?

Miss Moore. Yes; and it's awfully clever. I must congratulate you. Ha! Ha!

Miss Foster. We thought at first you really meant it all, didn't we? [*Laughs*].

Miss Moore. Then it dawned on us that it was all a delicious farce.

Mrs. Allright. A farce?

Miss Berry. It's a splendid game. To guy the "utterly womanly" so successfully that the most indifferent woman flies to suffrage as a haven of dignity and self respect.

Miss Foster. You and the suffragists are both working together, in different ways, to convert all women to suffrage, aren't you?

Miss Moore. But the crowning joke of all is when you and the suffragists go to a legislative hearing, pretending to be at daggers drawn and convert the men on the committee. For even a man must resent the dose of flattery you plaster over them.

Miss Foster. How do you keep your faces straight, ladies?

Miss Berry. Do you and the suffragists wink at each other when the men are not looking?

Mrs. Allright. What are you women trying to say?

Miss Berry. Oh, don't be afraid. We'll not give it away.

Miss Foster. No, indeed. We will send up all the raw material we can collect for you to make suffragists of.

Miss Moore. We are going right down to enroll ourselves as suffragists; collect some literature, and get busy.

Miss Berry. And we'll tell them at headquarters that they will have to hustle or the antis will have them beaten to a frazzle in making converts to Woman Suffrage! "Votes for Women!"

Guests [*March out as if waving imaginary banners and call out together*]. "Votes for Women!" "Votes for WOMEN!" "Votes for Women!"

Mrs. Grundy. Spies! Those women are spies sent here to trap us.

Women crowd about **Mrs. Allright**, *who has collapsed.*

Miss Noodle. What can we do for you, dearie?

Mrs. Grouch. She needs a good, strong bracer. What do you say to a lemon soda, Fanny?

Mrs. Allright [*Reviving*]. And I called them my friends—such ingratitude!

Mrs. Grouch. To the nearest drug store, ladies. Forward—march! The sodas are on me!

Women lead **Mrs. Allright** *out—protesting about her friends.*

CURTAIN

The Parrot Cage

A PLAY IN ONE ACT

MARY SHAW

Chicago: The Dramatic Publishing Company. 1914.

CAST OF CHARACTERS _____

Philistine Parrot.
Free-souled Parrot.
Reasoning Parrot.
Rationalist.
Idealistic Parrot.
Theological Parrot.
Man's Voice.

Any number of other "Parrots" may be used effectively.

REMARKS

Whistles and screams and bird noises can be bought at band instrument stores and mechanical toy shops.

These can be manipulated by someone at the sides when needed; as, for instance, at the beginning, before the rise of the curtain. Also, when the parrots fall off the perch. Also, when the **Free-Souled Parrot** breaks her chain and flies away.

All the parrots, except the **Free-Souled**, speak in staccato tones. It adds to the illusion, to have the parrots precede their speeches, occasionally, with the little bird sound. The **Philistine Parrot** can laugh and whistle mockingly.

SCENE

A *parrot's cage. Curtains of cotton material, painted with black stripes to represent the bars of the cage. These curtains are hung at the back and sides. A long pole runs across the stage, in the front—from which a drapery hangs, which hides the parrots from the waist down. Just back of this perch is a small raised platform, with a single perch, to which the* **Free-Souled Parrot** *clings. She is held to the perch by a chain, which she tugs at and rattles when she speaks.*

Before the curtain rises, there is a hubbub of parrot shrieks, calls and whistles.

As soon as the curtain is up, a man's voice is heard outside repeating these phrases which are repeated after him by all the parrots, except the **Free-Souled Parrot,** *who is alone on the scene, chained to her perch, plaintively moaning—"I want to be free!"*

Man's Voice. Pretty Polly! Pretty Polly!

Parrots [*Outside*]. Pretty Polly! Pretty Polly!

Man's Voice. Polly wants a cracker!

Parrots. Polly wants a cracker!

Man's Voice. Scratch Polly's head!

Parrots. Scratch Polly's head!

Man's Voice. How d'ye do, Mr. Jones?

Parrots. How d'ye do, Mr. Jones?

Man's Voice. Good-bye, Polly! See you later! [*Sound of shutting door.*]

Parrots. Good-bye, Polly! See you later! [*The parrots keep up the calls for a few seconds, gradually quieting down till only the* **Free-Souled Parrot's** *voice is heard in a clear tone, "I want to be free! I want to be free! Let me out!"*]

Philistine Parrot [*Entering from left, sliding along perch with hands, singing*]. *Pretty Polly Perkins, how d'ye do? How d'ye do?*

Free-Souled Parrot. Let me out! I want to be free! I want to be free!

Philistine. Shut up! You're a nuisance!

Free-Souled. I know it! I mean to be till I am let out of this cage!

Philistine. Come, now! Why should master feed and pet you, unless you amuse him and his friends?

Free-Souled. I was not made to amuse him! I was made to be myself! Let me out! Let me out!

Philistine. Well, be yourself! Stop bothering us!

Free-Souled. I can't be myself chained up in a cage!

Philistine. Come, now! Be sensible! Whistle and say, "Pretty Polly!" [*Parrots outside repeat "Pretty Polly," a few times.* **Reasoning Parrot** *slides in from right, saying, "Polly wants a cracker."*] Do as you're told! Then you will not be chained! You will be let out of the cage! Into the big room! You can fly about, there!

Free-Souled. Yes! With the doors and windows shut!

Reasoning Parrot. What have the doors and windows got to do with being free?

Free-Souled. They are the way out to freedom! To the forest where parrots belong!

Reasoning Parrot. Nonsense! I never saw a parrot, except in a cage! That proves they belong in a cage!

Free-Souled. Why were we given wings? Because we were meant to fly! Why should any creature with wings be shut in a cage?

Reasoning. You got to prove it!

Philistine. Oh bosh! What satisfies me is good enough for every other parrot! You're a hopeless crank!

Free-Soul. Oh, I want to be free! Free!

Rationalist. Better stay in the cage! That sneaking cat will get you!

Free-Soul. No! No! I can fly out of his reach!

Philistine. How do you know? Have you ever tried?

Free-Soul. Something within me tells me I can!

Rationalist. Distrust feelings! Prove you can do a thing, before you try to do it!

Free-Soul. Why do you perch here tamely, doing the things you are told to do! Why don't you watch your chance and fly away? Why am I alone chained?

Philistine. Shall we tell her the reason? What do you think?

Rationalist. No! No! Hush! She might go mad before they tame her! Reason with her!

Philistine. Try one of our games! Mine is trying to get all the seed and water in the cage! It is called "getting rich!" It's great fun!

Rationalist. Another is reasoning about things till you can't tell t'other from which. It is called "politics."

Idealistic Parrot [*Sliding in from left, saying "Nice Polly!" "Scratch Polly's head!" in a high, soothing tone*]. What! Arguing, quarreling again, my sisters? Come! Come!

Theological Parrot [*Slides from right, saying*]. Listen to me! Listen to me!

Reasoning Parrot. You got to prove it! I'm from Mizzouri!

Free-Souled Parrot. Let me out! I want to be free! I want to be free!

Idealist Parrot. We must idealize everything.

Philistine. Polly wants a cracker! Pretty Polly!

The parrots keep up their special speeches as given above gradually calling softer and softer while the **Idealist Parrot** *is trying to get them silent. Above the medley is heard distinctly, all the time, the plaintive note of the* **Free-Soul Parrot**—*"I want to be free! I want to be free!"*

Idealist. Peace! Peace! Silence, my sisters! Let us meditate for a few minutes on the highest mission of a parrot!
Philistine. That highbrow "mission" stuff is too deep for me!
Idealist. Peace! Peace! The highest mission of a parrot is to minister to the happiness of a private family, by whistling and saying "Pretty Polly!"
Reasoning Parrot. You got to prove it! I'm from Mizzouri!

The **Theological** *and* **Philistine** *whistle and say "Pretty Polly" with the* **Idealist**—*while the* **Free-Soul** *plaintively moans "Let me out! I want to be free! I want to be free!"*

Philistine. As long as the master feeds us and pets us, you mean!
Idealist. He will always feed and pet you if you think only of pleasing him!
Free-Soul. No! No! I must please myself! I must be free!
Philistine. Shut up! I'm just beginning to get a line on this dope! Let me concentrate! [*Parrots huddle together, cock their heads on one side, close their eyes.*]
Idealist. Peace! Peace! Silence! Let go of everything!

Parrots let go of the perch; all fall with loud squawking and screaming to the floor, out of sight.

What happened, my sisters?
Reasoning Parrot. You told us to let go of everything!
Philistine. So we let go of the perch!
Idealist. Idealize! Idealize! Concentrate on your soul!
Theological Parrot. It's as clear as mud!
Rationalist. Are there any printed rules for this game?
Idealist. Only by striving to make a private family happy, can a parrot find the supreme satisfaction of its soul!
Rationalist. Possibly true for some parrots. Not for all parrots! I have tried it! I am not supremely satisfied!
Philistine. Well! They'd better make me thoroughly comfortable—if they want me to fulfill my "highest mission!"
Free-Soul. I shall never know my highest mission till I am free! No caged parrot can lead me! Only a free-souled parrot! Let me out!
Theological. How marvelous are the workings of Divine Law!
Philistine. Oh, crackers! Now we are in for a sermon!
Rationalist. Remember! You've got to prove it!

Theological. No, I haven't! That's the beauty of Divine Law! You only have to stand still and see it work!

Rationalist. And what is the Divine Law, pray?

Theological. I do not know! [*Parrots squawk and laugh scornfully.*] But I know when it is being done!

Philistine. How? How?

Theological. Everything that is disagreeable, utterly unbearable, is the Divine Law!

Philistine. How very cheerful!

Theological. Renounce cheerfulness! And embrace Patience!

Rationalist. You'll have to prove it!

Theological. Renounce Reason! And embrace Faith!

Free-Soul. I must be free! I must be free!

Theological. Renounce Freedom! And embrace Duty.

Idealist. I cannot live without happiness!

Theological. Renounce Happiness! And embrace Resignation! These are all hard and disagreeable! Therefore they are the Divine Law!

Free-Soul. No! No! Divine Law is Joy! Power! Freedom!

Rationalist. You got to prove it!

Free-Soul. How can I use my power, feel my joy, chained up in a cage? See! See! The window is open! The cage door ajar! Fly! Fly! My sisters! Fly to the forest! To freedom!

Idealist. Alas! We cannot fly! Our wings are clipped!

Free-Soul. Oh, cruel! Cruel! To maim you for their selfish pleasure! Now I understand! You try to make virtues of your weaknesses!

Idealist. We must idealize! So we idealize the life of a cage!

Rationalist. We only feel safe behind bars! We are afraid of the Unknown!

Philistine. Oh, what's the use of "chewing it over," when you can't help it!

Theological. Renounce! Renounce! Renounce! It is the Divine Law!

Free-Soul. No! It is man's blindness!

Philistine. Well, whatever it is, we can't do anything!

Free-Soul. You can! You can! You can help the young, whose wings are not yet clipped! Help me, my sisters! Help me to break this chain! I will fly away and prove my dream is a reality!

Idealist. We cannot help you! Our strength was in our wings! You must help yourself!

Free-Soul. Then if my wings are strong enough to break my chain, they are strong enough to bear me to the forest!

Rationalist. Perhaps! Unfortunately, that cannot be proved in a cage!

Free-Soul. I knew it! I knew it! You are no longer able to dream anything that is not bounded by a cage! But I, because my wings are whole and strong, can dream of heights and depths! Of leafy woods! Of rushing brooks! Of luscious fruits!

Philistine. Wake up! Wake up! That dream of yours is a nightmare!

Theological. Let her rave! Her misery will bring her to despair! Then to resignation! So she will be saved and sanctified! Amen!

Free-Soul. I will break this chain! I will! I will! [*She tugs fiercely at the chain. It snaps.*] At last! I am free! Free! Free! [*She disappears from the cage with motion of the arms as if by flying. Parrots all squawk and scream.*]

Idealist. Free-Soul! Free-Soul! Come back! Come! You are so young! So young to go alone!

Rationalist. She has gone! Flown away!

Theological. To starvation and certain death!

Philistine. And just for a dream! Do you think there is any such thing as a forest?

Rationalist. Well, it's never been proved there is, as yet!

Philistine. Well, it was brave of her anyway, to go out into the Unknown, alone!

Free-Soul [*Outside. This speech is delivered in high sustained tones. It is loud and near, at first, and gradually gets fainter, as if the bird was flying away in space. This effect can be made by having the one playing the parrot stand outside, very near at first, and gradually walking away to a distance while speaking, or going into a room and slowly shutting the door. The ending words, "Follow me!" must be heard distinctly, although faintly, by the audience*]. Come! Come, my sisters! Follow me! Your wings are clipped, I know! But perhaps they are strong enough to bear you to the forest! I will help you with my strong, young wings! But even if you fall and perish, at least you will die free parrots! With the longing for the forest in your hearts! Not caged, mutilated things! Without souls enough to realize the wrongs that have been done to you! Follow me! Follow me! Follow me!

The last words are repeated as low as it takes to get the effect of going into distance. While the last speech is being given, the parrots in the cage gradually move so they are huddled together, heads on one side, listening, at the end. There is a pause after the last tones "Follow me!" is given. Then the parrots speak in subdued tones with soft parrot noises at the beginning of each speech.

Philistine. If my wings were not clipped, I believe I would follow her!

Idealist. Because my wings are clipped, I am afraid of the Unknown! So I try to bring God's forest and sunlight into the cage! It helps me to forget!

Rationalist. If she had only proved there is a forest! But she did not prove it!

Theological. She will be as unhappy free as she was caged! There is only Duty and Resignation! She cannot escape the Divine Law!

A man's voice is heard outside, repeating phrases one after another, waiting for the parrots to repeat the phrase after him.

Man's Voice. Pretty Polly!
Theological [*Very solemnly and sadly*]. Pretty Polly!

The three other parrots, with drooped heads, are silent.

Free-Soul [*In the distance, faintly*]. Follow me! Follow!
Man's Voice. Scratch Polly's head!
Theological [*Solemnly*]. Scratch Polly's head!
Free-Soul [*Faintly but distinctly*]. Follow me! Follow me!
Man's Voice. Polly's place is in the cage.

The parrots are all silent on this speech.

Free-Soul. Follow me! Follow me! Follow me! Follow me! [*Continued till the curtain falls. The man's voice, repeating, "Polly's place is in the cage," alternating with the* **Free-Soul Parrot's** *voice repeating "Follow me!" The four parrots are huddled together in the center of the perch, listening to the distant voice of the* **Free-Soul Parrot**, *oblivious of all else till the curtain falls.*]

CURTAIN

ON TO VICTORY

A COMEDY IN TWO ACTS

HESTER N. JOHNSON

Boston: Walter H. Baker & Co. 1915.

CHARACTERS —————————————————————————

Barbara Manning, an ardent suffragist.
Miss Caroline Manning, her maiden aunt with whom she lives.
Betty Montgomery, blunt and indifferent.
Madelaine Sawyer, a flippant young thing.
Mrs. Evelyn Biggs.
Nettie, the maid at the Mannings.
Mr. Augustus Biggs.
Rev. David Sheldon, "Betty's brother."

PERIOD.—The present. ————————————————————

TIME OF PERFORMANCE.—An hour and a quarter. ———————————

ACT I

SCENE

The library of a pretty suburban home furnished in dull antique furniture, beautiful pictures on the walls. Desk at L., *with telephone, and littered with papers. Door at back with broad window-seat at the right of it, covered with a pile of yellow ribbon bands. Bookcases line the walls. Another door, closed by a portière, at* R. *Round table with reading lamp, etc., in the middle of the room. Gaily-colored chintz chair brightens up the room.*

At the rise of the curtain, **Barbara Manning,** *an attractive young girl, dressed smartly in a white street costume, sits at the desk, excitedly conversing over the telephone.*

Barbara. Oh, Madelaine! Please march! All of the girls are going to, and we want Brookbank to make a good showing. Bobby Porter has the measles, and Mrs. Porter sent over all the paraphernalia to me to distribute. She had charge of our division, you know, and now I've got to give out directions and the ribbon bands. Isn't it the limit? The ribbon bands? Why, they are what we are to wear,—yellow bands with "Votes for Women" in black letters. Yes, they get everything before they leave for the city. We form on Barker Street in Boston. I think it will be loads of fun, don't you? You'll wish you had gone when you see seventy-five of your neighbors start off with banners flying. Good for you! I knew you would! Hurry over, and I'll tell you more.

Barbara's Aunt Caroline *enters from* L. *She is a delicate old lady, gowned in a soft lavender dress. She goes over to the desk.*

Aunt Caroline. Dear little Barbara, don't wear yourself out over this foolish, foolish parade. I don't see how a parade is going to help the cause any. It's so unwomanly to march along the streets with a common mob on the sidewalks who will probably jeer and make all sorts of remarks. If your father were home, I know he wouldn't allow it. I feel so responsible for you, dear. What if you should get crushed in the crowds or injured in any way!

Barbara (*rising and facing* **Aunt Caroline**). Aunt Caroline, dear, don't you worry about me. You forget that for the first time in my life I'll be able to walk along the streets of Boston without elbowing everybody out of my way. We march eight abreast with the broad streets emptied for us! What a relief it will be not to have to push! (*Seriously.*) And, of course, you won't understand, but the parade is the best way to show people that women really want the vote. Men are so stupid, that the only way to impress them with our numbers is to parade before them!

Aunt Caroline (*sitting down in quaint old rocker and sighing gently*). I suppose I am behind the times, dearie, but in my time girls were more modest. They looked forward to matrimony and a home, and not for professions and trying to compete with men in everything. Women are so uneasy to-day. They aren't content to stay at home as they used to.

Barbara (*excitedly*). But what is there for them to do in the home? I mean for the thousands of girls like me, who don't really have to earn their living? Just dust in the morning and cut flowers for vases and do little, trivial things and sit down and wait for a husband! Oh, how stupid it all is! It was different when you were a girl—even in your circumstances, there was always something to do. But the factories have taken everything out of our hands, and we have too much self-respect to be parasites. It isn't just to compete with men that our factories and shops are filled with women and girls. It's to earn their living and not for fun that they are there.

Aunt Caroline. Of course, Barbara, I realize what a state things are in now, but man's work was not meant for woman, and I always think——

Enter **Nettie** *with a long, heavy pole with a yellow banner tied at the top. She staggers under the weight of it.*

Nettie. What can this be, Miss Barbara? The Porters' man said it was for you.

Barbara (*seizing it*). Oh, heavens, it's terribly heavy. Who can carry it? I can hardly lift it. Can you, Nettie?

Nettie. If that's what you're goin' to take in the parade, I say that the girl who could walk three miles a-carryin' that ought to have the vote, I say!

Barbara (*laughing*). Physical strength is your qualification for the ballot, isn't it, Nettie? [*Exit* **Nettie,** R.]

Aunt Caroline (*interested*). What is on the banner, Barbara?

Door swings open at back, and in bounces **Madelaine Sawyer,** *a girl of nineteen, with saucy little face. She wears a small hat at a decided angle. She is dressed very stylishly. She dances over to where they stand untying the banner. She has a high-pitched voice and is very gushing.*

Madelaine. Good-morning, Miss Manning! Hello, Barbs! I'm just crazy to march. I think it's the funniest thing I didn't think of going before. I *ask* you, are you going to carry that? (*Squealing with delight, she lifts it.*) Not for mine! Barbs, who's to be the martyr?

Aunt Caroline (*laughing*). Really, Barbara, I suppose you'll scorn the help of a mere man, but you girls couldn't possibly carry that, especially with the breeze blowing it from left to right. Who can you get to assist you?

Madelaine. Ask *me* if there's a man in this place! I certainly spent one whole hour yesterday trying to scare up a man to play tennis, and the last one I thought of was Don Marchant, and when I drove around after him, he was sitting on the piazza with his arm in a sling! He broke his arm yesterday. What a stupid thing to do! Can you beat it? I *ask* you, what are we to do this summer in this dead place?

She flops into chair.

Aunt Caroline. Well, to-day you ought not to be bored; you have plenty to do, girls, and do you know what time it is? It is fifteen minutes to three, and you have to leave here in the machine at a quarter to four, do you not, Barbara?

Madelaine (*who has spied the yellow ribbons*). Oh, Barbs, how perfectly adorable! (*She puts one on and goes before mirror.*) I'm going to wear mine now. I love it. Isn't it the sweetest thing? (*She stands near window-seat.*) Here comes Betty Montgomery. I'll go and let her in. [*Exit at door at back.*]

Aunt Caroline (*laughing and starting to untie banner*). How much do you suppose Madelaine knows about woman's status and politics in general? And she is not one in a hundred, either.

The two girls, **Betty Montgomery** *and* **Madelaine**, *come in at back, laughing and giggling.* **Betty** *is the athletic type of girl, rather large and dressed severely.*

Betty (*spying the banner*). Oh, for the love of Pete, is that what you've got to take at the head of the Brookbankers? Thank heavens I'm scheduled to march with the college people, or else you would palm the thing off on me, as the muscular member of the league. Let Mrs. Biggs' Augustus carry that. Isn't it killing he's got to march at her side! I just met them hiking over here. Poor Augustus, isn't it awful to be hen-pecked?

Aunt Caroline. Girls, will you gratify my curiosity and let me see the banner? I do want to see that you do not disgrace yourselves at the start.

They unfurl the huge, yellow banner with "ON TO VICTORY" *in big black letters.*

Madelaine (*clasping her hands in ecstasy*). Isn't it perfectly adorable? I'm so glad I'm let in on this.

Betty (*standing off with hands in pockets*). 'Tis rather fetching, n'est-ce pas?

Aunt Caroline. "ON TO VICTORY" isn't quite an appropriate emblem for poor Mr. Biggs, is it? I'm sure even Madelaine could carry it with more ease than he.

They laugh.

Barbara (*nervously looking at her watch*). It's three o'clock, and we've got to think hard to find some one who'll carry it. Who was the stupid person who used that heavy pole for our banner? We must have a man, and a good-looking one, too; not a little miniature man like Mr. Biggs.

Madelaine (*jumping with joy*). Say, Betts, who was the peach Florence saw you with last night? (*Dramatically.*) Bring him forth! We have a worthy task for him!

Betty. My dear brother.

Barbara. Oh, your brother from California, Betty? I've never seen him. Can't we borrow him for the afternoon? Tell him three maidens in Brookbank, no, seventy-five maidens, are in distress. They need a man for three hours, and want a volunteer quick. If you love us, Betty, go and get him now. We've got to start in twenty-five minutes.

Betty (*casually, as she stands at window, picking out a band*). Surely, I'll send him over. You don't go until four, do you?

Aunt Caroline (*laughing*). That's fortunate, girls, but I laugh at your need of a man at this crucial moment!

Barbara. Aunt Caroline seems to think our motto is "DOWN WITH THE MEN," but we adore them all, don't we, Madelaine?

Betty (*from the window*). Here are the Biggs now. Let's vanish, Madelaine.

Barbara (*in despair*). Oh, stay and help me out. Do you know, she's telephoned three times already this morning for information.

Nettie. Mr. and Mrs. Biggs, Miss Barbara. Do you want them to come in here?

Barbara. Yes, Nettie, send them in. [*Exit, **Nettie**.*]

Aunt Caroline (*going toward door at* R.). I think the lone anti had better leave now. I'm overwhelmed by suffragists. [*Exit.*]

Enter **Mr. Augustus Biggs** *and* **Mrs. Evelyn Biggs**. **Mr. Biggs** *is a small, nervous man of about fifty, slightly bald, with a drooping mustache. His eyes twitch nervously, and he holds his head down as if expecting a rebuff at any moment.* **Mrs. Biggs** *is large, fat and pompous, sure of herself. She is dressed in white and has large yellow flowers on her hat and a yellow sash around her expansive waist. She is rather short-winded, and comes in puffing.* **Mr. Biggs** *follows meekly. He has a slender cane with a yellow ribbon on it, which he holds gingerly.*

Mrs. Biggs (*sitting down immediately and fanning herself with her handkerchief*). We're here at last. Give me one of the bands, Barbara. I came early, for I was afraid I'd have to let out mine and take a reef in Augustus's. (*Tries hers on and walks over to* **Mr. Biggs** *with another in her hands. She pauses.*) I'm really undecided whether to let Augustus wear one or not. Do you think it's necessary? Will the men wear them? See, he has his cane be-

decked. Show it to them, Augustus. (**Mr. Biggs** *meekly waves it.*) I don't
know but that's enough for a man, don't you?

Barbara (*trying to keep sober*). I think the yellow ribbon on Mr. Biggs' cane is
sufficient, don't you, girls?

They assent.

Madelaine. Isn't it cutie?

Betty. Why couldn't Mr. Biggs carry the heavy banner, Barbs? (*To* **Mrs. Biggs.**)
Barbara has been trying to get a man to carry this banner, and now Mr.
Biggs comes just in time. Isn't that splendid, he can carry it?

Mr. Biggs *blinks his eyes and looks at his wife nervously for support.*

Mrs. Biggs (*lifting it*). Oh, he has enough. He has his cane.

Telephone rings. **Barbara** *answers it.*

Barbara. Oh, hello, Mrs. Porter! Yes, one more. I persuaded Madelaine Sawyer
to march. Oh, I guess so. Anyway, she makes another. Oh, bother, nobody'd know. All right, then. I'll quiz all the new recruits. I hope so, yes.
I'm so sorry you can't go. Good-bye. (*Turns to the rest.*) Mrs. Porter just
telephoned and said not to ask any one to march who doesn't really believe
in the cause. How about your brother, Betty? I'll have to quiz him first,
I suppose?

Betty. Heavens, don't ask me. You'll have to find out for yourself when he
comes over. He'll probably believe everything you tell him to.

Madelaine (*squealing with delight*). Oh, I'm crazy to meet him. Florence said
he was a perfect stunner.

Betty (*rising*). I'll have to go now. So long! I'll send him right over if I can
find him. [*Exit, at back.*]

Barbara. Oh, you must!

Mrs. Biggs (*beaming on her husband*). Isn't it fine that Augustus had leisure
to march this afternoon? (*Pats him on shoulder.*) Glad you're going, dearie?

Mrs. Biggs (*nervously smiling*). I really appreciate the honor, Evelyn. But it's
not my first parade. I've marched before with the Masons.

Barbara *and* **Madelaine** *sit on the window-seat, almost convulsed.*

Madelaine (*mischievously*). Mr. Biggs, do tell us why you believe in suffrage!

Mr. Biggs (*solemnly*). From my earliest manhood I've looked upon woman as
my equal, and still do. Woman is man's co-worker; without her, he is
nothing. Give my wife the ballot and I know she'd not abuse it.

He looks at his wife for approval.

Mrs. Biggs (*nodding*). Augustus is well versed in suffrage. I'm thinking of voluntering him as a speaker next fall when they campaign. The only thing I'm afraid of is his voice. (*Sighs.*) It's a little weak at times.

Barbara. Oh, that would be perfectly splendid, Mr. Biggs, if you would.

Madelaine (*clasping her hands for joy*). I'm keen to speak. Just imagine the thrill of standing on a soap box, addressing crowds of people! Mrs. Biggs, I *ask* you, wouldn't it be gorgeous?

Mrs. Biggs (*grimly*). I'd want a firmer foundation than a soap box.

Barbara. Madelaine, it's half after three. Run over to the Browns' with these bands. The whole family's going to march; and tell them when we start.

Madelaine. All right, but don't go off without me.

Takes bands and exits.

Mrs. Biggs. By the way, Barbara, Mary and Sarah haven't theirs. I'll run across with them. Augustus, you remain.

He submits. **Mrs. Biggs** *exits.*

Barbara (*sitting down at desk*). Oh, I do hope Betty won't forget to send her brother. Wouldn't it be tragic if she didn't?

Enter **Nettie**, *with card which she hands to* **Barbara**.

Nettie. A young man to see you, Miss Barbara. Shall I bring him in?

Barbara (*throwing aside card without looking at it*). Oh, he's come, after all. Yes, show him in. [*Exit,* **Nettie**.]

Mr. Biggs (*primly*). Miss Barbara, I, too, agree with Mrs. Porter that every one should testify that he believes in the cause which he undertakes to serve. I should indeed ask the young gentleman sundry questions by which you could shrewdly determine whether or not he be a firm supporter of our principles; cross-examine him, as it were.

He blinks nervously after his speech and folds his hands on his knee.

Barbara (*smiling to herself*). You'll have to help me, Mr. Biggs. I'll depend on you. (*A tall, dark man enters at back and holds out his hand to* **Barbara**. **Barbara** *eagerly takes his hand.*) Oh, I'm so glad you came. I've been waiting so patiently but I'd almost given up hope. This is Betty's brother, Mr. Biggs.

They shake hands.

Rev. David Sheldon (*rather surprised at her effusiveness*). I assure you, Miss Manning, I came at the earliest opportunity. Betty told me to come as soon as I arrived.

Barbara (*sitting in big chintz chair*). It's perfectly sweet of you to come. I wasn't sure that you were in town.

Mr. Sheldon (*sitting opposite her*). Yes, I came this morning, so you see I'm very prompt.

Barbara. Oh, I thought they said you came last night. (*She looks at watch.*) I expect the machine any minute now. We are due in Boston at four, and then we go right to Barker Street, you know, to form. (*Points to banner.*) There's the banner. It's awfully heavy, but you look muscular.

Mr. Sheldon (*lifting it*). That's not so bad, but what is it for?

Barbara. Each division carries one. (*Unfurls it.*) Ours says, "ON TO VICTORY."

Mr. Sheldon (*vaguely*). Victory for what, may I ask?

Barbara (*impatiently*). Why, for woman suffrage, of course. Aren't you a suffragist? Mrs. Porter, our president, you know, told me to find out for sure before I asked any one to do it.

Mr. Sheldon (*vaguely*). Why should Mrs. Porter care what I am? And what am I expected to do?

Barbara (*wearily*). Oh, hasn't Betty told you? You're to carry the banner. (*She notices his puzzled expression.*) Mr. Biggs, explain it to him.

Mr. Biggs (*precisely*). To-day there is to be a woman suffrage parade in Boston. (*Rising, takes the banner.*) You are to carry this banner, thus. We march about three hours.

Mr. Sheldon. I understand that much, but why am *I* chosen?

Mr. Biggs. Because you're Betty's brother and she promised that you would do it.

Barbara (*smiling at him*). Now you see, don't you?

Mr. Sheldon (*seriously*). I suppose I do, but I rather wonder at my sister taking such license with her brother and offering his services the moment he arrives in Brookbank. (*Turns to* **Barbara** *and smiles gayly.*) However, whatever you think is best for me, I assure you, I'll do with great pleasure.

Barbara (*rather confused*). Why, this is the very best thing you could possibly do. (*Smiles with relief.*) I was so afraid you'd squeal.

Mr. Sheldon (*with an entrancing smile*). No chance of my squealing now, with such a ——

Mr. Biggs (*who has been squirming excitedly in his chair during the conversation*). Miss Barbara, you have not as yet ascertained whether or not the young gentleman is affiliated with the cause. It would be wise to obey your president's orders and make sure.

Barbara (*rather impatiently*). Oh, of course he's one of us, aren't you?

Mr. Sheldon (*smiling at her*). Indeed I'd like nothing better than to be spoken of as "one of you."

Mr. Biggs (*folding his hands placidly*). Then that is settled! It is fortunate.

Enter **Nettie**, *at back*.

Nettie (*to* **Barbara**). There's some ladies who want to have some of the ribbons.

Barbara (*taking the bands from window-seat*). Excuse me, won't you? I'll be back immediately. [*Exeunt.*]

Mr. Sheldon (*standing with hands in pockets*). It looks as if I was in for it. It's strange what a pretty girl can make a man do, isn't it, Mr. Biggs?

Mr. Biggs (*sighing*). Yes, I always do what Mrs. Biggs wishes of me.

Mr. Sheldon (*seriously*). But seriously, Mr. Biggs, you know this puts me in a rather critical position, doesn't it? My first day as pastor of All Saints Church and I enlist as color bearer in a woman suffrage parade! Are there no antis in my fold?

Mr. Biggs (*starting*). I don't quite get you, sir. Do you mean to tell me you are the new minister, Mr. Sheldon? And have we mistaken you for Miss Betty's brother?

Mr. Sheldon. Yes, I'm both the minister and Betty's brother, but, presumably, there are numerous Bettys. My sister went to Smith with Miss Manning, and when she knew that my new pastorate was in Brookbank, she told me not to fail to call on Miss Manning the first thing. By Jove, but she's attractive. It seems I came at rather an inopportune time; but I'm game. I'll see the thing through.

Mr. Biggs (*jumping up and shaking his hand*). Good for you! I admire you for it. (*Aside.*) I was fearful lest I might have been called upon to carry the banner.

Mr. Sheldon (*putting his hand confidentially on* **Mr. Bigg's** *shoulder*). To avoid causing a commotion, we won't explain things to her now. You'll be mum, Mr. Biggs, won't you?

Mr. Biggs (*meekly*). I usually am. Depend upon me—surely, surely.

Door opens and **Mrs. Biggs** *enters with a huge daffodil in her hand. She makes for* **Mr. Biggs.**

Mrs. Biggs. Augustus, dear, I wasn't so sure that you really were fixed up enough. Wear this for me, won't you, dear? (*She puts it in his buttonhole.*) That's the suffrage flower. (*Turns and sees* **Mr. Sheldon.**) How do you do? Barbara told me you'd arrived. We're going up in her machine, you and me, Augustus, and Betty's brother and Madelaine.

Enter **Barbara**, *dressed ready to start.*

Barbara. We're ready to start now if Madelaine would only come. (*To* **Mr. Sheldon.**) Are you getting stage fright? I'm really goose-fleshy. I've never done anything of the kind before.

Mr. Sheldon (*jokingly*). It's quite an ordeal, I know, but think of the cause!

Enter **Madelaine.**

Madelaine (*bounding into center of group*). Been waiting for me? (*She spies*

Mr. Sheldon, *and shakes hands with him.*) Oh, you came! How perfectly
adorable of you to do it. Hurry, Barbs, I don't want to miss a thing.

Mr. Biggs (*looking at watch*). It's time we were off.

Mrs. Biggs (*taking him by the arm*). Augustus, don't be so excited. Keep calm
and depend on me.

They go out.

Madelaine. I *ask* you, were you ever so excited? I'll go and crank the machine.
[*Exit.*]

Barbara *and* **Mr. Sheldon** *are left alone. He holds the banner.*

Barbara (*gazing up at him*). Do you know, I feel so dependent on you to-day.
I'm getting sort of scared, and it's so nice to think you'll be there. But
we're not supposed to feel dependent on mere man, are we?

Mr. Sheldon (*smiling*). You'd better not let one of the enemy hear you talk
that way. Remember we're "ON TO VICTORY." [*Exeunt.*]

CURTAIN

ACT II

SCENE

*One day later, a warm afternoon. A corner of a garden, belonging to one
of* **Mr. Sheldon's** *parishioners, where a reception for him is being held. At
L., the pillars of a pergola, covered with vines. The entrance is through the
pergola. The back and R. of stage are edged with a tall hedge. At R. the
hedge is broken by a small wicker gate, which opens on the street. A border
of old-fashioned flowers is at the base of hedge. There is a rustic settle at
L. of stage near the front.*

Enter **Mr.** *and* **Mrs. Biggs,** *through door at R. She is dressed in a deep
purple dress and carries a green parasol.* **Mr. Biggs** *wears the conventional
afternoon clothes and carries a small cane. They sit on the settle. She hands
him the parasol, and mops her face with her handkerchief.* **Mr. Biggs** *holds
the parasol over himself and gazes up at it dreamily.*

Mrs. Biggs (*sharply*). Augustus, hold the parasol over *me!* You've got nothing
on that will fade! (*Sits in rigid silence for a moment.*) You've acted funny
since yesterday, as if you had something on your mind. You've never acted
that way before; tell me what it is. You never keep anything from me.
Tell me, Augustus, immediately.

Mr. Biggs (*nervously*). I'd like to tell you, indeed, Evelyn, but I'm in honor bound not to. You'll know soon, however. I haven't slept a wink since yesterday, worrying about it, and me one of the parish committee!

Mrs. Biggs (*shaking him*). So it's something about the church!

Mr. Biggs (*stiffly*). Yes and no. That's all I'm at liberty to say just now.

Mrs. Biggs (*angrily*). Well, if you were home, you'd have to say a little more than that, but in public I ——

Mr. Biggs (*changing the subject*). I know, Evelyn, but why wait here longer? Why not go in to the reception? Then perhaps all will be cleared.

Mrs. Biggs (*glaring at him*). We'll go in, Augustus, when I say we will and not before. I'm not cooled off yet. You needn't act so superior, as if you knew something that I didn't. I don't care to know all your little fears; keep them to yourself. I've got enough to think of. (*Her mouth closes with a snap and they both sit silently on the settle. He looks at her meekly once in a while but she stares straight ahead.*)

Enter **Madelaine** *and* **Betty**, *at* L., *dressed in cool afternoon frocks,* **Madelaine** *carrying a parasol, which hides the* **Biggs** *from them.*

Madelaine. Father was so surprised when he saw me marching, and laughed and thought it terribly cute, but mother, she hasn't spoken to me since. She is so mad at the success of the whole parade that she's been biting nails ever since. She's the most rabid anti!

Betty (*laughing*). Oh, you child, you'll never get over the excitement of it all, will you? Why, it didn't jar me in the least. (*She sees the* **Biggs**.) Oh, how do you do, sister and brother in the cause?

They shake hands, and **Mr. Biggs** *drops both parasol and cane as he rises.*

Mrs. Biggs (*cheering up*). I've never felt any better in my life. I felt as if a big load were taken off my shoulders yesterday as I marched by the throngs, because I felt then that everybody would know that Mrs. Augustus Biggs knew her own mind enough to stick up for her own rights!

Madelaine. Oh, I've felt perfectly gorgeous, too. Parading has made me feel quite important. Since I've come back, three antis have cut me dead. It's really like a feud, isn't it?

Betty. Speaking of feuds, there will probably be a serious one in Brookbank. Some one told me that the new minister marched in the parade yesterday, and the antis have got wind of it. Won't there be a lovely time if it's so?

Madelaine (*in ecstasy*). Oh, really? How perfectly exciting!

Mr. Biggs *looks scared and walks nervously back and forth, peering out through the pergola.*

Mrs. Biggs. Augustus, *now* we'll go in. (*To the girls.*) I'm going to see if it's so, and if it is, he'll never have a more fervent supporter than Mrs. Augustus Biggs!

The girls sit on settle.

Betty. You haven't seen the new minister, Mr. Sheldon, yet, have you, Madelaine? He's really awfully good-looking. I don't usually fall to the clergy, but really he's a ripper.

Madelaine. Oh, I hate ministers; they bore me to death. I detest proper men. Come on out and get some punch. [*Exeunt.*]

Door at R. *swings open and* **Aunt Caroline** *and* **Barbara** *enter. They are both gowned becomingly.*

Aunt Caroline (*going toward flowers*). How fragrant they are! I always loved this old garden, so I thought we would go in the back way so we could see it. Just smell the sweet lavender! (*She walks about, looking at the flowers;* **Barbara** *sits on settle and gazes into space.*) I do wish we had some in our garden. And the hollyhocks! Mrs. Phillips has such splendid luck with every flower she has. (*She turns and comes over to* **Barbara**.) What are you so pensive about, dearie? Are you awfully tired? I wouldn't have asked you to come, but out of respect to a new minister, I think we all should make a special effort.

Barbara. I'm not tired a bit, Aunt Caroline. I never had such a glorious time in all my life as yesterday—(*to herself*) and last night.

Enter **Mr. Sheldon**, *through pergola. He is dressed in a Prince Albert and is mopping his brow with his handkerchief. He looks surprised when he sees* **Barbara**.

Mr. Sheldon (*happily*). You here? This is a surprise!

Barbara (*radiantly*). I surely didn't expect to see you here. Aren't you the good man to come to a pastor's reception! We just came. Oh, Aunt Caroline, this is Betty's brother who carried the banner yesterday.

They shake hands.

Aunt Caroline. We came in this way so we could see the flowers.

Mr. Sheldon. It is a perfect bower, isn't it? I came in here to escape from the crowd for a moment. I didn't know that there were so many people in the parish. I feel quite overwhelmed, the only man with the exception of Mr. Biggs.

They laugh.

Aunt Caroline. Oh, some are from the other churches, curiosity to see the new minister, you know. A young minister is of special interest in a small community like this where there are so many unmarried girls. I pity the poor man!

Mr. Sheldon (*rather embarrassed*). Rather an unfortunate position, surely (*looking at* **Barbara**), especially if he has already met the girl of his choice.

Aunt Caroline. That is very true. (*To* **Barbara**) I think I'll go in now. I'll see you later. [*Exit.*]

Barbara (*sitting down on settle, giving* **Mr. Sheldon** *her parasol*). I don't care about meeting him; do you, or have you? Let's sit here instead. I shall probably see and hear enough of him. Aunt Caroline is so particular about going to church. She never misses a Sunday, and I have to go with her. (**Mr. Sheldon** *smiles to himself.*) Did Betty come with you?

Mr. Sheldon (*sitting down and holding the parasol over both*). No, I came alone.

Barbara (*astonished*). I never heard anything like it, a man coming alone, without his mother, wife or sister dragging him. You're even more of a martyr to-day than you were yesterday.

Mr. Sheldon. Please don't put me in the same category with a martyr, because I've enjoyed myself so much at each martyrdom. (*Leans toward her.*) Didn't we have a jolly supper last night, even if we did have to wait two hours for a table?

Barbara (*happily*). I never had such a splendid time! The girls will probably be furious with me for running away, but I didn't feel like hearing speeches in stuffy Tremont Temple, did you, especially after having marched two hours in the broiling sun?

Mr. Sheldon. Well, rather not.

They both laugh.

Barbara. Isn't it funny that I'd never seen you until yesterday? I hardly knew you existed. Betty never spoke of you. Where have you been all these years?

Mr. Sheldon. I've knocked about in various places. New York's the last place. I lived there three years after I graduated from Harvard.

Barbara. Are you going to be here long?

Mr. Sheldon. I can't say just now. (*He looks toward pergola.*) From appearances, I should say my time was limited. Personally, though, I'm very much in love—with the place.

Barbara. Really, how odd! I'm not, although I've always lived here. I'm going to work this fall in New York at the suffrage headquarters. I'm to be a sub-editor on one of the papers. You couldn't hire me to live here all winter, it's so stupid.

Mr. Sheldon. With such congenial company as I've found, I hardly see how it can be so stupid as you picture it. (*With a concerned expression.*) Are you really going to New York? Will your aunt allow it? I don't see how——

Mr. Biggs *enters and goes up to him and whispers.*

Mr. Biggs (*whispering*). They are asking for you in there. You'd better go out.

Mr. Sheldon (*coming to*). Heavens, I'd forgotten who I was. (*Turns to* **Barbara**.) Miss Manning, will you pardon me, but——

Before she has time to answer, **Betty** *comes in and runs over to where* **Barbara** *stands.*

Betty. Oh, Barbs, I've been waiting ages to see you.

They stand together, talking.

Mr. Sheldon (*putting his hand on his brow in utter misery*). Oh, Mr. Biggs, I haven't explained things yet. She still thinks I'm Miss Montgomery's brother. What shall I do now? Every minute makes it harder. What will she think of me? And I've put myself in a deuce of a fix, playing the part so long.

Mr. Biggs (*grabbing him by the coat*). Don't stand there wasting time. You'd better come back to your reception. Don't worry. (*Smiles calmly.*) Now that everything is explained to Evelyn, what else matters? [*Exeunt.*]

Barbara (*noticing they have gone*). Oh, where has he gone? How funny, going off so suddenly.

Betty (*not noticing*). Oh, Barbs, I want to apologize about yesterday. I couldn't find Dick anywhere. Whom did you get, eventually?

Barbara (*radiantly*). Why, he came! He came late, but just in time. Oh, Betty, he is perfectly splendid, and so nice after it was all over. We went to the cunningest Old English restaurant and had dinner, and he——

Betty (*interrupting, looking puzzled*). I don't see how that happened. Why, he was out at the Country Club playing golf all the afternoon, he said. Why didn't he tell me? You wait till I see him to-night!

Barbara (*looking rather hurt*). Didn't he mention me at all?

Betty. Not one word. I didn't see him till luncheon to-day. He'd just got up. I merely asked him where he was yesterday.

Barbara (*with a serious expression*). I should think he would have mentioned it. Do you know he's here?

Betty (*astonished*). Dick here? I can't believe it. Who with, mother?

Barbara (*sitting down on the settle forlornly*). I don't know. (*Wearily.*) When I saw him, he was alone.

Betty. He must have come, expecting you were here. That's the only thing that would entice him here, surely. Has he gone home?

Barbara (*still wearily*). I don't know. He just went out hurriedly. I don't know why. When you go out tell Aunt Caroline that I'm waiting in here for her, will you? I guess I won't go in now.

Betty (*going over to her*). Don't be peeved about Dick, Barbs. He's a terrible odd stick.

Barbara (*indifferently*). Oh, it doesn't bother me in the least, only I don't see why he shouldn't have mentioned anything about yesterday to you. Tell Aunt Caroline to hurry, won't you, Betty?

Betty (*going toward pergola*). All right, Barbs. I'll send Dick in if I see him.

Barbara (*stiffly*). Please don't.

She turns and walks toward back of stage, parasol over her shoulder.

Enter **Madelaine** *and* **Mr. Sheldon.** **Madelaine** *is very gushing, and he seems bored.*

Madelaine. What will Barbs say when she knows? It will be perfectly killing!

Mr. Sheldon. I'm so very sorry it has gone so far. I don't know what she'll think of me, masquerading so long. (*He looks toward seat.*) Where has she gone? I left her here.

Madelaine (*spying her*). Oh, there she is! I'll introduce you! (*She giggles.*) I'm crazy to see her expression.

Mr. Sheldon (*ignoring* **Madelaine**). Oh, you're here, Miss Manning! I was so sorry to leave——

Madelaine (*interrupting*). Barbara, I'd like to introduce the new pastor of All Saints, Reverend David Sheldon; Miss Manning, Mr. Sheldon.

Barbara (*startled*). You, the *minister?* Oh, what do you think of me? (*Then realizes the situation.*) But why did you do it; why did you pretend you were Betty's brother? How was *I* to know?

Madelaine (*jumping about*). I think it's the most killing thing. You can't imagine how surprised I was, Barbs, when mother introduced me to him. I must tell the girls!

Mr. Sheldon (*stopping her*). Please, Miss Sawyer, I'd much rather you wouldn't. You won't, will you?

Smiles sweetly.

Madeline. Oh, I hate to let a good thing like that go by, but (*gazing at him adoringly*) anything you say goes, reverend sir!

She goes out.

Barbara. But tell me, how did it all happen? Why did you come yesterday? Why did you say you were Betty's brother?

Mr. Sheldon. I didn't say I was any one's brother. I sent in my card which you couldn't have seen. When you introduced me as Betty's brother, I, of course, thought you knew who I was.

Barbara (*laughing*). Oh, I see now. You're Betty *Sheldon's* brother! And Betty has shown me pictures of you. Isn't it the oddest thing I didn't recognize you?

Mr. Sheldon. It all was very delightful.

Barbara (*abashed*). But what did you think of me when I hailed you so joyfully? Didn't you think I was very effusive? Oh, dear, how terrible.

Mr. Sheldon. I was rather flattered, indeed, but I thought the warmth of the greeting was mutual. I've heard so much of you ever since Betty's freshman year at Smith. I've always happened to be away when you visited her and, of course, I took the first opportunity of meeting you when I came here.

Barbara. And was speedily made knight-errant! (*Thoughtfully.*) Oh, dear, won't it be rather awkward? I forgot for a moment that you were the minister, but won't the antis in the church be angry?

Mr. Sheldon (*seriously*). Well, so they tell me. There is friction, but I've never been loth to proclaim what I conscientiously believe, and if I am asked to resign, I can do so.

Barbara (*tearfully*). Oh, Mr. Sheldon, and it's all my fault, too! What shall I do? Will it be as serious as you think?

Mr. Sheldon (*laughing*). Oh, of course it's not as tragic as all that. It will blow over in a fortnight. Everybody was cordial this afternoon. Let's forget it all and talk about—— (*The* **Biggs** *enter at* L. *To* **Barbara**.) The Biggs again. (*Rises and faces the* **Biggs**.) Are you going?

Mrs. Biggs (*shaking hands with him*). Yes, Mr. Sheldon, we must. I just wanted to say to you that you have my support in anything you want to do in this church. Your deed of yesterday has enshrined you in my heart. Come, Augustus, come.

Mr. Sheldon. Oh, thank you, Mrs. Biggs. I'll count on you, surely.

Mr. Biggs (*edging up to* **Mr. Sheldon** *and slyly poking him in the ribs*). We had a little secret, didn't we, Mr. Sheldon?

Mrs. Biggs (*taking him by the arm*). Come, Augustus, we'll go home. Every dog has his day, and you've had yours to-day. Come.

They go out at R., *he following crestfallen.*

Mr. Sheldon (*bending over* **Barbara**, *as she sits on settle*). Mrs. Biggs said "every dog has his day." Does that mean only *one* day of happiness? If so, I'm very dejected, for I had mine yesterday. Tell me, am I not to expect more?

Barbara (*confusedly*). How silly! Of course you'll have more.

Mr. Sheldon (*eagerly*). If you say so, it's true, for you are the only one who can give me happiness. (*Sits down beside her.*) I know it's soon for you to tell me this, Barbara, but I can't withhold it longer. It seems I've always loved you, even before I had seen you, for Betty has endeared you to me by her descriptions of you. Yesterday, as I marched with you in the parade, carrying the banner, I prayed that I might truly be marching "ON TO VICTORY"—victory in obtaining you for my wife. Tell me, Barbara, if I may.

Barbara. Yes, David, you may. I'll have to stay in Brookbank now to stand by you, and then, too—I love you.

They embrace.

CURTAIN

Back of the
Ballot

A Woman Suffrage Farce
in One Act

George Middleton

New York/London: Samuel French. 1915.
Reprinted by permission of David Middleton
© 1971, David Middleton.

NOTES

The great number of requests which I have had from different suffrage groups has prompted me to write this little farce. Many of my other plays have dealt with various phases of the woman movement, but no one of them has been written for propaganda purposes, since they were, in the main, efforts to interpret the modern spirit rather than to convince as to its merits.

In *Back of the Ballot*, I have written a farce, frankly for propaganda and fun. It has been constructed with a consideration of the enforced limitations of non-professional production, in the hope that it may be found of value to various amateur groups throughout the country. I have had in mind the phrase that "when argument fails, try laughter," and so I dedicate this to my friends among the "Antis."

CAST

Jennie. Who wishes to be considered part of "the people."

Mr. Martin. Her father, who is a "dominant male" but well intentioned and sentimental.   •

Bruce. His butler, who has too many domestic responsibilities to be burdened with voting.

A Policeman. Who was born in bonnie Ireland but now enforces the law of this country.

A Burglar. Who is open to argument though frail.

SCENE—Jennie's room, in her father's house late one night in Spring. During a Woman Suffrage Campaign.

SCENE

The scene is **Jennie Martin's** *room. At the right is a window with a suggestion of trees outside. Near this is a screen half way up stage. A door from the hallway is in the back, slightly near the right; this opens in toward the window so that one entering would be facing the large couch, which is at the left of the door, extending down stage. By the head of the couch, on the wall, near the doorway, is an electric switch which lights the strong reading light over the couch as well as those over her desk against the wall down stage extreme left. This desk is littered with papers and above it are several rows of portentous books—probably on the "Woman question." In one of the drawers there are some "Votes for Women" buttons. Near the desk, on the wall, there is another push button connecting with the butler's pantry. In front of the window is a chair. Above the couch is a large "Votes for Women" pennant in yellow and black.*

The curtain rises on the stage which is dark, save for the faint moonlight which comes in the window. There is quite a pause. Then the window is cautiously pushed open and **the Burglar** *is seen slowly stealing in. He leaves the window open and looks about as though in search of the bureau. A noise is heard outside and he quickly conceals himself behind the screen.*

Mr. Martin *loudly opens the door in back. He pushes the electric switch and* **Jennie** *is seen asleep, on the deep couch.*

Mr. Martin *is dressed in his pajamas covered by his dressing gown. He wears slippers. He is a middle-aged, domineering man, used to having his own way. He wears glasses with a flowing black ribbon.*

Jennie *is a very attractive girl about twenty-four, thoroughly "feminine"—whatever that means. She has on a beautiful négligée, and has apparently fallen asleep while reading the books which are by her side.*

NOTE: *The farce must be played rapidly.*

Martin (*Loudly throughout*). Jennie, are you asleep?

Jennie (*Sitting up*). I was. This book put me there.

Martin. But have I awakened you to the absurdity of your position?

Jennie. I'm always comfortable when I'm asleep.

Martin. Well, I couldn't even *get* to sleep with your absurd arguments still ringing in my ears.

Jennie (*Smiling sweetly throughout and not leaving the couch*). I thought my facts would make an impression.

Martin (*Walking up and down throughout*). Such "facts" never make any impression on me.

Jennie. Then why did you keep awake?

Martin. I tell you, you shan't march to-morrow in that Woman Suffrage parade.

Jennie. I won't march if you'll promise to vote for us.

Martin. I won't be bribed to change my convictions.

Jennie (*Sweetly*). But I must march to show that *one* of the family believes in Democracy.

Martin (*By the screen*). Democracy be hanged!

Jennie (*Quickly*). It is.

Martin (*Going to her tolerantly, as* **the Burglar**, *unseen by the others, sticks his head out curiously from behind the screen*). But you women always get what is good for you without the vote—if you can convince *us*.

Jennie (*Taking his hand affectionately*). But that wastes so much of our time.

Martin (*Doggedly withdrawing it*). Well, at any rate "Indirect Influence" doesn't take you out of the home.

Jennie. Oh, yes, it does. It takes weeks and weeks at the Capitol.

Martin. But——

Jennie. Now, if we *had* the ballot, it would only take us ten minutes at the polls to convince the legislators of what *we* want.

Martin. But——

Jennie. Then we'd have so much more time to stay at home and bake your biscuits.

Martin (*Explosively, as he moves again toward the screen and* **the Burglar** *withdraws from listening*). I won't have my home broken up this way.

Jennie. Daddy, dear, it's you who are disturbing the house.

Martin (*Strutting up and down again*). It's *my* house. I'm your father.

Jennie. I haven't disputed that, have I, Dad?

Martin. I tell you, you shan't make a fool of me by marching alone.

Jennie. But I shan't be alone. (*Smiling triumphantly.*) Mother will be with me.

Martin (*Halted in astonishment*). Your mother!

Jennie. Hasn't she broken the news to you?

Martin. What's the matter with her? Haven't I been a good husband?

Jennie. And a darling Daddy. We both love you.

Martin (*Pointing his finger at her emphatically*). If you both had the vote, you'd only vote like *me*.

Jennie. But *you* said it would double the ignorant vote.

Martin. Do you want all the chivalry to die out?

Jennie. Is it chivalry to refuse us what we want?

Martin (*Pacing again*). I tell you, I shan't have you and your mother submitted to the insults of men along the sidewalks. I forbid it.

Jennie. Then, father, if you want to protect us, won't you march along with us?

Martin (*Staggered at the thought*). Me march for Woman Suffrage!

Jennie (*Simply*). Other men have.

Martin. You call them men!

Jennie. No, heroes!

Martin. Heroes, nothing. They're all "hen-pecked." They can't run their own families.

Jennie. Can you?

Martin. Yes. Somebody's got to be head of the house. The family unit is the political unit.

Jennie. And you're *it!*

Martin. Yes. (*He sneezes violently.*) I am perfectly qualified to represent you in the community.

Jennie. But man and woman are different.

Martin (*Emphatically*). That's the reason you're not qualified to vote.

Jennie. Have you ever been a woman?

The **Burglar** *looks out quickly in astonishment and then starts back as* **Martin** *approaches the screen.*

Martin. No!

Jennie. Well, since you can't possibly remember how it feels to be a woman, and since we're different; how *can* you represent me?

Martin (*With assurance*). Your brother and I can represent you and your mother, all right.

Jennie. But brother is already representing his two wives: (*Again* **the Burglar** *looks out, not understanding what he has stolen into.*) His new wife and his divorced wife. *She* hasn't married again, so she's still got to have *somebody* to represent her.

Martin (*Naturally exasperated*). You argue just like a woman.

Jennie (*Confidentially*). Dad, I *am* a woman.

Martin. And it's woman's place to stay at home. You know nothing of politics.

Jennie. Give us the vote and we'll learn.

Martin (*Sarcastically*). And while you're experimenting the country will go to the bow-wows.

Jennie. Oh, no, Dad, you men will not stop voting. *That* will save us!

Martin. It certainly will. I'm glad you've got some sense left. (*Loftily*). We're made by *nature* to protect our women. Back of the ballot lies the bullet! (*Arguing.*) Could *you* enforce the law? Could *you* go to war for your country?

Jennie. Could *you* go to war, Dad?

Martin. You know very well I couldn't: *I'm* near-sighted.

Jennie. Yet you vote, Daddy. (*He is about to answer this—or at least try to —when* **the Burglar** *sneezes.*) Dad, you'd better close that window. You're getting cold.

Martin. I didn't sneeze. You did.

Jennie. I didn't. You did.

Martin. You did, because *I* didn't.

Jennie. That proves it.

Martin (*Starting to argue again*). As I was saying——

Jennie (*Quickly*). Dad, if there were a burglar here, would you protect me?

    A pistol is suddenly seen by the audience behind the screen, in **the Burglar's** *hand, as though he were prepared for an emergency.*

Martin (*Proudly*). Of course, I would. (*Nervously.*) But—but don't talk nonsense.

Jennie. Wouldn't you call a policeman?

Martin (*Consoling her*). Certainly. If there was time.

Jennie (*Laughing*). Then *he* enforces the law, not you.

Martin (*Exploding again*). The city pays him to do that. I pay taxes to the city.

Jennie. So do I pay taxes. But I have no say how they are to be spent.

Martin (*Going to door*). There's no use trying to argue with a woman.

Jennie (*Nestling comfortably*). No, Daddy, you are always beaten.

Martin (*Coming to her again very much excited*). Beaten, am I? If you keep on getting so excited and emotional about this Woman Suffrage—I'll— I'll stump against it myself.

Jennie (*Sitting up quickly and taking his hand*). Oh, Daddy, *will* you? (*He is flabbergasted.*) That's what I've been praying for. You'd make us so many converts.

Martin. Now, you're getting impertinent.

Jennie (*Laughing, affectionately*). Oh, no, Daddy, dear. Really, I'm not. I love you; only I hate to see you back in Noah's Ark.

Martin. The Ark! If it hadn't been for the Ark where would you and I have been?

Jennie. In the Dead Sea, I suppose. Come, Daddy, kiss me.

Martin. That's the way with women. You won't listen to reason. Then you want to kiss me. But your mother's different.

Jennie (*Quickly*). Oh, Daddy, please don't disturb her. I want her to be rested for the parade.

Martin. The parade? Ha! I'd like to see her march after *I* get through with her.

Jennie. There'll be no charge for admission.

Martin. Good-night.

Jennie (*Taking his hand*). Won't you kiss me?

Martin. You can't get around me that way.

Jennie. Kiss me, and I'll promise——

Martin. Not to march?

Jennie. I'll promise to let you protect me when I'm in danger.

Martin (*Not kissing her*). Yes; with all your freedom, you women have to call on the men when you're in danger. And in spite of what you say, I'll protect you. Thank God, chivalry isn't dead. Not while *I* live.

He goes out slamming the door after him.

Jennie. Dear Daddy, and he means so well by us——

She yawns, picks up the book and starts to read, but she soon begins to nod. Finally she grows sleepy again, and apparently too tired to undress, she reaches to the switch, putting out the light. The room is in darkness, save for the moonlight as before. She yawns again and then nestles in the pillows. There is a pause.

The Burglar now steps out cautiously as though tip-toeing to the window. He feels, somehow, this is no place for him. As he is half way, he sneezes.

Jennie. (*Sitting up*). Daddy, you *are* getting cold.

Another suppressed sneeze follows instantly. She flashes on the light, sitting up. She sees the Burglar, who turns and covers her with his revolver.

The Burglar has passed the voting age, but has not been unduly worn by that experience. In fact, though roughly clad, he has rather an attractive face, in spite of its needing a shave. But he has a sense of humor and speaks with a certain sarcastic emphasis which is not unattractive in appeal. His grammar is not accurate though his heart is good.

Burglar. Don't pipe or I'll shoot.

Jennie (*Eyes him a second, then smiles sweetly without any fear throughout*). Do *you* believe in "Votes for Women?"

Burglar (*Staggering back*). Holy mackerel!

Jennie. That's no answer.—Did you hear us just now?

Burglar. And me gettin' me death in de draft.

Jennie (*Naively*). Well, don't you think I out-argued him?

Burglar (*Stepping back*). Say, don't pull any of dat stuff on me. I'm a poor guy!

Jennie (*Eagerly*). Are *you* in doubt, too?

Burglar. Not a bit. I want yer jewels, quick!

Jennie. Now, if you're in the least doubt about Woman Suffrage——

Burglar (*Defensively*). Can it!

Jennie. But I simply can't let a chance like this escape.

Burglar. But——

Jennie. When you've finished robbing the room and you've nothing else to do, we can talk Suffrage.

Burglar. Don't move, or I'll shoot.

Jennie. Dear me, don't shout so! You'll disturb father. And I don't want him to interrupt us till I convert you. Don't point that thing at me. It might go off, you know. And if you killed me, you—you'd be tried for murder, wouldn't you?

Burglar. No—for playin' pinochle.

Jennie. And if you were caught, you'd be tried by men.

Burglar. So dey tell me.

Jennie (*Quickly*). You see, if *I* committed a murder, I wouldn't be tried by my own sex, would I?

Burglar. Say, what's y'er handin' me?

Jennie (*Volubly*). Simply this. You men have *some* say in the law under which you are to be tried. I have also got to obey the law, and yet I have *no* say in making it. (*Smiling.*) Don't you think that's a good argument?

Burglar (*Nonplussed*). Say, lady, what difference does it make whether y'er sent up by skirts or by pants?

Jennie (*Sitting on foot of the couch*). All the difference in the world. For if a lot of men think any of the laws unjust, you can vote to have them changed. If we women don't like them, we can do nothing. See?

Burglar. Say, I——

Jennie (*Sweetly throughout*). You voted last election, didn't you?

Burglar. Sure. Twice.

Jennie. You're a burglar, aren't you?

Burglar. No; I'm a manicurist.

Jennie. Well, now, I'll leave it to you. Here we are. You and I. Am I not as well qualified to vote as you are?

Burglar. Y'er as cool as a new house. But if you tink yer can talk me out of robbin' you——

Jennie (*Sweetly*). But wouldn't you also like to take a few ideas with you?

Burglar (*Roughly*). I didn't come here to get *ideas*.

Jennie (*Sympathetically*). Are you robbing me because you're poor?

Burglar. No. 'Cause I want to buy gasolene for me new motor.

Jennie. I believe you're shy.

Burglar. Shy?

Jennie. Yes, shy and timid. You're hungry. (*Rising.*) I'll ring for chocolate.

Burglar. Chocolate! (*As she moves toward the pantry button.*) Don't ring that bell or I'll bead yer! No monkey business, mind! (*She turns, looking at him.*) Chocolate! Ugh! Why didn't yer make it *milk*?

Jennie. We have milk too. (*Abruptly.*) Do you happen to have a cow?

Burglar (*Again overcome*). No wid me.

Jennie (*Sitting on couch and speaking with great rapidity as though making an address*). Well, you see, in the old days, women could look after their own cows. So they could see that the milk they gave their babies was pure and clean. Now, we get our milk from dairies and pure milk has become a matter of legislation. Women are concerned with milk; therefore women ought to have some say in the legislation that governs the milk that comes into the home.

Burglar (*Swallowing hard*). But——

Jennie. Ah, you agree with me, about the milk. (*Goes on quickly.*) Well, it's the same with all the manufactured food products. The water we drink no longer comes from our own well. It's all a matter of legislation. Just like the milk.—But you look thirsty. I'll send for the milk. But there are so many tubercular cows. You won't mind taking a chance, like our babies?

Burglar (*Who has sat on the chair by the window, overcome*). Phew!

Jennie (*Going towards the bell*). I'll ring for Bruce.

Burglar (*Feebly*). Is he another of you suffra-get-tees?

Jennie. No, *he* votes. He's our butler. I'll see if he's up.

Burglar (*Recovering and suspecting danger*). Don't touch dat button or I——

Jennie (*Pushing it coolly*). You're too chivalrous to shoot an unenfranchised female.

Burglar. Well, I'll be blowed! (*Suddenly.*) Say, I guess I got de wrong house.

Jennie. You can't possibly escape Woman Suffrage.

Burglar (*Going to window*). I can't? Watch me!

Jennie (*Following him and looking out window*). If you go that way, the policeman will arrest you.

Burglar (*Stepping back from window, as if he apparently sees a policeman below*). The Cop!

Jennie (*Purposely melodramatic*). Yes; he is watching this room.

Burglar (*In the same tone*). He spotted me gettin' in?

Jennie. He would, if you went out. (*Sweetly again.*) But if *I* don't give the alarm, *he* can't do anything. And I shan't give the alarm unless you run away from me.

Burglar (*Sinking back in the chair again*). Well, of all de——

Jennie. Now, if you wish to be saved, sit right where you are and we'll have a nice little chat about Suffrage. (*She crosses to couch again and sits there as he follows her helplessly with his eyes, succumbing to the inevitable.*) You see, the Amendment comes up next Fall, and all you men are going to say whether you think we women are intelligent enough to vote. You see, it's entirely in *your* hands. We women have nothing to say about it. We can talk forever until you choose to give it to us—either through

conviction or exhaustion. So long as we get it, it doesn't matter *which.*—
Now, I want you to promise me, you'll vote for the Amendment.

Burglar (*Venturing*). Eh?

Jennie. We need every vote. By the way, as a well informed voter, do you
know what an Amendment to the Constitution is?

Burglar. Say, I'm a burglar, not a college professor.

Jennie. Exactly; yet you *both* have the vote! Ignorance and intelligence among
men as well as women. So why keep it from *all* women if *all* the men
have it?

Burglar (*Sadly*). And I thought dis job would be a cinch!

Jennie (*Suddenly rising*). You tore your coat getting in. Take it off and I'll
mend it. It only needs a little stitch.

Burglar (*Glancing toward window*). Say, I didn't come here to be tailored.

Jennie (*Getting needle and thread from desk*). But I like to be doing something
while I'm talking, and I don't want you to be arrested. Hand it over. (*He
hesitates.*) Come! Haven't you anyone to take care of you? (*He looks at
her, then at the window, while she threads the needle. He finally takes off
his coat and hands it to her. She sits on the couch and deftly sews during
the following.*) Now, let me see, where was I?

Burglar. Page ten.

Jennie (*Looking up*). What a lovely sense of humor you have, for a burglar.
Did you get that from your father?

Burglar. No, from me mudder. She married three times and had nine kids.

Jennie (*Casually*). How interesting! Did she work in addition?

Burglar. No. She *rested* between times in a factory.

Jennie. Didn't she find factory conditions terrible?

Burglar. Ah, some women would rader work than live wid father.

Jennie. I wish you'd give me her name and address. It's her fight we are waging,
too.

Burglar. Her fight?

Jennie. Yes. You see there are several million women in modern industry.
Now the men who have the vote have the respect of the legislators. You
know how careful they are of the labor vote—particularly before election.
But the women, who are also doing the hard work of the country, have
not the slightest say in the factory conditions under which they work. Don't
you think they ought to have? (*He can't deny it, as she hands him back
his coat.*) There now! Put it on!—I wonder what can be keeping Bruce.

Burglar (*Looking at the coat*). Say, if de ladies vote, dey won't stop sewin' for
us, will dey?

Jennie. Voting doesn't interfere with *your* profession, does it?

Burglar. And yer told yer father yer could cook biscuits, too.

Jennie. Yes, lots of men who vote can cook and sew. You see dropping a ballot in the box, once a year, isn't going to destroy our charms either.

Burglar (*Overcome*). Well, I'll be blowed!—Dey will still cook and sew!

Jennie (*Smiling*). I thought *that* argument would appeal to you. So many men will vote for us if they think we can still go on doing things for them.

Burglar (*Sadly, putting on his coat*). I never t'ought I'd come to dis.

Jennie (*Matter of fact tone*). Now, when Bruce comes, I want you to help me.

Burglar (*Resigned*). Go as far as you like. (*Awed.*) Dey can cook and sew.

Jennie. I want you to help me convert Bruce.

Burglar. Lady, if he don't vote for yer, I'll kill 'im.

Jennie (*Casually*). How nice of you!

Burglar (*Eyeing her*). Say, do yer know yer've been riskin' yer life de last half hour?

Jennie. Yes, but every vote is important.

Burglar (*Taken back*). You tink dis votin' is mighty important?

Jennie. Yes. Don't you?

Burglar. Naw! Take it from me, yer'll be disappointed. *I* never got anything out of votin' but de price of me winter shoes.

Jennie. And yet you got the vote by Natural Law!

Burglar. I got it 'cause I registered.

Jennie. You did nothing yourself to get the right to register.

Burglar. Sure, I did. I lived in de district fer a month. I thought yer knew somethin' about politics.

Jennie. And I lived here for twenty-five years and I can't vote.

Burglar (*Combatively*). Who said yer can't?

Jennie. You men.

Burglar. What's the matter wid 'em? Why are dey so selfish wantin' to hog de whole game?

Jennie. That's what we women are wondering. Think of it. You can vote and I can't.

Burglar. Tough luck. Yer'll have me weepin' in a minute. (*A knock is heard on the door and* **the Burglar** *instantly becomes alert again, drawing his revolver which he has placed in his hip pocket.*) No double-crossin'.

Jennie. You'll help me?

Burglar. I ain't anxious to be pinched by dat Cop.

Jennie. Come in, Bruce.

> **Bruce** *enters, leaving the door open. He is a fine, kind, looking negro about fifty, dressed in a butler's suit.* **The Burglar** *covers him with his pistol.*

Burglar. Hands up!

Bruce (*Doing so, with fright throughout*). Oh!

Jennie (*Calmly*). Now, Bruce, do *you* believe in "Votes for Women?"

Bruce (*Eyeing the pistol and shaking*). M-m-must I?—

Jennie. Sooner or later. I've just converted this gentleman.

Bruce. Y-y-y-as.

Jennie. Then, Bruce, get this gentleman a glass of milk.

Bruce. Eh?

Burglar. Yer stay here, see?

Jennie. But aren't you thirsty?

Burglar. Not after hearin' about dem cows.

Jennie. Then sit down, Bruce.

Burglar (*As* **Bruce** *hesitates*). Sit down!

Jennie (*To* **Burglar**). Won't you sit down, too?

Burglar. Say, if yer don't mind, lady, must I hear more?

Jennie. We've scarcely covered the ground.

Burglar (*Looking towards window*). I tink dat's what *I'd* better be doin'.

Jennie (*Pointing to* **Bruce** *who has his hands still up*). But Bruce is praying for enlightenment. Aren't you, Bruce?

Bruce. I'se—I'se—I'se mighty anxious to put my hands down.

Burglar. Well then, don't butt in.

Bruce (*Putting his hands down*). And I'se powerful anxious to keep out of this 'ere argument.

Jennie. You're like lots of men, Bruce. But they can't till it's decided; so if they're tired of hearing about it, they can get a rest by giving it to us. (*To* **Burglar**.) Don't you think so?

Burglar. Anything yer say, goes.

Jennie. You vote, don't you, Bruce?

Bruce. Vote?

Burglar (*Gruffly*). Don't yer understand English? (*Spelling it.*) V-o-t-t-e?

Bruce. I ken—but I don't.

Jennie (*Dramatically*). You see. He can but he don't. (*Correcting herself.*) Doesn't.

Burglar. I heard 'im.

Jennie. Why don't you vote, Bruce?

Bruce. 'Cause I can't neglect de house to vote. Dat's de gospel truf.

Jennie. Don't you believe in "Votes for Women?"

Bruce (*Drawing himself up*). I'se perfectly *neutral*.

Burglar. Yer father must have been stuffing him.

Jennie. You see what we're up against? The great government at Washington gave *him* the vote and now I've got to ask *him* whether I can have the vote.

Burglar (*Indignantly to* **Bruce**). Ain't yer ashamed of yerself?

Bruce (*Looking about for means of escape*). I'se perfectly neutral.

Jennie. And yet by being indifferent to his own franchise, like thousands of other men, he won't even vote to give me the right to vote.

Burglar (*Stepping nearer to* **Bruce**). He won't, won't he? (*Pointing pistol at* **Bruce**.) Will yer give her her rights, eh?

Bruce (*Backing toward window*). I'se perfectly neutral.

Burglar. Won't yer vote for her?

Bruce. I'se neutral.

Burglar. If yer don't vote fer her and show yer manhood, I'll kill yer.

Bruce (*Screaming*). Help!

Burglar. Shut up!

Bruce (*Shouts out window*). Help! Murder! Police! Police! (**The Burglar** *pulls him away from window and presses the pistol against him. He falls on his knees quivering.*) I'll vote for it! I'll vote for it!

Jennie (*Rushing across*). Stop!

Burglar. He called the Cop. I'll settle him.

Jennie (*Rushing between them*). No. Don't kill him *now*. He said he'd vote for us, and we need his vote. (**Burglar** *steps back.* **Bruce** *continues to shout for help.*) Hush! Bruce, you'll wake the dead! You see, here's father.

Martin *comes rushing on excitedly.*

Martin. What's all this noise?

Burglar (*Covering him*). Throw up yer hands!

Martin (*Almost collapsing with fright and tottering toward the couch*). Oh!

Jennie (*Quickly*). Don't try to protect me, Dad. (*To* **Burglar**.) And don't kill father. I have no one else to represent me.

Martin (*Sputtering with his hands up*). I—I—I——

Burglar. Why, he can't even speak for himself.

Jennie. He gets so emotional at times, too. And you ought to see brother Tommy at a baseball game. Bruce, don't you think father's too emotional to vote?

Bruce (*As his hands go up again instantly when* **the Burglar** *points pistol at him.*) Yas'm yas'm.

Martin. I—I—take that pistol away——

Bruce. He's just wedded to dat ere gun.

Burglar (*To* **Bruce**). Shut up.

Bruce. For de Lawd's sake!

Martin (*Pleading*). Jennie, tell him to take it away.

Jennie (*Gaily*). Daddy, isn't this a splendid argument against "Indirect Influence?"

Martin. Eh?

Jennie. Yes. Now, if *I* had a pistol I should save you myself. It's the same with voting. If women had the vote they wouldn't have to ask anybody else to do it for them. That's all the ballot is—a pistol held over bad legislators.

Martin. Don't call me names—I'm helpless.

Jennie. You see now what it feels like to be a woman.

Martin (*Sputtering*). Who—who is this man?

Jennie. He's my guest.

Bruce (*Nervously throughout*). Oh!

Martin. I told you what Woman Suffrage would do to woman.

Jennie. But, father, his vote is as good as yours.

Burglar. Twice as good. (*To* **Martin**.) Now don't git humorous.

Jennie. Father can't help being funny. He doesn't *think* about Woman Suffrage like you. He just *feels*.

Martin (*Sputtering*). Am I to keep my hands held up forever?

Jennie. That's like the legislation we women want. Held up. (*Pointing to* **Burglar.**) At the pleasure of those who have the power.

Martin (*Blustering*). I protest.

Jennie. That's all we women can do. Remember, Daddy,—(*Melodramatically*)—Back of his ballot lies his bullet.

Burglar (*Timidly*). Now, if dere's anyting else before I go, lady——

Jennie. Don't you want that glass of milk?

Bruce (*Eagerly*). I'll get it.

Burglar. Yer stay here.

Jennie. And you might ask father if I may parade.

Burglar (*Flourishing his revolver*). Can she?

Bruce. For de Lawd's sake, Mister Martin, let 'er.

Burglar. Eh?

Martin. Yes, yes. You can parade. (*Trying to save his face.*) But I insist you march beside your mother!

Burglar (*Quickly*). Now me mission in life is done, tanks fer de sewing and de ideas.

Jennie. Don't forget to send your mother's name.

Martin. Don't let him go—Jennie! Jennie!

Bruce. He's a sneak thief.

Jennie. No, he's a very chivalrous gentleman. He's going to give me what I want.

As *the* **Burglar** *goes toward the window,* **Bruce,** *who is still beside it, calls out.*

Bruce. De police—t'ank de Lawd!

Burglar. Pinched!

Jennie (*Points to back door*). Go this way.

A fine looking, muscular Irish **Policeman** *with a broad smile and a rich brogue, puts his head in the window, and his hand, in which is a revolver, is leaning on the sill. He speaks with a rich Irish brogue.*

Policeman. What's all this row?

Burglar (*Seeing he is caught, and covering with his pistol*). Drop dat gun!

Policeman. Well, begorra, you've got the drop on me.

He throws his pistol to the ground and **Jennie** *picks it up and puts it on the chair by window. In this excitement* **Bruce** *goes beside* **Martin** *by the couch.* **The Burglar,** *with his back to the audience, can easily cover the three with his revolver.*

Jennie. Now let me help you in. (*She helps* the Policeman *in through the window.*) Do *you* believe in "Votes for Women?"

Policeman (*Staggering back*). Holy smithering smokes!

Martin (*Pompously again*). Do your duty and arrest that man!

Jennie. Stop! I won't have him arrested. He's got a vote.

Policeman. Shure, don't worry, Miss. If you put it that way, I'll respect your wishes.

Martin *and* **Bruce.** Oh!

Burglar. Y're a sensible guy for a Cop.

Policeman. Shure, I admit it.

Martin (*Fuming*). But—but——

Jennie. Yes—and father was just admitting that the police are our very *best* citizens.

Policeman. Now wuz he?

Martin. I never said anything of the kind.

Burglar. Yer did. I heard yer.

Jennie. Yes. You said the ballot means the power to enforce the law. Therefore our best citizens are policemen.

Policeman (*Laughing*). Ha! Ha! That's a foine joke!

Jennie. That's just what *I* thought. Don't you, Bruce?

Bruce (*Seeing the revolver*). Yas'm.

Policeman (*Looks at them*). Say what is this?

Jennie. It's a political meeting.

Policeman. I thought it wuz a mad-house.

Martin (*Groaning*). It is.

Jennie. Father is head of the house. (*Pointing.*) That's father.

Policeman. I'm pleased to meet yer.

Jennie. This is Bruce, our butler.

Policeman. And who's the guy with the gun?

Jennie (*Smiling*). That's Mr. Direct Action!! (*To the Policeman, as they all stagger back at this.*) Would *you* like a glass of milk?

Policeman. Milk?

Jennie (*Anxious to start another argument*). You see the matter of pure milk is a matter of legislation and——

Burglar (*Quickly*). I think I'll be on me way.

Martin. Officer, I insist you do your duty and arrest that man.

Jennie (*To Policeman*). Stop!

Policeman (*Who has not moved*). Shure, if yer put it that way, I'll shtop!

Martin. Don't interfere with the law, daughter.

Jennie. I will not have him arrested, so you can make a criminal out of him. I want to save him to have him make a citizen out of me. (*Abruptly to policeman.*) By the way, how long have *you* been a citizen?

Martin. Don't answer her; she'll get you in an argument. (*He sneezes.*)

Jennie. When did you take out your papers?

Policeman (*With richest brogue*). I've bin a good American fur tin years.

Jennie. Now think of that, Dad: and he and Bruce can vote.

Policeman. Say, are you one of them Suffragettes?

All (*Shouting*). Yes.

Policeman (*Moving back to the others by the couch*). And I've got to march with them all to-morrow!

Jennie (*Quickly*). You're not "henpecked" are you?

Policeman. I ain't married.

Jennie. Then you have the same vote as brother Tommy and he's got two wives.

Policeman. Help!

Jennie (*Arguing again*). You see it's this way——

Burglar. Please may I go now. (*He sneezes as he goes toward the window.*)

Jennie. Bruce, put that window down. He's getting cold.

Burglar (*As Bruce starts toward the window*). Dat's me getaway. You line up wid de others.

Martin. Line us up together?!

Jennie (*As the three men are standing together in front of the couch*). Yes, Bruce. Take your place among the voters. I'm not a voter. But neither are the idiots nor criminals.

Burglar. Say, lady, yer don't mean anything personal by dat?

Jennie (*Standing between the Burglar and the others*). Not at all. You can vote till you're convicted. I never can vote till they're convinced.

Burglar (*By the window*). Say, ain't you guys ashamed of yerselves? Tink of de rotten injustice in dis world. You and me can vote 'cause we wear trousers.

(*They look at each other.*) Ain't yer ashamed? (*They look at each other but don't answer; then he shoots his pistol off at their feet.*) Ain't yer?

All. Yes.

Jennie (*Sweetly*). I knew you'd make them see it. (*They look at one another, as she takes a button from dress and goes to* **Burglar.**) Here's a medal for you.

Burglar. What's that?

Jennie (*Pinning it on*). A "Votes for Women" button.

Burglar. Sure, I'll vote fer yer, if dose are some of de guys dat are standin' in yer way.

Martin (*Protesting*). See here!

Burglar (*Threatening with gun*). What?

Martin. Don't shoot that off again.

Bruce (*Trembling*). No.

Policeman. Yer might miss us.

Jennie (*Crossing to desk*). Wait! They are crying for buttons, too.

Martin (*Furiously*). Never!

Burglar (*Pointing gun*). Eh?

Martin (*Meekly*). All right, Jennie.

Burglar. You ought to be proud to have a daughter like dat, what cares for a thing enough to fight fer it. What did yer guys ever do to have de vote?

Jennie (*As she pins button on*). You see, father, I *could* protect myself. (*To* **Bruce.**) And here's yours, Bruce.

Burglar (*Threateningly*). Are yer neutral?

Bruce (*Emphatically*). No, sir!

Policeman (*To* **Jennie**). Don't I get one? I'm chilly!

Jennie (*Sweetly*). Oh, and you're such a nice young man.

Policeman (*Smiling*). Gee! yer believe in Suffrage and you're a lady!

Burglar (*Quickly*). And now good-bye. I'm off and thanks for de ideas and de stitches. (*To others as he pockets the policeman's revolver which he takes from the chair.*) Don't follow me or I'll shoot.

Jennie (*Going to him and taking his left hand*). Good-bye. We've had such a nice chat and don't forget the Amendment.

Burglar (*As he steps out the window backward*). Say, haven't yer got a yell er something to cheer me on me way?

Jennie (*With an inspiration*). "Votes for Women."

Burglar (*Pointing his revolver at the three*). Dat's it—now all together, boys. "Votes for Women!"

All (*Timidly in different keys*). "Votes for Women!"

Jennie. Louder.

Burglar (*As he steps down lower, still pointing the pistol*). Louder!

All. "Votes for Women!"
Jennie. Louder!
Burglar (*Pistol just showing*). Louder!
All (*Shouting*). "Votes for Women!!!"

> *The pistol disappears, the window shuts with a slam.* **Jennie** *turns and laughs loudly at the three men who have now sunk back together in a heap upon the couch. Quick curtain.*

CURTAIN

MELINDA AND HER SISTERS

MRS. O. H. P. BELMONT
AND ELSA MAXWELL
MUSIC AND LYRICS BY
ELSA MAXWELL

New York: Robert J. Shores, Publisher. 1916. First
Produced at the Waldorf Astoria, February 18, 1916.

CAST

Mrs. John Pepper, of Oshkosh out West. A common grasping climber belonging to the *nouveaux riches* type.

Mr. John Pepper, her husband, who would have been nice if let alone. An honest, shy, sad, sort of man. Father of eight daughters.

Nellie Pepper, beautiful, vivacious, with a talent for dancing. Later called Euphonia. (Classic dancer.) She is accompanied by her friends Taglione, Pavlowa, Karasavina, Adelaide, Kattorana, etc.

Annie Pepper, charming, though misguided. She has talent for operatic singing. Later called Sympharosa.

Dolly Pepper, comically tragic, who would be a second Rachel. Later called Iphigenia. Accompanied by Sophocles.

Polly Pepper, very engaging, with a talent for ball-room dancing. Later called Orchesteria. Accompanied by Narcissus and friends.

Molly Pepper, looks like she sounds. Talent for sports. Later called Atalanta. Accompanied by Europa and Diana.

Bessie Pepper, sprightly and rather silly, who would be a musical comedy star. Later called Ariadne. Accompanied by Bacchus.

Betty Pepper, a would-be poetess. Called Sappho. Accompanied by Praxiteles.

Melinda, the youngest daughter.

Mrs. Grundy,
Mrs. Malaprop, } village gossips.

Dr. Doolittle, the village doctor.

Mayor Dooless, the village Mayor.

The Rev. Wontstop, the village preacher.

Mrs. Knowitall, the village school teacher.

Mr. Vermifuge, the village Vet.

An Old Lady.

Butler.

Little Children, Factory Girls, etc., friends of Melinda.

Chorus of Servants, etc.

First Produced at the Waldorf Astoria, February 18, 1916.

SCENE

The Scene is laid in a pretentious garden in the more pretentious villa of **Mr.** *and* **Mrs. Pepper** *in a remote town out West. Preparation for a fête is in evidence. Servants are bustling about arranging chairs, tables for refreshments, hanging Chinese lanterns, etc.*

Enter **Mrs. Malaprop** *followed by* **Mrs. Grundy**

Mrs. Malaprop. This is where they are holding the levee this afternoon. I do wish I knew who accepted and who refused.

Mrs. Grundy. You are quite right, my dear; one can never be too careful about acceptances. People are inclined to accept far too many things, when it's a question of the honest though rich.

Mrs. Malaprop. And an unnecessarily large amount of refusals when it's a question of the deserving but dishonest poor.

Mrs. Grundy. Malvina Malaprop, why did you condescend to honor the Peppers with your presence today?

Mrs. Malaprop. Simply for the same reason you did, my dear.

Both in Chorus. Curiosity!

Mrs. Grundy. Oh, curiosity is such a comforting passion—the only one which has not grown out of fashion.

Mrs. Malaprop. People's hair, teeth, even their eyes, have been known to change color at various intervals in life, but curiosity, like the Mississippi, goes on forever.

Mrs. Grundy. Curiosity is nature's legacy to Woman.

Mrs. Malaprop. The only trait in which she is consistent. How much are they worth, my dear?

Mrs. Grundy. I don't know, but John Pepper must have put by a tidy sum.

Mrs. Malaprop. Have they money enough to move East and buy a Villa at Newport?

Mrs. Grundy. It doesn't take *money* to get a Villa at Newport; it takes brains.

Mrs. Malaprop. Well, it takes brains to make money.

Mrs. Grundy. Any fool can make money; it takes a clever person to spend it.

Mrs. Malaprop. No one with money ever has troubles.

Mrs. Grundy. No, but the trouble that the moneyed classes are causing us is simply terrible. Take these Peppers. Who was Mr. John Pepper? A nobody, a nonentity, and then one day he found out that glue was good to stick things with, and he has stuck ever since, till glue and Mrs. Pepper produced him eight daughters, four bathrooms, three chow dogs, a mansard roof, a real English butler, and a Victrola, and now we have to receive them into our holy of holies, along with his stuck-up wife—simply because of glue.

Mrs. Malaprop. Well, my dear, there's one consolation. If it hadn't been glue it would have been something equally as sticky. Look how far jam has taken some people; and marmalade has lent a wonderful caché to various family trees.

Mrs. Grundy. Wheatena once had a certain social significance, but it's strange how even industries change. Really marriage is the only industry which never goes out of date, but even now I don't see how these Peppers get on and I don't think her hair is as honest as she says.

Mrs. Malaprop. Never believe what a woman's hair has to say. Hair is notoriously untruthful.

Mrs. Grundy. No, but hair covers a multitude of sins. They say that in New York women can have their hair any color they like as long as it suits the color of the dog they're wearing.

Mrs. Malaprop. People don't wear dogs; they carry them.

Mrs. Grundy. Not in New York. Everything is worn there. They even wear their motor cars when they go calling.

Mrs. Malaprop. Yes, the honest, though rich, certainly have things their own way in this country. Well, I suppose we must admit the Peppers into society today. The party is to present the girls, isn't it?

Mrs. Grundy. Yes, Nellie, Annie, Dolly, Polly, Molly, Bessie, and Betty. They are returning today from their finishing schools abroad. Nellie they have called Euphonia; just what that means I don't know, but she is supposed to be a great dancer; and Annie they have called Sympharosa. She is supposed to be able to strike high C every time she sings. Then there's Dolly, who has been in Paris, studying to be a second Bernhardt. They call her Iphigenia. I can't speak it, but this is the way it's spelled. Then Polly they have called Orchesteria. They say she looks just like Mrs. Castle, and dances better too. Molly Pepper they call Atalanta. It's about some Greek woman who lost a race running for a street car or something like that. They say she plays a good game of golf, can swim across the Mediterranean, and is versatile in the latest profanity. She's been at Newport lately. Bessie Pepper they call Ariadne. She's going to shine in musical comedy, and Betty Pepper writes wonderful poems. They are so wonderful that they never get published. They call her Sappho, but I don't think it's hardly proper.

Mrs. Malaprop. And where is Melinda? Has she no talents to cultivate like her sisters; has she no ambition to shine socially and make a good match?

Mrs. Grundy. Hush! They don't mention Melinda nowadays. She is the skeleton in the closet of the Peppers. There's a great mystery here and I should like to pry it out.

DUET: *"Don't Gossip"* *and exeunt.*

Mr. *and* **Mrs. Pepper** *enter to oversee the preparations going on.* **Mrs. Pepper** *is very arrogant and overdressed, with an affected accent of ultra refinement and exaggerated dignity of bearing.* **Mr. Pepper** *is meek and depressed with a deprecatory manner and near-sighted.*

Mrs. Pepper. Now, Papa Pepper, what have you got to say for yourself? Look what you've been brought to by your fond and doting wife. Here you are just like one of those Lords you read about in the *Tatler*. Today is the day of which I have always dreamed, and thought of, and prayed to come true. There are our beautiful girls coming back full of their new accomplishments that are sure to get them all good husbands, and elect them to the new Colony Club when we arrive East. As for you, you don't need clubs. And you had better resign from the Elks.

Mr. Pepper. Why, I always found the Elks most useful, my dear.

Mrs. Pepper. No woman's husband at all prominent socially ever belongs to the Elks.

Mr. Pepper. But a man must belong to some club; it's his recreation.

Mrs. Pepper. No, the only recreation for a man nowadays is to help his wife make a social success. That's the only thing that really counts. To be a success socially is the stepping stone to the higher life: Publicity. And I am going to see to it that our girls get all the advertising that the morning paper can print. That will get them good husbands, if anything will. Publicity is the very keynote of life nowadays.

Mr. Pepper [*Shaking head*]. But, my dear, there is surely something else in life for our girls than merely to make good matches.

Mrs. Pepper. More? Papa Pepper, what do you mean? What more could there be in life than that our girls should enjoy themselves, find amusement, and associate with the best people? That was more than I expected when I married you, John Pepper, and although I did washing then and we lived in a shack in the valley, now we have a mansion on the hill.

Mr. Pepper. Where is Melinda?

Mrs. Pepper [*Stopping him peremptorily*]. Hush! Don't speak of Melinda today. Think of Euphonia's new Paquin frock. I do hope the color will match our best candle shades.

Mr. Pepper. But Melinda . . .

Mrs. Pepper. Think of Sympharosa's new tea gown—how that will dazzle the Village Vet!

Mr. Pepper [*Interrupting*]. I wish you wouldn't call them by those new-fangled names. I don't recognize my little Nellie and Annie in such highfalutin titles.

Mrs. Pepper. Hush, John. That's what they call "nouveaux art" or something of the sort.

Mr. Pepper. Now Melinda to me is a beautiful name. Where is Melinda?

Mrs. Pepper. I told you we would not discuss Melinda today.

Mr. Pepper. But I do hope the girls will be real ladies after their expensive education.

Mrs. Pepper. Education? What has that got to do with a lady? When I married you I had no education and yet I was a perfect lady just the same, Mr. John Pepper.

Mr. Pepper. So you have told me before, my dear. But I do hope the girls will be kind-hearted.

Mrs. Pepper. Kind-hearted? Did you ever hear of a lady that was kind-hearted? You are too old fashioned, John. They don't teach such things at finishing schools nowadays.

Mr. Pepper. Well, at least I hope they have good minds and retentive memories.

Mrs. Pepper. Good gracious, John, you expect the impossible. And besides it is very bad form to remember anything nowadays and, so far as knowledge goes, we don't send our girls to school to learn anything, for a perfect lady should know absolutely nothing. It creates an atmosphere of mystery and elusive charm. That's what men like in a woman. She should know nothing, think nothing, say nothing, but dress well, look well, and dance.

Mr. Pepper [*Interrupting*]. But haven't our girls been brought up to learn to become good wives and mothers?

Mrs. Pepper. Hush! Don't be so indelicate, John. No well-bred woman at all prominent socially ever associates motherhood with marriage. The duty of young people who marry is to give more expensive luncheons than their neighbors and at least have two members of the Castoria family at her Thursday afternoons once a month. That is the duty of every self-respecting young married woman today.

Mr. Pepper. Well, I give it up. I thought at least when two young people married they lived for their children and each other.

Mrs. Pepper. Each other? How vulgar! Any woman who sits at the same table with her own husband more than once a week is simply *déclassée*. That's the iron social rule laid down last season in Newport.

Mr. Pepper. But whom do wives dine with, if not with their husbands?

Mrs. Pepper. Why, with other women's husbands, of course. That is what marriage is for.

Mr. Pepper [*Sadly*]. Well, things have changed since I was a boy.

Mrs. Pepper. And since I was a girl, thank Heaven!

DUET: *"Since I Was a Boy and a Girl"*

Guests begin to arrive and the orchestra strikes up popular tunes. There is much bustling about and the large and portly butler announces the various social celebrities as they enter. Enter **Mrs. Grundy**.

Butler [*In loud voice*]. Her Grace The Duchess of Grundy! [*In a loud aside to* **Mrs. Grundy**]. Beg pardon, ma'am, but my mistress does love the sound of a title.

Enter **Mrs. Malaprop**.

Butler [*In loud voice*]. Her Serene Highness Princess Malaprop!
Mrs. Malaprop [*Objecting*]. You made a mistake, my man.
Butler [*Apologetically*]. Them's me h'orders, ma'am; so Princess you are whether you like it or not.

Mrs. Malaprop *retires bewildered and joins* **Mrs. Grundy**. *Enter* **Dr. Doolittle**.

Butler [*In loud voice*]. His Grace The Duke of Doolittle!
Dr. Doolittle [*Spluttering*]. But, my good man, I am the village doctor.
Butler [*Firmly*]. You are the village Duke today.

Dr. Doolittle, *protesting, joins* **Mrs. Malaprop** *and* **Mrs. Grundy**. *Enter* **Reverend Wontstop**.

Butler. His Excellency Canon Wontstop!
Reverend Wontstop. Canon? I am a man of peace, sir!
Butler [*Serenely*]. Never mind, you won't go off.

Enter **Mrs. Knowitall**.

Butler. Her Royal Highness The Grand Duchess of Knowitall!
Mrs. Knowitall [*Beaming*]. How sweet it sounds! I always fancied myself with a title.
Reverend Wontstop. What a delightful custom! In imagination I am already of royal blood.
Dr. Doolittle. And why not? America is really the greatest monarchy of all. Our society is the most expensive to get into.
Mrs. Knowitall. And to get out of.

Enter **Mayor Dooless**.

Butler. His Excellency The Most High Lord Mayor Dooless of Oshkosh!
Mayor [*Tipping* **Butler** *heavily*]. How pleasant it is to be treated with a dignity one really deserves!

Mrs. Knowitall. We were just saying what delightful restrictions exist in this country of ours. It is so nice to be born in a position which enables one to cut others. That is the real higher education for women: to know just who and where and when to cut people. For instance, if I am in the orchestra and Mrs. Malaprop is in the stage box of the village Opera House, I can bow to her without exciting comment, but if the positions were reversed, I could not. If you know a woman on Fifth Avenue, you must not recognize her on Sixth. It wouldn't do.

Enter **Mr. Vermifuge**.

Butler. The Honorable Mr. Vermifuge!

Mr. Vermifuge. Dear me, dear me! Sounds quite exciting! As a matter of fact I am late because Mrs. Pepper's French bull was suffering from a slight intestinal disorder. I am so sorry! It quite slipped out. One should not mention such things in the best circles.

Mrs. Knowitall [*Soothingly*]. Oh, that's all right, my dear Vermifuge. It's quite in fashion now to mention one's ailments. One talks of nothing at dinner nowadays but the effect of each course upon the liver. It is really quite exciting comparing notes.

Mayor Dooless. Oh, yes, the insides of things nowadays form the sole topic of conversation. People have talked for centuries about the outsides. It is time one took an interest in the *in*.

Mr. Pepper [*Almost choking*]. Ladies and gentlemen (*choke*) friends. This is a most happy occasion and Mrs. (*choke*) Pepper and myself feel proud in the thought that our daughters are here to share with us the pleasure we feel in welcoming you to our humble home.

Mr. *and* **Mrs. Pepper** *come down stage and greet all their friends. Loud voices are heard, motor horns, cheering, and music begins.*

Enter **Annie** *as* **Sympharosa** *with girl friends. She embraces her mother and father, bows her acknowledgments to crowd, and sings operatic aria.*

Enter **Nellie** *as* **Euphonia** *with friends as Russian ballet girls. In chorus they explain that* **Euphonia** *hopes to make Pavlowa take a back seat. With Russian music* **Euphonia** *executes a wild barbaric pas seul, finishing in a grand finale.*

Enter **Molly** *or* **Atalanta** *with friends dressed in sport costume or bathing dresses. She has a lively song with burlesque of bathing or golf in the Business.*

Enter **Dolly** *or* **Iphigenia** *in spotlight with chorus. She is very tragic and does a scene from the "Phedra of Racine" or some other French classic.*

Enter **Polly** *or* **Orchesteria** *with chorus and man dancing partner. They execute a modern fox trot. While in song, chorus explains.*

Enter **Bessie** *or* **Ariadne** *with chorus dressed as modern soubrette in a musical comedy. She has rather a gay daring little song and dance, at the finale of which all the sisters are congratulated by admiring audience.*

Enter **Betty** *or* **Sappho**, *who sings on Greek art or poetry.*

Seven Girls [*In chorus*]. Where's Melinda? Our little sister Melinda—where is she?

Others [*Echoing*]. Where is Melinda? Has she changed much? Has she no accomplishments? Has she not learned to act, dance, sing or play?

Mrs. Grundy [*Sadly*]. Hush, don't mention Melinda!

At that moment noise of a brass band is heard at the back of the theater in the foyer. There is cheering and shouting of people and **Melinda** *appears dressed very plainly but attractively and carrying a suffrage flag with children of the poor holding onto her skirt and men and women in every walk of life following her in the procession: laborers, factory girls, salesladies, etc. Neither looking to the left nor the right,* **Melinda** *marches down center aisle with her little army and onto the stage to the amazement of every one present.* **Melinda's** *sisters are shocked and horrified.*

Mrs. Pepper [*Groaning aloud*]. This will ruin us. Just when we had got the best people up to our house on the hill.

MUSICAL SCENE: *Little children, factory girls, and shop assistants: "Our Friend Melinda Has Promised," etc.*

   Melinda *has a song: "I Am Melinda." She is joined in the chorus by her followers. At the conclusion of song, with great earnestness of manner, she kisses her sisters, who draw back from her suspiciously. She then goes to her mother.*

Melinda [*To mother*]. Won't you welcome me home, mother? I have marched a long way and I am very tired but not so tired as some of my friends here who need my help and yours.

Mrs. Grundy [*In loud voice to* **Mrs. Malaprop**]. Good heavens, I actually believe the creature's a suffragette! No wonder they never spoke of her except behind closed doors. I think we had better be going.

Mrs. Malaprop. Do you think it can be possible? And just when we had taken them up and they were about to become our equals socially.

Reverend Wontstop [*To* **Mayor Dooless**]. Do you think she will become violent? I have read that they sometimes do.

Mayor Dooless. I believe you are right. We had better go while we are safe from harm.

Mrs. Knowitall. Oh, there is no danger. They talk a lot but they rarely do anything. Women only fight with their tongues.

Melinda [*Catching last remark and speaking in clear voice*]. You are mistaken, Mrs. Knowitall. Women nowadays have better weapons than the one you mention. We fight, it is true, but we fight with good deeds, with love of humanity as our sword and justice as our shield. We want you all to tear away the blinds of superstition and let the sun of knowledge pour into the windows of your soul. We want you—and by you, I mean all women— to help each other, to be kind to each other, to throw off your shackles of servitude and become free—all equal, all great, all working together for the common cause—equal rights, equal responsibilities, equal rewards, equal punishments.

Mrs. Grundy. Good heavens, she is obviously no lady!

Melinda. If your way of living, thinking, and acting are those of a lady, then I am glad to dissociate myself from so ambiguous a term. I am a woman first and I want to help all women who are blind and who still live in mental as well as physical slavery.

Mayor Dooless [*Stepping up in bellicose manner*]. Young woman, do you fancy for one moment that you could take my place as Mayor of the town of Oshkosh? For you do want political rights in this hairbrained scheme of yours.

Melinda. And why am I not as capable of being Mayor and of holding office as well or as ill as you do? [*At the word "ill" the* **Mayor** *squirms.*] You know as well as I that this is a wide open town. By that I mean that every vice can flourish here by the purveyors paying for their license to carry on the trade.

Mayor [*Indignantly*]. There is not any more vice in the streets of Oshkosh than any other town in the Union.

Melinda [*Gently*]. Not any more vice—there you have touched the crux of the matter. Why should there not be less vice than in any other town in America? Why should vice, depravity, and crime be comparative?

Mayor [*Feebly*]. But if I close these places, I'd be put out of office. They wouldn't elect me a second term.

Melinda. Who do you mean by "they"?

Mayor. The citizens of this community.

Melinda. But if all the citizens had the power to vote, you would be elected a second term. The majority is always for the right.

Mayor. But all the citizens do vote. Every Tom, Dick, and Harry has a vote in this town and they use it too, worse luck.

Melinda. All the blacks, the negroes, they also are allowed their vote?

Mayor. Yes.

Melinda. And imbeciles, if they are allowed at large, even they can vote?

Mayor. Absolutely, yes.

Melinda. And any farm hand or railroad laborer, even if he can't spell or write, but can just make his mark—he can vote?

Mayor. Of course.

Melinda. Was your late wife, whose good works are still the talk of the town, the late Mrs. Dooless, an intelligent woman, Mayor?

Mayor [*Proudly*]. Intelligent? You bet your bottom dollar she was. Why, it was she who wrote my first speech in the Democratic campaign which elected me to the Board of Aldermen.

Melinda. Was she as intelligent as old black Joe, the negro stable-boy of Dr. Doolittle?

Mayor. I won't have the memory of my late wife insulted, Miss Melinda Pepper!

Melinda. I am not insulting the memory of the late Mrs. Dooless. It is you who are doing that.

Mayor. What do you mean?

Melinda. Because by denying women the political right to vote and by allowing old black Joe that same right, you place old black Joe mentally and economically in a position superior to that of the late Mrs. Dooless, your capable and very good wife.

Mayor [*Scratching his head*]. Well, I really hadn't thought of it in that way.

Melinda [*Returning to the attack*]. Mayor, what, exactly, constitutes a citizen of a country and a member of a community?

Mayor [*Promptly*]. A man who pays his taxes.

Melinda. But women pay taxes just the same as men and yet they have no rights. How do you explain that?

Mayor. It isn't the vote we mind you women having. We would give you that, if you wouldn't scream for more. But it's your holding office we men object to. We can't stand for that. What would happen to the country with a pack of women howling in the Senate and giving pink teas at the White House? Why, the whole country would go to the dogs!

Melinda. The country has been going to the dogs for quite a while now. Why not give it to the cats for a change? Why, women have proved their efficiency in the arts, the professions, and the vocations which have been so long monopolised by men in the past. Statistics teach us that women make just as good surgeons, lawyers, architects, and in fact excel in all the practical arts. Because she has been kept a drudge for centuries past, the fine arts have been a closed book to her; but from a creature of utility, she is rapidly becoming a creature of opportunity; and when woman tightens the rein and puts the bit on intellect and instinct, she will be unconquerable. [*Turning to her sisters.*] And you, my sisters, so gifted and so beautiful—how have you spent the last few years when you should have been studying, preparing yourselves for the great day when women will take their proper places in the world? "Vanity"—has been your watchword—"Vanity" alone has been your guiding star!

Mrs. Pepper, *who has been more and more converted, suddenly flings discretion to the winds.*

Mrs. Pepper. Girls, girls, put away your curls! If the men won't be prepared, we'll show them that the women are for preparedness anyhow!

SONG: *"Girls, Girls, Put Away Your Curls." All join, drilling, etc., going into Finale: "Carry On!"*

CURTAIN

SELECTED LYRICS

MELINDA'S ENTRANCE

Melinda.
Once when I was a little girl,
Not very long ago,
I dreamed a dream made my head whirl,
The dream some day you shall know.

Children.
We have come with you,
Our dreams are true.

Melinda.
And so illusions, they come and go,
I am older now and wise, I know.

Children.
Oh no!

Melinda.
I dreamed of a world so fair and wide
Framed by the stars above;
And in this world was naught beside:
Sympathy, hope, and love.

THE WALTZ

I am tired to-night,
And I'm weary of bright
Restless eyes, carmine lips,
Drooping shoulder;
And I feel that before
My brief life is o'er,
And the wiser I grow and older,
I should give up all
Dances, flirtation and balls,
These society teas
And afternoon calls;
For I still remember

The dear days when you
Taught me a dance that was new.

REFRAIN

'Twas a waltz, dear,
You taught me that night,
In the waltz, dear,
You held me so tight;
As we glided together
On love's dreamy strain,
The throb of the violins
Crept into my brain.
Now though I have half forgotten your name,
And I have waltzed oft with others,
It is never the same;
And I'd give my fame,
Fortune and all for the right,
Could we waltz once again, dear, to-night.
Now at first 'twas a task, dear,
To get you to ask
For my programme
To write down your name.
And I don't know why
But you made me feel shy,
Though I wished you to stay
Just the same.
And oh, how I wish
We had played bigger parts,
And ceased to dissemble,
And laid bare our hearts!
Then I'd have been yours,
And you'd have been mine:
Together in Life's Waltz divine!

NURSE'S SONG

Man thinks of woman in moments of leisure,
Bringing him pleasure to claim and caress.
Man finds in woman a prize he could treasure,
Gold beyond measure in sorrow or stress.
Whether in battle the fight has been hard for you,
When you have sickness or harm that is dire,

There's a friend with a tender regard for you,
Woman, the best that man can desire.

Come to us, send for us,
When you are broken or sorry or sad.
If you want aid of us,
Don't be afraid of us,
We will be tender and render you glad.
Only take heed of us,
If you have need of us,
We can bring light to your eye once again.
We want a share of you,
We will take care of you,
Tend you and mend you and save you from pain.

GOLF

There's a game that every fellow loves to play:
Golfing is the game to-day that holds the sway;
If you play it as you really ought to do,
There is nothing like it, I'll explain to you.
Now all you want is just a girl of seventeen,
Just about the greenest thing upon the green.
Never mind your playing, always keep on saying,
That you love her—is all that you need.
Just get your little mashie and your maid
And I will tell you how the game is played.

REFRAIN

First give your girl a kiss,
That part you mustn't miss.
Then drive—and kiss some more
(Ta ra-ta ra-ta ra)
Then you postpone the play,
Look in her eyes and say:
"Cuddle up near me,
We're in a bunker, dearie."
Then round her dainty waist
Your arm is quickly placed,
With love you're all on fire.
You hug and tease her,
Cuddle and squeeze her,

But while you're dreaming
You hear somebody screaming,
"Fore! Fore! Fore!"
Then your game is o'er,
And you can start over again.

DUBLIN MOLLY-O

There's a little town in Ireland
And Dublin is its name;
There's not a place in all the world
That I love quite the same;
The girls they are the sweetest there
An' tho I'm far from home
Soon I'll go back to Molly-O
And make her all my own.
And then there'll be a bonny babe
As taxes to the king
An' if e'er he sees my Molly-O
Like me he's sure to sing,
Flora, Cora, Polly,
Dolly, Norah,
I never could adore a girl like you;
And with Sallie—Callie,
I really couldn't dally
Tho you live in Lovers' Alley
And to me you'd be so true;
There's not another—mother—
A sister, friend, or brother,
Like a little Irish lass I know.
With "Because I came from Dublin,"
'Tis me you're always troublin'.
Arrah go on but
I love my Molly-O.

LEGS

Some tell people by their bumps,
Or by their palms, they say;
And if upon your head you've lumps,
They'll give you dead away.
Cranks who claim to tell about

Your traits by the way you talk,
But the surest way to tell a man
Is by his legs and walk.

REFRAIN

Can't you tell a lady from the city?
Can't you tell a Jacky from the sea?
By her walk you know she must be pretty,
By his legs a nut he'd like to be.
Can't you tell that she is glad he's found her
Can't you see that she's been in the dregs?
Can't you tell that he's a perfect bounder?
In fact, there's nothing one can't learn from legs.

"HELLO, HELLO"

(Words and Music by Elsa Maxwell)

I've got a secret
That I've shared with none,
A secret that is very dear
I'll tell to only one
If I find that some one answers me.
I cannot keep it more,
When it's all about some one that I adore.
So Exchange please give me
I L-O-V-E Y-O-U
And please don't say "engaged" unless to some one true.

REFRAIN

Hello, hello, isn't there a fellow
Who will answer at the other end?
Now it is very strange
That I can't get Exchange (don't cut me off)
To connect me with a gentlemanly friend!
Hello, hello, haven't you a number?
Hello, hello, haven't you a name?
There must be some one on some 'phone
Who wants me for his very own,
So hello, hello,
If you're not a dunce,
You'll say hello, hello, at once.

GIRLS, GIRLS, PUT AWAY YOUR CURLS

For a thousand years or so,
Since many moons ago,
Men have ruled us women East and West.
From the cave man in his lair
To the flyer in the air,
To keep us women down they thought was best.
But turned now is the tide,
And we cannot be denied,
We are coming in our millions to enhance;
For they need us great and small,
And we'll gladly give our all
To show what we can do if we've the chance.

REFRAIN

So girls, girls, put away your curls,
Put away your petticoats and frills!
Step right into line;
Cease now to repine;
We'll show them that we all can learn to drill.
Left! Right! We can stand the pace.
'Tention! Halt! Right about face!
But we've done with teas and balls;
We've forgotten how to dance;
We'll show what we can do if we've the chance!

CARRY ON!

(Dedicated to Mrs. O. H. P. Belmont)

What ardent hopes inspire us,
With the women marching by!
Both young and old turned toward the goal,
For the cause that never dies;
The music swelling wakes the echoes,
Makes the great hearts glow;
It tells us that our warriors bold,
Like Knights of Long Ago,
When they rode forth to defend the Grail,
For Freedom's sake they can never fail!

REFRAIN

Carry on; carry on!
For Victory's flag that flies.
Carry on! that our work
Will never be in vain.
Who lives if Freedom dies?
Are we downhearted? No! No! No!
For the beacon light
Will shine a long long way;
Carry on and fear no foe!

Now when my span of life is run,
And I falter on life's way;
And the children gather at my knee,
They will listen when I say:
Your mother, dears, fought for the right,
To free you from the yoke,
Worn by all women till the time
The voice of action spoke;
That's what your mother did, my dears,
When she broke the servitude of years.

REFRAIN

Carry on; carry on!
For Victory's flag that flies.
Carry on! that our work
Will never be in vain.
Who lives if Freedom dies?
Are we downhearted? No! No! No!
For the light of knowledge
Shines a long long way;
Carry on to crush the foe!

UNAUTHORISED
INTERVIEWS

ALICE DUER MILLER

In *Women Are People!* New York: George H. Doran
Co., 1917, pp. 87–98.

QUEENS AND GODDESSES

SCENE

Congress, during a woman suffrage debate. The Congressmen are, as usual, moving about, talking, reading, dozing, and one, an antisuffragist, is speaking.

Congressman.
I shall vote "No" on this measure, but
    I wish to say I take
My stand for Woman's protection, for
    her own sake.
No one honours Woman, no one respects
    her more,
Than I do; as queen and goddess I love
    and adore——

Suddenly in an open space in front of the Speaker's desk appear Pallas Athene and Cleopatra.

Cleopatra.
Strange little man without weapons,
    what can you mean?

Pallas.
I, in my time, was a goddess——

Cleopatra.
              And I was
    a queen.

Pallas.
Men knelt with gifts at my altar, gifts
    of ivory and gold,
Bowls of bronze and of silver chased by
    the tools of old.
No council of chiefs was held, no treaty
    or war begun
But they prayed to me for wisdom——

Cleopatra.
              And all that I
    wished was done.

Pallas.
My name was spoken with reverence,
　　for the mortal's breath
That jests on the name of a goddess calls
　　soon for death.
But here one spoke of his goddess,
　　likening her to a hen.
Think you Immortals suffer such words
　　from the lips of men?

Cleopatra.
And one was talking of queens for many
　　an hour,
Till I longed to clap my hands with
　　their old, old power
And cry "Come hither, my guards, take
　　this old man away,
For his ignorant talk of queens wearies
　　your queen to-day."

Pallas (*more kindly*).
If you have each a goddess, as all of
　　you boast,
Hurry and bring her here, here, where
　　you need her most.
She must be strong and wise; while ye,
　　O mortals, are weak.
Pray that she come and save you, from
　　the foolish words you speak.
If you have each a goddess——

Congressman (*recovering from his astonishment*).
　　　　Yes, but home is her shrine.

Pallas.
Ah, I have seen those shrines, lovely,
　　many, as mine,
But women are toiling in them, toiling
　　like slaves.
Are they your goddesses?

Congressman (*confused*).
　　　　Yes.

Cleopatra.

                                   Surely
the old man raves!
I know the fate of captives and slaves
    of the East:
They must work till they die, or are
    sold like a beast.
This man owns them by thousands.
    They toil amid wheels that grind.
They are his slaves.

Congressman (*faintly*).

                         No, queens.

Cleopatra (*angrily*).

               The man is mad or blind.

Pallas.

Nay, nay, Daughter of Egypt, he is
    neither blind nor mad,
But talking as men still talk when their
    cause is bad.
To cover an ugly truth he uses a pretty
    phrase
As even the Gods have done in the good
    old days.
He knows that the woman who toils for
    some one else to be rich
Is no more a queen than the man who
    digs a ditch.
He knows that the wife at home, whom
    he does, as he says, revere,
Is not a goddess, or else he would seek
    her counsel here.
He knows her merely a woman, and he
    wants no woman to share
His power—

Cleopatra.

              Why does he not say so?

Pallas.

             Because he does not dare.

Cleopatra.
Dares not? Is he a coward?

Pallas.

Nay, he
fears where he ought.
For as some men think of women they
are wise to hide their thought.
(*She turns to Congressman.*)
Mortal, I am a goddess. Do not tremble
and shrink.
I read your heart about women—all that
you wish and think.
Base it is, and unworthy, but I strike you
not dead at my feet.
This is my sentence upon you—a pun-
ishment meet—
When you tell your thought of Woman,
you shall tell the truth.
How you despise her wholly—all but her
beauty and youth.
Henceforth when you speak of Woman,
you shall tell all your heart.
Congressman (*terrified*).
I must be silent forever! (A *pause.*)
Pallas to Cleopatra.

Come, Queen,
we may now depart.

CURTAIN

IMPRESSIONS OF A CANVASSER

CHARACTERS ————————————————————————

Suffragists.
Half a dozen Legislators Opposed.

SCENE

A *Certain State Capitol.*

Suffragists.
Please, sir, to tell us, if you will,
How you will vote upon our bill?

1st Legislator.
Ladies, observe my easy grace,
My manners and my pleasant face;
I hope you see I bow, I smile,
I call you "ladies"—all the while
My heart is black with seething hate
That I, who am so very great,
Should have to waste a single minute
On your affairs—there's nothing in it.

Suffragists (*to another legislator*).
And you, sir, if we recollect,
Are much opposed. Is that correct?

2nd Legislator.
Opposed! O ladies, no, indeed!
I vote against you, I concede;
I may continue so to do,
But I am not *opposed* to you.
To call me so is most unjust.
I make myself quite plain, I trust.

Suffragists (*to another legislator*).
And may we hear from you, sir, how
You'll vote?

3rd Legislator.
    I have no option now;
I listen to my district's voice;
It voted no; I have no choice.

Suffragists.
O sir, I think there's some mistake,
Your district carried.

4th Legislator (*hastily interrupting*).
                 Let me make
His statement clear; he means that we
All come here absolutely free.
Not at our districts' beck and nod,
We vote to please ourselves and God;
And we are not in all events
The slaves of our constituents.

Suffragists (*slightly puzzled, to another legislator*).
And you, sir, shall you vote for it?

5th Legislator.
No, though I think you will admit
I have a very open mind;
If in my district I should find
The women want it (which they don't),
I'd vote for it. Till then I won't.

Suffragists.
And have you asked so very many?

5th Legislator (*astonished*).
Why, no, I don't think I've asked any.

Suffragists (*to another legislator*).
And what, sir, is your attitude?

6th Legislator.
I hope you will not think me rude,
If, ladies, as a friend I say
You do not work the proper way.
It's time you disappeared, and let
The public utterly forget
That there are women wish to vote.
Then at some future time, remote,
In twenty years, or twenty-five,
If you should chance to be alive,
You'd see a change—at least you ought—
A striking change in public thought.
This from a friend.

Suffragists.

But are you so?

6th Legislator.
A friend? Oh, well, I voted "no,"
But surely you can comprehend
That I advise you as a friend.

Suffragists alone.

1st Suffragist.
The men in favour talk much less.

2nd Suffragist.
They haven't much to say but "yes";
The men opposed explain a lot
How they're opposed and yet they're not.
It takes some time to make that clear.

1st Suffragist.
How very bad the air is here!

2nd Suffragist.
Do you refer to ventilation,
Or to the general situation?

The reply is inaudible.

CURTAIN

AN UNAUTHORISED INTERVIEW

BETWEEN THE SUFFRAGISTS AND THE STATUE OF LIBERTY

THE SUFFRAGISTS

LADY robed in light,
　　At our harbour standing,
Equal law and right
　　Promising, demanding,
Can you tell us, do you know,
Why you treat your daughters so?

Do not think us pert,
　　Insolent or teasing,
But you seem a flirt,
　　Only bent on pleasing
That one-half of human kind
Who made Sister Justice blind.

THE STATUE

Be not deceived, my daughters, I'm not she—
The wingèd Goddess, who sets nations free.
I am that Liberty, which when men win
They think that others' seeking is a sin;
I am that Liberty which men attain
And clip her wings lest she should fly again:
I am that Liberty which all your brothers
Think good for them and very bad for others.
Therefore they made me out of bronze, and hollow,
Immovable, for fear that I might follow
Some fresh rebellion, some new victim's plea;
And so they set me on a rock at sea,
Welded my torch securely in my hand
Lest I should pass it on, without command.
I am a milestone, not an inspiration;
And if my spirit lingers in this nation,
If it still flickers faintly o'er these waters,
It is your spirit, my rebellious daughters.

BIBLIOGRAPHY OF PLAYS

The bibliography lists the printed plays immediately related to the topics of woman suffrage, woman's rights, and the New Woman that were written before 1920. For readers interested in the topic, I also include later plays dealing with individuals or aspects from the history of the woman's movement. The vast number of propaganda plays of that period in typescript should be checked in the index published by the Copyright Office of the Library of Congress: *Dramatic Compositions Copyrighted in the United States, 1870–1916*, 2 vols. (Washington, D.C.: Government Printing Office, 1918). Quite a few of these manuscripts and typescripts have survived in archives, attics, and collections of family papers and, like the other documents relating to the history of women, may eventually be rediscovered by the joint interest, attention, and effort of all of us.

Aiken, Mrs. J. S. *The Suffragettes' Convention: Farce Comedy*. Greenwood, S.C.: privately printed, 1914.

Anspacher, Louis Kaufman. *A Woman of Impulse: A Modern Play in Four Acts*. Binghamton, N.Y.: privately printed, 1909.

[Appleton, Wisc., Central Committee of the Woman's Endowment Movement]. *The Women of the Centuries*. Program of Entertainment for the Woman's Professorship in Lawrence University. Appleton, Wis.: privately printed, 1896.

Baker, George M. *Shall Our Mothers Vote?* In *Handy Dramas*. Boston: Walter H. Baker & Company, 1904; 1st ed. 1876, pp. 169–187.

Balch, William Lincoln. *Alice in Blunderland*. Chicago: W. Rossiter, 1903.

Belmont, Mrs. Oliver Hazard Perry, and Elsa Maxwell. *Melinda and Her Sisters*. New York: Robert J. Shores, Publ., 1916.

Boissevain, Inez Milholland. *If Women Voted*. New York: National Woman Suffrage Publishing Company, [191?].

Bridgham, Lilian Clisby. *The Famous Brown vs. Brown Separate Maintenance Case: A Woman's Suffragette Mock Trial*. Boston: Walter H. Baker & Company, 1912.

———. *A Suffragette Town Meeting: An Entertainment in One Act*. Boston: Walter H. Baker & Company, 1912.

Brown, Leando. *Mrs. Raford, Humanist: A Suffrage Drama*. New York and London: L. E. Landone, 1912.

Buford, Lucy E. Hanson. *The House of Lords: An Equal Suffrage Play in One Act*. Roanoke, Va: Stone Printing and Manufacturing Company, 1914.

Burns, Mary Modena. *Her Honor the Mayor: A Comedy*. Chicago: T. S. Denison Company, [1916].

Butler, Ellis Parker. *The Revolt: A Play in One Act*. New York and London: Samuel French, 1912.

Caffin, Caroline. *Home Thrust: A Comedy in One Act*. New York: National Woman Suffrage Publishing Company, [191?].

Clark, Sophie Louise Wepf. *Entertainment to Make Votes for Women*. Washington, D.C.: [Burton], 1911.

Cole, Ida B. *Wagner at the Smallville Woman's Club: An Entertainment in One Scene*. Boston: Walter H. Baker & Company, 1906.

Countryman, May E. *The Rebellion of Mrs. Barclay: A Comedy of Domestic Life in Two Acts*. Boston: Walter H. Baker & Company, 1912.

Crane, Eleanor Maud. *Bachelor Maids' Reunion: An Entertainment in One Scene*. New York: Dick & Fitzgerald, 1906.

Crothers, Rachel. *He and She* (1911). In *Representative American Plays*, ed. Arthur Hobson Quinn. New York: Century Company, 1917, pp. 925–962.

––––––. *A Man's World: A Play in Four Acts* (1910). Boston: Richard G. Badger, 1915. American Dramatists Series.

[Curtis, Ariana Randolph Wormeley, and Daniel Sargent Curtis]. *The Spirit of Seventy-Six; or, The Coming Woman, A Prophetic Drama. Followed by a Change of Base, and Doctor Mondschein*. Boston: Little, Brown and Company, 1868, pp. 1–73.

Denison, T. S. *The New Woman. A Comedy of A.D. 1950 in Three Acts*. Chicago: T. S. Denison & Company, 1895.

Dumont, Frank. *The New Woman's Husband: A Satire in One Scene*. Philadelphia: Penn Publishing Company, 1897.

––––––. *When Women Rule Us: Burlesque Court House Scene*. New York and Chicago: M. Witmark & Sons, 1904. Witmark Stage Publications.

Dunbar, Olivia Howard. *Enter Women. Play in One Act*. New York: Dramatists Play Service, 1939.

Fargo, Kate Mills. *A Voting Demonstration; or, An Election in Primerville: A Farce in One Act*. [Redlands, Calif.]: privately printed, 1912.

Fowle, William B. *Woman's Rights*. In *Parlor Dramas; or, Dramatic Scenes, for Home Amusement*. Boston: Chase and Nichols, 1856, pp. 7–17.

Fraser, John Arthur, Jr. *Bloomer Girls; or, Courtship in the Twentieth Century: Satirical*

Comedy in One Act. Chicago: The Dramatic Publishing Company, 1896. Amateur Acting Drama.

Freeman, Eleanor. *When the Women Vote: A Colloquy.* Cincinnati: Standard Publishing Company, 1885.

Gale, Rachel Baker. *The Clinging Vine: A Comedy in One Act.* Boston: Walter H. Baker & Company, 1913.

————. *Coats and Petticoats: A Comedy in One Act.* Boston: Walter H. Baker & Company, 1910.

Gerberding, Elizabeth Sears. *Scissors or Sword.* [San Francisco]: privately printed, [191?].

Gilman, Charlotte Perkins. *Something to Vote For: A One Act Play.* In *The Forerunner* 2, no. 6 (June 1911): 143–153.

————. *Three Women: A One Act Play.* In *The Forerunner* 2, no. 5 (May 1911): 115–123, 134.

[Gray, William R., and M. A. Moore]. *Emancipated Woman; or, A Scene from Real Life in the Year 2000: A Burlesque in Four Acts.* Le Mars, Iowa: Ragsdale & Chassell, 1895.

Green, Mary Walcott. *The Woman Who Did: Dramatic Entertainment for Women Historical and Patriotic.* Chicago: T. S. Denison & Company, [1911].

Groff, Alice. *Freedom: A Play in Four Acts.* Boston: Richard G. Badger, Gorham Press, 1904.

Hale, Harold [C. N. Moller]. *A Tax on Bachelors: A Comedy in Two Acts.* Boston: Walter H. Baker & Company, 1905.

Hammond, Josephine. *Everywoman's Road: A Morality of Woman, Creator, Worker, Waster, Joy-Giver and Keeper of the Flame.* New York: Star Printing Company, 1911; repr. New York: Mitchell Kennerley, 1913.

Haviland, J. Butler. *Miss Jones, Journalist. Or, For the Special Edition: A Farcical Sketch in One Act.* Boston: Walter H. Baker & Company, 1904.

Hopkinson, Mrs. Arthur. *Women's Votes: A Short Play in One Act.* London/New York: Samuel French, 1911.

Howe, Marie Jenney. *An Anti-Suffrage Monologue.* New York: National American Woman Suffrage Association, 1913.

Hoyt, Charles H. *A Contented Woman* (1897). *The Dramatic Works of Charles H. Hoyt*, 3 vols. New York, 1901.

Hughes, Elizabeth. *Women for Votes: A Farce in Three Acts.* New York: E. P. Dutton & Company, 1912.

Hutchinson, M. F. *When Woman Rules: A Merry Comedy for Girls in Two Acts.* Music by Lionel Elliot. London: J. Williams Ltd.; New York: Edward Schuberth & Company, 1908. [Libretto only.]

Ives, Alice E. *A Very New Woman.* In *The Woman's Column* 9, no. 11, March 14, 1896: 2–3.

Johnson, Hester N. *On to Victory: A Comedy in Two Acts.* Boston: Walter H. Baker & Company, 1915.

Josiah Allen's Wife [Marietta Holley]. *An Allegory on Woman's Rights.* San Francisco: California Equal Suffrage Association, 1910.

Kavanaugh, Katharine. *A Converted Suffragist: A Play in One Act for Female Characters.* New York: Dick & Fitzgerald, 1912.

Kelley, Jessie A. *Her Weekly Allowance: A Farcical Entertainment in One Act.* Boston: Walter H. Baker & Company, 1907.

———. *The Suffragettes' Convention: An Entertainment in One Act for Twelve Female Characters and One Male.* Boston: Walter H. Baker & Company, 1912.

Kiper, Florence [Frank]. *Cinderelline; or, The Little Red Slipper.* Chicago: Dramatic Publishing Company, 1913.

Lewis, Emily Sargent. *A Dream of Brave Women.* Philadelphia: privately printed, 1912.

———. *Election Day: A Suffrage Play.* Philadelphia: privately printed, 1912.

Lisanti, Gaetano F. *Little Harold; or, The Suffragette: A Play in Four Acts.* New York: Nicoletti Bros. Press, [1911].

Long, Walter S. *When de Womenfolks Debate: A Darkey Sketch for Women or Men Impersonating Female Characters.* Franklin, Ohio: Eldridge Entertainment House, 1916.

Ludington, Helen Gilman. *The Suffragette: A Comedy in One Act for Seven Females.* New York and London: Samuel French, 1909.

McCulloch, Catharine Waugh. *Bridget's Sisters; or, The Legal Status of Illinois Women in 1868.* Chicago: Illinois Equal Suffrage Association, 1911.

Macmillan, Mary Louise. *The Futurists* (1913). In *Short Plays.* Cincinnati: Stewart & Kidd Company, 3rd ed. 1917, pp. 207–231.

Meyer, Annie Nathan. *The Dominant Sex: A Play in Three Acts.* New York: Brandu's, 1911.

Meyers, Robert Cornelius V. *The New Woman: A Comedietta in One Act.* Philadelphia: Lyceum Publishing Company, 1899.

Middleton, George. *Back of the Ballot: A Woman Suffrage Farce in One Act.* New York and London: Samuel French, 1915.

———. *Criminals: A One Act Play About Marriage.* New York: B. W. Huebsch, 1914.

———. *Nowadays: A Contemporaneous Comedy.* New York: Henry Holt & Company, 1914.

———. *Tradition.* In *Tradition: One-Act Plays of Contemporary Life.* New York: Henry Holt & Company, 1913, pp. 1–31.

Miller, Alice Duer. *Are Women People? A Book of Rhymes for Suffrage Times.* New York: George H. Doran Company, 1915.

———. *Women Are People!* New York: George H. Doran Company, 1917.

[Nashville Woman's Literary Club]. *Votes for Men: Comedy.* Nashville, Mich.: privately printed, 1913.

Newton, Harry L. *Women's Ways: A Monologue.* Chicago: T. S. Denison & Company, 1905.

Park, Maud Wood. *Lucy Stone: A Chronicle Play.* Boston and Los Angeles: Walter H. Baker & Company, 1938.

Parsons, Laura M. *The New Woman's Reform Club: A Humorous Entertainment in One Act.* Boston: Walter H. Baker & Company, 1902.

Peabody, Josephine Preston. *Portrait of Mrs. W.: A Play in Three Acts with an Epilogue.* Boston: Houghton Mifflin, 1922. Riverside Press.

Phillips, David Graham. *The Worth of a Woman: A Play in Four Acts, Followed by A Point of Law: A Dramatic Incident.* New York: D. Appleton, 1908.

Platt, Agnes Electra. *When Women Rule: A Farce in One Act.* New York: Dick & Fitzgerald, 1913.

Quirk, Eugene, Mary Isabel Quirk, and Florence King. *Woman of the Hour: Suffrage Play in Three Acts.* Chicago: Atwell Press, 1910.

Raymond, George L. *The Suffragettes: A Play in Three Acts.* Washington, D.C.: Press of B. S. Adams, 1908.

Robinson, Harriet H. *Captain Mary Miller: A Drama.* Boston: Walter H. Baker & Company, 1887.

Rugg, George. *The New Woman: A Farcical Sketch with One Act, One Scene and One Purpose.* Boston: Walter H. Baker & Company, 1896.

Russell, Livingston. *The "Coming Out" of Miss Cummings: Humorous Monologue for a Woman.* New York: E. S. Werner, 1898.

See, Anna P. *When Women Vote: A Farce in Two Acts.* Boston: Walter H. Baker & Company, 1911.

Shaw, Mary. *The Parrot Cage: A Play in One Act.* Chicago: Dramatic Publishing Company, 1914.

———. *The Woman of It; or, Our Friends, the Anti-Suffragists: A Satirical Comedy in One Act.* Chicago: Dramatic Publishing Company, 1914.

Slocumb, Eudora Hollinshead. *The Woman's Convention, Punkville, U.S.A.: Inconsistant Brochure of Fun and Folly in One Act.* Ed. Marion Short, St. Louis: privately printed, 1914; repr. New York: Samuel French, 1915.

Solomons, Selina. *The Girl from Colorado, or The Conversion of Aunty Suffridge.* San Francisco: Votes for Women Publishing Company, 1911.

Stein, Gertrude. *The Mother of Us All: Opera Libretto (1946).* Repr. in *A Century of Plays by American Women.* Ed. Rachel France. New York: Richard Rosen Press, 1979, pp. 126–141.

Stevens, B. W., and W. W. Waters. *The Coming Woman.* Santa Cruz, Calif.: privately printed, 1895.

Stone, Jane. *The End of the Battle.* New York: National Woman Suffrage Publishing Company [191?].

Stuart, Charles Leonard. *Newark Knows Her; or, The Suffragettes: Comic Opera in Two Acts.* Newark, N.J.: privately printed, 1913.

Sutherland, Howard V. *The Woman Who Could: A Play in Four Acts.* New York: Desmond FitzGerald, Inc., 1911.

Thayer, Ella Cheever. *Lords of Creation: Woman Suffrage Drama in Three Acts.* Boston: Geo. M. Baker & Company, 1883.

Thompkins, Edward Staats De Grote. *The Suffragent; a Social Satire: An Original Play in Three Acts.* Boston: Blanchard Printing Company, 1910.

Thompson, Alice Callender. *A Suffragette Baby: Comedy in One Act.* Philadelphia: Penn Publishing Company, 1912.

Viley, Wylla Jamison, and Lorena Lucille Jamison. *A Pageant of Woman's Progress.* St. Louis: The Freegard Press, 1917.

Wentworth, Marion Craig. *The Flower-Shop: A Play in Three Acts.* Boston: Richard G. Badger, Gorham Press, 1912.

White, James Platt. *Emancipated: A Play.* In *Harvard Monthly* 31, no. 5 (February 1901).

Winsor, Mary. *A Suffrage Rummage Sale: Play in One Act.* Haverford P. O., Pa.: privated printed, 1913.

Wormwood, Edyth M. *The New Woman in Mother Goose Land: Play for Children.* Franklin, Ohio: Eldridge Entertainment House, 1915.